Introduction to Economics

*An Integrated Approach to
Fundamental Principles*

Second Edition

John Craven

Basil Blackwell

Copyright © John Craven 1984, 1990

First published 1984
Reprinted 1984, 1988, 1989
Second edition 1990

Basil Blackwell Ltd
108 Cowley Road, Oxford, OX4 1JF, UK

Basil Blackwell, Inc.
3 Cambridge Center
Cambridge, Massachusetts 02142, USA

British Library Cataloguing in Publication Data

A CIP catalogue record for this book is available from the British Library.

Library of Congress Cataloging in Publication Data

Craven, John, 1949–
    Introduction to economics : an integrated approach to fundamental
principles / John Craven. —2nd ed.
        p.   cm.
    Includes bibliographical references.
    ISBN 0–631–16567–3 — ISBN 0–631–16568–1 (pbk.)
    1. Economics.   I. Title.
HB171.5.C8673   1990
330—dc20   89–18201
                                                                              CIP

Typeset in 10 on 12 pt Times
by Photo·graphics, Honiton, Devon
Printed in Great Britain by Dotesios (Printers) Ltd

For Laura
with love and gratitude
beyond all measure

Contents

Preface to the second edition

The first edition of this book was published in 1984 and was the product of increasing dissatisfaction with the tendency of many introductory courses to divide economics into two parts, macroeconomics and microeconomics. This separation is confusing to students, many of whom continue to believe that economics is, in effect, two subjects that have little in common. This second edition revises the first in substance but not in spirit. Apart from the updating of tables and other information, the main change in this second edition is the merger of the sections on the mixed and open economies. In the current state of, particularly, the UK economy, it is important to recognize the interrelationship between government policies and international aspects of the economy. Therefore, part IV of this edition combines much of the material of parts IV and V of the first edition. This reorganization has some other consequences, and so some of the rest of the material has been reordered.

The reorganization does not alter the basic structure. The book builds macroeconomic conclusions from microeconomic foundations, and chapters on macroeconomic topics do not appear in a separate section from those on microeconomics. Instead, the book is divided into parts, each of which involves both macro and micro topics. Part I introduces basic concepts and methods that are fundamental to all economic analysis. Chapters 5 and 6 give some information on the state of the UK economy in 1988. Parts II, III and IV deal with increasingly complex economic systems. In part II we examine a simplified market economy in which it is relatively easy to study individual decisions (the basis of microeconomics) and the consequences of their interrelationships (macroeconomics). Part III examines a more complex economy, but still without government intervention. Part IV examines government policies in the context of an open economy. These parts therefore build on those that come before, although it is possible to work through the book omitting some of the intermediate chapters, or considering them only briefly. Finally, part V brings in two less well related, but still important, topics: developing economies and planning.

A course of study can be devised that avoids taking too much on trust without losing the message that economics is a single subject that fits together in a coherent and interesting way. Such a course would include part I as a basic requirement and then chapters 8, 11, 12, 15, 16, 17, 19 and 21.

The only mathematical background required is the ability to cope with very simple algebra – little more than the use of notation for clarity and simplicity.

A few topics, dealt with in separate boxes, require more mathematical knowledge but none of these topics is essential and they are included mainly to illustrate the variety of ways in which mathematical methods can be used in economics. Since the publication of the first edition there has been an increase in the number of students of economics who are studying mathematics at the same time, but many do not find mathematics easy and are relieved to find that they can understand the basic principles of economics without much mathematical work.

Each chapter ends with topics for discussion and most chapters include some problems. The topics extend the discussion and seek opinions on the merits of policies that might be used; the problems illustrate the techniques used in the text. Answers to numerical problems are provided at the end of the book. The glossary of main terms can be used both for reference and for revision: it contains a number of important terms with which students should be familiar. Of course, such a glossary cannot explain how the terms are used in any detail, but it can list the major ideas and concepts that are needed to study economics.

I owe an enormous debt of gratitude to my teachers, my colleagues and my students, mainly at the University of Kent at Canterbury, but also at Guelph in Canada where much of the first edition was written. Colin Cannon, Jim Hughes, John Peirson, Bill Smith, Clive Southey, Tony Thirlwall and Roger Vickerman all helped with the first or second editions by supplying information and making suggestions. A number of students have pointed out errors and ambiguities in the first edition. Alan Carruth and Richard Disney read the manuscript of the first edition and have continued to offer suggestions and comments on teaching basic economics. I have taught the Kent first year course with Richard for six years, and learned a lot from his influence.

Technology moves on; the first edition was largely prepared on a typewriter, with a first generation word processor appearing at the end. The second edition has been prepared entirely on an Apple Macintosh and typeset direct from a floppy disk. Elizabeth Oxborrow provided a crucial link between the two, by persuading an ageing disk drive to work and to transmit the files containing the first edition in a form legible to my Apple. This means that I cannot thank my secretary for typing the manuscript. Much more importantly, since I have been Dean of Social Sciences, Lynne Curran has helped guard such time as I have for writing books, and released me from many time consuming chores by her own superb efficiency. To Lynne, a special vote of thanks. Mark Allin of Basil Blackwell suggested the second edition, and added his name to those others at Blackwell who have helped, encouraged and shown patience through two editions.

I am very grateful to everyone who has helped, although they are entirely absolved from errors and obscurities that remain. These are my own responsibility.

Finally, and most importantly, my thanks to Laura, for all her help and support, and to Matthew and Rebecca for being there still.

John Craven

Author's note

The sources of information used are listed in the bibliography. One billion equals one thousand million. Official statistics are revised (often for several years) after they first appear so that those used in this book (generally published during 1989) may not correspond exactly to those published later.

Chapter One

Scope and method of economics

Allocation and distribution — methods in economics — individual behaviour — assumptions — models — value judgements

---

1.1 Introduction

No one comes to economics as a traveller to an unknown land. Much of our everyday experience is of economics: spending money, budgeting, looking for jobs, working, paying taxes, collecting pensions, voting and arguing about what the government should do all involve economics, and all involve topics discussed in this book.

The familiarity of the subject matter has an advantage and a disadvantage. The advantage is that studying economics is extremely relevant to very important issues that involve everyone. This book discusses unemployment, inflation, wages, poverty, taxes, banks, nationalized industries, foreign currencies, aid to less developed countries and a great number of other important topics. The disadvantage is that everyone who studies economics comes to the subject with opinions based on his or her past experience and political and moral beliefs. On some occasions it is difficult to separate differences of opinion on what *should* be done from differences of opinion on what *can* be done. In principle, these two are separate sources of debate: for example, people disagree about whether the government *should* attempt to reduce the inflation rate by limiting wage rises even though they may not disagree about whether limiting wage rises *does* reduce the inflation rate. In political argument, however, this distinction is often blurred.

A very important aspect of the study of economics is the attempt to examine what does happen in certain circumstances without allowing views of what should be done to intrude. This does not mean that all economists agree on the consequences of an event or government policy. In this book, we shall see that there is a variety of views on a number of extremely important economic issues. This variation in views stems not from differences of opinion on what should be done, but from differences of opinion about what follows from a particular event or decision.

How do these differences arise? Why does economics differ from some other subjects in which there is much less disagreement about the consequences of particular circumstances. For example, physicists do not have different views of the consequences of bringing together two pieces of uranium with a total mass that exceeds a critical level – even though physicists have different views on the desirability of deploying nuclear weapons.

Economics gives rise to differences of opinion on what happens because economic events (such as an increase in unemployment or an increase in the price of sugar) are the outcome of a very large number of individual decisions. Many people (not only the unemployed) are affected by an increase in unemployment, because the incomes of the newly unemployed are reduced, and so they spend less money in shops, which then buy fewer goods from factories and employ fewer shopworkers, and so on. Most people are affected by an increase in the price of sugar and the consequences of the price increase are determined by the reactions of those who buy sugar and of farmers who grow sugar beet. Study of the consequences of an economic event may be complex, because it involves the behaviour of a large number of people.

Economists react to this complexity by trying to isolate the most important aspects of the problem under discussion, and by trying to summarize conclusions on economic questions into **economic principles**. These principles are relatively straightforward statements and are general, in that they do not apply only in one specific circumstance. For example, we shall derive principles that apply not only to the price of sugar but also to the prices of many other things.

The simplifications that underlie economic principles can be a source of disagreement about the consequences of economic events (such as price changes) and about what the government can do, even in the absence of disagreement about what should be done. We shall see, for example, that the topical argument about the effects of government policies on unemployment and inflation between free-market economists and Keynesian economists arises partly from a difference of view about the speed with which firms change their prices when their sales rise or fall. In the UK in the 1980s, this argument has been the basis of the disagreement between the Conservative government, which wants to reduce government involvement in the economy because it believes that this will reduce unemployment, and some of its opponents, who want the government to spend more because they believe that this will reduce unemployment.

One principle usually used by free-market economists is that firms change their prices quickly when they sell less or more: they cut prices when they sell less, and increase prices when they sell more. Keynesian economists, on the other hand, base their analysis on the principle that firms do not change their prices very quickly, and respond to an increase in sales by producing more, and to a decrease in sales by producing less.

1.2 Allocation and distribution

The subject matter of much of economics is familiar, but the idea that economics is concerned with employment, prices, inflation, poverty, exchange rates between countries, taxes and so on concentrates only on the outcome of a range of economic behaviour that we look at in this book. The subject matter of economics is rather deeper than this list of topics might imply.

Economics is concerned with the **economy** or **economic system**, which is a way of describing the consequences of a very large number of individual decisions, and the ways in which those decisions interrelate. We shall discover that there is a variety of types of economic system that differ according to the extent of government intervention, ranging from systems in which the government intervenes very little to those in which the government attempts to plan most important aspects of industrial and agricultural production.

Economic systems arise because people can be much better off it they co-operate, so that people do not have to produce everything they need for themselves. Much more can be produced if everyone does the job that he or she is best at than if each person tries to do every kind of job (see chapter 2). The economic system determines what job each person does, and how much he or she gets in return for doing it. The system also determines how the nation's **resources** of land, machinery, oil, raw materials and so on are used. In economists' language:

> a country's economic system determines the **allocation** of the nation's resources of labour, land, machinery, materials etc. between their alternative possible uses.

The problem of allocating resources is a central theme of economics, because most resources are **scarce**. A resource is scarce if it is possible to find desirable uses for more of it than is available.

The economic system also determines what people receive in return for working in various jobs, what they receive in return for providing land, machinery or materials that they own, and what they receive for other reasons (for example, a person in the UK who is sick, old or unemployed is likely to be eligible to receive money from the government). The system also determines the amount that each person pays in taxes (this depends on tax rates, the incomes that people receive and the goods that they buy). In economists' language:

> a country's economic system determines the **distribution** between the individuals in the nation of that which is produced using the nation's resources.

The allocation of resources and the distribution of the product of those resources are a major part of the subject matter of economics. The great issues, such as the level of unemployment, the inflation rate and the extent of poverty, are the consequences of the economic system, and of the way in which it allocates and distributes. We need to know how an economic system attempts to solve the problems of allocation and distribution before we can see why there is unemployment, inflation, poverty and so on. In this book, we build up our examination of the consequences of the economic system from an examination of the decisions of people and companies that determine the allocation of resources and the distribution of the product of those resources.

1.2.1 The international economic system

The same questions of allocation and distribution arise when one considers international economic issues. The world's resources are allocated to the production of many things, and the things that are produced are distributed between and within countries. The use of resources, and the question of which country or group does or should gain economic benefits, are the source of many international disputes – and lead quickly to discussions of international conflicts, boundary questions, the consequences of imperialism and many other issues that seem, at first sight, to be mainly political. There is very often an economic question behind a political dispute.

1.2.2 Definitions of economics

On the basis of the previous paragraphs, we can define economics as follows:

> Economics is the study of methods of allocating scarce resources and distributing the product of those resources, and the study of the consequences of these methods of allocation and distribution.

Such a definition includes most, if not all, of the topics discussed and examined by people who call themselves economists.

An alternative definition of economics might be that it is concerned with the uses of money. In Western economies many resources are allocated to whoever is willing and able to pay the most for them. The distribution is determined by the amounts of money paid as wages, rent and other forms of income. As we shall see in chapter 3, money has an extremely important role to play in economic systems, including those planned economic systems (in Eastern Europe and elsewhere) in which many resources are allocated, and much of the product is distributed, according to a government plan. However, it is possible to argue that, although money is extremely useful in allocating and distributing, the problems of allocation and distribution remain even if money is not used, such as when prices are increasing so rapidly that no one is prepared to accept a banknote. Allocation and distribution are more fundamental aspects of an economic system than the use of money.

1.2.3 Macroeconomics and microeconomics

The list of topics that economists discuss is often divided into:

(a) **Microeconomics**, which is the study of individual decisions and the interactions of these decisions. Microeconomic topics include consumers' decisions on what to buy, firms' decisions on what to produce and the interactions of these decisions, which determine whether people can buy what they would like, whether firms can sell all that they produce and the profits that firms make by producing and selling.

(b) **Macroeconomics**, which is the study of the whole economy, mainly using general economic magnitudes, and their interactions. These magnitudes include the total of everyone's income, total unemployment, the average rate of price increases (the inflation rate), the total extent of companies' capacities to produce goods and the total amount of money in use in the country.

It is often convenient to divide topics between microeconomics and macroeconomics, but perhaps not as convenient as some traditional approaches to the subject imply. The study of economics cannot be divided rigidly into two parts, because the general economic magnitudes of macroeconomics are the result of the individual decisions of microeconomics. Macroeconomics is built up from a foundation of microeconomics.

1.2.4 Economics and other subjects

An all-embracing definition of economics is not essential to anyone beginning to study the subject, particularly because everyone has his or her own interests and is likely to examine those parts of economics that are relevant to these other interests. Economics has a number of near neighbours among the social sciences and beyond, including:

(a) Political science, because economists are concerned with the organization of society, and with government policies.
(b) Psychology, because economists are concerned with the behaviour and decisions of individuals in a variety of situations.
(c) Accounting, because economists are concerned with the activities of companies and with the effects of the information that companies provide about their profits and other financial matters.
(d) Law, because the decisions that people take and the government's actions are affected by legal restrictions on various activities, and by the legal protection available to various groups of individuals.
(e) History, because current events are affected by past decisions, and, equally importantly, current decisions are likely to be influenced by decisions taken in the past, and by attitudes inherited from the past.
(f) Engineering, because the allocation of resources between alternative uses requires technical information on the ways in which resources can be used.
(g) Mathematics, because mathematical reasoning is often used to examine complex economic problems.
(h) Statistics, because economists want to answer questions that begin 'how large . . .' – these answers involve the measurement and analysis of numerical information, and the testing of hypotheses using statistical data.

The fact that economics has other disciplines as near neighbours implies that there is an overlap between topics studied in economics and those studied in other disciplines. This emphasizes the conclusion that it is impossible to draw a hard and fast boundary between that which is economics, and that which is something else.

1.3 Methods in economics

All areas of study have methods for examining important questions. These methods form the **methodology** of the subject. For example:

(a) Physicists and chemists test ideas by setting up experiments to examine the effects of a particular event (such as a change in temperature). Experiments are usually designed to eliminate, as far as possible, the chance that some other influences may affect the outcome of the experiment.
(b) Some literary critics discuss books by finding out the major influences on the author at the time of writing.
(c) Meteorologists make weather forecasts by comparing the current situation with historical records of similar patterns of air pressure, wind speed etc.

Economists also have methodologies that influence what they examine and how they examine it. Controlled experiments are generally impossible, because it is not possible to isolate the effects of a single cause in the way that natural scientists do in laboratory conditions. The decisions made by people as consumers, or as the managers of firms, and the policies pursued by governments are influenced by a number of simultaneous events. For example, a consumer may change what she buys from one year to the next, both because she has become richer and because the prices of the things that she buys have changed. It is not usually possible to set up an experiment to see what she would do if only one of these changes occurred.

At times, economics has much in common with meteorology, because the use of conclusions based on past events is an important part of economics. The analysis of data from the past involves the use of statistical methods and **econometrics** (measurement in economics). In chapters 5 and 6, in particular, we discuss some important problems of measurement in economics, including those involved in measuring unemployment, inflation and the extent of poverty.

The basis of the methodology of this book is that general principles can be derived from simple statements about how individuals behave in various circumstances. So we have a general principle that:

all economic questions can be analysed by examining the decisions of individuals and the outcome of those decisions.

This general principle differs from that used by other economists who examine economic questions by deriving principles from the behaviour and interaction of groups of people. The **Marxist** analysis of Western economies is based on the interrelations between social classes – **workers** and **capitalists** (see section 10.9) – whose interests and behaviour are regarded as uniform enough for a whole class to be seen as a single unit.

Our methodology requires that, in theory, we can trace the cause of all economic events (such as an increase in unemployment, or a fall in the number of dollars that can be bought for a pound) back to individual decisions. However, although this is possible in principle, we shall not always do so in practice, because it is often more revealing to trace causes back to general macroeconomic magnitudes, such as the total of everyone's income, the level of unemployment or the total of everyone's saving. In principle, changes in these totals can in turn be traced back to individual decisions, but there are occasions when this additional stage would unnecessarily complicate the discussion. Indeed, much of conventional macroeconomics deals with general magnitudes without discussing their roots in individual decision-making.

1.3.1 The government

Government actions could also, in principle, be traced back to the decisions of individual politicians and civil servants. However, these decisions are not ordinarily included in the study of economics, and we shall follow a tradition in economics that treats the government as an entity that may attempt to influence decisions taken by individuals as consumers, workers, managers, taxpayers and so on.

1.4 Individual behaviour

Our methodology is to examine economic questions first by looking at the individual decisions that underlie them. These decisions have two components:

(a) The **opportunities** available to the individual.
(b) The **motivations**, or **preferences**, of the individual that determine his or her choice from the available opportunities.

The opportunities open to an individual are likely to be limited in a variety of ways. For example, a consumer who is deciding what to buy has opportunities that depend on the range of items available, on his information about them, on the prices of the things he would like to buy, and on the amount of money that he can spend. The manager of a firm who is deciding how much to produce has opportunities that are limited by the quantities and qualities of materials, land and machinery that are available to her, by the number and skills of workers that she can employ, and by the costs involved in paying for materials, land, machinery and labour.

Motivations come from a variety of sources. Economists usually presume that people are strongly influenced by **materialist** motives, so that they prefer to have more material objects rather than fewer. This simple materialist motivation may be tempered by the desire not to work for too many hours, or in conditions that are unpleasant. In addition, people may not want to take too many risks to obtain as much as possible. For example, they might not put all of their savings into one risky venture that could give them a very high income, but that could instead cause them to lose everything.

We must also recognize that some preferences have other roots. People may be unwilling to move to a higher paid job that is available if they must move house, disrupt their social lives or interrupt their children's education. Managers of firms may not aim simply for the highest possible income, because they may be interested in prestige or power, or in having a relatively easy life.

Most of our discussion in this book concerns economies where the government does not attempt to plan major parts of industrial and agricultural production. The motivations of individuals are important in a planned economic system also. The planners detail how and where goods should be produced, and issue instructions to the managers of factories and to workers. However, the managers and workers may choose not to do what the planners want them to do, unless they are suitably motivated or their range opportunities is so limited that they have no alternative. Given the enormous range of activities in an industrialized economy, it is very difficult for planners to give instructions that are detailed enough to ensure that no one has the opportunity to do something contrary to the needs of the plan. So the planners must try to make sure that people are motivated by incentive schemes to do as the plan requires.

1.5 Assumptions

We cannot examine separately the behaviour of every individual in a large population. Instead, economists make **assumptions**, and try to reflect the most important aspects of behaviour in **models**. Assumptions and models are used to simplify the examination of a problem under discussion and thus to emphasize its main features. The choice of assumptions must attempt to avoid:

(a) Oversimplification, which removes an important aspect of the situation under discussion.
(b) Undersimplification, which leaves the important aspects obscured by too much detail.

Much of the art of economics involves the choice of assumptions that give the most useful simplification of a particular situation – and there is considerable scope for disagreement about what is most useful.

1.5.1 Types of assumption

Assumptions involve a variety of aspects of a situation, depending on the purpose of the discussion. We can make assumptions about:

(a) The number of people and number of items involved. For example, in chapter 2 we look at the behaviour of two people who can make only two things. This is obviously a great simplification of the real world, but the purpose of the discussion is to examine the gains that people can make when their abilities differ. The assumption that there are two people producing two things is the logically simplest case that we can construct, and it is possible to illustrate important conclusions using this simplification. If we tried to use a more realistic example, the conclusions would be hidden by the greater detail involved. The two-person assumption is not useful in other contexts. For example, two people can get together to bargain about the distribution of the items that they produce, but it is impossible for a much larger group to do so. We would not learn much about the distribution of the product of a society's resources if we were to limit our examination to a society in which only two people were involved.

(b) The issues that are omitted entirely. Despite its apparent irrelevance, it is very useful to discuss an economic system in which the government has a very limited role and/or in which there is no overseas trade. Parts II and III of this book make precisely these assumptions, and contain some very important analyses that are useful for understanding the more realistic economic systems examined in part IV.

(c) The opportunities open to decision-makers. These assumptions may involve legal restrictions on what people or firms are allowed to do, or the economic restriction of what people can afford to do. Limitations on opportunities also arise from lack of information. For some purposes we assume that people have sufficient information to know of all of the opportunities that are open to them. For other purposes we assume that people do not have all of this information, either because they are ignorant of some current opportunities or because they are uncertain about the future. Uncertainties about the future affect many current decisions. For example, a firm's decision to build a new factory depends on its view of the likelihood of selling more in the future. We shall discuss the implications of uncertainty in chapters 13 and 14.

(d) The motivation of decision-makers. Economics is particularly concerned with materialist motivation, and so most of our analysis is based on an assumption that people want to obtain as much as possible, allowing that they will want to limit the number of hours that they work.

(e) The decisions made by consumers, workers, managers and so on. Sometimes we make assumptions that do not separate opportunities from motivation, but instead state what people do. For example, if the managers of a company discover that more people want to buy its product, they have the opportunity to sell more without changing the price that is charged, the opportunity to increase the price charged without losing sales, or the opportunity to increase both sales and price to some extent. The actual decision taken depends on the motivations of the managers, but we could make an assumption about what they decide to do without making separate assumptions about their opportunities or motivations.

(f) The decisions made by the government. These assumptions are often the starting point for discussion of policy issues. For example, we could assume that the government reduces the rate of income tax, and ask what then happens to unemployment, inflation, the amounts of goods imported and so on.

(g) **Ceteris paribus** (with other things equal). Questions in economics often concern the effects of one change on people's behaviour or on the outcome of the economy. For example, we discuss theoretically the extent to which a consumer buys more or less of something when he or she becomes richer. When we do this, we assume that there is no change in the prices of anything that is bought, so that we can isolate the effects of the increase in income. Economists use the *ceteris paribus* assumption when they are examining a problem theoretically; that is, when they are not using evidence from a real world situation. The difficulty of doing controlled experiments in economics implies that this assumption often cannot be used when we are assessing the implications of information on what people have actually been observed doing.

1.6 Models

A model consists of assumptions, and conclusions reached from those assumptions. There are at least three ways of reaching conclusions from a number of assumptions:

(a) Using **verbal arguments** to trace out the logical implications of the assumptions.
(b) Illustrating the assumptions in a **diagram**, and drawing conclusions from the diagram.
(c) Writing the assumptions in a **mathematical form**, and deriving conclusions using mathematical methods.

In this book we favour the first two methods, because most of the conclusions reached do not require the use of mathematics. In some places we use shortened notation for magnitudes involved (such as S for saving or I for investment) and reach conclusions using very simple algebraic manipulations. Some conclusions are derived in separate mathematical sections, using calculus or somewhat less straightforward algebra. These sections show to those who have the necessary background that mathematics can be very useful in some areas of economics, but none of them is essential to understand later material. However, the use of mathematics is essential for exploring some areas of economics beyond a simple level: the bibliography lists some introductory and further reading that involves much more mathematics than is used here.

1.6.1 Choosing a model

We can build models using a variety of assumptions, but not all models are equally useful. What distinguishes a more useful model from a less useful model? We build models with two main purposes in mind:

(a) To **explain** why something has occurred, and perhaps to provide a single explanation for a number of events.
(b) To **predict** what will happen in the future.

So a 'good' model is one that provides a convincing explanation and/or one that provides predictions that turn out to be accurate.

Explanation and prediction are not unrelated aims, because we are likely to be more confident about predictions from a model that provides a convincing explanation of a number of past events, and we are more likely to be convinced by an explanatory model if it predicts future events with reasonable accuracy. However, explanation and prediction do not necessarily lead to the use of the same model.

Given the general principle adopted in this book, that economic events are the outcome of individual decisions, a model can provide a convincing explanation only if it makes assumptions on opportunities, motivations and behaviour that are not too unrealistic. So, for example, an explanation of why many people have no job that is based on the assumption that the unemployed do not want to work for a wage of, say, £80 per week, would not be convincing if we were to find in a survey that many people would like to work for £80 per week but cannot find a job. This does not imply that a good explanation must reflect all aspects of everyone's behaviour, however eccentric – unless, of course, eccentric behaviour is important to the issue at hand. An attempt to build an explanatory model that reflects every aspect of behaviour leads to a similar problem to that of a geographer who wants to draw a completely accurate map of a city, and finds that she can do so only by using a scale of one metre to one metre. A good explanation, like a useful map, tries to capture the essential features without becoming overburdened with detail.

If we choose a model according to its ability to predict, we are not necessarily concerned with the realism of the assumptions that it makes about individual behaviour. A model for prediction is likely to be judged on its 'track record' rather than its realism. For example, we might find that we can make reasonably accurate predictions of the inflation rate next year using a model that assumes that next year's inflation rate equals the rate of increase in the amount of money in use this year. If such a model proved to be reasonably accurate over a number of years, people would use it, even though it gives no explanation based on individual behaviour of how the amount of money affects inflation in the next year. This does not imply that there is no such explanation, only that the use of the model for prediction does not *require* that there is such an explanation.

1.6.2 Competing models

There are often rival models in use, and we shall discuss a number of areas in which there are several competing models. This multiplicity of models stems partly from differences of view about the realism of particular assumptions. All models involve some use of the *ceteris paribus* assumption, and someone may believe that a model would provide a good explanation or prediction if only the *ceteris paribus* assumption held in reality. For example, we might have a model that predicts that people buy less cheese if the price of cheese increases, assuming that other things (including incomes and the prices of goods that people might buy instead of cheese) remain unchanged. If it is observed that, over a number of years, people buy more cheese, even though the price has increased, some might say that the model is not useful. Others might say that the increased purchases of cheese have occurred because people have more money to spend, or because the prices of meat and eggs have risen even more than the price of cheese, so that the model does not reflect actual circumstances. The former view implies that the model is not useful, and should not be used; the latter view implies that the model might be useful when the circumstances assumed in it occur in reality.

Another reason for the multiplicity of models is that it is not easy to establish criteria for 'the most accurate' prediction. Many models are used to predict a number of magnitudes (such as the extent of unemployment, the inflation rate, exchange rates between currencies and increases in incomes), perhaps over several years. It is likely that, if there are several rival models, each will be more accurate in some of the predictions, and there is scope for disagreement on which is the most accurate overall.

Finally, economists and politicians may be reluctant to discard models because they have political views that are supported by the explanation given by the model. This is particularly true in discussions of government intervention. Some models imply that some government policies are ineffective in achieving their aims, and those who support attempts to achieve the aims may not be willing to use these models. Conversely, anyone who opposes government intervention (for example, because they believe that it is an infringement of individual liberty) might, but not necessarily would, be unwilling to use models that imply that government intervention could be very effective in solving some problems.

1.6.3 Models used in this book

This book is arranged so that, broadly speaking, the main simplifying assumptions used become more realistic as the book proceeds. This pattern can be justified only because the use of highly simplifying assumptions allows us to reach relevant conclusions in a simple framework. So the general pattern of the assumptions is that:

(a) In part II we make simplifying assumptions about behaviour, the sizes of firms and the information available, and that people and firms react quickly to take advantage of profitable opportunities. In particular, we assume that there is very little government intervention in the economy, and that there are no economic transactions (such as imports and exports) with other countries.

(b) In part III we retain the assumptions of very restricted government activity and no international transactions, but we modify the other assumptions made in part II. This allows us to look at the behaviour of large firms facing considerable uncertainty, and at circumstances in which firms do not necessarily react quickly to profitable opportunities.

(c) In part IV we allow for significant government intervention in the economic system and for international transactions. This allows us to examine government policies that might be implemented to try to change the outcome of the economy (for example, to control inflation or to reduce unemployment).

1.7 Value judgements

We have seen that economists can differ in their choice of model because they make different judgements about the important aspects of individual behaviour. Once a model is chosen, we can make three different kinds of statement:

(a) **Positive** statements of what the model predicts, or how it explains. These statements are based only on logical deductions from the assumptions of the model.

(b) **Prescriptive** statements, which say what can be done (according to the model) to achieve a particular aim.

(c) **Normative** statements, which say what should be done (based on the prediction or explanation of the model).

A normative statement involves a **value judgement**, which is an opinion that one situation is better than another. This value judgement is additional to the judgement that leads to the choice of the model. People disagree, and there is no logical way to say that one opinion is better than another. A prescriptive statement does not directly involve a value judgement, because it does not make a statement that one situation is better than another. Instead, a prescriptive statement states the best course of action if an individual or the government has a particular aim, based on a value judgement of what is important. Positive statements involve no value judgement: if two people use the same model, they reach identical conclusions on the basis of logical argument.

We can illustrate the distinction between these three types of statements using the following example:

(a) If the government increases the tax on cigarettes, people smoke less. This is a positive statement that can be reached by a logical argument from assumptions about how people behave.

(b) If the government wants to reduce the amount smoked, it should increase the tax on cigarettes. This is a prescriptive statement. It does not assume that the government wants to reduce smoking, but tells it what it can do if it wants to reduce smoking.

(c) The government should increase the tax on cigarettes. This is a normative statement because it involves a value judgement that the situation after the tax increase is better than the situation before the tax increase.

This is not a polemical book; it is not designed to say what individuals or the government should do. Thus normative statements have no place in our analysis. We avoid normative statements because the book examines the implications of various assumptions for major economic issues and, by extension, the ways in which the government can change the outcome of the economy if it so wishes. Thus we do not avoid prescriptive statements. We do, of course, make judgements when we choose assumptions that we believe are likely to give the best explanations or predictions, but these are not judgements on the relative merits of different outcomes of the economic system.

1.8 Summary

On one level, economics is concerned with everyday issues, such as unemployment, inflation, poverty, money, prices, wages, imports and exports. However, these topics can be discussed as implications of a society's method of allocating resources and distributing the product of those resources. The everyday issues are the outcome of more fundamental events.

When we study the principles of economics, our starting point is individual behaviour. This behaviour is determined by opportunities and motivations, and economists assume that materialist motivations are of major importance.

Economists use assumptions to build models, both for explanation and for prediction, but there is no universally agreed way of identifying a good model. Our study of economic principles involves positive and prescriptive statements, but not normative statements.

Topics and problems

(1) What are the most important national and international economic issues?
(2) In what ways is your behaviour constrained other than by what you can afford to do?
(3) In what ways are you motivated, other than by materialist objectives? Why do people give time and money to charities?
(4) Is explanation important, or is prediction the only reason for studying economics?
(5) 'All good economists should be rich, because they should be able to make money through accurate predictions of share prices on the Stock Exchange.' Discuss in the light of the evidence that many economists are not rich.
(6) 'Higher education benefits society and should be freely available to all who are qualified for it.' 'People with qualifications get paid more so they should pay the full cost of their tuition.' Which of these views do you support?
(7) Suppose that the following positive statement is true: 'If the value of notes and coins in circulation decreases, prices will decrease'. What prescriptive and normative statements can be made using this positive statement? (Note that the truth or otherwise of the positive statement is discussed in several later chapters.)

Part I

Basic principles and issues

In this part we introduce the most basic aspects of economic analysis. These are the building blocks for future sections that form the core of all courses in economics and the vocabulary of economics. This vocabulary degenerates too often into jargon, but some parts of it are essential to ensure a clear understanding of concepts and a common language for discussion. The basic principles, vocabulary and concepts that we introduce include:

(a) The division of labour and the pattern of specialization in an economy.
(b) The principles that underlie beneficial exchanges of goods.
(c) Why money is used.
(d) How the legal system affects economic decisions and actions.
(e) How prices and wages are determined through supply and demand in markets.
(f) How the total amounts produced in a country can be combined in the national accounts to calculate national income and gross national product.
(g) The concepts of saving and investment, government activity and the balance of payments, and their roles in the national accounts.
(h) Definitions and categories of unemployment.
(i) Major themes of growth, inflation, poverty and the standard of living.

Chapter Two

Specialization and the division of labour

Specialization — opportunity cost and comparative advantage — many people and many goods — co-operation in production — specialization in the UK — disadvantages of the division of labour — specialization and economic systems

2.1 Introduction

This chapter answers the question 'What is the economic reason why people live together in social groups?' by examining two ways in which a group of people can produce more using the same effort than they could if they did not co-operate. The two reasons are, in brief:

(a) Each person in a society can **specialize** in the tasks that he or she does best, and exchange what he or she produces for things produced by other people. An isolated individual must do a variety of jobs to meet his or her needs, including jobs that he or she does badly; he or she must be **self-sufficient**.

(b) The joint efforts of a group of people can exceed the sum of their individual powers. People who **co-operate** can do jobs that no one could do alone.

2.1.1 Goods and services

Goods are things that are produced (the term 'commodity' is sometimes used). People produce both material, tangible goods, such as cars, steel and corn, and intangible items, such as health care, education and bus journeys. The intangible items are **services**, and economists often refer to 'goods and services'. However, it would be cumbersome to include 'and services' on each of the many occasions we use 'goods' and so, in this book, 'good' and 'goods' include both tangible and intangible items.

2.2 Specialization

In chapter 1 we discussed why economic arguments often involve simplifications, and we now meet our first example of this. We examine how people can produce more if they specialize than if each person is self-sufficient. The simplest possible case is where two people produce two goods and, fortunately, this simplest case illustrates many of the principles that apply to realistic situations in which many people produce many goods.

Our two people, Alan and Bill, produce two goods, food and cloth. We suppose (see table 2.1) that Alan can either gather 30 kilograms of food or make 60 metres of cloth in a year. Alan decides that, when he is self-sufficient, his needs are best met by spending one-half of each year on each activity, so that he has 15 food and 30 cloth. (Note, for brevity, we do not repeat 'kilograms of food' or 'metres of cloth'; the units of measurement are always implied.) Bill can produce either 20 food or 80 cloth in a year and he decides that, when he is self-sufficient, his needs are best met by dividing his time equally so that he has 10 food and 40 cloth. In total, Alan and Bill produce 25 food and 70 cloth when they are self-sufficient.

These totals are less than Alan and Bill can produce if Alan spends the whole year making food and Bill spends the whole year making cloth. If they specialize in his way, they produce a total of 30 food and 80 cloth, and so

Specialization can increase total outputs.

Specialization does not necessarily increase total outputs. Some patterns of specialization increase outputs, while others decrease them. For example, if Alan specializes in producing cloth and Bill specializes in producing food, they

Table 2.1 Annual production possibilities for two people

	Annual food production (kg)		Annual cloth production (m)
Possibilities			
Alan	30	or	60
Bill	20	or	80
Self-sufficiency (1/2 time on each)			
Alan	15	and	30
Bill	10	and	40
Total	25		70
Specialization			
Alan	30	and	0
Bill	0	and	80
Total	30		80

produce a total of 20 food and 60 cloth, which is less than their total production when they are self-sufficient.

2.2.1 Efficient outputs

We can extend the example to allow for the possibility that Alan and Bill do not want 30 food and 80 cloth. Suppose that both are content with the amounts of cloth that they have if they are self-sufficient. What is the maximum food that they can produce, given that 70 cloth is wanted? If Bill produces the 70 cloth, he spends 7/8 of his time making cloth, and can spend 1/8 of his time producing food. So Bill produces $1/8 \times 20 = 2.5$ food and Alan produces 30 food, so that there is total production of 32.5 food and 70 cloth. More food is produced than when they are self-sufficient. In this way we can work out the maximum food production for a given target of cloth production, or the maximum cloth production for a given target of food production. A combination of goods that involves the greatest production of one good, given a target for the other (or for all other goods if there are more than two), is an **efficient output level** for the economic system. The production levels when Alan and Bill are self-sufficient do not form an efficient output level, because it is possible (by specialization) to increase the total output of one good without reducing the total output of the other.

Figure 2.1 shows the possible output levels for Alan and Bill in our example. Point A represents the combined outputs when Alan and Bill are self-sufficient;

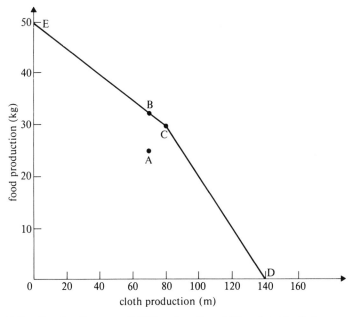

Figure 2.1   Production possibilities for the skills of table 2.1
A represents outputs when self-sufficient; EC and CD represent all efficient output levels.

C represents outputs when Alan specializes in food and Bill in cloth; B represents the maximum possible output of food (32.5) when cloth output is 70. Line CE represents the efficient output levels that can be reached if Alan specializes in food production, and Bill divides his time between the two activities (at E both specialize in food production; with zero cloth, the maximum food output is 50). Line CD represents the efficient output levels that can be achieved if Bill specializes in cloth production, and Alan divides his time between the two activities. Lines CD and CE form the **production possibility frontier** for the two people:

> The production possibility frontier represents all the possible efficient output levels for an economy using fixed amounts of resources.

2.2.2 Variable resources

In our example, the resource used by Alan and Bill is the time during which they work. This time is divided between the two tasks. In more realistic cases, people use a variety of resources (land, machines, skills that they have learned, strength and so on) and they could produce more if they used more resources. To allow for this possibility, we amend the definition of an efficient output level. When the total amounts of resources used can be varied, the economy operates at an efficient output level if it is possible to increase the output of one good only by either reducing the output of some other good or using more resources.

2.2.3 Skills and wants

The **skills** of the two people determine which patterns of specialization produce the greatest outputs. If they want an efficient output level, at least one of them should specialize in producing a single good. Alan should produce no cloth if Bill is producing any food (positions on CE in figure 2.1); Bill should produce no food if Alan is producing any cloth (positions on CD). However, there are many different combinations of food and cloth on lines CD and CE in figure 2.1 and, if we know only the people's skills, we cannot say which of these combinations is produced. We need to know in addition what is wanted.

In a simple example with two people and two goods, it is likely that Alan and Bill can decide on the combination of goods they produce by negotiation or bargaining. However, direct negotiation or bargaining becomes much more complicated when there are many people and many goods. With many people, impersonal mechanisms such as **markets** (see chapter 4) or a **central plan** (see chapter 24) determine the combination of goods that is produced.

2.3 Opportunity cost and comparative advantage

2.3.1 Opportunity cost

We can examine the gains from specialization in a slightly different way in order to introduce the idea of **opportunity cost**. In the example in table 2.1, each person spends one-half of his time on each task when they are self-sufficient. Suppose that Alan produces 1 more food by devoting an extra 1/30 of the year to food production. He therefore must reduce his output of cloth by 60/30 = 2. Bill increases his time spent producing cloth to make up for this reduction of 2 cloth; Bill must therefore spend an extra 1/40 year producing cloth. This reduces his food production by 20/40 = 1/2. The net result is shown in table 2.2, where we see that cloth production stays the same and food production increases by 1/2. The output of one good increases without reducing the output of the other, and this is a more efficient use of resources.

Food production increases because, although Alan produces 2 less cloth when he produces 1 more food, Bill reduces his food output by less than one unit when he produces 2 more cloth. They have different opportunity costs of producing food in terms of cloth. In general, if people can produce several goods, then, for any two goods:

A person's opportunity cost of producing good 1, measured in units of good 2, is the reduction in his production of good 2 when he increases his production of good 1 by one unit.

In our example, Alan's opportunity cost of producing food is 2 (metres of) cloth; Alan's opportunity cost of producing cloth is 1/2 (kilogram of) food. The corresponding figures for Bill are 4 and 1/4.

Alan's lower opportunity cost of producing food measured in units of cloth implies that it is better that he, and not Bill, should produce food, because less cloth is sacrificed if Alan produces a unit of food than if Bill does. Similarly, Bill's opportunity cost of producing cloth measured in units of food is lower than Alan's, so that less food is sacrificed if Bill produces a unit of cloth than if Alan does.

This example takes advantage of these differences in opportunity cost by increasing Alan's food production and reducing Bill's food production, without

Table 2.2   Output changes reflecting opportunity costs

	Change in annual food production (kg)	Change in annual cloth production (m)
Alan	+1	−2
Bill	−1/2	+2
Total	+1/2	0

changing the amount of cloth produced. Outputs can be increased whenever it is possible to take advantage of differences in opportunity costs, and a pattern of specialization results in an efficient output level only if society has taken advantage of all differences in opportunity costs. In our example, Alan should continue to produce more food, and Bill more cloth, until at least one of them is specialized to produce only one of the goods.

2.3.2 Comparative advantage

A difference in opportunity cost implies that one person has a **comparative advantage** over another. A comparative advantage may be found for any two people, and any two goods:

> Person A has a comparative advantage over person B in the production of good 1 compared to the production of good 2 if A has a lower opportunity cost than B in the production of good 1 measured in units of good 2.

Comparative advantages reflect differences in skills and in opportunity costs. People have taken advantage of all differences in their opportunity costs when they have specialized according to their comparative advantages. So:

> An efficient output level is achieved if people specialize according to their comparative advantages.

In the example in table 2.1, Alan has a comparative advantage over Bill in the production of food compared to the production of cloth, and Bill has a comparative advantage over Alan in the production of cloth compared to the production of food. These comparative advantages imply that to reach an efficient output level at least one person should specialize. They do not reach an efficient output level if Alan produces some cloth and Bill produces some food. The requirement that people specialize according to their comparative advantages rules out inefficient patterns of specialization. It does not imply that there is a single efficient pattern.

2.3.3 Absolute advantage

The definitions of opportunity cost and of comparative advantage do not refer to the total amounts that people can produce, but to the sacrifice that each needs to make to produce an additional unit of a good. In table 2.3, Alan's abilities are the same as in table 2.1, but Bill can produce only one-tenth as much as in table 2.1. Both people's opportunity costs are the same as in table 2.1, but in table 2.3 Bill is less efficient than Alan in the production of both goods. Alan has an **absolute advantage** over Bill in the production of both goods, because he is better at producing both. Alan also has a comparative advantage over Bill in the production of food compared with the production of cloth, but Bill has a comparative advantage over Alan in the production of cloth compared with the production of food.

Table 2.3 Annual production possibilities with absolute advantage

	Annual food production (kg)		Annual cloth production (m)
Possibilities			
Alan	30	or	60
Bill	2	or	8
Self-sufficiency			
(1/2 time on each)			
Alan	15	and	30
Bill	1	and	4
Total	16		34
Specialization			
Alan	16	and	28
Bill	0	and	8
Total	16		36

Suppose that in table 2.3 each person spends half of his time in each activity when he is self-sufficient. Total outputs are 16 food and 34 cloth. If Bill specializes in cloth production, he produces 8 cloth; if Alan spends 8/15 of the year producing 8/15 × 30 = 16 food and 7/15 producing 7/15 × 60 = 28 cloth, total outputs are 16 food and 36 cloth, which exceed the outputs when they are self-sufficient. The people's absolute abilities determine how much can be produced in total (less in the example of table 2.3 than in that of table 2.1 because Bill is less efficient in table 2.3), but they do not affect the conclusion that outputs can be increased if people specialize according to their comparative advantages. So, although it might be thought that there could be no gain from specialization in this situation, because Bill can produce so much less than Alan, the theory of comparative advantage shows that this is not so. An alternative interpretation is that an economy has not reached an efficient output level until every individual's abilities have been used to best advantage.

Problem 14 at the end of this chapter demonstrates that there is no gain from specialization if people have identical skills, or if their opportunity costs are the same but they can produce different amounts. For example, there is no gain from specialization if Alan is twice as efficient as Bill in the production of both goods.

2.3.4 International specialization

All the examples and conclusions in sections 2.2 and 2.3 apply to international specialization and to comparative and absolute advantages between countries, or regions of countries. Different countries or regions have different abilities to produce because they have different natural resources of minerals, energy and fertility of land, because they have different climates and because their people have different skills and different machines with which to work.

Replace Alan by country Alpha and Bill by country Beta, and the same examples illustrate that the world production (in a world of two countries) of two goods can be increased if countries specialize according to their comparative advantages – this applies whether or not one country has an absolute advantage over the other in the production of both goods. If one country does have an absolute advantage, more is produced if the rich or well endowed country specializes and, by implication, obtains some goods from much poorer countries. Indeed, the expansion of trade between rich and poor countries may be one of the most effective ways in which richer countries can help poorer countries to develop their economies and to increase their standards of living (see section 23.4).

David Ricardo (born in London in 1772, died in 1823; MP for Portarlington, Ireland, from 1819 to 1823) is generally credited (although, as often in economics, others may have prior claim) with being the first to demonstrate explicitly the benefits that can be achieved by specialization according to comparative advantages and, in particular, that these gains arise even when one person or country is more efficient in producing all goods than another. Ricardo made fundamental contributions to economics in a variety of areas, including taxation, the discussion of the rents paid for using land and other aspects of the sources and sizes of people's incomes.

2.4 Many people and many goods

When two people can each produce two goods, there are four possible patterns of specialization in which each person produces one good (two patterns in which they produce different goods, and two in which they produce the same good), and it is also possible for one person to specialize while the other produces both goods. The number of possible patterns of specialization increases considerably when we consider more people and more goods. For example, when there are four people and five goods, there are $5 \times 5 \times 5 \times 5 = 625$ patterns in which each person produces one good, and many more ways in which some can specialize in producing one good while others produce two or more goods. So when there are many people who can produce many goods, it is not easy to examine each possible pattern of specialization to see whether it increases or decreases outputs compared to a situation in which everyone is self-sufficient. In addition, two-dimensional figures, such as figure 2.1, cannot be drawn when there are more than two goods.

Fortunately, it is not necessary to examine each of the many possible cases to discover whether specialization can increase outputs. The lessons of the simple example carry through to more complex cases. We can examine opportunity costs or comparative advantages to see whether gains can be made. A person who can produce several goods has several different opportunity costs of producing, say, food. If he can produce food, cloth, paper and chairs, he can increase his output of food by reducing his output of any of the other goods. He has an opportunity cost of producing food measured in terms of any other good that he can produce. If we take any two goods and any two people who have different opportunity costs of producing one good, measured in units of the other, then we can work out possible increases in production exactly as we did in the example in section 2.3.1. The definition of comparative advantage is unchanged.

For example, suppose that Alan and Bill have the abilities given in table 2.4. Alan has two opportunity costs of producing food: these are 2 cloth and 4 chairs. The equivalent figures for Bill are 3 cloth and 2 chairs. Therefore Alan has the lower opportunity cost and a comparative advantage over Bill in producing food compared with cloth. Table 2.4 shows how specialization (in that Alan produces no cloth and Bill produces no chairs) can increase the outputs of all goods compared to a situation in which both are self-sufficient, and each spends 1/3 of his time producing each good.

2.4.1 Equipment and land

Our discussion has not yet taken account of the machinery, tools, land and buildings that are used in the production of goods. In this book, we generally refer to machinery, tools and buildings as **equipment**. The quantity and quality of the equipment and land available make a considerable difference to the quantities of goods that can be produced. People's skills, and hence comparative advantages, depend on the equipment and land that they have available, and the achievement of an efficient output level requires that these resources are used in the best possible way.

The items that we have referred to as equipment are also known as **capital** or **physical capital**. Economists also refer to **financial capital**, which is the value of money and some other assets (such as bank accounts, shares and savings

Table 2.4 Annual production possibilities with three goods

	Annual food production (kg)		Annual cloth production (m)		Annual chair production (units)
Possibilities					
Alan	24	or	48	or	96
Bill	30	or	90	or	60
Self-sufficiency (1/3 time on each)					
Alan	8	and	16	and	32
Bill	10	and	30	and	20
Total	18		46		52
Specialization					
Alan	8	and	0	and	64
Bill	12	and	54	and	0
Total	20		54		64

bonds) held by a person or a company. To avoid a possible confusion between these two separate uses of the word capital, we use the term 'equipment' as defined above for machinery, tools and buildings.

The availability of equipment and land affects the amounts that people can produce. Differences in the available amounts of these items help to explain why people in some countries are able to produce much more than people in others. This is only a superficial explanation of the great differences in production levels between rich and poor countries, because we need to explain how some countries have in the past been able to produce (or buy from abroad) a much greater amount of equipment than others (see chapter 23).

2.5 Co-operation in production

In our discussion of specialization, people co-operate by agreeing to specialize, but our examples suppose that those who specialize use the same methods of production as they would if they were self-sufficient. For example, in table 2.1, Alan can produce 30 food in one year, 15 food in half a year, 3 food in 1/10 of a year and so on. His efforts are **divisible** with no loss of efficiency.

This divisibility is improbable in practice. A person who spends all her time doing one job is likely to be more efficient than if she changes jobs, if only because she wastes no time moving from one job to another. It is also likely that greater experience of a particular job leads to greater efficiency through greater experience and on-the-job learning.

Time savings and experience add to the advantages that result from specialization. Furthermore, even if two people produce cloth equally efficiently, time saving and learning imply that they are likely to produce more if one specializes in one part of the process of producing cloth and the other specializes in the other part. Specialization can go beyond a situation in which each person produces one good, to a situation in which each person specializes in a part of the process of production of a good.

This further specialization, and the need for co-ordination and supervision, requires that people work together in groups, or **factories**. For example, it would be very inefficient if 10 people each specialized in a different part of the process of producing paper and each worked in a different town. The partly made paper would have to be moved frequently from town to town. So production processes are likely to be integrated within a factory, within which each person has his or her own specialized task within an overall structure. The concentration of work in one place also allows people to take advantage of the fact that combined strengths or abilities are needed for some jobs: for example, 10 people can lift heavier things than one person. Similarly, a surgeon and an anaesthetist are required to perform operations, and the skill of each is required for the other to do his job.

The advantages of co-operation in production may increase as more people work together. More combined effort is available for some jobs, and people can specialize in smaller parts of a process of production. For example, in small-scale car factories, one person may be responsible for assembling the engine of each car, but in a very large factory, using techniques of **mass production**, each person may have just a single operation to perform. The mass production factory can produce more cars per worker than the small-scale factory. This is an example of **economies of scale** (or **increasing returns to scale**), which occur when an increase of *x* per cent in the amounts of resources that are used in a factory leads to an increase of more than *x* per cent in the output from the factory.

The pattern of specialization between and within factories is known as the **division of labour** in society. This name goes back at least to Adam Smith (born in 1723 in Kirkcaldy, Scotland, died 1790; professor of moral philosophy at the University of Glasgow). Smith's most famous book, *An Enquiry into the Nature and Causes of the Wealth of Nations*, was published in 1776, and was one of the first major books largely devoted to the study of economic principles. Smith lived during the industrial revolution, when the concentration of work into factories and the use of machinery (compared to the previous methods of local, small-scale production) became widespread. One of the most famous passages in the *Wealth of Nations* describes production in a pin-making factory, where Smith observed 10 workers who could make a total of 48,000 pins per day, whereas a single worker would be unlikely to make even 20.

2.5.1 Factories, firms and industries

We have referred to the places where goods are produced as factories, but people also work together in farms, hospitals, shops, oil rigs, schools, offices, mines and so on. To avoid listing all of the places where people work, we refer to them all as factories.

A factory (or plant) is a place where people work in groups; a **firm** (or **company**) may operate several factories producing similar goods, or components of a good, or even producing very dissimilar goods. Firms may be owned and controlled by private individuals, or they may be under the control of central government (for example, the nationalized coal and railway firms in the UK) or of local government (for example, state schools in the UK). So, broadly speaking, the main topics of interest in discussing factories are the division of labour and the technical aspects of production, but decisions on matters of finance and the control of operations are the concern of firms. It is, of course, quite possible that a firm owns only one factory, and in this case the two can be discussed together.

An **industry** consists of all of the factories (in a country, unless we refer specifically to, for example, the world oil industry or the European steel industry) that produce a particular good or, more usually, a range of related goods. An industry may consist of one or more factories controlled by one or more firms. A firm may operate in more than one industry. For example, British Petroleum operates in both the oil and the chemicals industries.

The extent of an industry is not clear-cut. For example, at times we may refer to the food industry; at other times it may be necessary to distinguish the milk industry from the potato industry. The range of goods to be included in an industry is a matter of convenience and judgement in a particular context.

2.5.2 Transport costs and economies of scale

Although it makes sense to combine parts of a process of production in a single plant, some industries (for example car production) can make use of economies of scale to such an extent that it may be impractical to integrate all the production activities in a single plant. Firms may therefore produce components in several different plants and bring them together for assembly elsewhere. In Europe, this process may cross national boundaries. Ford, for example, produces car components in several countries. The economic advantages of this style of production depend on the extent of the possible economies of scale and the ease of transporting the components from one factory to another. Major changes in transport systems (such as the international rail link provided by the Channel Tunnel) may lead to significant changes in production patterns as the cost of transporting components is significantly reduced.

2.6 Specialization in the UK

The pattern of specialization in practice is very complex, and no economy uses all of its resources as efficiently as it might. An obvious example of a resource that is not fully used is unemployed labour. Table 2.5 shows the considerable rise from 1972 to 1987 in the proportion of the workforce that was unemployed, and the increase over the same period in the proportion that was self-employed rather than employed by firms: self-employment has increased from 7.75 per cent in 1972 to 10.26 per cent in 1987.

Table 2.6 shows, for a similar period, the shift from employment in agriculture (including fishing and other food production), manufacturing industries (which produce many of the tangible goods; see section 2.1) and construction (building) to employment in distribution, producing services of various kinds and employment by the government. This is a part of a continuing process in the UK, which is resulting in a major switch from the production of tangible goods

Table 2.5   Employment in the UK, 1972–87

	1972	1977	1982	1987
Workforce (thousands)	25,627	26,209	26,663	27,887
% unemployed	3.04	5.19	10.39	10.42
% employed	89.21	87.55	81.47	79.32
% self-employed	7.75	7.26	8.14	10.26

Source: *Annual Abstract of Statistics*

Table 2.6 Division of labour in the UK, 1967–87

% of employed people in	1967	1977	1987
Agriculture, forestry and fishing	1.90	1.73	1.48
Manufacturing	38.18	32.41	23.59
Construction	6.82	5.59	4.62
Transport and communications	6.99	6.39	6.13
Distribution (retailing and wholesaling)	12.26	12.07	15.37
Professional, scientific and other services	23.57	31.53	37.16
Government (except armed forces)	6.12	7.20	9.33
Other	4.16	3.08	2.32

Source: *Annual Abstract of Statistics*

in traditional industries (for example, iron and steel, textiles and motor vehicles) to the production of services.

2.7 Disadvantages of the division of labour

So far, our discussion has implied that specialization has nothing but advantages to offer to society. However, there is a variety of problems that may arise in a highly specialized society, and some people may want to sacrifice some of the additional outputs that specialization can bring to reduce or remove these problems.

The division of labour can lead to several problems, such as:

(a) An individual who specializes in a narrow range of activities may become bored or careless. Someone who spends too long at his job may be less effective at it than he would be if he took time off to do something else.

(b) Large factories may be prone to interruptions if a few crucial workers are absent, or if some vital piece of equipment fails.

(c) An individual specialist working on her own can control the quality of her product, and benefits directly in prestige and self-esteem from satisfying her customers. A worker in a large factory does not have this advantage, because the quality of the final product depends on many other people, and relations with customers are the concern of those who specialize in selling the product. In consequence, a worker may become dissatisfied with his job, because he has no control over the quality of the product. This dissatisfaction may reduce the quantity and/or quality of the goods produced.

(d) If people specialize, they contribute in different ways to the production of goods that people want. It is difficult (probably impossible) to find a society in which there is no difference in prestige between different jobs, and in which no people are considered (or consider themselves) to be more important, of higher class or greater status than other people. These differences can lead to social tensions between classes, races etc., and are a source of the social stratification discussed by sociologists.

(e) Changes in the pattern of specialization are needed from time to time because new equipment is introduced that changes people's abilities or that requires new skills. Changes also occur because workers retire or die, and others who begin to work have different abilities from those who have stopped working. These changes imply that some people change their jobs, and that some people's abilities are no longer wanted. Inevitably, some people are left without jobs when these changes take place. Some may be able and willing to retrain to do new jobs and to move to different areas, but others may be unemployed for long periods. Changes in the pattern of specialization both within and between countries are an important cause of unemployment, and a major reason why the level of unemployment is higher in some areas than in others. For example, changes in the method of producing steel and reductions in the amount of steel wanted have reduced employment in the UK iron and steel industry from 390,000 in 1972 to 147,000 in 1985. This reduction in employment is, of course, concentrated in towns where iron and steel were produced.

These disadvantages lead some to argue that it would be better to produce goods in small-scale factories, or even to abolish specialization so that people could be self-sufficient. The extent to which a society relies on production in very large factories depends in part on what is produced. In the UK in 1985, 68 per cent of all employees in manufacturing industries were employed in factories where at least 100 people worked. This figure had fallen from 84 per cent in 1979, mainly because of the decline in the proportion of the labour force working in those manufacturing industries in which large factories are more frequently found.

As economists, we cannot say how much output should be sacrificed to balance the advantages and the disadvantages of the division of labour, because each person makes his or her own value judgement on the benefits from having more goods and the disadvantages that have been discussed.

2.7.1 Disadvantages of international specialization

If a country specializes in producing a few goods, it relies on other countries to produce many of the goods that its citizens need. The possibility that another country will be unable to – or will refuse to – supply the goods that a country needs is likely to reduce enthusiasm for complete specialization according to comparative advantages. Most countries have some strategic reasons either for not specializing completely or for holding stocks of goods that come from abroad to reduce dependence on a single supplier. Conversely, of course, any country that is the sole supplier of a good is in a very strong strategic position. The desire of oil producers to co-ordinate their producing strategies through

OPEC (Organization of Petroleum Exporting Countries) is an example of the potential power of single suppliers.

The other major disadvantage of international specialization is linked to one of the disadvantages of individual specialization. The pattern of skills and/or natural resources changes, and so the pattern of specialization that accords to comparative advantages changes. Countries that have traditionally produced a particular good may find that other countries gain a comparative advantage, and so compete successfully with domestic firms. The domestic industry declines, and there is likely to be unemployment among its workers. Very often, this unemployment is concentrated in particular regions. For example, the decline of the UK car industry and increase in car imports over the past 20 years has contributed greatly to unemployment, particularly in the Midlands.

2.8 Specialization and economic systems

A country's **economic system** is its way of organizing economic activities, including the ways in which people come to specialize in particular tasks. There is a variety of economic systems, which can be divided into three groups:

(a) **Market** or **decentralized** economic systems, in which economic decisions are taken by individuals, and the outcome (including the pattern of specialization) is the result of the interaction of these decisions.
(b) **Planned** or **centralized** economic systems, in which economic decisions are taken by government planners.
(c) **Mixed** economic systems, in which many economic activities are organized in a decentralized way, but in which the government takes some of the most important economic decisions.

In practice, every economic system is mixed to some extent, but it is very useful to distinguish those (decentralized) in which government involvement is very limited and those (centralized) in which the government takes virtually all the major economic decisions.

2.8.1 Specialization in a planned economic system

In a planned system, decisions are made by a central, government appointed body. In principle, the planners must make very detailed decisions so that they can tell each person what to do, and determine exactly how each factory is to operate. To do this, planners would need information on everyone's abilities and the potential production of each factory, and they would have to decide how much of each good was wanted. In practice it is impossible to make such a detailed plan for the working of the economic system, and factory managers and individual workers are left to take many decisions. For example, a factory manager may have considerable scope to decide what is to be produced in his factory, and his decision depends on his motivation and on the range of choice allowed him by the planners.

2.8.2 Specialization in a market economic system

In this economic system, the pattern of specialization is the result of many individual decisions that are not co-ordinated by a plan. Each person chooses her specialization on the basis of her motivation and the opportunities available to her. A person may have skills that she could use in a one-person business, she may be able to do jobs offered by people who own factories, or she may be able to set up her own factory and employ other people. The reward from a one-person business is a combination of the profits from selling goods and the satisfaction of 'being one's own boss', offset by the possibility that the enterprise may fail. Jobs in factories pay wages, but may be boring or of little prestige. Running a factory may bring financial rewards and perhaps prestige, but also brings the risk that the costs of producing goods may exceed the proceeds from selling the goods produced, so that the factory owner makes a loss, and the employees lose their jobs.

If planners are equipped with powerful computers and a lot of detailed information they may be able to work out a pattern of specialization in accordance with comparative advantages. A market economic system does not have the deliberate co-ordination of a planned system, but it is not operating in an entirely random fashion. The following three observations imply that there is some tendency for the pattern of specialization in a decentralized economic system to reflect comparative advantages and to produce goods that people want, although these observations do not imply that specialization is necessarily extensive enough to give an efficient output level:

(a) Those who own factories want to employ the most suitable people, and so they are likely to offer wages that encourage those with the most appropriate skills to work for them.
(b) Workers choosing between jobs are likely to want to work where their skills are best rewarded.
(c) Self-employed specialists and the owners of factories can sell goods only if people want to buy them, and so they try to produce the goods that other people want.

The first two observations imply that it is likely that people work where their skills are used best, so that they may specialize according to their comparative advantages. The third observation implies that individual decisions on what goods are wanted may be reflected in decisions on what to produce.

Much of this book examines market economic systems. Part II is concerned with a simplified economic system in which it can be shown that individual decisions lead to a pattern of specialization in accordance with comparative advantages. In part III we discuss various features of economic systems that make the analysis more complex, and that imply in particular that people do not specialize according to their comparative advantages. These complications are a major reason for government intervention to modify many individual decisions and to transform a decentralized economic system into a mixed economic system.

2.8.3 International economic systems

The pattern of international specialization is, in part at least, the outcome of the international economic system (although political and strategic considerations are also important). There is plainly no equivalent of a central plan in international economic relations, but there are some international agreements that alter the effects of decentralized markets. In particular, there are agreements that encourage **free trade** by reducing restrictions that one country may place on the goods that other countries can sell to it. On the other hand, there are some arrangements that hinder free trade, and that are therefore likely to affect the pattern of international specialization.

Free trade has a variety of potential disadvantages, including:

(a) Some strategically important goods may not be produced if firms do not find it profitable to do so and, indeed, the cheapest source of these goods may be a potential political enemy. So free trade has political and military implications, and the government may restrict imports and subsidize domestic firms to ensure that the country's strategic interests are met. Strategic interests sometimes affect exporters also. For example, the USA restricts sales of high-technology products to Warsaw Pact countries.

(b) Comparative advantages do not remain unchanged because, for example, a country accumulates more machinery, its workers become better or worse educated compared with workers in other countries or new sources of raw materials, oil and coal are discovered. Established industries might therefore face foreign competition, causing unemployment among their workers.

(c) A country may find it difficult to establish a domestic industry in which it will eventually have a comparative advantage but that is not able to compete with established foreign firms during its early years. The government may restrict trade to protect these **infant industries**.

(d) A country that specializes may be vulnerable to events outside its control. For example, Caribbean countries that used to export sugar to the UK have suffered from the increased production of sugar beet in Europe; Mexico borrowed a large amount of money (over US$100 billion) to finance an ambitious development plan after the price of oil increased in 1979. The later fall in the oil price has given Mexico great problems in continuing to repay these loans.

2.9 Summary

The fundamental economic advantages gained by living in social groups are increases in outputs that result from specialization and the division of labour. The gains from specialization are the result of differences in opportunity costs, or comparative advantages. These gains do not depend on the absolute levels of people's efficiencies, but on their relative efficiencies. A society achieves all the gains from specialization, and reaches an efficient output level, if people specialize according to their comparative advantages.

Within a factory, people may specialize in part of a production process, and this division of labour can give rise to economies of scale. However, specialization may lead to boredom and alienation, and a specialist may be vulnerable to unemployment if his or her skill is no longer needed.

Countries also have comparative advantages and specialize, and gains can be made from international specialization even between rich and poor countries. The extent of specialization may be reduced for strategic reasons and also by the unemployment that can arise when comparative advantages and the pattern of specialization change.

Some societies plan their economic systems and may come near to achieving an efficient output level if the plan is detailed enough. Other societies do not plan in this way and the pattern of specialization is then the outcome of many individual decisions.

Specialization occurs in all economic systems and is one of the main reasons why people live together in societies. However, a person is unlikely to specialize if he or she cannot obtain the goods produced by other people. In chapters 3 and 4, we shall discuss how people obtain the variety of goods that they need. This discussion indicates how much each individual gains from the advantages of specialization and how an economic system determines how much of each good is produced. In chapter 5 we shall discuss ways of measuring the total production in an economy, which indicates, to some extent, the size of the benefits from specialization and the division of labour. In chapter 6 we shall make a preliminary examination of some other outcomes of economic systems, such as unemployment, inflation and poverty. We shall build on these introductory ideas in later parts of the book.

Topics and problems

(1) Is it possible to be completely self-sufficient? Is it desirable?

(2) At what age, if at all, should people be encouraged to specialize in their choice of educational courses? At what age do intellectual comparative advantages become apparent?

(3) What criteria are relevant in your own choice of occupation?

(4) In a planned economic system people may not be free to choose where they work or what they produce. Is this too high a price to pay for the central co-ordination of economic decisions?

(5) Should people receive the full benefit from what they do, however rich this makes them and however poor other people may be? If not, how should decisions on taking from some to give to others be made?

(6) Why is a greater fraction of the work-force likely to be employed producing services as time goes on? Is this desirable?

(7) What is the microelectronic revolution (in particular, the introduction of less expensive computers and communication equipment) likely to imply for the pattern of specialization in the UK?

(8) What does the theory of comparative advantage tell us about the benefits or otherwise of exports of subsidized food from rich to poor countries?

(9) What problems might a poor country face if it specializes in producing a single foodstuff?

(10) Cars are produced in most EC countries. Does this imply that countries are not specializing according to their comparative advantages?

(11) What are the likely economic effects of economic sanctions (involving refusal to trade) against a country?

For problems 12 to 17, consider the production possibilities of table 2.7.

Table 2.7 Production possibilities for problems 12 to 17

Case	Person	Food	Cloth	Chairs	Paper
1	Alan	150	50	—	—
	Bill	200	40	—	—
2	Alan	15	5	—	—
	Bill	50	20	—	—
3	Alan	50	20	—	—
	Bill	50	20	—	—
4	Alan	50	20	—	—
	Bill	100	40	—	—
5	Alan	150	50	—	—
	Bill	200	40	—	—
	Colin	250	20	—	—
6	Alan	120	160	50	—
	Bill	80	80	100	—
7	Alan	240	400	100	90
	Bill	160	200	90	60
8	Alan	120	100	60	—
	Bill	90	200	60	—
	Colin	90	300	20	—

(12) Draw diagrams to represent the efficient output levels that can be achieved by specialization in cases 1 to 5. What is produced in each case if the people are self-sufficient and each spends 60 per cent of his time producing food and 40 per cent producing cloth?

(13) What comparative advantages does one individual have over another in each case?

(14) Why is there no advantage to be gained from specialization in cases 3 and 4?

(15) In which cases does one person have an absolute advantage in the production of all (or both) goods?

(16) What is the maximum food production given a target of 25 cloth in cases 1 to 5?

(17) In cases 6 and 8, what is the maximum output of chairs given targets of 100 food and 60 cloth?

(18) A factory produces pins, and the weekly output is related to the number of people employed according to table 2.8. Draw one diagram to represent the information in table 2.8 and another to show the relationship between average output per worker and the number of workers. Give possible reasons for the shapes of the curves.

Table 2.8 Output levels for problem 18

Number of workers	Output per day (pins)
1	10
2	40
3	90
4	160
5	250
6	340
7	420
8	480
9	520
10	550

Chapter Three

Exchange and money

3.1 Introduction

Specialization and the division of labour can increase the outputs of goods, but an individual who specializes produces few of the goods that he or she wants. People would not agree to specialize if each person was forced to use only the goods that he or she produced, so an economic system requires a method for distributing goods to people. A planned economy might, in principle, distribute goods using a complete rationing system in which everyone is allocated goods according to a plan; an unplanned system relies on **exchanges** that result from individual decisions.

3.2 Voluntary exchange

We begin by examining decentralized economic systems in which the distribution of goods is governed by the **principle of voluntary exchange**:

People exchange goods voluntarily only if the exchange makes each of them better off than if they do not exchange.

The principle of voluntary exchange places limits on the quantities of goods that people exchange. We can illustrate this using the example in table 2.1, in which Alan can produce either 30 food or 60 cloth, and Bill can produce either 20 food or 80 cloth. If Alan produces food and Bill produces cloth, Alan wants to exchange food for cloth made by Bill and Bill wants to exchange cloth for food made by Alan, provided that this makes each of them better off compared with self-sufficiency. AB in figure 3.1(a) illustrates Alan's abilities to produce when he is self-sufficient. His opportunity cost of producing 1 food is 2 cloth.

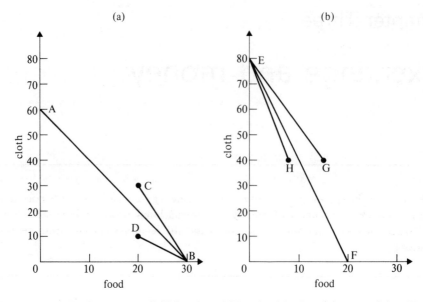

Figure 3.1   Exchange possibilities for skills of table 2.1 (a) Alan (b) Bill
AB represents Alan's production possibilities. At C he gains from trade; at D he does
not. EF represents Bill's production possibilites. At G he gains from trade; at H he
does not.

If Alan specializes in producing 30 food (so that he starts at B) and exchanges
some food for cloth made by Bill, he wants to have a combination that lies
outside line AB, such as point C. To achieve C, he must exchange 10 food
for 30 cloth, which is an **exchange ratio** of food for cloth of 1:3. Starting from
B, Alan reaches a point outside AB as long as the exchange ratio is 1 food
for more than 2 cloth. If he exchanges 10 food for 10 cloth (an exchange ratio
of 1:1) he reaches point D and is worse off than if he is self-sufficient.

Bill has a similar decision to make. EF in figure 3.1(b) shows his production
possibilities when he is self-sufficient and if Bill specializes in producing 80
cloth (so that he starts at E) he reaches a point outside EF as long as he
exchanges 1 cloth for at least 1/4 food. For example, if he exchanges 40 cloth
for 15 food, he has 15 food and 40 cloth (point G), and he is better off than
if he is self-sufficient. If he exchanges 40 cloth for only 8 food, he reaches
point H and is worse off than if he is self-sufficient. So Bill exchanges
voluntarily if the exchange ratio gives him 1 food for less than 4 cloth.

These two decisions show that Alan and Bill voluntarily specialize and
exchange only if the exchange ratio of food for cloth is between 1:2 and 1:4.
These limits on the exchange ratios at which voluntary exchange occurs are
determined by the opportunity costs of producing food measured in units of
cloth. Alan's opportunity cost of food is 2 cloth, and Bill's is 4 cloth. This
illustrates the general principle that:

Two people voluntarily exchange two goods only if the exchange ratio of good 1 for good 2 lies between their opportunity costs of producing good 1 measured in units of good 2.

The problems at the end of this chapter show that this principle applies even when one person has an absolute advantage in the production of both goods, and that it applies when there are more than two goods and/or more than two people.

3.2.1 Who gains from specializing?

In our example, Alan and Bill specialize voluntarily only if the exchange ratio of food for cloth is between 1:2 and 1:4. If the ratio is 1:2, Alan is no better off (and no worse off) than if he is self-sufficient. He can obtain the same combinations of food and cloth by producing food and exchanging it for cloth as he can if he is self-sufficient. So Bill obtains all the benefit from specialization if the ratio is 1:2. Similarly if the exchange ratio is 1:4, Bill is no better off and no worse off than if he is self-sufficient, and Alan gets all the benefit from specialization. If the ratio is near 1:2, then Bill gets most of the benefit; if it is near 1:4, Alan gets most of the benefit. The example illustrates the principle that:

The distribution between individuals of the benefit from specialization depends on exchange ratios.

3.2.2 Uncertainty and voluntary exchange

The principle of voluntary exchange implies that a person specializes and exchanges if she is certain to be better off by doing so. However, she may not do so if there is even a small chance that she will be much worse off. This possibility is particularly relevant to people in less developed countries. In principle, a poor person may have much to gain from specializing, but he will not do so voluntarily if he fears that he may be unable to obtain some of the goods vital to life. A person who obtains little more than a subsistence income from farming may, in most years, do much better by specializing in producing a single crop or in some non-agricultural activity. However, he may fear that in some years either his own crop will be very small or the crops of those who specialize in growing other goods that he needs will be small. In the former case, he has little to exchange for other goods; in the latter case the other goods that he wants are not available. He may feel that he is more likely to survive in these bad years if he grows a variety of crops for himself, and does not rely on other people.

3.2.3 Forced exchange

An exchange ratio must be between the exchangers' opportunity costs if they exchange voluntarily. The exchange ratio can be outside this range if one person forces the other to exchange at an unfavourable ratio. The most obvious force is physical violence: if Alan is physically stronger than Bill he might force Bill to specialize in cloth production, and to exchange say 5 cloth for 1 food. Then, if the possibilities are as in table 2.1, Alan could obtain 45 cloth in exchange for only 9 food and would have 21 food and 45 cloth. Bill would have 9 food and 25 cloth, which is less of both goods than he could have if he were self-sufficient. Alternatively, Alan may be able to enforce an exchange ratio that is very favourable to him because he can prevent Bill from producing food. Alan can do this if he claims ownership of all of the fertile land, and can successfully defend the land from Bill's attempts to use it. In this case Alan can take advantage of his **monopoly power** (see chapter 12) over the land, which arises because he is in sole control of a useful and valuable resource.

3.3 Money and the coincidence of wants

We have so far discussed a **barter** economic system in which goods are exchanged when each of two people has something that the other person wants. In the example with two people and two goods this **coincidence of wants** occurs because Alan, who has food and wants cloth, exchanges with Bill, who has cloth and wants food. They must, of course, agree on the exchange ratio, but at least they can find each other easily (if they could not they would not specialize). However, if many people specialize, the coincidence of wants is much more difficult to establish. Someone who specializes in making shoes and wants wood and food might spend a long time finding a woodcutter and a farmer who want shoes in exchange for their products. If this searching takes too much time, many of the benefits of specialization would be entirely lost. There is in fact no certainty that the shoemaker could ever find a woodcutter and a farmer who both want shoes. She might have to exchange her shoes for, say, bricks because the only person who wants shoes is a brickmaker. Then the shoemaker would exchange these bricks for the goods that she wants if she can find a woodcutter and a farmer who want bricks. Each individual might spend a lot of time arranging intermediate trades so that he or she can finally get what he or she wants.

The need to establish a coincidence of wants takes time and effort because each person must find others who want to exchange. The operation of an economic system can be made much more efficient by using an **intermediary** in exchange. This intermediary or **medium of exchange** is **money**. Money is paid to buy goods and is received when goods are sold, so that goods are not directly exchanged as they are in a barter system.

The **price** of a good is the amount of money for which it is bought or sold. Prices are related to exchange ratios: if the price of an apple is £1 and the price of a banana is £2, then a person who sells one banana can buy two apples. The implied exchange ratio is two apples for one banana. In general:

The exchange ratio of good 2 for a unit of good 1 is given by the price of good 1 divided by the price of good 2.

3.3.1 Other transactions

A modern economy involves many monetary transactions that do not involve buying and selling goods. For example:

(a) Money is used to pay wages to people who work in factories, and profits to people who own shares.
(b) Money is borrowed and repaid with interest at a later date.
(c) Taxes are collected in the form of money.
(d) The government uses money to make transfer payments, such as unemployment benefit and pensions.

In a mixed economy (where the government intervenes by, for example, levying taxes), some transactions are not voluntary; however, when a transaction involves two or more people who agree, the principle of voluntary exchange applies. For example:

(a) An employer pays a worker only if the employer gains more (from selling the goods produced by the worker) than he or she has to pay in wages to the worker. The worker takes the job only if the wage payment enables him to buy more goods than he could have if he were self-sufficient or in some other job.
(b) A person borrows if she will become better off by having more money now, taking into account that she must repay with interest later; a person lends if she will become better off by delaying spending her money and gaining interest, so that she can spend more in the future.

The fact that someone agrees to a transaction because she is better off doing so than not doing so does not tell us anything about how much better off she is made by the transaction. She may sell what she has produced for a low price, or work for a low wage, but still be better off than if she were self-sufficient. Exchange ratios determine how much each exchanger gains from a voluntary exchange. When money is used, prices, wages, interest rates and other payments determine how much each person gains in the economic system as a whole. We shall discuss in chapter 10 how the distribution of incomes depends on prices, wages, interest rates and other monetary payments.

3.4 Properties and uses of money

Money is used in a variety of transactions because it is widely **acceptable**. A person accepts money as long as he is confident that others will accept the money when he wants to spend it. Money must be **durable**, because people do not want it to deteriorate between the time that they receive it and the time that they spend it. Something that deteriorates rapidly is not useful as money because it cannot serve as a **store of wealth**.

Money is acceptable if people believe that they can use it to buy goods whenever they choose to do so. The acceptability of money would be undermined if the prices of goods were to change so rapidly that people could buy much less if they were to spend their money tomorrow than they could if they spent it today. There have been episodes, usually during or after wars, in which prices have risen so rapidly that people have lost confidence in using money. For example, prices in Greece at the end of November 1944 were 855,000 times higher than at the beginning of the month, and so anyone who held money throughout the month found that it was virtually worthless at the end. These exceptional circumstances, in which prices rise so rapidly that people lose confidence in the use of money, are known as **hyperinflations**.

Even though people lose confidence in the use of money when prices increase very rapidly, money is used in circumstances where prices rise much more rapidly than has ever occurred in the UK. The greatest annual price increase in the post-war period in the UK was 24 per cent between 1974 and 1975, whereas people in Argentina, Brazil and Israel have continued to use money despite the fact that prices have doubled in each of several recent years.

3.4.1 Unit of account

The money used for making transactions takes several forms: for example, notes, coins, cheques drawn on bank accounts and credit cards. In whatever way a transaction is made it is in the same **currency unit** or **unit of account** (the pound sterling in the UK, the dollar in the USA). The prices of goods, wages, interest payments, rents and so on are all measured in the unit of account. So, in addition to being the medium of exchange, money provides a way of simplifying the process of quoting prices and of measuring wealth, because everything can be measured in the same units. It is much easier to examine and compare the profits of firms when they are reported in money than it would be if, for example, farmers reported their profits measured in kilograms of corn and brickmakers reported profits measured in thousands of bricks.

3.4.2 Money and information

We saw in section 3.2 that exchange ratios determine how much each person gains from specialization. To gain the most, an individual wants to obtain as much as possible of what others produce for each unit of his own production. In terms of money, he wants to sell his own goods at the highest possible price, and buy from others at the lowest possible price. He therefore needs as much information as possible on the prices of the goods offered by other people. However, the amount of information that he needs is much less if all goods are exchanged for money than if he lives in a barter economy.

For example, suppose that a shoemaker wants to obtain milk. In an economy where money is used, she needs to know only who will pay the most money for her shoes, and who will sell milk at the lowest price. In a barter system she needs to know not only who will exchange milk for shoes, but also about all the indirect ways of obtaining milk for shoes. For example, she could exchange shoes for pencils, and pencils for milk, and she would want to do this if she could get more milk per shoe in this indirect way than by direct exchange. If each shoe could be exchanged for 20 pencils and each pencil for half a litre of milk, she can obtain 10 litres of milk per shoe. If she can find no one who wants to make a direct exchange of 10 litres of milk for a shoe, she would use the indirect method. So, in the barter system, she needs to know about many exchange ratios in addition to those affecting direct exchanges of shoes for milk. In an economic system where money is used, she needs to know only the prices at which people buy shoes, and the prices at which people sell milk. The information requirements for effective decision-making are much less.

3.4.3 Liquidity

Many people hold some money so that they can buy goods in an emergency. As long as no emergency arises, the money remains unspent: it is saved. People hold savings in forms other than money: for example, they buy shares, savings certificates and goods such as gold and houses. However, money can be used instantly to buy goods, whereas other forms of savings cannot. Shares and goods must be sold before savings can be used, and some savings certificates must be held for a specified period before the money is repaid. So these other forms of saving are not available as quickly as money when an emergency arises. Money is therefore useful because of its **liquidity**. Other forms of saving are less liquid than money because they cannot be used immediately to buy goods. In general:

> The liquidity of an item is measured by the speed with which it can be used to pay for other things.

3.5 Creation of money

The total money in an economy includes anything that plays most or all of the roles of money described in the previous section. Plainly, notes and coins are money, and an individual who can draw cheques on a bank account regards that account as money because the cheques can be used to pay for things. Note that the money in a bank account includes any money that may have been borrowed: to the person who can spend it, a bank loan or overdraft is money. Credit cards also represent money, and there is a variety of other ways of paying for goods, such as credit notes and IOUs, that are effectively money as long as they are acceptable.

3.5.1 Privately produced money

In some societies, people are allowed to produce the item used as money. For example, gold has been privately produced and used as money. Some produce money directly, and others obtain money indirectly by producing and selling other goods. If people specialize according to their comparative advantages, people produce goods if they can make more money producing goods than producing money. So it is certainly not true that, if no one is prevented from producing cash, everyone would choose to do so (for example, many people did not join the gold rushes of history), even if we, who are not allowed to print our own banknotes, are tempted to think otherwise.

3.5.2 State created money

In many countries the state prevents people from producing notes and coins. The government produces notes and coins at a production cost that is far below the face value of the money produced. So it makes a profit (known as **seignorage**) from its production of money and, as we discuss in chapter 17, the government can use this profit to pay for some of its expenditure.

3.5.3 Banks and money

The government can produce notes and coins, but banks make decisions on, for example, whether to create money by lending to individuals. A bank cannot create indefinitely large amounts of money by making loans to customers. In simple terms, a bank knows that some of its customers will want to withdraw notes and coins from their accounts. If 10 per cent of the money held in bank accounts is withdrawn in cash each day, then a bank cannot lend money and thus allow accounts to build up beyond 10 times the amount of notes and coins that it has available. So the fact that the government controls the amounts of notes and coins available means that there is an upper limit on the total size of bank accounts – and hence the total amount of bank lending is restricted.

The government has some control on total bank lending (which creates money) because it controls the production of notes and coins. In chapter 18 we shall see that the financial relationships between banks and the government are more complex than this simple argument allows, but the principle that there is a limit on banks' abilities to create money remains.

3.5.4 Measuring money

Few subjects in economics generate as much controversy as the measurement of the amount of money in circulation. Official statistics include a variety of measures, ranging from very **narrow** definitions – that money is just notes and coins – to very **broad** definitions – that the total money available includes a variety of bank and building society accounts that may involve less liquidity than a normal current or chequing account. For some purposes, an account that requires three months' notice of withdrawal is not liquid enough, but for predictable expenditures, an individual may regard the contents of such an account as money. Table 3.1 gives a number of different measures of the amount of money in circulation in the UK, and we discuss these in greater detail in chapter 18.

3.6 International trade

International specialization implies that countries must exchange goods, and the principle of voluntary exchange implies that countries specialize and trade with one another willingly only if both countries gain compared with a situation in which they are self-sufficient.

3.6.1 Terms of trade

The decision to trade and the distribution of the gains from trade depend on exchange ratios. In international trading, the amount that a country gains from trade depends on the prices at which it sells its exports and the prices that it must pay for imports. This ratio is the country's **terms of trade**:

A country's terms of trade is the average price of the country's exports divided by the average price of the country's imports.

Table 3.2 shows how the UK terms of trade have changed since 1980. Note that the average prices for imports and exports are for a representative collection of goods that cost £100 in 1985. The figures for the terms of trade are the average price of exports as a percentage of the average price of imports in the same year. The figure of 102.2 in 1981 implies that the UK could buy more imports with the money gained from the collection of exports in 1981 than it could in 1985. The figure of 95.6 in 1986 implies that the UK could buy fewer imports with the money gained from the collection of exports in 1986 than it could in 1985.

Table 3.1   Measures of the UK money supply (averages, January to March 1989)

	£ million	Cumulative £ million
Notes and coins	14,466	14,466
Instant access bank accounts	94,395	108,861
Other bank accounts	124,768	233,629
Building society accounts	138,851	372,480

Source: *Financial Statistics*, 1989

Table 3.2 UK terms of trade, 1980–8 (figures are index numbers with 1985 set at 100, so that each figure is a percentage of its 1985 level)

	Average price of exports	Average price of imports	Terms of trade
1980	69.7	68.9	101.2
1981	75.9	74.2	102.2
1982	81.0	80.4	100.8
1983	87.6	87.8	99.8
1984	94.8	96.1	98.7
1985	100.0	100.0	100.0
1986	91.8	96.0	95.6
1987	95.5	98.5	97.0
1988	97.1	98.8	98.3

Source: *Annual Abstract of Statistics*

A country's terms of trade improve if the average price of its exports increases relative to the average price of its imports (as occurred in the UK between 1986 and 1988). This implies that the country can buy a larger quantity of imports with the money obtained by selling a given quantity of exports, and so more goods are available for use in the country. If a country's terms of trade deteriorate (as between 1981 and 1984 in the UK), it must export more to obtain a given quantity of imports, which implies that fewer goods are available for use within the country. In general, changes in the terms of trade reflect changes in the extent to which a country gains from international trade, in terms of the goods that are available for use within the country.

The effect of a change in a country's terms of trade is analogous to the effect of a change in exchange ratios when individuals exchange goods (see section 3.2). The terms of trade determine the distribution of benefits from international specialization; exchange ratios determine the distribution of benefits from individual specialization and exchange.

If a country is able to produce all the goods it needs, it can become self-sufficient and would want to do so if the terms of trade deteriorate far enough (just as an individual wants to be self-sufficient if the exchange ratio is sufficiently unfavourable to him or her, see section 3.2). However, few countries have all the materials and energy that they need, and in some countries people are unable to grow sufficient food to allow the country to become self-sufficient. So the option of self-sufficiency is not available to many countries, and they must trade even if the terms of trade are very unfavourable to them.

The terms of trade of most oil-importing countries deteriorated during the 1970s, because the price of their imports of oil increased. Despite this worsening of their terms of trade, these countries were not able to cease trading internationally, because they needed oil. So the conclusion that countries trade only if they gain from trade is modified by the fact that many have no alternative to trading, even at unfavourable terms of trade.

3.7 Currencies and exchange rates

Within a country, virtually all transactions are made, and accounted for, in terms of the national currency. In international trade there is no uniquely acceptable way of making payments because each country has its own currency. The **exchange rate** between two currencies is the amount of one that can be bought for a unit of another: it is the price of one currency in terms of the other. These exchange rates are a vital ingredient of the international economic system. For example, when a French-made good is imported into the UK, either the importer must obtain French francs to pay the producer, or the producer is paid in pounds and then converts these into francs. Similarly, if a UK-produced good is exported to France, either the buyer must obtain pounds in exchange for francs to pay for the good, or the exporter is paid in francs and then converts these into pounds. The number of francs that can be exchanged for a pound affect the profitability of the trade.

An exchange rate can be quoted in two ways: for example, that between the pound and the dollar can be quoted in £ per $ or in $ per £. An exchange rate of $1.65 per £ is also a rate of £0.61 per $.

The pound **depreciates** against another currency if it loses value against the other currency. For example, the pound depreciates against the dollar if there is a reduction in the number of dollars received in exchange for one pound. The pound **appreciates** against another currency if it gains value against the other currency. For example, the pound appreciates against the dollar if there is an increase in the number of dollars received in exchange for one pound.

3.7.1 Exchange rates and the gains from trade

The prices of goods traded internationally, and hence the gains from trade, depend on exchange rates between currencies. Table 3.3 gives an example of production possibilities for the UK and the USA. The comparative advantages suggest that the UK should specialize in food production and the US in cloth. Suppose that the UK price of a kilogram of food is £5, and the US price of a metre of cloth is $4.

(a) The exchange rate is £1 = $2. The UK sells 1 food to the USA for £5 = $10 with which it can buy 2.5 cloth. The UK gains from this trade because it could gain only 2 cloth per unit of food if it were self-sufficient.
(b) The exchange rate is £1 = $1.2. The UK sells 1 food to the USA for £5 = $6 with which it can buy 1.5 cloth. The UK does not gain from this trade because it could gain 2 cloth per unit of food if it were self-sufficient.

As well as affecting the gains from trade, changes in exchange rates can have major effects on a country's economy. For example, if the pound depreciates against other currencies, then:

Table 3.3 Production possibilities
for the UK and the USA

	Food		Cloth
UK	30	or	60
USA	20	or	80

(a) An importer must pay more pounds to buy foreign currency to buy a
quantity of goods from abroad. Imports become more expensive in terms
of pounds, and an increase in the prices of goods imported to the UK may
contribute to inflation in the UK.

(b) An exporter receives more pounds for each unit of foreign currency that
he or she receives by selling abroad. Exporting becomes more profitable,
so firms are encouraged to export more. More labour is needed to produce
the additional goods for export, and this may contribute to a reduction in
unemployment.

3.7.2 Actual exchange rates

Trade and the distribution of gains from trade depend on currency exchange
rates, and historically these have been very volatile. Since 1945, the exchange
rate between the US dollar and the UK pound has varied from £1 = \$4.03
(between 1945 and September 1949) to £1 = \$1.08 (in January 1985). Table
3.4 shows the exchange rates of the pound with some other currencies between

Table 3.4 Selected exchange rates of the pound sterling, 1978–89

Year	US dollars	French francs	W. German marks	Japanese yen	Trade-weighted index (1975 = 100)
1978	1.92	8.65	3.86	402.73	81.5
1979	2.12	9.03	3.89	465.55	87.3
1980	2.33	9.83	4.23	525.99	96.0
1981	2.03	10.94	4.56	444.63	95.3
1982	1.75	11.49	4.24	435.20	90.7
1983	1.52	11.55	3.87	359.93	83.2
1984	1.34	11.63	3.79	316.80	78.6
1985	1.30	11.55	3.78	307.08	78.3
1986	1.47	10.16	3.18	246.80	72.8
1987	1.64	9.84	2.94	236.50	72.6
1988	1.78	10.59	3.12	227.98	82.0
1989	1.63	10.50	3.06	225.20	72.8

Source: *Financial Statistics*

1978 and 1989; it also shows the average exchange rate of the pound with the currencies of countries with which the UK trades. In this **trade-weighted index**, each country's currency is weighted according to the amount of trade between that country and the UK.

3.8 Economic transactions and the legal system

The gains from specialization and co-operation in economic activities are not the only reasons why people live together in social groups. A society has a code of laws that have important economic consequences.

3.8.1 Contracts

Many agreements between people would not be made if there were no way in which they could be enforced. For example, a borrower usually signs a **contract** to repay a loan; an employer often signs a contract that requires him or her to pay for work done; a tenant signs a contract to pay rent for a specified period. If these and other contracts could not be enforced, people would be unwilling to lend money, to work or to rent out their property.

The legal system provides ways of enforcing contracts and of obtaining compensation if a contract is broken. The legal system in the UK does not protect all contracts in all circumstances. For example, someone who is owed money by a firm that goes bankrupt may be unable to obtain full payment even though there is a contract.

3.8.2 Prohibitions and restrictions

Some exchanges are illegal in the UK. There are many goods that people may not buy: for example, heroin, plutonium and anti-aircraft missiles. Other goods, such as shot guns, can be bought legally only by people who have a licence.

Slavery is a major prohibition that few of us think about as our ancestors did. In the UK no individual can buy or sell another individual, and no one is allowed to sell himself or herself into slavery. All employees have the right to leave their jobs (perhaps after giving notice), a right that was denied to slaves in the British West Indies until 1833 and in the southern United States until 1865.

3.8.3 Property rights

The legal system protects and restricts **property rights**: it helps to protect goods against theft and to restrict the uses of goods that people possess. For example, planning laws may prevent a farmer from selling farmland for building; it is illegal to drive a car at more than 70 m.p.h. in the UK. Restrictions on property rights may change a person's view on whether an exchange is worthwhile or on the price at which it is worthwhile. We are accustomed to thinking of the legal system (police, courts, prisons etc.) as a part of the activities of the state, but some private firms protect property and collect debts for other people. We discuss the view that all legal services could and should be provided by private firms in section 22.5.1.

3.9 Rationing and planning

Rationing is a method of distributing goods that is used in countries of Eastern Europe, and was widely used in the UK during the Second World War. In principle, a rationing system could distribute a different quantity of goods to each person according to individual needs and wants. However, rationing systems usually operate by giving a basic ration to each person, supplementing the ration in particular cases. For example, a child received a greater ration of milk than an adult in the UK during the Second World War.

However detailed the system of rationing may be, the amounts of goods allocated must not exceed the amounts of goods available. There are at least two reasons why it may not be easy to ensure this:

(a) The rationers need detailed information on the amounts of goods that are available, but they may be unable to obtain this information because they need to decide the sizes of rations before the goods are produced. Events such as a bad harvest may upset their calculations.
(b) People may work harder if they are content with their rations, and some ways of allocating goods between people may lead to greater production than others. For example, people may be unwilling to do difficult jobs if their rations are no greater than those allocated to people who do easier jobs.

The second difficulty may be made worse if the planners make mistakes. If, by mistake, they tell people that they can have more goods than are actually available, it is likely that people will waste much time queueing at the places where the goods are distributed. In extreme cases, the time spent in queues may reduce the time spent at work, so that fewer goods are produced, which may cause even greater shortages.

People are likely to make voluntary exchanges of goods even if a rationing scheme is effective, because two people can both gain if each has received goods that the other wants. A non-smoking wine-drinker may exchange his ration of cigarettes for the wine allocated to a teetotal smoker. So even in countries that use rationing exclusively, individual decisions to exchange goods affect the quantities of the goods that people finally obtain.

3.10 Summary

People or countries that are not self-sufficient must obtain goods from each other. They do so through voluntary transactions (buying and selling) only if both the buyer and the seller are made better off by the transaction. This voluntary exchange occurs if the exchange ratios are within limits determined by exchangers' opportunity costs. In an economic system where money is used, an exchange ratio is a ratio of prices. The exchange ratio, price wage or interest rate involved in a transaction determines the extent to which each person or country gains from the transaction.

The use of money removes the need to find a coincidence of wants. Money must be something that is acceptable and durable. The prices of goods must not change so rapidly that people lose confidence in the use of money. Money is also used as a unit of account and as a form of saving. There are several definitions of money, depending on the items included.

The possibilities for international trade depend on the terms of trade and on exchange rates. Changes in exchange rates may have major effects on a country's economy.

The legal system helps to enforce contracts and to protect property. It also restricts some transactions that the government decides are socially undesirable.

The distribution of goods by rationing may lead to problems of co-ordination. Rationing does not remove all scope for voluntary transactions.

A system of voluntary exchange involves exchanging goods at prices. We have seen that price ratios are limited by opportunity costs, but we have not yet said how prices are determined within these limits. This is the subject of chapter 4. Once we know how prices are determined we can discuss the outcome of the economic system in terms of what is produced, the extent to which each person benefits, and other aspects such as unemployment and inflation. We return to discuss money as a form of saving and its role in government policy in chapters 11, 14, 17 and 18.

Topics and problems

(1) In a system of voluntary exchange, no one is forced into any economic transaction. Is such a system therefore fair?

(2) People in the UK are required to go to school, to pay for education through taxation and to join the national insurance scheme. Can you justify these involuntary transactions? What other involuntary transactions can you think of? Can you justify them?

(3) What exchanges are prohibited by laws? For what reasons?

(4) Every adult in the UK is given one election vote. Should people be allowed to sell their votes to buy goods that they value more?

(5) Should people have unrestricted property rights to do what they like with the goods that they own?

(6) What would happen if people suddenly lost confidence in the use of money?

(7) Which, if any, of the following might be suitable for use as money: cheese, sand, cows, stones, cigarettes, potatoes?

Use the information in table 3.5 on total production levels of each person to answer problems 8 to 11.

Table 3.5 Production levels for problems 8 to 11

Case	Person	Food	Cloth	Chairs
1	Alan	80	50	—
	Bill	40	100	—
2	Alan	80	50	—
	Bill	10	25	—
3	Alan	80	50	—
	Bill	40	25	—
4	Alan	80	50	30
	Bill	40	100	50
5	Alan	80	40	—
	Bill	20	40	—
	Colin	100	20	—
6	Alan	0	90	150
	Bill	240	0	120
	Colin	60	300	0

(8) What is the range of possible exchange ratios in each case? (N.B. when there are three goods, there are three possible exchange ratios for each pair of people.) Explain the relation between your answers to cases 1 and 2. Explain your answer to case 3.

(9) In case 5, suppose that the prices of food and cloth are £1 and £2 respectively. Who is willing to exchange what with whom?

(10) In case 4, suppose that the exchange ratios are 5 food for 4 cloth and 6 food for 4 chairs. What is the only exchange ratio of cloth for chairs that ensures that no pair of indirect exchanges is better than a direct exchange?

(11) In case 6, suppose that Alan specializes in chairs, Bill in food and Colin in cloth. What exchanges ensure that each person obtains one-third of the total output of each good? Would the use of money simplify these exchanges?

Chapter Four

Markets and prices

Markets — supply — demand — market equilibrium — competition and monopoly — using partial equilibrium analysis — elasticities — using elasticities — many markets: general equilibrium — markets and economic systems

---

4.1 Introduction

In a decentralized economic system, prices, wages, interest rates and other amounts of money involved in economic transactions are the result of the interaction of decisions in **markets**. In this chapter we examine markets using a fundamental method of economics: **supply and demand analysis**. This method is divided into two parts:

(a) **partial equilibrium analysis**, which examines a single market
(b) **general equilibrium analysis**, which examines all markets at once.

We examine both parts of the method in this chapter.

In simple examples of barter, such as those of Alan and Bill in chapter 3, an exchange involves the simultaneous sale of one good and purchase of another. When money is used, decisions to buy and sell need not be co-ordinated in so simple a way, and we separate the discussion of decisions to sell from that of decisions to buy. The people, firms or government agencies involved in a single market are divided into:

(a) **suppliers**, who want to sell
(b) **demanders**, who want to buy.

The analysis of supply and demand is probably the most famous and widely used method in economics. It may be reasonable to say that it is the most widely misused too.

Alfred Marshall (born in London, 1842, died 1924; professor of political economy at the University of Cambridge 1885–1908) established the principles underlying partial equilibrium analysis in his *Principles of Economics* (first published in 1890). This book was, for many years, the main text used in economics education in the UK. As well as making major contributions to the principles of economics, Marshall was concerned with less theoretical matters, and was a member of the 1891–4 Royal Commission on Labour. He was particularly concerned with poverty, and he wrote in the *Principles* that 'the study of poverty is the study of the causes of the degradation of a large part of mankind'. His most famous pupil, at least among economists, was J. M. Keynes (see section 17.5.1), who wrote in his obituary of Marshall in the 1924 *Economic Journal*: 'Marshall is the father of Economic Science as it exists in England today'. Economic science has expanded in the past 65 years (not least through the work of Keynes), but Marshall's contribution to supply and demand analysis remains the foundation of a large part of economics.

4.2 Markets

To an economist a market is not necessarily a place where buyers and sellers meet in person. Instead:

> A market is the totality of all acts of buying and selling a particular good in a given period of time.

A market may be limited geographically (for example: the French market for shirts or the London silver market), but there is no need for buyers and sellers to meet. Mail-order, telephone and computerized Stock Exchange transactions, for example, are all included in markets.

4.2.1 Goods markets

One problem involved in discussing markets concerns the extent of the range of goods to be included in a single market. For some purposes it may be useful to discuss 'the housing market' in broad terms, but for other purposes we may need to discuss 'the market for four-bedroomed country cottages within 10 miles of York', or the 'market for north-facing studio flats in Chelsea'. Similarly, we may sometimes want to discuss the food market, on other occasions we may need to limit the discussion to the meat market or to the fruit market, and sometimes we may need to limit it further to the beef market or the apple market.

There are many occasions in this book when we discuss broadly defined markets, but in this chapter we examine basic ideas and for this purpose it is generally better to think of narrowly defined markets. In this case two items are involved in the same market if they are close substitutes for one another, in the sense that a potential buyer of one would be equally satisfied with the other whenever the two items have the same price. For example, this definition would be likely to include different brands of petrol in the same market, but would involve separate markets for different types of cars.

4.2.2 Labour markets

Labour time is bought by employers from employees, although the workers themselves are not bought (unless they are slaves). It is frequently useful to distinguish markets for different types of labour, so that there are separate markets for computer programmers' labour time, plumbers' labour time and so on.

4.2.3 Other markets

Land, equipment and natural resources that are used in production are bought and sold in markets, and there are also markets in which land, housing and equipment are rented. The markets for land, labour and equipment (which are known as **factors of production**, or simply as **factors**) are **factor markets**.

Financial assets, such as shares in firms, are bought and sold on the **stock market**. Individuals, firms and the government borrow in the **loan market** from those who want to lend. Sometimes it is useful to sub-divide these markets by discussing the market for one firm's shares, or for loans of a particular duration (for example, 20 year mortgage loans).

Currencies are bought and sold on **foreign exchange markets**, and it is possible not only to buy, say, US dollars (in exchange for pounds) for immediate use on **spot markets**, but also to contract now to buy dollars which will be provided in three months' (or six months' or some other specified period) time on **futures** or **forward markets**. Futures markets also exist for a number of basic goods, such as oil, wheat and copper, and we discuss their role in helping firms to be more certain about their future prospects in chapter 14.

4.3 Supply

We saw in chapter 2 that people specialize voluntarily only if they can obtain more goods through exchange than they can obtain if they are self-sufficient. So more people want to specialize in producing a good if they can sell it for a high price than when they get little money for it. Those who organize firms are also likely to want to produce more when they receive a high price. The supply of a good is the quantity of it that people and firms want to sell at a particular price. It is usually true that:

The supply of a good increases if its price increases.

The relation between the supply of a good and its price is given by its **supply schedule** and is represented by a **supply curve**. An example is given in table 4.1 and figure 4.1.

Note that, in all diagrams involving supply and/or demand curves, price is measured on the vertical axis and quantity on the horizontal axis. This is a convention that economists have long used. It is usual to join the points with

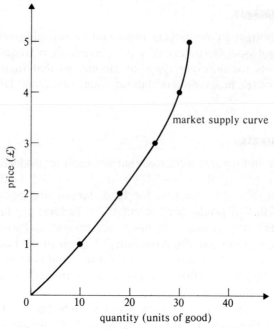

Figure 4.1 Market supply curve for schedule of table 4.1
The quantity supplied increases as price increases.

Table 4.1 Supply schedule relating quantity of good supplied to its selling price

Selling price (£)	Quantity supplied (units)
0	0
1	10
2	18
3	25
4	30
5	32

a smooth curve to approximate the response of suppliers and/or demanders to fractional prices.

The supply curve that we have drawn is the **market supply curve**, which shows the total amount that people and firms want to supply at each price. We can also draw a supply curve for each individual and firm, showing the amount of the good that he or it is willing to supply at each price. The market supply is found by adding the supplies of all individuals and firms.

4.3.1 Other influences on supply

The supply curve shows how supply depends on price, but supply is also influenced in other ways. The quantity supplied at each price depends on:

(a) The technology available to producers. Supply increases if a new method of production is invented that enables firms to produce more cheaply.
(b) The costs of factors of production used to produce it. If these costs increase, supply is likely to fall because some suppliers can no longer make a profit and so are likely to go out of business.
(c) The prices of other goods that people and firms could supply instead. A supplier may switch from producing good 1 to producing good 2 if the price of good 2 increases; hence the supply of good 1 depends on the price of good 2. This switching is most likely to occur when a firm can produce different goods with similar factors. For example, farmers switch from growing wheat to growing barley if the price of barley increases but the price of wheat does not.
(d) Random events, including the weather which affects production in the agricultural and building industries in particular.

A supply curve represents the relation between the supply of a good and its price under the assumption that all these other influences are unchanged. If any of these influences changes, the supply curve shifts.

(a) An increase in supply at each price implies that the supply curve shifts outwards (as from SS to TT in figure 4.2). This shift could be caused by a change in any of the other influences, such as by a reduction in production costs following an invention or a fall in the prices of factors of production used to produce the good, by a fall in the prices of other goods that could be produced instead or by weather that is favourable for producing the good.
(b) A reduction in supply at each price implies that the supply curve shifts inwards (from TT to SS in figure 4.2). This shift could be caused by, for example, an increase in the prices of factors of production, an increase in the prices of goods that could be produced instead, or unfavourable weather.

4.4 Demand

The **demand** for a good is the quantity of it that people and firms want to buy at a particular price. It is usually true that

The demand for a good falls if its price increases.

The relation between the demand for a good and its price is given by its **demand schedule**, and is represented by a **demand curve**. An example is given in table 4.2 and figure 4.3. (Note that we have not specified the demand when

Figure 4.2   A shift in the supply curve
The supply curve shifts from SS to TT because firms are willing to supply more at each price.

Table 4.2   Demand schedule relating quantity of good supplied to buying price

Buying price (£)	Quantity demanded (units)
1	38
2	30
3	25
4	21
5	18
6	16

the price is zero. A good with a zero price is freely available, and so people may demand an enormous quantity at no cost to themselves.)

The demand curve that we have drawn is the **market demand curve**. We can also draw a demand curve for each individual or firm. The market demand is found by adding the demands of all individuals and firms.

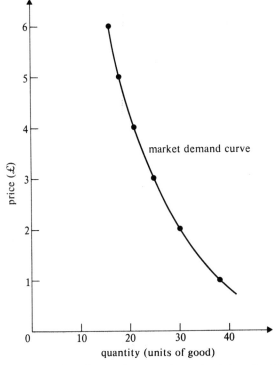

Figure 4.3 Market demand curve for schedule of table 4.2
The quantity demanded falls as price increases.

4.4.1 Other influences on demand

The demand curve shows how demand depends on price, but demand is influenced in other ways too. The quantity demanded at each price depends on:

(a) The incomes of those who buy the good. Generally, if people's incomes increase, more goods are demanded (we discuss exceptions to this statement in section 9.3).
(b) The prices of other goods. People demand less of a good if the price of a similar (or **substitute**) good falls. They buy more of a good if the price of a **complementary** good falls (for example, people buy more accommodation in hotels if the price of air travel falls because they take more holidays).
(c) People's **tastes**, which is a way of summarizing other influences on demand, such as opinion, the effects of advertising, the example of friends etc.

A demand curve represents the relation between the demand for a good and its price under the assumption that all other influences are unchanged.

The demand curve shifts if one of these influences changes. For example, the demand curve shifts outwards from DD to EE in figure 4.4 if there is a

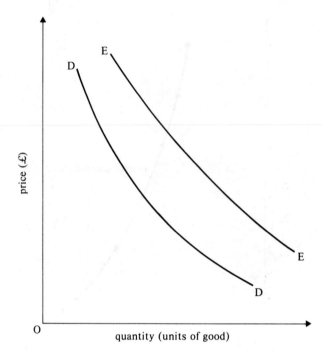

Figure 4.4 A shift in the demand curve
The demand curve shifts from DD to EE because people demand more at each price.

successful advertising campaign for the good or if there is an increase in the prices of substitute goods. The demand curve shifts inwards if there is a reduction in demand at each price.

4.4.2 Unusual slopes

The reasons that we have put forward for the upward slope of the supply curve and the downward slope of the demand curve are in line with common sense. Upward-sloping supply curves and downward-sloping demand curves are used in most applications of supply and demand analysis in this book and elsewhere. However, it is possible that curves have 'perverse' slopes. For example, people may demand more of a good when its price is high than when it is low if the good has some snob or status appeal. There is no point in showing off that one can afford to buy something that is very inexpensive, and so the demand for such a good is low when the price is low. On the supply side, it is possible that some people are capable of producing only one good. When its price is high, they can buy all the other goods that they want by producing only a little. If its price is low, they must produce and sell much more to generate an income that is sufficient to buy what they want. In this case, more is supplied at a lower price than at a higher price. It is a useful exercise to see which of our arguments in this and other chapters can be carried through when one (or even both) of the curves has other than the usual slope.

4.5 Market equilibrium

If we combine figures 4.1 and 4.3 into a single diagram (figure 4.5), we can see that in this case demand equals supply when the price is £3. The market is in **equilibrium** at that price:

The **equilibrium price** is that for which demand equals supply

In equilibrium, the market **clears**: suppliers can sell the quantity that they want to sell and demanders can buy the quantity that they want to buy. The quantity bought and sold at the equilibrium price is the **equilibrium quantity**. In figure 4.5, the equilibrium price is £3 and the equilibrium quantity is 25.

If the price is £4, there is a situation of **surplus** or **excess supply**, because the supply (30) exceeds the demand (21), and so some sellers sell less than they want to sell. Some suppliers may decide to store some of the goods that

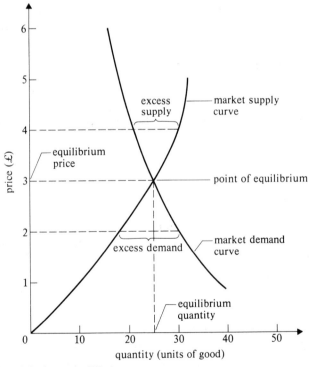

Figure 4.5 Market equilibrium
Demand equals supply at the equilibrium price. When price exceeds the equilibrium there is excess supply (a surplus); when price is lower than the equilibrium price there is excess demand (a shortage).

they had hoped to sell, and others may try to attract buyers away from other sellers by reducing the price that they ask. Some suppliers are unable to sell the quantity that they would like to sell when the price is £4, and so the market is not in equilibrium.

If the price is £2, there is a situation of **shortage** or **excess demand**, in which demand (30) exceeds supply (18), and so some demanders buy less than they want. Some demanders may buy another good, and others may hold their money for longer than they would wish. Some suppliers may take advantage of the shortage and recognize that they would not sell less if they increased the prices that they ask. The market is not in equilibrium because some demanders are unable to buy what they would like to buy when the price is £2.

An equilibrium price is not necessarily fair or desirable simply because the market clears. For example, the price of houses may be at its equilibrium level, but that level may be more than some people can afford. Without government intervention to provide subsidized housing, some people would be homeless when the housing market was in equilibrium. Many people might make the value judgement that this is not a desirable situation.

Note that in the definition of market equilibrium we consider only the price of the good in question. The price of the good may fall when there is excess supply, assuming that all other prices are unchanged. Partial equilibrium analysis of this kind makes great use of the *ceteris paribus* assumption.

4.5.1 Actual and equilibrium prices

A market clears when everyone buys and sells at the equilibrium price, but we have not established that it is possible or likely that the *actual* price is at the *equilibrium* level. There are two questions that we can ask in this context:

(a) Does everyone buy and sell at the same price?
(b) Do the prices at which people buy and sell move towards the equilibrium level?

We can give positive answers to these two questions provided that:

(a) Each demander buys from the supplier who sells at the lowest price. This requires that each demander knows who the cheapest supplier is, and has no reason (such as a personal prejudice) not to buy from that person.
(b) Each supplier reduces the price that she asks when she has unsold goods, and increases her price when she cannot supply all that her customers want.

If, in these circumstances, some suppliers charge more than others, those who charge higher prices have no customers, and so they reduce their prices. Suppliers who charge a lower price find that people are queueing up to buy from them, and they increase their prices to profit from the demand for their goods. The differences between the prices charged by different suppliers are reduced until everyone buys and sells at the same price.

4.5.2 Price movements towards equilibrium

If the price at which people buy and sell exceeds the equilibrium price, the quantity supplied exceeds the quantity demanded (for example, price £4 in figure 4.5). Suppliers have goods that they cannot sell, and an incentive to reduce their prices. So:

> If the actual price exceeds the equilibrium price, the actual price falls towards the equilibrium.

If the actual price is below the equilibrium price (for example, price £2 in figure 4.5) more is demanded than is supplied, and so some demanders are not satisfied. Suppliers respond to the shortage by asking for higher prices and, although some people are then dissuaded from buying, the suppliers can still sell all they want to sell. So:

> If the actual price is below the equilibrium price, the actual price increases towards the equilibrium.

We have demonstrated that if demanders buy from the cheapest supplier, and suppliers increase their prices in response to a shortage and reduce their prices in response to a surplus of the good, the actual price moves towards the equilibrium price. The equilibrium is said to be **stable** because of this tendency for the actual price to move towards its equilibrium level.

4.5.3 Why bother with equilibrium?

The behaviour of demanders and suppliers is influenced by actual prices, and not by equilibrium prices. Why, then, do we bother to analyse market equilibrium? The answer is simplicity: the equilibrium price of a good depends on the demand and supply curves that represent the amounts that people and firms want to buy or sell at each price. Actual prices also depend on these curves, but they are affected by the speed with which suppliers respond to shortages and surpluses, and the speed with which demanders find the cheapest supplier. So the analysis of actual prices is more complex than the analysis of equilibrium prices, and the analysis of equilibrium prices is a major part of the analysis of actual prices.

4.5.4 The speed of price changes

Our arguments on the stability of the equilibrium do not tell us how quickly the actual price moves towards the equilibrium price. The speed of movement may be very important because the equilibrium price changes if either the supply curve or the demand curve shifts. These shifts may be quite frequent, particularly in markets where supply or demand is affected by the weather (such as markets for harvested food and for ice-cream). If the actual price moves only slowly towards the equilibrium, the equilibrium price may change before the actual price has reach its equilibrium level.

4.5.5 Price and quantity adjustments

If the price in a market does not rapidly reach equilibrium, many goods will be bought and sold at non-equilibrium prices. Then either there is excess demand, and so some buyers are constrained so that they buy less than they would like, or there is excess supply, and some sellers are constrained so that they sell less than they would like. Buyers or sellers must adjust the quantity that they buy or sell away from what they want: they must make a quantity adjustment in what they do. This may lead to other quantity adjustments as, for example, a seller who cannot sell all he wants might decide to produce less and make some workers redundant. If the price does not move rapidly to the equilibrium level, there are **quantity adjustments** that bring the amount bought into equality with the amount sold.

The speed of price movements towards equilibrium is a fundamental aspect of economic behaviour. In part II, we examine economic systems in which we assume that prices move very rapidly to their equilibrium levels. Changes in demands and supplies in any market, including labour markets, lead to rapid **price adjustments** and a new equilibrium outcome. There are no persistent excess demands or supplies. In chapter 13 we examine markets in which suppliers are slow to respond to shortages and surpluses because, for example, they believe that the shortage or surplus may only be temporary, so that the equilibrium price will soon change, or because they want to avoid annoying regular customers by frequently changing their prices. In these markets, there are quantity adjustments instead.

The assumption that is made on the speed of movements towards equilibrium is one of the fundamental points of disagreement on the causes and cures for unemployment. **Free market economists** believe that if there is unemployment (that is, if more labour is supplied by individuals than is wanted by firms), then the price paid for labour (that is, the wage) will fall rapidly towards a new equilibrium where demand and supply are equal. Unemployment is then quickly reduced. **Keynesian** economists believe that such rapid wage movements do not occur (we discuss why they believe this in part III) and so unemployment persists. This single paragraph is, of course, inadequate to describe the persistent and passionate debate between these two schools of thought (and there are several variants of each in practice). However, it alerts us to the consequences of the speed of price changes and its importance in macroeconomic contexts.

4.6 Competition and monopoly

Our analysis of price movements towards equilibrium assumes that each supplier announces the price at which he or she is willing to sell, and that each demander decides how much to demand from each supplier, given these announced prices. This is a realistic assumption for many of the goods that we buy, although buyers often negotiate the prices of houses, cars and some other goods. **Price-takers** are people who make a decision on whether to buy or sell at a given price; **price-setters** are people who can change the price at which they buy or sell.

The distinction between price-setters and price-takers becomes blurred if a price-setter is forced by the actions of others to change his price unless he is willing to accept the consequences of not doing so (for example, the consequences might be that he fails to sell anything if he does not reduce his price). For example, if there are several sellers of petrol in a town, one is unlikely to sell much petrol if he does not reduce his price when his rivals do. Although he can announce whatever price he chooses, he is forced by his rivals' action to reduce his price or sell no petrol. In principle he is a price-setter, but in practice he has little opportunity to set his price at an independent level: all price-setters take similar decisions in these circumstances, and no individual has much power to act differently.

The ability of a price-setter to act independently depends on the extent of **competition** in the market. A supplier has very little scope to set her price in an independent way if she has many close competitors. In part II we examine markets in which there is **perfect competition** because there are so many sellers, each of whom can supply only a very small fraction of the total, that none can effectively change his or her price from the level charged by all the others. If one supplier increases his price, all his customers go elsewhere; if one supplier reduces his price, every demander wants to buy from him, and he cannot meet the demand. He makes more profit by selling his limited supply at the price charged by all the others than by selling it at a lower price. This **market structure** is unrealistic, but it is very convenient to assume that no seller has any **market power** in this way. We can then isolate the effects of a change in demand without considering the possibility that different firms may react in different ways.

An equally idealized market structure is **monopoly**, in which the single seller faces no competition and so need not be concerned with the prices set by rivals. She can announce whatever price she wants and sell whatever is demanded at that price. The individual supply curve and the market supply curve are identical. Monopoly is also unrealistic, because there is always some substitute for any good – even if it is not very close – and the price set by suppliers of that substitute affects the demand for the good. However, an examination of monopoly focuses on the effects of market power, as we shall see in chapter 12.

Between perfect competition and monopoly there are other market structures, including **monopolistic competition** and **oligopoly** (see chapters 12 and 13). In these market structures, sellers set prices with some degree of independence, but most take some notice of the prices set by their rivals. The analysis of oligopoly focuses particularly on the fact that one price-setter is uncertain of the reaction of his rivals to his own price-setting behaviour.

Perfect competition, monopoly, monopolistic competition and oligopoly are theoretical market structures that are useful for isolating different aspects of the behaviour of price-setters. In perfect competition there are very many firms; in monopolistic competition there is also a considerable number; in oligopoly there are a few (*oligo* is Greek for 'few'); in monopoly, there is a single firm. In practice, the number of firms selling a particular good is only a rough guide to the freedom of each seller to set an independent price. This number is reflected in a **concentration ratio** for an industry, which is the percentage of total sales of a good made by the largest *n* firms (where *n* is usually 3, 5 or 10). If the ratio is low, then even the largest firms sell only a small percentage of the total, and so there are many competitors – the market is not far from perfect competition. If the largest five firms supply nearly all the market, then there is an oligopoly. Table 4.3 shows some concentration ratios for UK industries.

4.7 Using partial equilibrium analysis

The analysis of a single market can help us to answer many questions on the behaviour of prices, wages, interest rates and other aspects of the economy. We discuss some examples here.

Example 4.1

Suppose that the price of meat increases, and so people buy more cheese. The old and new demand schedules and the unchanging supply schedule for cheese are shown in table 4.4 and the supply and demand curves are shown in figure 4.6. The equilibrium price of cheese increases from £4 to £5, and the equilibrium quantity increases from 800 to 900. Note that the equilibrium quantity increases

Table 4.3 Concentration ratios for selected UK industries (1980)

Industry	% of total output supplied by largest five firms
Cement	86
Glass	63
Basic industrial chemicals	57
Hand tools and finished metal goods	14
Cycles and motor cycles	80
Precision instruments	18
Brewing	60
Tobacco	100
Clothing, hats and gloves	12
Furniture	12

Source: *UK Census of Production* (1980)

Table 4.4 Supply and demand schedules for example 4.1

Price (£ per kg)	Old demand (kg)	New demand (kg)	Supply (kg)
2	1,350	2,025	600
3	1,050	1,575	700
4	800	1,200	800
5	600	900	900
6	450	675	1,000
7	350	525	1,100

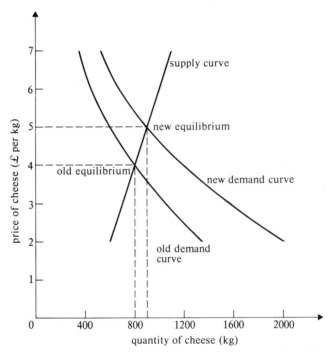

Figure 4.6 Supply and demand curves for example 4.1
Demand increases at each price, and the equilibrium price increases.

by only 12.5 per cent, even though the quantity demanded at each price increases by 50 per cent. Some of the increase in demand is 'choked off' because the equilibrium price has increased.

Example 4.2

Suppose that an invention reduces the cost of producing a computer by 50 per cent. The old and new supply schedules and the unchanging demand schedule are given in table 4.5 and illustrated in figure 4.7. For example, firms that

Table 4.5 Supply and demand schedules for example 4.2

Price (£)	Old supply (number of computers)	New supply (number of computers)	Demand (number of computers)
800	1,500	6,500	10,750
1,200	4,000	10,000	10,000
1,600	6,500	13,000	9,250
2,000	8,500	15,500	8,500
2,400	10,000	17,500	7,750
2,800	11,500	19,000	7,000
3,200	13,000	20,000	6,250

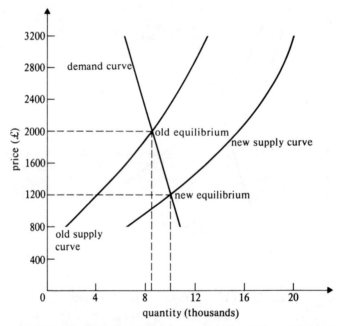

Figure 4.7 Supply and demand curves for example 4.2
Supply increase at each price, and the equilibrium price falls.

were willing to supply 10,000 computers at £2,400 become willing to supply that quantity at £1,200. The equilibrium price falls from £2,000 to £1,200. Some of the 50 per cent reduction in the cost of producing a computer is offset by the increase in the equilibrium quantity from 8,500 to 10,000.

Example 4.3

A large number of school-leavers enter the labour market, so that the supply of labour increases. The supply curve for labour shifts from SS to TT in figure

4.8, and the equilibrium wage falls from E to F. The increase in the size of the labour force causes the equilibrium wage to fall.

Example 4.4

The increased use of cars increases the demand for oil, causing an increase in the equilibrium price of oil from X to Y in figure 4.9. However, the higher price eventually leads to more exploration for oil, and to the exploitation of oil fields that were unprofitable at the old lower price. So in the **long run** the supply curve for oil shifts from SS to TT, and the equilibrium price falls to Z. Some of the initial increase in the equilibrium price of oil is offset by the long-run increase in supply. The curve EF that joins the initial equilibrium to the long-run equilibrium may be thought of as the **long-run supply curve** (because it allows for the supply of oil from new fields). Curves SS and TT are **short-run supply curves** (each from a fixed number of fields). This example illustrates that:

> where some effects of a price change take place only after an interval of time, the eventual change in the equilibrium price is less than the immediate change.

Example 4.5

Suppose that more American tourists decide to take their holidays in the UK. The tourists may pay their hotel and other bills in pounds. So the demand for

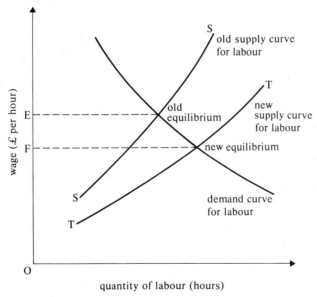

Figure 4.8 Supply and demand curves for example 4.3
More people want to work at each wage, and the equilibrium wage falls.

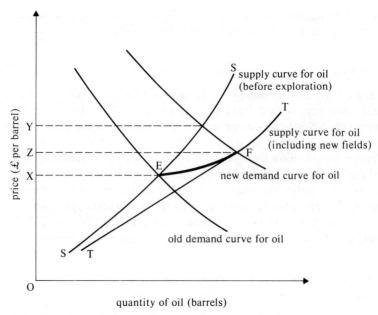

Figure 4.9 Supply and demand curves for example 4.4
Demand increases at each price, so the equilibrium price increases from X to Y in the short run. This stimulates exploration, so that the equilibrium price falls from Y to Z in the long run. The long-run supply curve is EF.

pounds by those who hold dollars increases, shifting the demand curve from UU to VV in figure 4.10(a). The equilibrium price of a pound in terms of dollars (that is, the equilibrium exchange rate) increases from £1 = \$2 to £1 = \$2.5: the increased demand for pounds causes an **appreciation** of the pound relative to the dollar. We can also analyse this in the market for dollars, where the American tourists increase the supply of dollars by buying pounds. The supply curve for dollars moves from WW to XX in figure 4.10(b), and the equilibrium price of a dollar in terms of pounds falls from \$1 = £0.5 to \$1 = £0.4. The increased supply of dollars causes a **depreciation** of the dollar relative to the pound. The movements of the exchange rates are equal and opposite since one is the reciprocal of the other. (Note also that governments often have policies to offset these market changes in order to maintain exchange rates at target levels: see section 21.4.4.)

4.8 Elasticities

The examples of the previous section involve shifts in one or both of the demand and supply curves. The direction of the change in the equilibrium price, wage or exchange rate follows from the fact that we have drawn downward-sloping demand curves and upward-sloping supply curves. The size

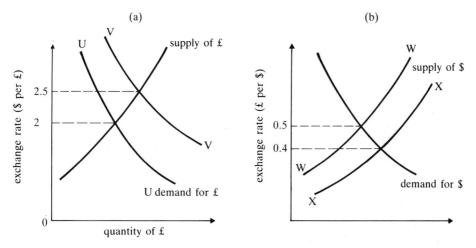

Figure 4.10 Supply and demand curves for example 4.7.5 (a) market for pounds (b) market for dollars
The demand for pounds rises from UU to VV and the pound appreciates relative to the dollar. Equivalently, the supply of dollars falls from XX to WW.

of the changes in the equilibrium price and quantity in a market depends on the shapes of the curves and the extents to which they shift.

Economists have traditionally used the concept of **elasticity** to describe the effects of a change in supply or demand. If a change in one item (x) leads to a change in another item (y), then

The elasticity of y with respect to x (or the x-elasticity of y) is the percentage change in the size of y following a 1 per cent change in the size of x.

For example:

The **price-elasticity of supply** is the percentage increase in the quantity supplied following a 1 per cent increase in the price of the good.

The **price-elasticity of demand** is the percentage decrease in the quantity demanded following a 1 per cent increase in the price of the good.

The **income-elasticity of demand** is the percentage increase in the quantity demanded following a 1 per cent increase in the incomes of those who buy the good.

So, if a 1 per cent increase in the price of a good causes a 2 per cent increase in supply and a 3 per cent reduction in demand, the price-elasticity of supply is 2 and the price-elasticity of demand is 3.

It is usual (but not universal) to define an elasticity so that it is positive, even though the curve may describe a negative relationship (x increases and *y* falls). For example, supply usually increases and demand usually decreases when price increases, so that the definition of price-elasticity of supply involves an increase in quantity and that of price-elasticity of demand involves a decrease in quantity when the price increases.

The terms 'price-elasticity of supply' and 'price-elasticity of demand' are sometimes abbreviated to 'elasticity of supply' and 'elasticity of demand'. These abbreviations may lead to ambiguity, because the *cause* of the change in the quantity supplied or demanded is not specified. We shall refer to the elasticities of other influences on supply and demand, and so we shall continue to use the full names of the price-elasticities.

4.8.1 Elastic and inelastic curves

It is convenient to use the terms **elastic** and **inelastic** to distinguish curves of different elasticities. The most common uses are:

(a) **Perfectly inelastic** – elasticity equal to zero.
(b) **Inelastic** – elasticity between zero and one.
(c) **Unit of unitary elasticity** – elasticity equal to one.
(d) **Elastic** – elasticity greater than one, but not infinite.
(e) **Perfectly elastic** – infinite elasticity.

For example, a perfectly inelastic demand curve is vertical in our diagrams, because a price change causes no quantity change. A perfectly elastic demand curve is horizontal, because even a tiny reduction in the price is sufficient to increase the quantity demanded without limit. Clearly, we could never know if this occurs in practice, because we cannot know whether an elasticity is infinite or very large but finite. However, perfectly elastic curves are often useful approximations for constructing a simplified model (for example, see chapter 8).

4.9 Using elasticities

4.9.1 Shift in the demand curve

Suppose that the demand for a good increases because, for example, the price of a substitute good increases, so that people switch from buying the substitute good. For example, people switch from buying butter to buying margarine when the price of butter increases. Figure 4.11(a) and (b) shows alternative supply curves for the good, together with the old and new demand curves. The old equilibrium price is A and the new equilibrium price is B.

Given the shift in the demand curve, the size of the change in the equilibrium price depends on the slope of the supply curve. If this is very nearly horizontal (figure 4.11(a)), the equilibrium price changes very little. If the curve is almost vertical (figure 4.11(b)), the equilibrium price changes considerably. These facts of geometry are confirmed by common sense: if the supply curve is nearly horizontal, then suppliers are willing to sell much more even if the price only

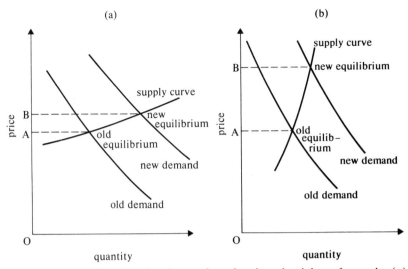

Figure 4.11 An increase in demand and price-elasticity of supply (a) high price-elasticity of supply (b) low price-elasticity of supply
An increase in demand at each price causes an increase in the equilibrium price that is greater when the price-elasticity of supply is lower.

changes a little. If the curve is nearly vertical, suppliers are very unwilling to increase the quantity that they sell even if there is a substantial increase in the price; an increase in demand is followed by an increase in the equilibrium price that limits demand to the almost fixed supply.

A nearly vertical supply curve has a very low price-elasticity of supply (very close to zero), because the quantity supplied increases very little when the price increases by 1 per cent. A nearly horizontal supply curve has a very high elasticity, because a 1 per cent increase in price causes a very large increase in supply. So an outward shift in the demand curve increases the equilibrium price by a small amount if the price-elasticity of supply is high, and by a large amount if the price-elasticity of supply is low. A larger price-elasticity of supply implies a larger change in the equilibrium quantity, and a smaller change in the equilibrium price.

4.9.2 Shift in the supply curve

Suppose that the supply of a good increases because, for example, firms introduce a more efficient method of producing it. Figure 4.12(a) and (b) shows alternative demand curves for the good, together with the old and new supply curves. The old equilibrium price is Q and the new equilibrium price is P.

The size of the change in the equilibrium price and quantity depends on the price-elasticity of demand. If this elasticity is near zero, the demand curve is nearly vertical because there is only a small fall in the quantity demanded

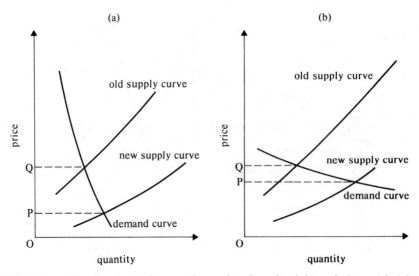

Figure 4.12   An increase in supply and price-elasticity of demand (a) low price-elasticity of demand (b) high price-elasticity of demand
An increase in supply at each price causes a reduction in the equilibrium price that is greater when the price-elasticity of demand is lower.

when the price increases (figure 4.12(a)). If the price-elasticity of demand is very large, the demand curve is nearly horizontal because a very large reduction in the quantity demanded results from a small increase in the price (figure 4.12(b)). A large price-elasticity of demand implies a large change in the equilibrium quantity and a small change in the equilibrium price when the supply curve shifts.

4.9.3 Arc and point elasticities

A demand schedule and elasticity calculations are given in table 4.6. If the price is initially £10, the quantity demanded is 25. The table does not tell us the result of a 1 per cent increase in price to £10.1, but we do know the effect of a 5 per cent price increase to £10.5. This causes a reduction in demand by 2 units to 23, which is an 8 per cent fall (2/25 = 0.08). The best estimate that we can make of the price-elasticity of demand is 1.6 (8/5). This estimate assumes that, if a 5 per cent price increase causes an 8 per cent reduction in demand, then a 1 per cent price increase would cause a 1.6 per cent fall in demand. This method of estimation gives an **arc-elasticity** according to the formula:

  arc elasticity = percentage change in quantity/percentage change in price

If we have information about the change in demand for a very small price increase (for example an increase of 0.05 per cent), the arc-elasticity becomes a very good approximation to the **point-elasticity**, which is the elasticity of the

Table 4.6 Calculating an arc elasticity

1	2	3	4	5	6	7
Price (£)	Change in price	% change in price	Quantity demanded (units of good)	Change in demand	% change in demand	Price elasticity of demand (col.6/col.3)
8.5			37			
	0.5	5.9		5	13.5	2.29
9			32			
	0.5	5.6		4	12.5	2.23
9.5			28			
	0.5	5.3		3	10.7	2.02
10			25			
	0.5	5.0		2	8.0	1.60
10.5			23			
	0.5	4.8		1	4.3	0.90
11			22			

curve at a single point (see box 1). Arc-elasticity is so called because it is calculated from knowledge of two points on the demand curve, representing demands before and after the change in price. When the price change is quite large, the curve forms an arc between them and we calculate the arc-elasticity; when the two points are very close together, they almost coincide and we calculate the point-elasticity.

4.9.4 The elasticity of a straight line

The demand schedule of table 4.7 gives the straight line demand curve of figure 4.13. We know the demands at £1 intervals, and we can calculate the price-elasticity of demand at each price. Notice that for a £1 increase in price there is a different percentage increase depending on the price before the increase. So the elasticity calculated when the price increases from £1 to £2 is

Table 4.7 Price-elasticity of demand for a straight line

Price	% change in price	Quantity demanded	% change in demand	Price-elasticity of demand (col.4/col.2)
1		60		
	100		8.3	0.083
2		55		
	50		9.0	0.18
3		50		
	33.3		10.0	0.3
4		45		
	25		11.1	0.44
5		40		
	20		12.5	0.625
6		35		
	16.7		14.3	0.856
7		30		
	14.3		16.7	1.168
8		25		

Box 1 Mathematics of elasticities (requires elementary calculus)

A supply curve illustrates a supply function, in which the quantity supplied S of a good is expressed as a function of the price p of the good:

$$S = f(p)$$

A demand curve illustrates a demand function, in which the quantity demanded D of a good is expressed as a function of the price p of the good:

$$D = g(p)$$

The equilibrium price p^* is that for which:

$$f(p^*) = g(p^*)$$

If the price increases from p by Δp, the percentage increase in the price is $100(\Delta p/p)$. If this price increase causes an increase in supply of ΔS, the percentage increase in supply is $100(\Delta S/S)$. So the arc price-elasticity of supply is given by:

$$E_{Sa} = (\Delta S/S)/(\Delta p/p) = (\Delta S/\Delta p) \times (p/S)$$

If the price increase and the increase in supply are both very small, the point price-elasticity of supply is given by:

$$E_{Sp} = (dS/dp)(p/S) = p\,f'(p)/f(p)$$

where f' is the first derivative of the supply function f.

Similarly, if a price increase Δp causes a change in demand ΔD, the arc price-elasticity of demand is given by:

$$E_{Da} = -(\Delta D/\Delta p) \times (p/D)$$

The minus sign is used because D is negative if demand falls when price increases, and elasticities are usually quoted as positive numbers. The point price-elasticity of demand is

$$E_{Dp} = -(dD/dp) \times (p/D) = -p\,g'(p)/g(p)$$

where g' is the first derivative of the demand function g.

So, for example, if a demand curve is a straight line given by

$$D = g(p) = a - bp$$

(where a and b are positive constants), the point price-elasticity of demand is

$$E_{Dp} = -p\,g'(p)/g(p) = bp/(a - bp)$$

which is zero when the price is zero, and approaches infinity when the price approaches a/b (when $p = a/b$, $D = 0$).

The demand function

$$D = Ap^{-b}$$

(where A and b are positive constants), has a price-elasticity equal to b at all prices, because $dD/dp = (-b)Ap^{-b-1}$.

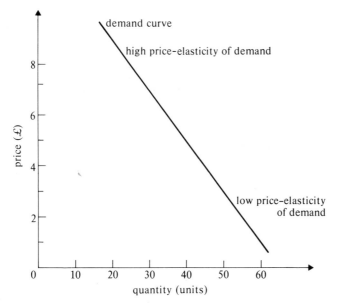

Figure 4.13 Price-elasticity of demand along a straight line demand curve (schedule in table 4.7)
The price-elasticity of demand falls as price falls.

0.083; when the price increases from £6 to £7 the elasticity is 0.856. Figure 4.13 shows that the elasticity increases as the price increases.

4.10 Many markets: general equilibrium

The analysis of supply and demand in a single market determines a single price and does not consider the effects of the change in one market on another. However, there are in reality many interactions between markets. For example:

(a) An increase in the price of petrol reduces the demand for cars. These goods are complements. An increase in the price of a good reduces the demand for its complements.
(b) An increase in the price of butter increases the demand for margarine. These goods are substitutes. An increase in the price of a good increases the demand for its substitutes.
(c) An increase in the price of steel reduces the supply of cars, because the cost of producing a car is increased.
(d) An increase in the price of wheat increases the supply of straw. These goods are joint products. An increase in the supply of a good increases the supply of goods produced jointly with it.
(e) An increase in wages increases the cost of production of most goods, and so affects their supplies.

Some interactions between markets are not as obvious as these. For example, if the price of bread increases substantially, people are likely to reduce their demands for less necessary goods, such as umbrellas, so that they can continue to buy food. So there is an interrelation between the markets for bread and for umbrellas. In this way, many apparently unrelated goods are, in fact, complements because an increase in the price of one good reduces the demand for the other.

4.10.1 Cross-elasticity of demand

Figure 4.14(a) and (b) illustrates the effects of a change in the price of a good on its substitutes and complements. The elasticities of these curves are the **cross-elasticities of demand** (or cross-price-elasticities of demand):

> The cross-elasticity of demand for good 1 with respect to the price of good 2 is the percentage increase in the demand for good 1 caused by a 1 per cent increase in the price of good 2.

For example, the cross-elasticity of demand for bacon with respect to the price of eggs is the percentage increase in the demand for bacon caused by a 1 per cent increase in the price of eggs. If bacon and eggs are substitutes (people eat more bacon and fewer eggs when eggs become more expensive) then the cross-elasticity of demand is positive; if bacon and eggs are complements (people eat them together so that the demand for both goods falls when the price of eggs increases), the cross-elasticity of demand is negative.

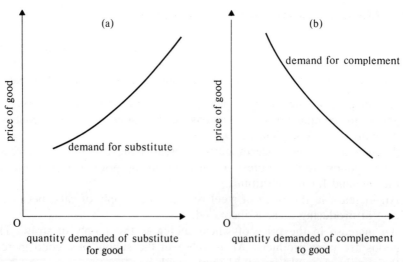

Figure 4.14 Demand for (a) substitute good (b) complementary good
When the price of a good increases, the demand for a substitute increases and the demand for a complement falls.

4.10.2 Equilibrium in many markets

Interrelations between markets imply that the analysis of supply and demand in a single market is an insufficient description of the way in which prices are determined. When we consider several markets at once, an equilibrium is a situation in which supply equals demand in all markets simultaneously. There is an equilibrium price in each market, and our search for these equilibrium prices must allow for the interrelations between the prices of some goods and the demands and supplies of others.

Unfortunately, we cannot find general equilibrium prices and quantities by considering supply and demand diagrams, because the supply and demand curves for one good are drawn assuming that the prices of other goods do not change. When we consider several goods, the general equilibrium prices and quantities can be established only by complex numerical computations.

Leon Walras (born in Evreux, France, in 1834, died 1910; professor at the University of Lausanne, Switzerland, 1870–92) was the principal founder of general equilibrium analysis. In his *Elements of Pure Economics* (1874), he set out the problem of obtaining equilibrium simultaneously in many markets. He recognized that this is a mathematical problem (see box 2) involving the solution of simultaneous equations representing the condition that supply equals demand in each market.

Box 2   General equilibrium in simultaneous equation form

In principle, the supply and demand for each good depend on the prices of all goods:

$$S_1 = f_1(p_1, p_2, p_3, \ldots, p_n) \qquad D_1 = g_1(p_1, p_2, p_3, \ldots, p_n)$$
$$S_2 = f_2(p_1, p_2, p_3, \ldots, p_n) \qquad D_2 = g_2(p_1, p_2, p_3, \ldots, p_n)$$
$$\vdots \qquad\qquad \vdots \qquad\qquad \vdots \qquad\qquad \vdots$$
$$S_n = f_n(p_1, p_2, p_3, \ldots, p_n) \qquad D_n = g_n(p_1, p_2, p_3, \ldots, p_n)$$

where $S_1, S_2, \ldots, S_n$ are the supplies of the n goods, $D_1, D_2, \ldots, D_n$ are the demands for the n goods, and $p_1, p_2, p_3, \ldots, p_n$ are the prices of the n goods.

The general equilibrium prices $(p_1^*, p_2^*, p_3^*, \ldots, p_n^*)$ are found by solving (if possible) the following n equations:

$$f_1(p_1^*, p_2^*, p_3^*, \ldots, p_n^*) = g_1(p_1^*, p_2^*, p_3^*, \ldots, p_n^*)$$
$$f_2(p_1^*, p_2^*, p_3^*, \ldots, p_n^*) = g_2(p_1^*, p_2^*, p_3^*, \ldots, p_n^*)$$
$$\vdots \qquad\qquad\qquad \vdots$$
$$f_n(p_1^*, p_2^*, p_3^*, \ldots, p_n^*) = g_n(p_1^*, p_2^*, p_3^*, \ldots, p_n^*)$$

4.10.3 Using general equilibrium analysis

When we consider a single market in partial equilibrium analysis, we can establish the direction of the change in the equilibrium price after a shift in the supply or demand curve. When we use general equilibrium analysis, we cannot be sure how a change, such as a technical advance in the production of a good or a change in people's tastes, will affect the equilibrium prices of goods. For example, an improvement in the method of making steel has implications for the demand for coal, which is used in making steel, and for the supplies of goods made from steel. There may be feedbacks to the steel price through these other markets. For example, if less coal is used to make steel, because of the technical improvement, fewer tools are needed in the coal industry. So less steel is needed to make the tools and equipment used in the coal industry, so that the demand for steel is reduced.

4.10.4 Movement towards equilibrium

The simple partial equilibrium demonstration that the actual price moves towards its equilibrium level cannot be used in the analysis of general equilibrium. The response of a price-setter to a surplus or shortage in one market may make worse the surplus or shortage in some other market. We cannot be sure that the combined effects of the responses to shortages and surpluses bring all prices towards their equilibrium levels. It is possible that the general equilibrium is **unstable**.

Equilibrium prices are a useful guide to actual prices only if actual prices move towards their equilibrium levels. So when we use general equilibrium analysis we assume that the equilibrium is stable – even though we do not demonstrate that it is stable. Such demonstrations can be very difficult (when they are possible at all) because of the many interrelations between markets. In our examination of market economies in part II, we assume that the general equilibrium of all prices (including wages and interest rates) is re-established quickly after any change in the economy. This assumption has profound consequences, as we shall see in part II.

4.11 Markets and economic systems

In chapters 2 and 3 we examined some fundamental features of economic systems. We identified two broad categories: those that are planned, and those in which the outcome is the result of individual decisions that are not co-ordinated by a plan. In the latter category of economic systems, decisions by individuals and firms to supply and demand goods, labour, loans and so on interact in markets. These interactions determine the prices, wages, interest rates etc. at which the transactions are made, and so determine the amounts that each individual and firm buys and sells, and how much of the benefits of specialization each person receives.

Markets are principally associated with a **capitalist** economic system (**capitalism**) in which capitalists and **landlords** own the equipment and land, employ workers and make decisions on the goods to supply. Some capitalists and landlords rent their equipment and land to **entrepreneurs** who run factories, employ workers and make decisions to supply goods. The entrepreneurs receive the profit, or suffer the loss, made by their firms. There is, in principle, a distinction between the capitalist who owns the equipment and land, and the entrepreneur who makes the decision on how to use them and who pays the capitalist for the right to use them. The entrepreneur takes the risk that the venture might fail – with the compensating reward that it might succeed with great profit. In practice, many small businesses are run by entrepreneurs using their own equipment or land, and so the distinction is often blurred. Of course, a capitalist may suffer loss if the entrepreneur makes so large a loss that he cannot meet his obligations to pay for the equipment or land that he uses. Similarly, workers may also suffer a loss if the entrepreneur is unable to pay their wages.

Markets can operate in other circumstances. There have been some worker-controlled firms and co-operatives in the UK (such as the Meriden motor cycle factory, which was established as a co-operative in 1975 and which ceased operations in 1982). These firms are owned by their workers, who decide how much to supply and what factors and materials to demand, and receive the profit or suffer the loss made. Some goods in the UK are produced by nationalized firms, which are owned by the government and run by people appointed by the government.

4.11.1 Markets in planned economic systems

It is possible for planners to try to allocate goods to people by deciding the prices at which people can buy goods. The supplies of goods are determined by the planners, but people have some freedom to choose what they buy. The planners may alter prices to reflect surpluses and shortages, trying to emulate the mechanism that brings about stability in a single market. However, a shortage (caused by a price being set below its equilibrium level) often results in queueing rather than a price increase. A shortage can also lead to a **black market**, in which people who have scarce goods resell them illegally at a higher price. The higher black market price reflects the fact that the official price is below its equilibrium level.

4.11.2 Market analysis

The analysis of equilibrium prices and quantities in markets is one of the main ways in which we examine the consequences of individual decisions for an economic system as a whole (such as the inflation rate and the level of unemployment). This method, which is known as **market analysis** (see section 11.7.1), is useful as long as prices move rapidly to their equilibrium levels in all markets. We shall see in part III that market analysis is not the only useful method for examining macroeconomic issues in the economy.

4.12 Summary

Decisions on what to buy and what to produce determine supplies and demands in markets for goods, loans, labour time, other factors of production and foreign currencies. Partial equilibrium occurs when supply equals demand in one market; general equilibrium occurs when supply equals demand in all markets.

There is a shortage if the price of a good is less than its equilibrium level; there is a surplus if the price is above its equilibrium level. If price-setters increase the price of a good for which there is a shortage and reduce the price of a good in surplus, the price in a single market moves towards its equilibrium level. The extent to which a price-setter has freedom of action is determined by the market structure. If there is much competition, a price-setter is likely to be very constrained. If there is a monopoly, a price-setter has considerable freedom to set the price, subject only to the constraints set by market demand.

Supply and demand diagrams tell us the direction of the change in an equilibrium price when there is a change in some influence on supply or demand. The price-elasticity of supply and demand tell us the size of this change.

Market analysis can be used to examine the outcome of economic systems as a whole. Market analysis assumes that actual prices move rapidly to their general equilibrium levels.

Topics and problems

(1) A market is not necessarily a meeting place. What other forms can a market take?

(2) Are there any goods for which demand increases when the price increases? Why might this 'perverse' behaviour occur?

(3) For what goods are sellers not the price-setters? Who sets wages, rents, interest rates etc. in factor and loan markets? Who sets prices in stock and foreign exchange markets?

(4) What happens to the supply, demand and equilibrium price of

(a)	Coffee	when the coffee-bean harvest is reduced by frost
(b)	Tea	when the coffee-bean harvest is reduced by frost
(c)	Houses	when the mortgage interest rate falls
(d)	Beef	when the cost of cattle feed increases
(e)	Cheese	when the price of milk increases
(f)	Slide rules	when the calculator is invented
(g)	Mopeds	when the price of petrol increases?

Would you expect actual prices to follow equilibrium prices in these circumstances? If so, how quickly would you expect actual prices to change? Are long-run effects different from short-run effects? What determines the size of the change in the equilibrium price in each case?

(5) Trace the major general equilibrium effects of the introduction of word-processors into offices in the UK.

(6) What is the effect of an increase in the price of oil on the equilibrium wage of coal-miners in a country that imports oil?

(7) What is the effect of a increase in the price of oil on the equilibrium wage of coal-miners in a country that exports oil?

(8) The *Economist* magazine has suggested that the price of a Big Mac hamburger is a better measure of the purchasing powers of different currencies than the official exchange rate. Why might exchange rates established in markets imply that people in different countries pay very different amounts for basic goods? What good or collection of goods might replace the suggested hamburger as a useful 'standard of value' for comparing the worth of currencies?

(9) What are the likely implications for the prices and sales of blank and pre-recorded tapes of a levy on blank cassette tapes?

Answer problems 10 to 14 using the information in table 4.8.

Table 4.8 Supply and demand schedules for problems 10 to 14

Price	Quantity supplied	Quantity demanded
1	24	60
2	28	55
3	32	50
4	36	45
5	40	40
6	44	35
7	48	30
8	52	25
9	56	20
10	60	15

(10) Draw supply and demand curves for the good on one diagram.

(11) What is the equilibrium price of the good?

(12) What are the arc price-elasticities of supply and demand when the price is (a) 3 (b) 5?

(13) What is the equilibrium price if there is a 60 per cent increase in demand at each price? Why does the equilibrium quantity not increase by 60 per cent?

(14) Find, from your diagram, the equilibrium price if there is a 50 per cent reduction in supply at each price. What assumption have you made to obtain your answer?

Answer problems 15 to 17 using the information given in table 4.9, given that the supply of good 1 is 10 units and that of good 2 is 15 units. These supplies are unaffected by price changes.

Table 4.9 Demands for use in problems 15 to 17

Price of good 2	Price of good 1				
	1	2	3	4	5
1	10,24	8,27	6,30	4,33	2,36
2	11,18	9,21	7,24	5,27	3,30
3	12,12	10,15	8,18	6,21	4,24
4	13,6	11,9	9,12	7,15	5,18
5	14,0	12,3	10,6	8,9	6,12

Each entry in the table reports first the demand for good 1, and second the demand for good 2. So, for example, when the price of good 1 is 4 and the price of good 2 is 5, the demands are 8 units of good 1 and 9 units of good 2.

(15) What are the equilibrium prices of the two goods?
(16) What are the arc cross-elasticities of demand for the two goods when the markets are in equilibrium?
(17) Draw demand and supply curves for good 1 when the price of good 2 is 1. Draw demand and supply curves for good 2 when the price of good 1 is 4. What are the partial equilibrium prices that you find in your diagrams? Why are these two partial equilibrium prices not the general equilibrium prices?

Chapter Five

National income and the national accounts

Circular flow of national income — domestic product — expenditure method — income method — net and gross domestic product — national product and national income — public sector accounts — balance of payments — simplifications of the national accounts

---

5.1 Introduction

One method of assessing how well an economic system operates is to calculate how much is produced in total. Plainly, this calculation cannot tell us everything we want to know about the efficiency of an economic system. For example, a country with a favourable climate and many natural resources, such as coal and oil, may produce a similar total of goods to a less well endowed country, because the latter uses its resources more efficiently and ensures that its people specialize according to their comparative advantages. Both countries produce similar totals but one operates more efficiently than the other. However, despite shortcomings of this kind, it is very useful to know how much is produced, at least as a starting point for a discussion of the efficiency of an economic system and to help us to assess the standard of living of the people of the country. The total produced in a country in a year is recorded in the **national accounts**; the construction of these accounts is a part of **national accounting**.

The UK national accounts are published each year in *UK National Accounts* (formerly *National Income and Expenditure*), commonly known as the Blue Book, and we use figures for 1988 in this chapter.

5.2 Circular flow of national income

A fundamental feature of national accounting is that the same items might be recorded in several ways. Expenditure on goods by consumers generates revenue for the firms that sell the goods. This revenue is used to pay incomes to those who work for the firms or provide other services to them. So money flows from households to firms as payment for goods, and from firms to households as payment of incomes. This is the **circular flow of national income** illustrated in figure 5.1. Because incomes and expenditures circulate in this way we can calculate the total amount produced in an economy directly (by somehow adding up the value of everything that is produced), by looking at the **expenditures** of those who buy what is produced, or by looking at the incomes that are paid out of the revenues of the firms that sell the goods produced.

The simplified circular flow illustrated in figure 5.1 does not contain many of the flows of money in a modern economy. In particular:

(a) Households receive transfer payments and interest from the government, save, pay taxes and buy goods from abroad.
(b) Firms pay taxes, buy imported goods and sell exports.
(c) The government receives taxes, buys goods, pays pensions and other state benefits and pays interest on money that it has previously borrowed.

We can categorize these additional items into **withdrawals** from and **injections** to the simple circular flow of national income.

5.2.1 Withdrawals from the circular flow

These are:

(a) **Savings**, mainly by households, although firms save when they have **undistributed profits**, which are the part of their revenues that they do not pay out as incomes.

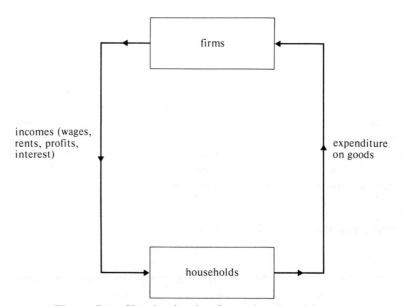

Figure 5.1   Simple circular flow of national income

(b) **Taxes** of all kinds, paid by households and firms.

(c) **Imports** of goods from abroad by households, firms and the government.

All these items involve the withdrawal of money from the circular flow of national income. For example, savings by households is money that flows to them in the form of income, but that does not flow back to firms in the form of expenditure.

5.2.2 Injections to the circular flow

These are:

(a) **Investment** by firms in machinery and buildings that will help them to produce goods in the future.

(b) **Government expenditure** on goods, state benefits and interest.

(c) **Exports** by firms to other countries.

All these items involve the introduction of money into the simple circular flow of national income. For example, a firm that exports a good from the UK receives money that is not an expenditure by a UK household. Figure 5.2 shows the circular flow including these items.

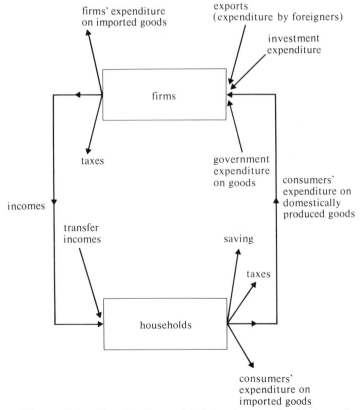

Figure 5.2   Circular flow with injections and withdrawals

5.2.3 Saving and investment

It is very important to note how economists use the terms **saving** and **investment**. The common use of these terms is often different from economists' use, and the distinction between the two is vital in many aspects of macroeconomics.

Saving occurs when a household does not spend all of its income (after paying taxes) on consumer goods.

Investment occurs when a firm buys equipment or materials that it intends to use for producing goods in the future.

Thus a household that buys shares, puts money into a bank or pays contributions to a pension fund commits an act of saving (although we talk of 'investing in shares' in common parlance; economists avoid this phrase). There may be very different influences on saving and investment: for example, if interest rates rise, people may decide to save more to take advantage of the higher interest payments available; firms may invest less because they need to borrow money to buy new equipment, and this borrowing becomes more expensive as interest rates rise.

5.3 Domestic product

One method of reporting how much is produced in a country in a period of time, say a year, is to list all the goods produced in that period. However, so great a variety of goods is produced in a modern economy that it is impossible to interpret a list of this kind as an indication of economic efficiency. It is difficult to make comparisons of such lists from one year to the next because some outputs increase, others fall and new goods are introduced. We need to combine (or **aggregate**) the quantities of goods produced into some more easily manageable form, so that we can see whether the increases outweigh the decreases from one year to the next. However, we cannot directly add quantities of goods as varied as carrots, haircuts, economics classes, tractors and oil to one another, because they are not measured in the same units (no physical measurement such as weight or length is appropriate to all of them). One function of money is to act as a unit of account (see section 3.4.1), and this allows the calculation of total output in terms of money. Each good is valued at a price that may be its market price, its market price net of taxes and subsidies, or indeed any other price that is considered 'correct' for the good – although it is hard to use prices that are not related in some way to market prices.

A fundamental item in the national accounts is **domestic product**:

Domestic product is the sum of the quantities of each good produced in a period multiplied by its price.

For example, if an economy produces 50 cloth and 25 food in a year, and the prices of cloth and food are £4 and £6 respectively, domestic product is

$$(50 \times £4) + (25 \times £6) = £350$$

More generally, if quantities $q_1, q_2, q_3, \ldots, q_n$ of goods 1 to n are produced, and their prices are $p_1, p_2, p_3, \ldots, p_n$, then

$$DP = p_1 q_1 + p_2 q_2 + p_3 q_3 + \ldots + p_n q_n \tag{5.1}$$

where DP is the symbol that we use to denote domestic product.

5.3.1 Intermediate goods and double counting

The calculation of domestic product involves a potential problem caused by the production of goods that are used in the production of other goods. This can be illustrated using an example. Suppose that a baker produces 100 loaves using 50 kilograms of wheat which he buys from a farmer for £4 per kilogram. He sells the loaves for £3 each. If we add together the values of the outputs of wheat and bread, the contribution to domestic product would be $(50 \times £4) + (100 \times £3) = £500$. However, the wheat is counted twice: first in the production of wheat by the farmer, and second in the production of bread by the baker. The size of domestic product is overstated, as we can see by considering a slight change in the example.

Suppose that the same production of wheat and bread takes place elsewhere, where the baker and the farmer are parts of a single firm. There is no sale of wheat because it moves from one part of the firm to another, and the national accounts would record only the production of the bread. It would appear that domestic product is lower by £200 in the second situation, even though the quantity of bread produced is exactly the same, and the same quantity of wheat is used to produce it. If we double count the wheat in the first example, the contribution to domestic product is higher despite identical production.

Double counting can be avoided in two ways:

(a) We can identify **final goods** and ignore all of the others. In our example, bread is a final good because it is not used to produce anything else, whereas wheat is not a final good (it is an **intermediate good**) because it is used up in making some other good. If we do this, the contribution of the production of bread to domestic product is £300 in both examples.

(b) We can add together the **value added** at each stage of production. This requires that every producer records the value of the goods that it sells minus the cost of intermediate goods bought to use in production. This is the producer's value added, and total value added is domestic product, because it includes final goods, but excludes intermediate goods. In our example the value added by the farmer in the first example is £200 (assuming for simplicity that he uses no intermediate goods) and the value added by the baker is the value of bread sold minus the cost of the intermediate good, wheat, i.e. £300 − £200 = £100. Total value added is then £300, which is the same as the value added by the farmer-and-baker firm in the second example, which sells goods for £300 and buys no intermediate goods.

In a way, the value-added method seems to be more complicated than the method of identifying final goods, but it has the advantage that firms need not separate their production of final goods from their production of intermediate goods. This separation may be quite difficult for some firms. For example, coal is used to heat houses, in which case it is a final good, and to produce electricity, in which case it is an intermediate good. The coal-producer may have no idea what the coal is to be used for. There is no need to separate these when we use the value-added method, because the value of coal used to produce electricity is a part of the value added in the coal industry, and is subtracted from the revenue from electricity sales in calculating the value added in the electricity industry, so that it is not double counted.

5.3.2 Income and expenditure methods

Equation 5.1 is difficult to use as a measure of domestic product because it requires a very considerable amount of information. Some of this is recorded in the *UK National Accounts*, but usually one of two alternative methods is used. These alternatives are available from the circular flow of national income:

(a) The **expediture method**. Every sale of a good is also an expenditure by whoever buys it, and domestic product can be calculated by adding these expenditures.
(b) The **income method**. When a good is produced and sold, the seller receives a revenue that is used to pay for materials, to pay wages to those who have worked to produce the good, to pay interest to those who have lent money and to pay rent for land and buildings. Any revenue in excess of these payments is retained by the seller as his or her profit from the sale. So the total value of goods produced, which is domestic product, includes the incomes paid to those who are in some way involved in producing goods. Domestic product can be calculated from the total of these incomes.

5.4 Expenditure method

To use the expenditure method to calculate UK domestic product, we add together expenditures by four categories of buyers:

(a) Households (including individuals and families) who buy consumer goods. This **consumers' expenditure** is divided between **non-durable** goods, such as food and petrol, that can be used only once, and **durable** goods, such as cars and televisions, that can be used many times.
(b) Firms that buy **investment** goods and intermediate goods. Investment goods are buildings and equipment that are bought to be used to produce goods

in the future. Intermediate goods are not included in total expenditure, to avoid double counting.

(c) The government buys goods and provides them to individuals. For example, the construction of public sector hospitals and prisons is a part of **government expenditure** on investment goods; the food eaten by patients and prisoners is a part of government expenditure on consumption goods. Government expenditure on the wages of civil servants is included in domestic product, and the value of the output produced by a civil servant (which is not usually sold) is, by convention, defined to be equal to his or her wage. Government expenditure also includes **transfer payments** (such as pensions and unemployment benefits) and interest on borrowed money. These are not payments to buy goods produced, and so they are not a part of domestic product.

(d) Foreign buyers of exported goods.

5.4.1 Stocks and work in progress

Total expenditure in 1988 includes expenditure on goods sold in 1988 that were produced in previous years (and which should be included in domestic product for the year in which they were produced), and excludes goods produced in 1988 that are sold in 1989 or later (which should be included in domestic product for 1988). At the start of each year firms have **stocks** or **inventories** of unsold goods, and they have stocks of different sizes at the end of the year. If the stocks at the end of the year are larger than at the beginning, more was produced in 1988 than was sold in 1988. The production of goods that are added to stocks is a part of 1988 domestic product, and so we must add the increase in stocks to total expenditure when we calculate domestic product.

The same problem arises because some goods are partly finished at the end of a year (partly built houses, for example), so that although they are partly produced in the year there is no expenditure on them in that year. If the amount of **work in progress** at the end of 1988 exceeds that at the start of 1988, the expenditure method understates domestic product. A particular difficulty with allowing for work in progress is that partly finished goods are not sold, and so they have no price and it is difficult to place a monetary value on them. For example, if a house is partly completed on 31 December 1988, and is completed and sold in 1989, what fraction of its selling price is included in the domestic product for 1988, and what part in 1989? In practice, the monetary value of work in progress is estimated, causing some inaccuracy in domestic product figures.

We can now write the following equation

$$TE = C + I + GE + X + S_{inc} \tag{5.2}$$

where TE is total final expenditure, C is consumers' expenditure, I is investment expenditure, GE is government expenditure (excluding interest and transfer payments), X is exports and S_{inc} is the increase in stocks and work in progress.

Some final expenditure is on goods imported from abroad, and these are not included in domestic product, which is the total of goods produced within the country. Thus, to calculate domestic product using the expenditure method, we use the equation:

$$DP = TE - M \qquad (5.3)$$

where M is imports.

Table 5.1 gives the 1988 figures for UK domestic product by the expenditure method.

5.4.2 Market prices and factor cost

Expenditure on goods includes taxes levied by the government when goods are sold. In the UK and other countries of the European Community, many goods are subject to value added tax (VAT), and the UK government levies additional taxes on sales of cars, petrol, alcohol and tobacco. In the USA and Canada sales tax is charged on many goods. If any of these taxes is increased, expenditure increases, even if the quantities of goods bought are unchanged. So if we use selling prices to aggregate the quantities produced, a tax increase

Table 5.1   UK domestic product (at market prices) in 1988, by the expenditure method

Item	£ million
Consumption	293,569
Investment (private)	79,599
Government expenditure	
on investment goods	9,152
on consumer goods	91,847
Exports	108,533
Increase in stocks and work in progress	4,371
Total final expenditure	587,071
Imports	−125,194
Domestic product	461,877

In *UK National Accounts* 'gross domestic fixed capital formation' (investment) includes public investment by central and local government and nationalized industries. By our convention, this is included in government expenditure; the table reports government investment separately so that it can be included in either way.

Source: *UK National Accounts*

would appear to increase domestic product, even if no more goods are produced. This problem does not arise if these taxes are excluded from total expenditure, and we can distinguish two methods of calculating domestic product:

(a) Domestic product at **market prices**, which includes taxes.
(b) Domestic product at **factor cost**, which excludes taxes.

The opposite of a tax on a good is a **subsidy**, whereby the government pays a firm whenever it sells a good. A subsidy reduces the market price of a good compared to its level without a subsidy. So domestic product at market prices is reduced if subsidies are increased, but this does not happen to domestic product at factor cost. So

domestic product = domestic product − taxes on + subsidies
   at factor cost   at market prices   expenditure

Table 5.2 shows the **factor cost adjustment** for the 1988 UK national accounts: domestic product at factor cost is approximately 85 per cent of domestic product at market prices.

5.5 Income method

The income method of calculating a country's domestic product involves adding together all the incomes generated in firms producing goods in the country. These incomes are paid out of firms' value added and so domestic product, which is the sum of values added, equals the sum of these incomes. The major categories of income are:

(a) **Wages** (incomes from employment). This category includes salaries, contributions paid by employers for benefits (national insurance, pensions, etc.) received by employees and fringe benefits such as company cars.
(b) **Incomes from self-employment**.
(c) **Interest** received by those who have lent money to firms.

Table 5.2 Factor cost adjustment for the UK in 1988

Item	£ million
Domestic product at market prices	461,877
Taxes on expenditure	−75,029
Subsidies	5,883
Domestic product at factor cost	392,731

Source: *UK National Accounts*

(d) **Rent**, which is the income received by those who hire out land, buildings and equipment (excluding any costs involved in doing so).
(e) **Profits** made by all firms, whether they are privately owned or government owned.

All these incomes are calculated before any income taxes and national insurance contributions are paid from them.

We can then write the following equation:

$$TDI = W + SE + P + Int + R \qquad (5.4)$$

where TDI is total domestic income, W is wages, SE is income from self-employment, P is profit, Int is interest paid by firms and R is rent.

Firms pay wages, profits and rents out of the money that they receive from selling goods; these receipts equal expenditures on goods, plus subsidies received by firms, minus taxes on goods. So the income method calculates domestic product excluding taxes on goods and including subsidies; that is, domestic product at factor cost. This helps to explain the term 'factor cost', because the incomes that are added in the income method are the incomes of the suppliers of factors of production.

5.5.1 Stock appreciation

Some of the income from self-employment and from profit and rent is the result of increases in the prices of goods held in stocks (**stock appreciation**). The owner of a stock of a good gains if the price of the good increases while he or she holds it (this may, indeed, be one reason for holding the stock). For example, any firm that held a stock of oil for a year from April 1978 benefited from an increase in the price of oil of approximately 30 per cent by April 1979. A firm would therefore have made a profit if it had bought oil in 1978 and sold it in 1979. This profit is a part of total domestic income, but it does not correspond to the output of any good. So we must exclude stock appreciation from total domestic income when we calculate domestic product. Therefore

$$DP = TDI - S_{app} \qquad (5.5)$$

where S_{app} is stock appreciation.

Table 5.3 shows the 1988 figures of the UK domestic product calculated by the income method.

5.5.2 Statistical discrepancy

Domestic product at factor cost calculated using the income method (table 5.3) is slightly different from that calculated using the expenditure method (table 5.1). There are inevitable inaccuracies in the figures because, for example, the valuation of the change in stocks and work in progress and the calculation of stock appreciation are unlikely to be accurate. The UK national accounts include an average estimate (which is based on income, expenditure and output based measures), and there is a **statistical discrepancy** between the average

Table 5.3 UK domestic product 1988, income method

Item	£ million
Wages	249,775
Income from self-employment	42,617
Profits and interest	77,458
Rent	27,464
Other	3,408
Total domestic income	400,722
Stock appreciation	6,116
Domestic product (income method)	394,606
Statistical discrepancy	1,875
Domestic product (expenditure method)	392,731

Profits and interest include the gross trading profits of companies plus the gross trading profits of public corporations plus the gross trading surplus of general government enterprises. A firm's trading profit (or surplus if it is government owned) equals the money that it receives from selling goods minus payments for wages, materials and rent that it would make whether or not it had borrowed money in the past. Interest on borrowed money is paid out of trading profits. Trading profits also include undistributed profits.

Source: *UK National Accounts*

estimate (£1,875 million for the UK in 1988) and the income and expenditure calculations of domestic product.

5.6 Net and gross domestic product

In our discussion of investment expenditure, we ignored a basic distinction between two uses of investment goods. Some equipment and buildings are bought to replace those that wear out: this is **replacement investment**. Other equipment and buildings are bought to increase the amounts available for use: this is **net investment**.

Gross investment is the sum of replacement investment and net investment.

Net investment gives the potential for an increase in domestic product in future years; replacement investment ensures that the domestic product is not reduced by the wearing out of some physical capital.

Using this distinction we can calculate **gross domestic product** (which is the figure used in tables 5.1 and 5.3) including goods produced for replacement investment, and **net domestic product**, which excludes replacement investment. These two calculations have different uses:

(a) Gross domestic product tells us how much is produced in total, and is therefore one indication of the efficiency of an economic system.
(b) Net domestic product tells us how much is available to satisfy the needs and wants of the population so that the economy's ability to produce in the future is not depleted. In an emergency, such as a war, a country may not replace worn-out equipment and buildings, so that current production of the most essential goods is increased at the expense of future production.

The expenditure method calculates net domestic product by including net investment in total expenditure, and it calculates gross domestic product by including replacement investment as well. To use the income method, we must distinguish between **gross rent** and **net rent** and between **gross profit** and **net profit**. A part of the gross annual rent or profit of the owner of a building or equipment compensates him for the fact that the asset partly wears out during the year. He can, if he wishes, set aside this part of his income to buy a replacement asset when it has finally worn out. The remainder of the owner's income is his net rent or net profit. Net rent and net profit are included in net domestic product; gross rent and gross profit are included in gross domestic product.

The value of buildings and equipment that partly or wholly wear out during a year is **depreciation**. In practice it is difficult to calculate depreciation, even for the equipment used by a small firm (indeed, even for a car or a television). So a firm's accountants calculate its depreciation according to some rule. For example, a simple rule assumes that a particular machine will last for five years and in each year one-fifth of the price paid for the machine is recorded as depreciation. This accounting figure is used to calculate the difference between gross and net investment expenditure in the domestic accounts, even though the machine does not necessarily produce 20 per cent fewer goods each year. These calculations of depreciation are the basis of the **allowance for capital consumption** in the national accounts. This is the estimated value of replacement investment, and is the difference between gross and net domestic product.

The figures for investment and domestic product reported in tables 5.1 to 5.3 are gross. Table 5.4 shows the difference between gross and net domestic product for the UK in 1988.

5.7 National product and national income

The UK national accounts distinguish between net and gross domestic product (**NDP** and **GDP**) and **net** and **gross national product** (**NNP** and **GNP**). The difference arises because:

(a) UK residents receive incomes from abroad, because they work abroad, own shares in foreign firms, or lend money abroad.

Table 5.4 UK gross and net domestic product, 1988

Item	£ million
Gross domestic product at factor cost	392,731
Depreciation	−54,769
Net domestic product at factor cost	337,962

Source: *UK National Accounts*

(b) UK firms pay incomes to residents of other countries who have supplied them with factors of production or lent them money.

The difference between incomes received from abroad and incomes paid to foreign residents is **net property income from abroad**, and:

$$NNP = NDP + NPA \qquad (5.6)$$

$$GNP = GDP + NPA \qquad (5.7)$$

where NPA is net property income from abroad. So domestic product is the value of incomes generated within the country whether they are paid to residents or foreigners. National product is the value of incomes received by residents, wherever they may be generated. The difference between these two figures will be considerable if many residents receive incomes generated abroad (because they cross a national boundary to work) so that national product exceeds domestic product, or if many firms within the country have foreign shareholders so that domestic product exceeds national product.

Table 5.5 shows the 1988 figures for UK net and gross national and domestic products.

Table 5.5 UK gross and net national and domestic products, 1988

Item	£ million
GDP at factor cost	392,731
Net property income from abroad	5,619
GNP at factor cost	398,350
NDP at factor cost	337,962
Net property income from abroad	5,619
NNP at factor cost (= national income)	332,343

Source: *UK National Accounts*

The definition used in the national accounts is that

National income is net national product at factor cost.

However, 'national income' is often used to refer to the value of goods produced in the economy – that is to domestic product (thus ignoring net property income from abroad). The distinction between national product and domestic product is important in the compilation of the national accounts, but not so important in the discussion of the principles that determine major economic magnitudes (including national income). These principles, rather than national accounting, are the central feature of macroeconomics in this book, and so we use 'national income' in its conventional rather than official sense.

5.7.1 National income and total incomes of households

National income is not equal to the total of the incomes of all households for two main reasons:

(a) Many people receive incomes from transfer payments (for example, unemployment benefit, pensions, student grants) and from interest paid on money that they have lent to the government. These incomes are not paid directly out of firms' value added, and so they are not included when incomes are added together to calculate national output using the income method.

(b) Some of a firm's value added may not be paid as income to anyone. The surplus of a firm's value added over payments of wages, rents and interest is the firm's profit, some of which is paid to its owners. However, some **undistributed profit** may be retained in the firm, usually to meet future contingencies and to pay for investment projects. Value added exceeds incomes paid to the extent of undistributed profits.

So

$$Y = HI - TP + UP \tag{5.8}$$

where Y is national income (NNP at factor cost), HI is total incomes of households (before deducting income taxes), TP is transfer payments and interest paid by the government, and UP is undistributed profits. Note that the letter Y is almost universally used to denote national income (since I is reserved for investment).

Table 5.6 shows figures for incomes of households in the UK in 1988.
Total household income is divided between consumption expenditure, saving and tax payments. So:

$$HI = C + S + T \tag{5.9}$$

where HI is total household incomes, C is consumption expenditure, S is saving and T is tax payments by households. Table 5.7 shows this division of household incomes for the UK in 1988.

Table 5.6   Household incomes in the UK, 1988

Item	£ million
Wages	249,775
Income from self-employment	42,617
Rent, dividends and interest (including interest from the government)	40,878
Transfer payments	54,207
Other	2,350
Total incomes of households	389,827

Source: *UK National Accounts*

Table 5.7   Use of household incomes in the UK, 1988

Item	£ million
Consumption	293,569
Income tax payments and national insurance contributions	80,341
Saving	13,601
Transfers abroad and other	2,316
Total incomes of households	389,827

Source: *UK National Accounts*

5.8 Public sector accounts

The difference between total government expenditure and its receipts from taxation is the government's **budget deficit**. If taxation exceeds government expenditure, there is a **budget surplus**. If the two are equal, there is a **balanced budget**.

The government covers a budget deficit by:

(a) **Borrowing** from the public, from the banking sector of the economy and from abroad.
(b) Selling assets in **privatization** issues involving shares in previously **nationalized** industries (note that in the published national accounts the UK government treats receipts from privatization as negative expenditure; this procedure disguises their true role in financing a deficit and makes the deficit smaller than our definition implies).

(c) Issuing more **money**, by authorizing the central bank (the Bank of England in the UK, the Federal Reserve in the USA) to print more notes and coins. The profits from issuing money are substantial as long as the government has a monopoly on the production of notes and coins (see section 3.5.2).

The consequences of different methods of financing a budget deficit are of great importance in macroeconomics – and cause considerable controversy between different schools of thought in economics. We shall return to this issue in part IV.

The UK government had a budget surplus in 1987, 1988 and 1989, in contrast to virtually every other year since 1945. The government can use such a surplus to repay some of the loans that it has previously acquired, and this helps to reduce future government expenditure by reducing the total of interest payments on the remaining government debt. Table 5.8 shows the major items of taxation and expenditure for the UK in 1988.

5.9 Balance of payments

A country's transactions with foreign countries are recorded in its **balance of payments account**.

Table 5.8 UK government income and expenditure, 1988

Item	£ million
Government income	
Taxes on incomes	61,123
Taxes on expenditures	75,029
Social security contributions	31,686
Sale of privatization shares	6,076
Other government income	12,286
Total government income	186,200
Government expenditure	
Consumer goods	91,847
Investment goods	9,152
Transfer payments	57,476
Interest	18,027
Other	6,243
Total government expenditure	182,385
Surplus (income – expenditure)	3,815

Source: *UK National Accounts*

5.9.1 Balance of trade

Imports and exports are major items in the balance of payments account, and the difference between total exports and total imports in a year is the country's **balance of trade**. In 1988, the UK exported goods to the value of approximately £108 billion (30 per cent of national income) and imported goods valued at approximately £125 billion.

A country's overseas trade is often classified as:

(a) **Visible trade** in goods (but not services: see section 2.1). The difference between visible exports and visible imports is the balance of visible trade.
(b) **Invisible trade** in services. The difference between invisible exports and invisible imports is the balance of invisible trade.

5.9.2 Current account

The 'invisibles' in the balance of payments also include net property income from abroad (see section 5.7), which is the difference between payments of incomes to and from the UK. These incomes include wages, dividends, interest and rent paid by foreign firms and governments to UK residents (this is an inflow of money), and similar payments by UK firms to residents of other countries (an outflow of money).

The sum of the balance of visible trade, the balance of invisible trade and net property income from abroad is the balance on the **current account** of the balance of payments.

5.9.3 Capital account

The remaining part of the balance of payments account is the **capital account**. This includes:

(a) Overseas investment in the UK, which includes the inflow of money when residents of other countries buy shares and other financial assets in the UK, and the inflow of money when a foreign-owned firm sets up a factory in the UK (the latter is known as **direct investment** in the UK).
(b) UK private investment overseas, which includes both the purchase by UK residents of financial assets in other countries and direct investment abroad by UK firms.
(c) **Official financing**, which includes government borrowing from other governments, and withdrawals from the UK **reserves**. These reserves consist of currencies of other countries, gold and assets known as **special drawing rights** issued by the **International Monetary Fund**. Negative official financing includes lending to other countries and increases in the UK reserves.

The balance of payments must balance, in that the total inflow of money (including withdrawals from the reserves) must equal the total outflow of money (including additions to the reserves). The process of collecting the information needed to construct the account is subject to many inaccuracies, particularly because some payments are unrecorded and many payments for imports and exports are made some time after the goods are delivered. The published UK figures change considerably as more information reaches the government, and the errors and omissions are collected together in the balancing item. This figure is calculated to be exactly the amount needed to ensure that the balance of payments account balances.

Table 5.9 shows the UK balance of payments account for 1988, as recorded in 1989. The errors and omissions noted above imply that the figures for 1988 are likely to change considerably over the succeeding two or three years.

5.9.4 The UK and the EC

Since 1973, the UK has been a member of the **European Community** (EC). The 12 member countries contribute to the EC budget, which is spent in several ways. The **Common Agricultural Policy** (CAP) guarantees prices for some farm products. The regional fund makes grants to poorer areas in an attempt to equalize the income distribution within the Community. The EC raises money to pay for these policies from:

Table 5.9   UK balance of payments, 1988

Item	£ million	£ million
Current account		
Visibles: exports	+80,602	
imports	−101,428	
Visible balance		−20,826
Invisibles: inflow	+87,233	
outflow	−81,024	
Invisible balance		6,209
Balance on current account		−14,617
Capital account		
Overseas investment in UK	+11,985	
UK investment abroad	−24,937	
Borrowing abroad by UK banks (net)	+14,595	
Increase in UK reserves (see note)	−2,761	
Other	+3,452	
Balance on capital account		+2,334
Balancing item		12,283

The increase in UK reserves has a negative sign since it is a payment from the capital account to the reserves.

Source: *UK Balance of Payments*

(a) Import duties that are designed to reduce imports of goods from outside the EC, and so to increase the amount of trade within the Community. These duties are effectively taxes on goods brought in from outside, and are levied only on goods that can be produced in sufficient quantity within the EC. Agricultural goods imported from outside the EC are subject to levies that increase their prices to a level comparable to those guaranteed by the Common Agricultural Policy.

(b) A fraction of each member country's revenue from value-added tax (see section 20.4), which is charged on most goods. The EC's policy to achieve a **single European market** by 1992 is likely to include some movement towards harmonizing value-added tax rates between member countries.

Table 5.10 shows the financial transactions between the UK and the EC for 1988. This table illustrates the extent to which the UK is a net contributor to the EC.

5.10 Simplifications of the national accounts

We shall use the national accounts frequently in later chapters. When we do so, it will be useful to make some simplifications:

(a) Include the increase in stocks and work in progress in investment expenditure (S_{inc} included in I).

(b) Include incomes from self-employment in wages and profit. In principle this income can be divided between wages and profit by regarding as wages the amount that a self-employed person would be paid if he or she were employed. The remainder of his or her income is profit (SE included in $W + P$).

Table 5.10   UK transactions with EC 1988

Item	£ million
Payments to EC	
Levies and customs duties	1,748
From UK VAT	1,164
Other	613
Total	3,525
Receipts from EC	
Agricultural policy	1,379
Social and regional funds	647
Other	161
Total	2,187

Source: *UK Balance of Payments*

(c) Include undistributed profits in total household incomes. These profits belong to the owners of firms, and are not spent on consumer goods. If we include undistributed profits in total household incomes, any part of undistributed profits that firms pay in tax is a part of households' tax payments, and the remainder is a part of household saving because it is not spent on consumer goods (UP included in HI).

(d) Subtract stock appreciation from profit and rents, so that these categories include incomes other than those obtained from holding stocks of goods of which the prices are increasing (S_{app} deducted from $P + R$).

(e) Ignore net property income from abroad (for the UK in 1988, this was less than 1.7 per cent of national income) (assume NPA = 0).

(f) Regard I as net investment, because national income is net national product.

If these simplifications are applied to the national accounting equations 5.2 to 5.9, we have the following:

(a) Using simplifications (a) and (e), and the fact that Y = NNP at factor cost:

$$Y = C + I + GE + X - M \tag{5.10}$$

(b) Using simplifications (d) and (e) and the fact that Y = NNP at factor cost:

$$Y = W + P + Int + R \tag{5.11}$$

(c) Using simplification (c):

$$Y + TP = C + S + T \tag{5.12}$$

From these:

$$C + I + GE + X - M = C + S + T - TP \tag{5.13}$$

Cancelling C from both sides of equation 5.13 and rearranging terms gives

$$I + GE + TP + X = S + T + M \tag{5.14}$$

If we now substitute G (total government expenditure) for GE (government expenditure on goods) + TP (transfer payments + interest paid by the government), equation 5.14 becomes

$$I + G + X = S + T + M \tag{5.15}$$

This tells us that:

total injections to the circular flow of national income ($I + G + X$) equal total withdrawals from the circular flow ($S + T + M$).

The government's budget deficit is $G - T$; $X - M$ is the balance of trade, which may be in surplus (if X exceeds M) or in deficit (if M exceeds X). So equation 5.15 implies that

$$S - I = G - T + X - M \tag{5.16}$$

$S - I$ is the **private sector balance**, because it reflects the withdrawals and injections that result from decisions made by private individuals and firms within the country. So:

private sector balance = budget deficit + balance of trade surplus

5.10.1 Closed economy with no government

In parts II and III of this book we shall discuss a model of an economy in which no goods are imported or exported (the economy is **closed**) and in which government expenditure and taxation are also zero. So G, T, X and M are all zero, and equation 5.15 simplifies to:

$$I = S \qquad (5.17)$$

This case is a simplification, and there is no reason why investment expenditure should equal saving in an **open economy** in which there is government activity so that G, T, X and M are all not zero. In such an economy, I equals S if the government's budget is balanced and if there is a zero balance of trade (or if the government deficit exactly equals the balance of trade deficit).

5.10.2 Equations and identities

It should be noted that some of the equations in this chapter are in fact identities, because they are true by definition. For example, saving is defined to be the amount of household incomes remaining after consumption expenditure and tax payments, so that the statement

$$HI = C + S + T$$

is an identity. The distinction between equations and identities is not important in our discussion of the national accounts, although it is useful to remember which of the relations discussed are true by definition.

5.11 Summary

Many of the conclusions of this chapter are summarized in the equations in the text, and the definitions and notation are listed in the Glossary. The circular flow of national income is the flow of money from firms to households and back to firms. Injections to the flow are investment expenditure, government expenditure and exports; withdrawals from the flow are saving, taxation and imports.

Domestic product is the sum of the values of all final goods produced in the economy in a particular period. Domestic product can be calculated in three ways: by adding the values of final goods, by adding expenditures on goods and by adding incomes generated in firms. The value of final goods produced equals the sum of values added in all firms (both exclude expenditure on intermediate goods). Gross domestic product exceeds net domestic product by the amount of replacement investment expenditure.

The government's deficit is the difference between its expenditure and taxation; the balance of trade is the difference between exports of goods and imports of goods.

Topics and problems

(1) What are the most important aspects of an individual's standard of living? How well does national income measure the standard of living of people in a country?

(2) Does an increase in national income necessarily imply that more goods are produced?

(3) To what extent can we compare the national outputs of two countries given that they are evaluated in different currencies and that the countries may produce different goods?

(4) Which of the following items are not included in the UK national accounts:

> Food produced by farmers and eaten by their families
> Food produced by farmers and eaten by other people
> Services of housewives
> Services of domestic servants
> The work of students in schools and colleges
> Consumption of alcohol
> Do-it-yourself activities
> The output of smoke from power stations?

Are the exclusions important? How, if at all, might national accountants take account of those items not now included?

(5) What would be the effects of the following changes on the items of the national accounts reported in tables 5.1 to 5.9:

> An increase in value-added tax (or sales tax)
> An increase in pensions financed by an increase in income taxes
> An increase in the amount of investment goods bought by firms
> An increase in the number of houses with foundations laid (a) in December 1987 (b) in December 1988.
> An increase in the number of American tourists coming to the UK
> An increase in the production and exports of oil?

(6) Many citizens of Lesotho are employed in South Africa, and send back a part of their wages to support their families in Lesotho. How do these payments affect the national accounts of the two countries concerned?

(7) The Ruritanian national accounts for 1988 (consisting of the equivalent of our tables 5.1 to 5.7) were accidentally destroyed. To what extent can they be reconstructed from the following information salvaged from the destruction (all figures in millions of Ruritanian dollars)?

Consumption: 243,567
Government expenditure on consumer and investment goods: 75,879
Exports: 46,210
Value of stocks on 1 January 1988: 73,491
Value of stocks on 1 January 1989: 71,211
Increase in the value of work in progress: 1,007
Imports: 51,061
Taxes on expenditure: 68,980
Wages: 222,222
Profits and interest: 76,576
Other income: 0
Total domestic income: 332,564
Stock appreciation: 5,981
Depreciation: 21,905
Net property income from abroad: −98
Residual error: 107

(8) How much more of the national accounts can you reconstruct if you know that Ruritania had a balance of trade surplus of 893 million dollars in 1988?

Chapter Six

Unemployment, poverty, growth and inflation

Unemployment — poverty and income distribution — economic growth — inflation — changes in national income — standard of living

---

6.1 Introduction

The national income of a country gives one indication of the efficiency with which it uses its resources. However, the size of national income does not tell us everything that we might want to know about the way in which the system operates. Other indications include the extent of **unemployment**, the extent of **poverty**, the **inflation rate** and the **growth of national income**. We take a preliminary look at these issues in the context of the UK in this chapter.

6.2 Unemployment

A country's economic system does not use its resources very efficiently if a large number of people want a job but do not have one, or if many people work fewer hours than they would like. Some of the country's resources of labour are being wasted, and national income could be increased if these resources were employed.

To measure the extent of this inefficiency, we need to measure unemployment. There are many definitions of unemployment; a definition that captures the difference between what people want to do and what they are able to do is:

Unemployment is the total number of hours that people want to work in a period, minus the number that they actually do work.

In practice, unemployment is measured in a less detailed way – usually by categorizing individuals as employed or unemployed, without considering whether they are working the number of hours that they would like. Furthermore, some people who are counted as unemployed may not actually want to work at the current wage for their skills but are counted as unemployed because they are observed not to work.

6.2.1 Supply of labour

The number of hours that people want to work depends on the wages that they would receive (after they have paid income tax), for at least three reasons:

(a) A very low wage may give someone a lower income than he could receive from the social security system, so that he would not want to work at all. The lowest wage for which a person is better off working than not working depends on his or her entitlement to social security payments.
(b) An increase in the wage increases the reward for each hour worked. The incentive to sacrifice an hour of leisure is increased, and this incentive makes it more attractive for a person to work longer hours when his or her wage increases.
(c) A person may work less when his wage increases because he can achieve a reasonable income in fewer hours.

The first two effects increase the number of hours of labour supplied when the wage increases; the third effect causes a reduction. Whatever the overall outcome of these three effects, the total number of hours that people want to work is likely to depend on wages. The labour supply is shown as the curve SS in figure 6.1, where we have supposed that labour supply falls when the wage increases beyond A, so that at these high wages the third effect is dominant. We shall discuss influences on the labour supply curve in greater detail in chapter 10.

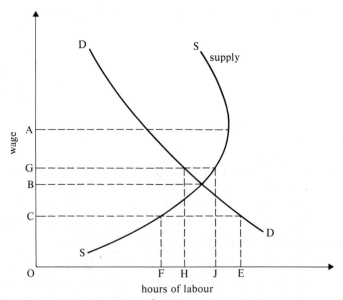

Figure 6.1 Labour market
The equilibrium wage is B. If the wage exceeds B, some people who want jobs cannot find them. If the wage is below B, some firms that want to employ workers cannot do so.

6.2.2 Demand for labour

The demand for labour comes from firms that decide how many hours they want to employ according to the employment cost. This includes the wage (before income tax is deducted) and other payments that the firm must make, such as pension and national insurance (social security) contributions. A firm is likely to employ more labour if the employment cost falls. If tax and other payments do not change, an increase in the wage received by workers (after income tax is paid) causes an increase in the employment cost, and so the demand for labour falls. This relation is shown by curve DD in figure 6.1. Note that a firm's demand for labour also depends on its **productivity** (that is, how much each worker produces). This is likely to change over time.

6.2.3 Actual and equilibrium wages

If the wage is at its equilibrium level (at wage B in figure 6.1), the supply of labour equals the demand. The number of hours that people want to work is equal to the number that firms want to employ, so that there is a job available for everyone who wants one. In practice, even in this situation, there is likely to be some **frictional unemployment** of a short duration that arises during the period when people change jobs and when school and college leavers look for their first jobs. This unemployment lasts for a few weeks at most if the labour market is in equilibrium.

If the wage is below its equilibrium level (at C for example), more labour is demanded (E) than is supplied (F). In these circumstances there is again a job available for everyone who wants one. Unemployment is only frictional, and likely to be of very short duration because there are more job vacancies than people seeking them.

If the wage is above its equilibrium level (at G for example), the supply of labour (J) exceeds the demand (H). Some people who want a job cannot find one, and others who work part-time would like a full-time job but cannot find one. Unemployment is more than frictional. In figure 6.1, unemployment is JH when the wage is G.

In figure 6.1 we have combined all types of labour into a single labour market. In reality there are markets for many different types of labour because people have different skills. If the wage in labour market 1 is at A in figure 6.2(a), there is unemployment of BC. If the wage in labour market 2 is at D in figure 6.2(b), there is a shortage of type 2 labour, and people who are unemployed in labour market 1 may train to acquire the necessary skills and supply labour in market 2. The supply curves of labour shift from S_1 to T_1 and from S_2 to T_2, so that unemployment at wage A in market 1 falls to EC and the shortage of labour in market 2 is reduced. We shall say more about this aspect of labour markets in chapter 10.

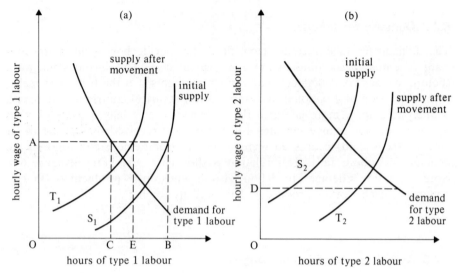

Figure 6.2   Movement of labour from market 1 to market 2 (a) market 1 (b) market 2

Initially, the wage in market 1 exceeds its equilibrium level, and workers who cannot find jobs move to market 2. This reduces the supply in market 1 and increases the supply in market 2.

6.2.4 Real and money wages

An individual works for a wage in order to be able to buy goods, and so her decision on how much labour to supply depends on her wage in relation to the prices of the goods that she can buy. So we assume that if all wages double and the prices of all goods double, individual decisions on labour supply will be unaffected because a given supply of labour time would continue to buy the same quantities of goods.

A firm employs labour to produce goods for sale, and so the profitability of employing labour depends both on the wage paid and on the price of the goods produced. Again, if wages and all prices double, the firm's decision on the desirability of employing a particular worker will not change; if it was profitable to do so before the doubling of prices and wages, it remains profitable after the doubling.

Thus decisions on both the supply of labour and the demand for labour depend on the **real wage**, which measures the wage relative to the prices of goods. If the **money wage** (which is the actual amount of money paid for an hour of work) doubles and all prices double then the real wage is unchanged. So in times of inflation a person's money wage may increase without any increase in his real wage because the prices of goods that he buys increase (on average) at the same rate as his money wage.

If, contrary to our assumption here, an individual decides her labour supply on the basis of the money wage, regardless of any changes in prices, she is said to experience **money illusion**. Her decision is based on an amount of money and not on the goods that can be bought with it, and the individual has an illusion that she is better off when her money wage increases, even though she may be able to buy no additional goods because prices have risen. We shall suppose in this book that people (and firms in making labour demand decisions) experience no money illusion because they react as quickly to changes in prices as they do to changes in money wages.

6.2.5 Causes of unemployment

Unemployment arises for a variety of reasons, including the following (which are not mutually exclusive):

(a) Changes in the pattern of demand for goods that reduce the demand for labour in those industries where demand for goods has fallen. These changes may result because people switch from buying one good to buying another (because, for example, there is a change in fashion), or by switches from domestically produced goods to cheaper goods imported from abroad. Unemployment that arises from this source and that affects people working in some industries but not in others is known as **structural unemployment**.

(b) Changes in technology, which may reduce the demands for the skills of some groups of people. New technology is likely to increase the demand for some types of labour, but this increase is likely to be for different skills from those displaced, and the displaced workers may not be able to train to take up the new jobs. For example, the microelectronic revolution of recent years has increased the demand for workers who can program and operate computers, but the resulting automation reduces the demand for workers on production lines in factories. Unemployment that arises from this source is known as **technological unemployment**.

(c) A general reduction in demands for goods that causes a reduction in the demand for most or all types of labour. This may occur if households spend less or if firms buy less new equipment. The general unemployment that arises from these reductions in the demands for goods is known as **demand deficient** (or **mass** or **Keynesian**; see section 16.2) **unemployment**.

(d) An increase in the supply of labour that arises because more workers enter the labour market than retire from it. A likely cause of this is a change in the age structure of the population, but it may also be the result of changes in social conditions that, for example, cause more married women to look for jobs. This is **demographic unemployment**.

Both structural and technological unemployment are likely to be concentrated in particular areas of the country. Regional unemployment arises when there are differences between the levels of unemployment in different parts of the country. Seasonal unemployment arises when people have jobs (say in holiday hotels, building or agriculture) for only part of the year.

6.2.6 Unemployment in the UK

Table 6.1 gives figures for unemployment in the UK from 1971 to 1988. Since 1982 these figures have recorded the numbers of people receiving social security payments because they have no job. Previously, the figures recorded the number of people who registered as unemployed with the government employment service, whether or not they were eligible for unemployment benefit. These figures do not record the level of unemployment as defined at the beginning of this section. There are at least three reasons for this:

(a) The figures report a number of people and not a number of hours. So, for example, people who have a part-time job but want a full-time job are excluded.
(b) Some people register as unemployed so that they can receive unemployment benefit, but are not actively looking for a job.
(c) Some people (of which the largest group is married women) want a job, but do not register with the government because they are not eligible for unemployment benefit.

On balance, most economists believe that the last category is the most important, so that the government figures understate the extent of unemployment. Despite

Table 6.1   Measured unemployment in the UK 1971–88

Year	Working population (thousands)	Unemployed (excluding students) (thousands)	Percentage unemployed
1971	25,207	696	2.76
1972	25,267	778	3.08
1973	25,614	557	2.17
1974	25,658	528	2.06
1975	25,878	838	3.24
1976	26,093	1,265	4.85
1977	26,224	1,359	5.18
1978	26,358	1,343	5.10
1979	26,627	1,234	4.63
1980	26,839	1,513	5.64
1981	26,741	2,395	8.96
1982	26,677	2,770	10.38
1983	26,610	2,984	11.21
1984	27,265	3,030	11.11
1985	27,797	3,179	11.44
1986	27,985	3,229	11.54
1987	28,206	2,905	10.30
1988	28,552	2,434	8.44

Source: *Monthly Digest of Statistics*

this understatement, it is obvious that there has been a very substantial increase in unemployment over the period covered in the table.

Unemployment is calculated in different ways in other countries. For example, in the United States the level of unemployment is calculated from a survey in which a sample of the population is asked whether they are looking for a job. If this method of measuring unemployment was used in the UK, the reported unemployment figure would be higher because the group omitted from the UK figures (including married women) would be included in the survey.

6.3 Poverty and income distribution

In a market economy, a person's income depends on:

(a) The wage for his skill, if he is employed.
(b) Income from renting out or using land, equipment and buildings that he owns.
(c) Interest on money that he has lent.
(d) Profits and dividends from firms, or shares in firms, that he owns.

It is sometimes convenient to combine the second, third and fourth sources of income into **property income** (or **unearned income**, or **investment income**) because they are derived from assets owned.

In a market economy in which there is little government intervention, someone who is unemployed and has no property income has no income. The social security or welfare system of a mixed economy attempts to provide incomes for people who would otherwise have little or nothing.

In principle, the income distribution is described by a list of every person's income (or every household's income, which in most cases indicates the extent of poverty and riches better than individual income). This list can be assembled in part from income tax returns and from surveys of the population, but other incomes must be estimated if we want to measure the income distribution. In any case, there are many million households in the UK, and so any practical discussion of the income distribution, and of the effect of the social security and taxation systems on it, requires that we summarize the list in some way.

The simplest summary of the list is the **average income**, which tells us nothing about income distribution. The average income in the UK in 1985–6 was approximately £10,000, but this average can arise from a variety of distributions. For example, the average income is £10,000 if half the households have incomes of £8,000 and the other half have incomes of £12,000; the average is the same if 1 per cent of the households have incomes of £505,000 and 99 per cent have incomes of £5,000. In fact, of course, there is a range of household incomes in the UK, ranging from very low (perhaps zero if, for example, people do not claim social security benefits) to very high. The average tells us nothing about this range.

6.3.1 The Lorenz curve

A frequently used method of summarizing a list of all incomes into a single measurement involves drawing a **Lorenz curve**.

> A Lorenz curve shows the percentage of total household incomes received by successively larger fractions of the population, starting with the poorest group.

An example is given in table 6.2 and figure 6.3. Columns 3 and 6 in table 6.2 show that the poorest 10 per cent of the population receive 3.28 per cent of national income; the poorest 35 per cent receive 19.67 per cent of national income, and so on. These figures are represented by points A, B, C and D in figure 6.3; point E represents the fact that 100 per cent of the housesholds receive 100 per cent of the income. The Lorenz curve is drawn by joining O to A, A to B, B to C, C to D and D to E. In our example, we have six points (including O and E), but in real world examples we may have more points, depending on the amount of detail in the information provided. For example, we may have sufficient information to calculate the fraction of national income received by the poorest 1 per cent of households, by the poorest 2 per cent of households, and so on. We can then represent all these points in a diagram, and join them to give a Lorenz curve. However we divide up the population, the Lorenz curve shows the fraction of national income received by successively larger groups of households.

The Lorenz curve represents the income distribution by showing the fraction of income received by each fraction of the population. If everyone has a very similar income, the poorest 10 per cent of the population receive almost 10 per cent of national income, the poorest 20 per cent receive almost 20 per cent of national income, and so on. In these circumstances, the Lorenz curve is nearly a straight line, as in figure 6.4(a). At the other extreme, if a very few people, say the richest 5 per cent, receive most of national income, the poorest 95 per cent of households receive a small fraction of national income. Figure 6.4(b) shows the Lorenz curve in these circumstances: the fact that 5

Table 6.2 Example of unequally distributed incomes

1	2	3	4	5	6
Group	% of population	Cumulative % of population	Average income (£)	% of national income	Cumulative % of national income
Poorest	10	10	2,000	3.28	3.28
Next poorest	25	35	4,000	16.39	19.67
Next	30	65	6,000	29.51	49.18
Next	20	85	8,000	26.23	75.41
Richest	15	100	10,000	24.59	100.00

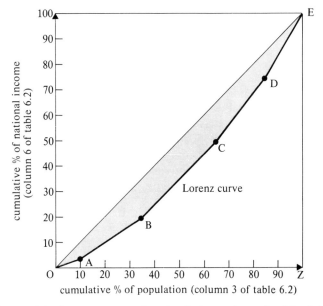

Figure 6.3   Lorenz curve for the information of table 6.2

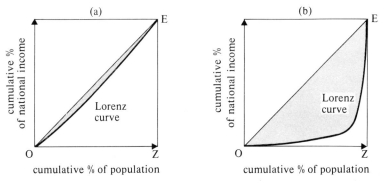

Figure 6.4   Extreme cases of the Lorenz curve (a) nearly equal incomes (b) very unequal incomes

per cent of the households are very much richer than the other 95 per cent is represented by the sharp change in the slope of the Lorenz curve.

6.3.2 The Gini coefficient

The two extreme cases of figure 6.4 suggest how we might make a numerical summary of the income distribution. When people have very similar incomes the Lorenz curve is close to the line joining O and E and the area between the Lorenz curve and line OE is a small fraction of the area of triangle OEZ. When a few households are much richer than the majority, the Lorenz curve is far from the line OE, and the area between the Lorenz curve and OE is almost the same as the area of OEZ.

The Gini coefficient is the area between the Lorenz curve and line OE divided by the area of OEZ.

In figure 6.3 the Gini coefficient is approximately 0.22; in figure 6.4(a), the Gini coefficient is almost 0; in figure 6.4(b) the Gini coefficient is almost 1. A Gini coefficient near 0 represents almost equal incomes; a Gini coefficient near 1 represents very unequal incomes.

Table 6.3 gives some information on the distribution of incomes in the UK both before and after payment of income tax. The figures are derived from a sample of income tax returns. They do not reflect the distribution of all incomes in the UK because:

(a) Some people, particularly with low incomes, do not pay income taxes.
(b) Some income is not declared on income tax returns (legally, in the case of incomes such as interest on National Savings Certificates; illegally in other cases).

The fact that the figures are taken from only a sample of tax returns implies that they should not be regarded as absolutely accurate, even allowing for these two limitations on their scope.

Table 6.3 Distribution of incomes in the UK, 1985–6

Range of income before tax (£)	% of people in group	Before tax		After tax		% of income paid in tax
		Average income in group (£)	% of total income	Average income in group (£)	% of total income	
Up to 3,000	8.10	2,583	2.16	2,514	2.60	2.7
3,000–5,000	19.20	4,006	7.92	3,635	8.92	9.3
5,000–7,000	18.27	5,944	11.19	5,099	11.90	14.2
7,000–10,000	21.95	8,432	19.06	6,949	19.49	17.6
10,000–15,000	17.81	12,151	24.62	9,835	24.71	19.1
15,000–20,000	8.23	17,062	14.47	13,559	14.26	20.5
20,000–50,000	5.96	26,911	16.53	19,984	15.22	25.7
Above 50,000	0.48	81,346	4.05	47,019	2.90	42.2
All	100	9,707	100	7,827	100	19.4

The information used to construct this table is based on tax returns. People who pay no tax are therefore excluded, biasing the results by reducing the number of lower incomes.

Source: *Annual Abstract of Statistics*

The Gini coefficient of incomes before tax is 0.362; the Gini coefficient of incomes after tax is 0.325. According to this measurement, the income tax system helps to reduce the disparity of incomes.

6.3.3 Value judgements and the income distribution

If the Gini coefficient of the income distribution falls, perhaps because of a change in the social security or taxation systems, incomes become more equally distributed. It is a value judgement that not everyone shares to say that this equalization is desirable. In many circumstances, people are likely to disagree in their judgements of the effects of policies on the income distribution because some gain from the policy (if they receive more benefit) and others lose (if they pay more tax). Some of those who lose may approve of the policy because it helps others, but there are likely to be some who disapprove. In section 19.7 and chapter 22 we shall discuss how, if at all, the government might decide whether the benefits to the gainers outweigh the losses to the loser, so that it can choose the best policy.

6.4 Economic growth

Over the period from 1954 to 1987, UK national output approximately doubled. Of course, in that time the outputs of all goods did not increase by 100 per cent; indeed, some outputs have fallen and some goods were produced in 1988 that were not produced in 1954. The statement that output has doubled reflects the *average* growth of outputs.

Outputs can increase because:

(a) More workers are employed, because the population has grown or because unemployment has fallen.
(b) Output per employed worker (which is **labour productivity** or **productivity** for short) increases because **technical progress** (or **innovation**) introduces more efficient methods of production, because firms buy more equipment, or because workers become better educated and trained, so that they are better at using the equipment that they have.

Increases in outputs are referred to as **economic growth** and, as long as output increases more rapidly than the population, economic growth allows each person to consume more goods. Alternatively, economic growth allows the government to implement policies to increase the incomes of some people without reducing the incomes of other people.

6.4.1 Cycles

Figure 6.5 shows the actual annual rates of economic growth in the UK from 1952 to 1987. The average rate (2.3 per cent) is a compromise between years when outputs increased rapidly (the maximum rate was 6.5 per cent in 1972), years when there was little or no growth and years when outputs fell (the greatest rate of decline was 2.3 per cent in 1979). Most economies experience an uneven pattern of economic growth, and the pattern of increases and decreases in the rate of economic growth forms the **trade cycle** (or **business cycle**).

During a trade cycle, outputs increase quickly during the upswing but fall, or increase more slowly, during the downswing. The number of people employed is likely to follow a similar pattern. Unemployment is at its lowest level during the **boom** phase of the cycle, and at its highest level in the **slump** (or **recession**, or **depression**) phase.

6.4.2 Sectoral growth

As people get richer, they tend to change the pattern of their consumption expenditures. In broad terms, people spend a larger amount, but a smaller fraction of their incomes, on manufactured goods and food as they get richer. Correspondingly, they spend a greater fraction of their incomes on services. Table 6.4 shows these changes in the composition of consumption expenditure in the UK in the 30 years to 1987, and also changes in the composition of UK national output. To some extent, the change in the composition of national output is a consequence of changes in the composition of consumption. However, output changes also reflect changes in international comparative advantages and the ability of UK industries to compete with similar industries abroad. Changes in the pattern of outputs have been much greater than changes in the pattern of consumption as manufacturing industries have declined relative to service industries. This radical shift in the UK economy from manufacturing to service industries is known as **deindustrialization**.

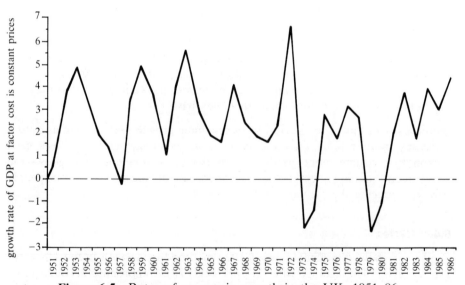

Figure 6.5   Rates of economic growth in the UK, 1951–86

Table 6.4 Composition of consumption expenditure and national output in UK, 1957–87

	% of total			
Item	1957	1967	1977	1987
Consumption expenditure				
Food	27.8	21.7	19.1	13.7
Drink and tobacco	13.2	12.3	12.2	10.2
Housing	9.0	11.9	13.8	15.9
Transport	8.3	9.9	15.1	17.7
All others	41.7	44.2	39.8	42.5
Output (GDP)				
Agriculture/forestry/ fishing	4.4	3.2	2.6	1.7
Manufacturing and construction	47.1	45.5	42.2	37.3
Services (private sector)	33.0	35.3	33.7	39.9
Services (public sector)	9.5	11.1	15.7	16.1
All others	6.0	4.9	5.8	5.0

Source: *Annual Abstract of Statistics*

6.5 Inflation

Inflation is an increase in the average level of prices.

If all prices increase at the same rate there is **pure inflation**, but the prices of different goods usually change at different rates. The inflation rate is then the average of these price increases.

The usually quoted inflation rate in the UK is the change in the average prices of consumer goods, which is the **Retail Prices Index**. This index is constructed by averaging the increase in the prices of consumer goods, weighting each price by the average amount that is bought by each consumer. For example, in 1987 approximately 7.2 per cent of the total expenditure of the average consumer was spent on energy products, and 3.6 per cent on beer. So an increase in the prices of energy products has twice as great an effect on the Retail Prices Index as a similar increase in the price of beer. The Retail Prices Index is not an average of all prices in the economy because it does not include the prices of investment goods, but it is the index of greatest relevance to consumers, and to workers and trades unions who are trying to negotiate money wage increases to maintain their real wages in the face of inflation.

Table 6.5 shows the annual inflation rates in the UK from 1971 to 1989. The inflation rate reached a peak for the period since the Second World War

Table 6.5 UK inflation rates, 1971–89

Year	Inflation rate (% per year)	Cumulative price increases from 1970 (%)
1971	9.4	9.4
1972	7.1	17.2
1973	9.2	28.0
1974	16.1	48.5
1975	24.2	84.4
1976	16.5	114.9
1977	15.8	149.0
1978	8.3	169.6
1979	13.4	205.8
1980	18.0	260.8
1981	11.9	303.6
1982	8.6	338.3
1983	4.6	358.6
1984	5.0	376.5
1985	6.1	399.4
1986	3.3	413.0
1987	4.1	430.2
1988	4.9	451.3
1989 (estimated)	7.5	485.1

Source: *Annual Abstract of Statistics*

in 1975, and the average increase in prices from 1970 to 1980 (260.8 per cent) was much greater than the increases during the 1950s (49.0 per cent) and the 1960s (48.8 per cent). The inflation rate has fallen in the 1980s. We shall discuss various explanations for variations in the inflation rate in chapter 21.

6.5.1 Consequences of inflation

In the 1970s and 1980s governments of many countries have tried to reduce the inflation rate. The need to reduce inflation has been supported by a variety of views, including that:

(a) Inflation causes unemployment.
(b) Inflation affects the poor more than the rich.
(c) Inflation reduces the value of past savings.
(d) Inflation reduces confidence in the use of money. In section 3.4 we discussed the possibility of hyperinflation, when prices rise so rapidly that people no longer use money because its purchasing power falls rapidly. The UK has not experienced a hyperinflation, but people may fear that the inflation rate will increase – perhaps to hyperinflationary levels – if the government does nothing to reduce it.

6.5.2 Inflation and unemployment

We discuss the relationships between inflation and unemployment in several later chapters. To some extent these suggest that an increase in the inflation rate increases unemployment; to some extent they suggest the opposite. The recent UK evidence (see figure 6.6) tends to support this ambiguity in the relationship between the inflation rate (table 6.5) and the level of unemployment (table 6.1). (See also problem 6 at the end of this chapter.)

6.5.3 Inflation and income distribution

Table 6.6 shows the extents to which the prices of different goods have risen in the UK in recent years. Fuel prices have increased by an average of 1.75 per cent more per year than all prices. It is estimated that for one group of relatively poor people, one-person pensioner households, expenditure on fuel and light is approximately 18.2 per cent of their total expenditure, compared with approximately 7.2 per cent for the population as a whole. The prices of durable consumer goods, on the other hand, have increased at an average of 2.76 per cent less each year than the average of all prices. Approximately 10 per cent of pensioners' expenditure is on these goods, compared with approximately 14 per cent for all consumers. On this evidence, this poorer group experiences a higher inflation rate than the average consumer.

6.5.4 Inflation and savings

The purchasing power of a sum of money falls when prices increase, but this may be offset by the interest received when the sum is lent. If the interest rate for a year is 12 per cent, someone who lends £100 for the year receives

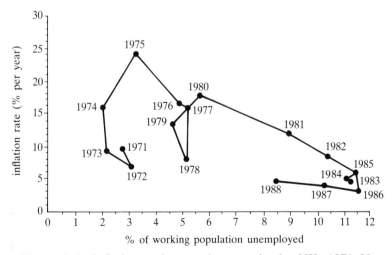

Figure 6.6 Inflation and unemployment in the UK, 1971–88

Table 6.6 UK price increases 1974–89 for selected categories of goods

Category	Annual average price increase (%)
All	10.06
Food	9.54
Drink and tobacco	10.58
Housing	12.75
Fuel and light	11.81
Durable consumer goods	7.28

back £112. If the inflation rate is less than 12 per cent she can buy more goods with £112 at the end of the year than she could with £100 at the start of the year. For example, if the inflation rate is 7 per cent for the year, goods that cost £100 at the start of the year cost £107 at the end of the year, so that with £112 she can buy goods that would have cost £112/107 = £104.67 at the start of year. She can buy 4.67 per cent more goods if she is prepared to wait a year for them. The **real interest rate** is 4.67 per cent, compared to the **nominal interest rate** of 12 per cent. These two interest rates and the inflation rate are related by the formula:

$$1 + r = (1 + n)/(1 + i) \tag{6.1}$$

which can be written as

$$r(1 + i) = n - i \tag{6.2}$$

where r is the real interest rate, n is the nominal interest rate and i is the inflation rate. (Interest and inflation rates are quoted in the usual percentage form in the text. They are used in decimal form in the equation, so that 4.67 per cent = 0.0467, 12 per cent = 0.12 etc.)

If the inflation rate exceeds the nominal interest rate, the real interest rate is negative, and savers can buy fewer goods at the end of the year than they could if they had spent their incomes at the start of the year.

The real interest rate is sometimes calculated using the formula:

$$r = n - i \tag{6.3}$$

so that the term ri in equation 6.2 is ignored. Equation 6.3 gives a close approximation if r and i are small: in the example above, this formula gives a real interest rate of 5 per cent per year (12 − 7). When the nominal interest rate and the inflation rate are large, the formulae give very different answers. For example, if the inflation rate is 100 per cent and the nominal interest rate is 110 per cent, equation 6.1 gives r = 5 per cent, while equation 6.2 gives r = 10 per cent. However, for much lower values of n and i, the two equations give similar answers and, given that the inflation rate is the average of numerous price increases, the apparent inaccuracy (5 per cent compared to 4.67 per cent, for example) is usually not important.

6.6 Changes in national income

National income can be calculated from the sum of the quantity of each good multiplied by its price (see section 5.3). So an increase in national income can be the result either of increased outputs of goods – that is, of economic growth – or of inflation. If we know that national income has increased from one year to the next, how can we separate the effect of economic growth from the effect of inflation?

The following example shows that there is no straightforward answer to this question, because there are (at least) two equally satisfactory answers. Table 6.7 gives the quantities of two goods produced and the prices of these goods in 1989 and 1990. In 1989, national income is (3×20) + (5×28) = £200; in 1990 national income is (6×16) + (7×40) = £376, which is an increase of 88 per cent over the 1989 national income. We can use two methods:

(a) Method 1 calculates the inflation rate from 1989 to 1990 as the increase in the cost of buying the goods made in 1989. Using 1989 prices, the goods produced in 1989 cost £200; using 1990 prices, these goods would cost (6×20) + (7×28) = £316, so that prices have increased, on average, by 58 per cent from 1989 to 1990. So 58 per cent of the increase in national income can be attributed to inflation. The remainder, that is the increase from £316 to £376 (19 per cent), can be attributed to the increase in outputs – to economic growth.

(b) Method 2 calculates the inflation rate from 1989 to 1990 as the increase in the cost of buying goods made in 1990. Using 1989 prices, the goods produced in 1990 would cost (3×16) + (5×40) = £248; using 1990 prices, these goods cost £376, so that prices have increased on average by 51.6 per cent from 1989 to 1990. So 51.6 per cent of the increase in national income can be attributed to inflation. The remainder, that is the increase from £200 to £248 (24 per cent) can be attributed to economic growth.

These two methods are illustrated in figure 6.7: method 1 by a clockwise movement from box 1 to box 3 via box 2, and method 2 by a counter-clockwise movement from box 1 to box 3 via box 4.

Both methods give a figure for the increase in national income due to economic growth. Using method 1, economic growth increases **real national**

Table 6.7 Price and quantities in two years

| | Quantities produced | | Prices (£) | | % price increase |
	1989	1990	1989	1990	
Apples	20	16	3	6	100
Brushes	28	40	5	7	40

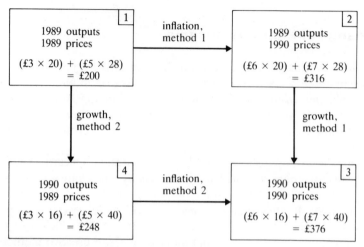

Figure 6.7 Separating inflation from economic growth

income in 1990 prices from £316 to £376 because both years' outputs are evaluated using 1990 prices. Using method 2, economic growth increases real national income in 1989 prices from £200 to £248 because both years' outputs are evaluated in 1989 prices.

The UK national accounts are published in both **current price** form and **constant price** form. The current price figures report each year's income valued at that year's prices (so, in our example, national income at current prices rises from £200 in 1989 to £376 in 1990). The constant price figures report national income from a series of years valued at the prices for some base year (1985 for the accounts published in 1989) to eliminate the average effects of inflation. Recent figures for UK national income in current prices and in constant 1985 prices are given in table 6.8. National income in current prices more than doubled between 1979 and 1987, while national income in constant prices increased by only 16 per cent in the same period. The final column of table 6.8 shows the implied inflation rate derived from the current and constant price figures. This figure is found from the annual change in national income in current prices divided by the annual change in national income in constant prices. It records the influence of inflation on national income, while the change in the constant price figures records the effect of economic growth. The implied inflation rate is not the same as that derived in table 6.5, which is the average rate of change of prices of consumer goods. The rate in table 6.8 includes the change in the prices of investment goods as well as those of consumer goods.

6.6.1 Index numbers

National income is also quoted in **index number** form. To calculate an index number the value of national income for some year is set equal to 100, and the figures for all other years are scaled accordingly. This can be done for

Table 6.8 UK national income 1979–88 in current and constant prices

Year	Current prices National income (£ million)	Index	Constant 1985 prices National income (£ million)	Index	Implied economic growth rate (%)	Implied inflation rate (%)
1979	151,182	56.7	250,327	93.8	—	—
1980	172,361	64.6	240,848	90.3	−3.8	18.3
1981	187,766	70.4	238,261	89.3	−1.0	10.2
1982	205,546	77.1	242,160	90.8	1.6	7.7
1983	227,106	85.1	252,599	94.7	4.3	5.8
1984	245,107	91.9	258,055	96.7	2.2	5.8
1985	266,736	100.0	266,736	100.0	3.4	5.2
1986	284,217	106.6	278,344	104.4	4.4	2.1
1987	312,176	117.0	291,183	109.2	4.6	4.9
1988	345,637	129.6	303,928	113.9	4.4	6.2

Source: *UK National Accounts*, 1989

national income in either current price form or constant price form, and also for the implied inflation rate. Table 6.8 shows UK national income figures in index number form, with national income in 1985 set at 100, and the others scaled accordingly. So, for example, the index for national income in constant prices for 1987 was 108.8, because national income in 1987 was 8.8 per cent higher than national income in 1985.

The use of index numbers makes percentage changes easy to read. Many economic magnitudes are quoted in index number form; perhaps the most famous is the Retail Prices Index, which was used to calculate the inflation rates in table 6.5. Note, however, that the use of index numbers does nothing to solve the problem raised in the example of figure 6.7: different index numbers for national output are derived according to the method used for calculating the change in national income.

6.7 Standard of living

In this chapter we have examined several of the possible outcomes of the operation of an economic system: unemployment, inflation, economic growth, income distribution and so on. However, each household is likely to be most concerned by its own **standard of living**. To a large extent, this depends on the household's income and the prices of goods that it buys, but it is likely to be affected by other issues. For example, most people hope for an increase, or at least no decrease, in their incomes, and this can be achieved only if there is economic growth. A high level of unemployment may make people less confident of their future prospects, or those of their children. Other issues that we have not discussed in this chapter, such as pollution and the availability of medical services and education, may also affect opinions about the standard of living.

There is little point in trying to include all these issues in a single numerical measurement of the standard of living. Each person can make his own evaluation of the benefits of economic growth, the disadvantages of unemployment, pollution and so on, and reach his own conclusion on whether he is better off or worse off than at some previous time. People make subjective evaluations of their standards of living because they make value judgements of what is important. As economists, we can try to provide objective information on issues such as economic growth and unemployment that are likely to influence subjective views.

6.8 Summary

To measure the extent of labour that is available but unused, we need to know the number of hours that people want to supply and the number that they actually supply. In practice, measured unemployment takes no account of hours worked, excludes some people who want to work and have no job, and includes some people who have no job because they do not want to work at the current wage.

The income distribution is a list of households' incomes. It can be summarized in a variety of ways, including the Lorenz curve and the Gini coefficient. A Gini coefficient of near 0 implies near equality of incomes; a Gini coefficient near 1 implies great inequality.

Economic growth is the increase in the outputs of goods; it arises from improvements in technology, better educated workers, investment in new equipment and population growth. Inflation is an increase in prices. Some of the effects of inflation may be offset by increases in money wages and in interest rates. Inflation and economic growth both increase national income. There are at least two methods of separating their effects that give rise to different estimates of the inflation rate and of the rate of economic growth.

Topics and problems

(1) Is complete equality of incomes desirable? If not, to what extent would you want to equalize incomes? Could you justify inequalities by telling a poor person that his or her poverty relative to some other people is for the social good?

(2) Should students on vacation and available for work be counted as unemployed?

(3) 'Inflation does not matter if everything goes up at the same rate because then no relative prices or incomes are altered.' 'Inflation is a major threat to economic prosperity.' Is either of these statements true?

(4) Draw Lorenz curves for each of the income distributions listed in table 6.9. Can you compare the extents of equality in the distributions?

Table 6.9 Distribution of incomes for problem 4

Group	Average income of people in group (£)		
	Case 1	Case 2	Case 3
Poorest 20%	1,000	2,000	1,000
Next 20%	2,500	5,000	2,000
Next 20%	5,000	7,500	7,500
Next 20%	10,000	12,500	8,000
Richest 20%	31,500	23,000	31,500

Answer problems 5 to 8 using the information given in table 6.10 for an economy in which three goods are produced.

Table 6.10 Data for problems 5 to 8

	Food	Drink	Machines
Price in 1988 (£)	20	15	75
Price in 1989 (£)	20	30	100
Total output in 1988	100	60	40
Total output in 1989	120	50	40
Total consumption in 1988	100	60	0
Total consumption in 1989	120	50	0
Household 1			
Consumption in 1988	8	6	0
Consumption in 1989	8	6	0
Household 2			
Consumption in 1988	9	15	0
Consumption in 1989	9	15	0

(5) What is the increase in national income at current prices from 1988 to 1989?

(6) Use the two methods of section 6.6 to separate the effects of inflation and of economic growth between 1988 and 1989.

(7) What is the average rate of increase of the prices of consumer goods, weighting the price changes by: (a) the quantities of goods consumed in 1988; (b) the quantities consumed in 1989?

(8) Which of the two households listed experiences the greater average inflation rate?

(9) Figure 6.6 illustrates the simplest possible relation between unemployment and inflation. We might instead put forward the views that:

(a) A high inflation rate in one year causes unemployment to increase from that year to the next.
(b) A high level of unemployment in one year causes a large increase in the inflation rate from that year to the next.
(c) A high level of unemployment is caused by a high average inflation rate over the previous three years.

Use the information given in tables 6.1 and 6.5 to draw diagrams illustrating these possible relationships. What are your conclusions?

Part II

Perfect economies and market analysis

Economic events are the outcome of individual decisions and their interactions. We can examine the behaviour of individuals as managers and owners of firms, as consumers and as workers most easily if we make a number of simplifying assumptions. In this part, we make unrealistic simplifying assumptions in order to bring out clearly basic aspects of individuals' behaviour and their interactions. So we assume that there is no significant government activity in the economy (the economic system is decentralized and capitalist), and economic decisions to produce and consume goods, and to supply and demand labour interact in markets. We refer to an economic system of this kind as a perfect market economy – although the word 'perfect' should be interpreted with care (see section 7.1), because it is used in a positive, not a normative sense. The economic system discussed in this part is simplified also by ignoring international economic transactions, including importing and exporting. Later parts of the book remove the less realistic assumptions and build on the basic material of this part to provide a general overview of the operation of economies in which government activities and international trade occur.

Chapter Seven

Perfect market economies: the invisible hand

Conditions for a perfect market economy — supply and comparative advantages — the importance of being small — efficiency and equilibrium

7.1 Introduction

In this chapter we ask a question that is fundamental to a discussion of market economies. It is important also as a basis for government policies in mixed economies. The question is:

Can individual decisions in a market economy result in specialization according to comparative advantages?

This is a very important question because it would seem that the system is not a good way of organizing economic activities if individual decisions imply that people's skills are not used in an efficient way (although such a conclusion would not tell us that any other system is better).

The answer to the above question is 'yes, in certain circumstances'. In this chapter we specify what these circumstances are, and in the remainder of this part we shall elaborate on them and their implications. The special circumstances that we introduce define a **perfect market economy** (also known as a **competitive market economy**, a **perfectly competitive market economy** or, perhaps confusingly, a **free market economy**).

The word 'perfect' is used in economics in a particular way. It does not imply that the economy is faultless, nor even that everyone, or most people, would want to live in a perfect economy if that were possible. Instead, 'perfect' implies that the economy has the features that we list in section 7.2. Some aspects of a perfect market economy are perfect in the normative sense of the word: for example, we shall see that in a perfect market economy people have all the information that they need for making economic decisions, so that the procedures for obtaining economic information cannot be faulted. Other aspects of a perfect market economy may be undesirable: for example, it is possible that some people are very rich and others very poor (see chapter 10). So someone who cares a lot for the equality of incomes may judge a perfect market economy to be very undesirable.

Market economies that do not satisfy the conditions of a perfect market economy are **imperfect**; they have **imperfections** (see part III). Just as a perfect market economy may be judged to be undesirable, so imperfections may be regarded as advantages. No value judgement is implied by the use of the terms 'perfect' and 'imperfect' in economics; they are used only to describe.

7.2 Conditions for a perfect market economy

A market economy co-ordinates individual decisions to supply and demand goods and factors of production in markets. These decisions are the result of decision-makers' motivations and their opportunities. The simplifications made to define a perfect market economy radically affect the nature of the decisions that are taken by individuals and by firms. These assumptions are:

(a) Each person is motivated entirely by material objectives (we refer to this as **material motivation**).
(b) There is no legal restriction on the goods that any person may buy or sell, or on the job that any person may do (**freedom of action**).
(c) Each person and firm has all the information that it wants to make economic decisions (**perfect information**).
(d) The supply or demand by each person in each market is so small that no action by a single person or firm can affect the price (or wage, rent or interest rate) in that market. Furthermore, people and/or firms do not collaborate in groups to affect prices (**smallness**).
(e) No person or firm has any direct effect on the opportunities of any other person or firm (**no external effects**).
(f) Actual prices, wages, rents and interest rates move rapidly to their general equilibrium levels after any change in conditions affecting supplies or demands (**market clearing**).
(g) Government activity is restricted to basic functions of maintaining law and order and its activities have no effect on prices, wages, rents or interest rates determined in markets (**minimal government**).
(h) No goods are exported or imported, and there is no borrowing from or lending to other countries (**no foreign transactions**).

These assumptions are sufficient to ensure that markets operate in an unregulated environment (minimal government, freedom of action) without interference from large firms or trades unions seeking to manipulate the system to their own ends (smallness, no external effects), or from those who might seek to restrict access to information (perfect information). Individuals seek to take advantage of profitable opportunities (material motivation) and do so in such a way that markets reach equilibrium quickly (market clearing), so that suppliers and demanders have no further profitable opportunities to change the prices that they charge or offer.

The assumption that there are no foreign transactions limits the scope of the analysis to a single country with a **closed economy**. However, it is possible to extend the analysis of a perfect market system to an **open economy** and to examine issues in international trade operating in a similarly unregulated environment, again free from the influence of large firms or national governments.

The unrealism of these assumptions is obvious. However, it is very valuable to begin our examination of the detailed operation of economic systems in this simplified model. It gives us a relatively simple context in which we can examine the determinants of decisions to demand and to supply and their interactions in markets. This gives the background for the rest of the book, where we build in much greater complexity (and realism). It also gives the analytical background to the belief of some economists and politicians that freely operating markets are desirable, and that economic policies should be devised to make the real economy look more like the simple model of a perfect market economy. The extent to which imperfections are effective in making the conclusions of this part irrelevant to the real world is an important issue in economic policy debates. Some say that the real economy is – or could be, given suitable government policies – sufficiently like a perfect market economy that the conclusions from it are highly relevant. Others deny this, but even the analysis of their position requires that we know what conclusions they criticize.

7.2.1 Material motivation

This assumption implies that each person sells goods at the highest possible price, buys goods at the lowest possible price and works for the highest wage, given the hours that he or she wants to work. Firms want to make the maximum profit, and employ whoever will do a job for the lowest wage. This assumption rules out behaviour such as loyalty to a supplier even when some other supplier will sell at a lower price, and the employment of friends or relations rather than more efficient or cheaper strangers.

7.2.2 Freedom of action

Legal restrictions on what people may do might prevent them from specializing according to their comparative advantages. For example, in the UK no woman is allowed to work underground in a coal mine, and this restriction prevents society from achieving an efficient output level if there are women who have a comparative advantage over male miners in producing coal compared with the good that the women produce instead.

7.2.3 Perfect information

This assumption implies that every buyer knows which supplier charges the lowest price, and every seller knows which buyer will pay the highest price.

Every person and firm knows of every job available, and every firm knows of every potential worker. The assumption also implies that every firm can predict accurately what it will be able to sell in the future, so that its decisions to invest in new equipment are not affected by the fear that the additional goods produced may not be sold profitably. This assumption is plainly unrealistic: in the real world, people lack information and are uncertain about the future (see chapters 13 and 14).

7.2.4 Smallness

This assumption implies that there are many suppliers and demanders in each market, whose supply or demand is a small fraction of the market supply or demand. Each person and firm is small in the sense that none has any influence over prices, wages, rents or interest rates. A firm is not small if it can influence the selling price of the good that it produces and/or the prices at which it buys its factors of production. A person (for example, a star entertainer) is not small in this sense if she possesses a skill possessed by no one else, because she can then influence the wage that she receives for her labour.

The decisions of a large number of people can affect supplies and demands in markets, and can therefore affect prices, wages and interest rates. The smallness assumption rules out co-ordinated actions by groups of individuals and firms to affect prices. An important implication is that workers do not act together in trades unions to influence wages in a perfect market economy. This is an unrealistic assumption that we shall discuss again in section 12.7.

7.2.5 No external effects

An external effect (or **externality**) occurs when the action of one person or firm affects the opportunities open to others. For example, a factory that discharges poisonous waste into a river causes an external effect because people downstream cannot drink the river water or use it for fish farming, at least without using resources to clean the water. A beekeeper gives rise to an external effect because his bees enable others to grow more fruit.

The most important aspects of external effects involve government policy: how can harmful external effects, such as water pollution, be controlled, and how can beneficial external effects be encouraged? We shall examine external effects more closely in section 19.6.

The assumptions of smallness and no external effects imply that the actions of one person or firm do not affect the opportunities open to others in any way. Thus individuals' economic decisions are affected by prices in markets, but no individual can affect the price in a market on his or her own, and no individual or firm can affect economic decisions in any other way. No supplier or demander can affect the price that anyone else pays for a good, or the wages, rents and interest rates that determine other people's incomes. So we can examine the decisions made by each person and firm in isolation from decisions made by others.

7.2.6 Market clearing

This assumption implies that we can examine problems by looking at general equilibrium prices and quantities. The assumption that prices move rapidly to equilibrium requires that the general equilibrium is stable (see section 4.10), and that price-setters respond rapidly to surpluses and shortages. They have information about these surpluses and shortages, and are materially motivated to take advantage of them by altering prices. Given these assumptions, it is reasonable to suppose that the response is rapid, and that markets clear quickly.

7.2.7 Minimal government

This assumption implies that we can examine the decisions of people and firms without considering ways in which the government can modify these decisions or their consequences. We shall discuss government policies in part IV.

7.3 Supply and comparative advantages

We begin our analysis of a perfect market economy by considering an even simpler version in which everyone is a self-employed specialist. We examine firms and the employment of labour in chapters 8 and 10.

The smallness assumption implies that each person reacts to prices knowing that he can do nothing to change them. The assumption of material motivation implies that each person chooses to specialize in producing the good that gives him the greatest income, and we can show that, in consequence, people specialize according to their comparative advantages and the economy reaches an efficient output level. This conclusion demonstrates the **invisible hand** operating in a perfect market economy.

The phrase 'invisible hand' is from Adam Smith's *Wealth of Nations*:

> By directing [his] industry in such a manner as its produce may be of the greatest value, he intends only his own gain, and he is in this . . . led by an invisible hand to promote an end which was no part of his intention. (Book 4, chapter 2)

The end that he (every individual) promotes is the 'interest of society', which in this case is the efficient use of resources.

We can illustrate this conclusion using an example in which there are two goods and many people (because each person must be small). Suppose that a person's opportunity cost of producing food is 2 cloth. He can increase his income by producing one more food and two less cloth, provided that the price of food is more than twice the price of cloth. If the prices of food and cloth are £5 and £2, he adds £1 to his income by producing one more food and two less cloth. In general:

A person specializes in producing good 1 rather than good 2 if the ratio of the price of good 1 to the price of good 2 exceeds his opportunity cost of producing good 1 measured in terms of good 2.

In our example, the ratio of the price of food to the price of cloth is 5/2, which exceeds the person's opportunity cost of producing food, measured in terms of cloth. So he produces food.

The quantities of goods that people supply change when prices change, as in the example of table 7.1. Alan chooses to produce food as long as the ratio of the price of food to the price of cloth exceeds 2/3. When the ratio is 2/3, Alan does not mind which good he produces, so that he may produce either or some of both, and when the ratio is less than 2/3 he produces cloth. Bill produces cloth as long as the ratio of the price of food to the price of cloth is less than 3/4; he produces food when the ratio exceeds 3/4.

Notice that the absolute levels of the prices are irrelevant to their decisions – each person makes the same decision when the price of food is £7 and the price of cloth is £10 as he does when the price of food is £35 and the price of cloth is £50. Only the price ratio is relevant to their decisions.

7.3.1 Prices and comparative advantages

In table 7.1, Alan has a comparative advantage over Bill in the production of food and to achieve an efficient output level the pattern of specialization should obey the following rules:

Table 7.1 Maximum outputs per period

	Food	Cloth
Alan	6	4
Bill	8	6

(a) Alan should produce no cloth if Bill produces food.
(b) Bill should produce no food if Alan produces cloth.

Their decisions are in line with these rules because if the ratio of the price of food to the price of cloth is:

(a) Less than 2/3, both produce cloth.
(b) Between 2/3 and 3/4, Alan produces food and Bill produces cloth.
(c) More than 3/4, both produce food.

There is no price ratio for which Alan produces cloth *and* Bill produces food, and so they choose to specialize according to their comparative advantages. The same conclusion applies to any two people and to any two goods. Note that, in table 7.1, Bill has an absolute advantage over Alan in the production of both goods, but this is irrelevant to the conclusion because the attainment of an efficient output level depends only on comparative advantages.

We have a general conclusion that:

In a perfect market economy, people choose to specialize according to their comparative advantages, and the economy achieves an efficient output level.

7.4 The importance of being small

The smallness assumption is important in deriving this conclusion, as the example of table 7.2 shows. Charles has a comparative advantage in producing cloth, David in producing food. Charles can influence the price ratio between the goods because he produces a large fraction of the market supply of whichever good he chooses. Suppose that, if he produces food, the price of food is £10 and the price of cloth is £10. If he produces cloth, the supply of food falls and the supply of cloth increases. This increases the price of food to £12, because less food is supplied, and reduces the price of cloth to £7, because more cloth is supplied. So if Charles produces food, his income is £10 × 160 = £1,600; if he produces cloth, his income is £7 × 200 = £1,400. Assuming that he wants to spend most of his income on goods with prices he cannot influence, Charles chooses to produce food, and the prices of both goods are £10. David is small, and has no influence on any price, so that, when the prices are £10 and £10, he chooses to produce cloth because this gives him the higher income. So Charles chooses to produce food and David chooses to produce cloth, contrary to their comparative advantages.

The recognition that people or firms that are not small may seriously affect the pattern of specialization can be found in Smith's *Wealth of Nations*. He commented that producers may collude to influence prices:

People of the same trade seldom meet together, even for merriment and diversion, but the conversation ends in conspiracy against the public, or in some contrivance to raise prices. (Book 1, chapter 10).

Table 7.2 Maximum outputs per period (one person with market influence)

	Food	Cloth
Charles	160	200
David	8	9

7.5 Efficiency and equilibrium

An economy is **efficient** if:

(a) It produces an efficient output level (see section 2.2.1).
(b) Each person buys what he wants to buy, and sells what he wants to sell given his income and prices.

The first condition requires that people specialize according to their comparative advantages and that resources are allocated efficiently, so that it is not possible to produce more of one good without producing less of another or using more resources. The second condition requires that the quantities of goods supplied equal the quantities that are demanded so that no one is prevented by a surplus from selling what he or she wants to sell at the going price, and no one is prevented by a shortage from buying what he or she wants to buy at the going price. Shortages and surpluses are rapidly eliminated when markets clear.

So, at least in the case in which everyone is an individual specialist, we can conclude that:

A perfect market economy is efficient.

This important conclusion is the basis of some proposals for government policies that are designed to bring the actual economy closer to perfection. The desire of the UK government in the 1980s to reduce its influence by privatization of nationalized industries and to reduce the power of trades unions are examples of such policies.

We should note that efficiency is only one aspect of an economic system, and it is quite consistent with, for example, extreme poverty. People with little ability may have low incomes and if we judge an economy by examining its income distribution as well as its efficiency we may judge a perfect market economy to be an undesirable way of organizing economic activities (see section 10.9).

7.6 Summary

A perfect market economy is characterized by seven assumptions: material motivation, freedom of action, perfect information, smallness, no external effects, market clearing, minimal government. For convenience we have dealt with a closed economy with no foreign transactions.

In a perfect market economy where everyone is an individual specialist, the invisible hand leads everyone to specialize according to their comparative advantages. The economy is in equilibrium and so a perfect market economy is efficient. This conclusion may not hold if someone is not small and so can influence prices.

Topics and problems

(1) In what important ways do the assumptions of a perfect market economy fail to hold in the real world? In what ways are people not small?

(2) Would you want to live in a perfect market economy? Would you want to live in such an economy if (i) you had great ability, or if (ii) you had little ability in any job, so that everyone else had an absolute advantage over you in the production of all goods?

(3) Which views of politicians reflect either a belief that the assumptions of a perfect market economy do hold fairly closely in the real world, or that the government should try to ensure that they do hold?

Problems 4 to 6 use data from table 7.3.

Table 7.3   Alternative maximum production levels for problems 4 to 6

Case	Person	Food	Cloth	Paper
1	Alan	24	16	—
	Bill	18	10	—
2	Alan	24	16	20
	Bill	18	10	30
3	Alan	24	16	—
	Bill	20	20	—
	Colin	16	24	—
4	Alan	24	16	10
	Bill	20	24	0
	Colin	16	20	24
	David	12	24	16

(4) List all the comparative advantages in each case.

(5) What is the market supply of each good in each case when the price of food is £10, the price of cloth is £12 and, where it is relevant, the price of paper is £8. What happens to the supply of each good if all prices increase by 50 per cent. What happens to the supply of each good if the price of cloth increases to £16, with the other prices at £10 and £8?

(6) Confirm that, in each case, people specialize according to their comparative advantages.

Chapter Eight

Perfect competition

Revenue — cost — profit — profit maximizing — perfect competition in the long run — perfect competition and efficiency — investment decisions: discounting and net present value

---

8.1 Introduction

In the previous chapter we examined a perfect market economy in which everyone is an individual specialist. In this chapter we extend the analysis to include firms. The assumptions of a perfect market economy imply:

(a) Material motivation: anyone who sets up a firm does so to make as large a profit as possible. The owners of a firm are **profit maximizers**. (Note that for simplicity we refer to actions and decisions made by a firm when, in principle, we should refer to decisions made by the owners or managers of the firm.)

(b) Freedom of action: there is no restriction that prevents any individual from setting up a firm to produce any good. All firms have **freedom of entry** to all markets, and they have **freedom of exit** so that they can cease to produce a good at any time.

(c) Perfect information: each firm has all the information that it needs to make decisions without uncertainty on prices, wages and other issues that affect it. Each firm knows how much each worker can produce in the time for which he or she is paid, and knows that he or she will produce it.

(d) Smallness: each firm produces a very small fraction of the total supply in the market, and no firm can influence the price of its product by increasing or decreasing the amount that it supplies. Each firm has many competitors that supply similar goods, and no firm buys enough of any material or factor of production to affect the price that it pays.

We make one further simplification: each firm operates only one factory and produces only one type of good. This excludes the possibility that a firm can subsidize the loss made producing one type of good out of the profits made on another.

Industries in which there are many small firms that have freedom of entry and exit are **perfectly competitive**, and the firms are in a situation of **perfect competition**. The use of the term 'perfect' in this context is the same as its use in the perfect market economy: it involves no value judgement.

8.2 Revenue

A firm in perfect competition is small, and so cannot affect the price at which it sells its products. If the price of the good is £5, the firm can receive £5 for each unit however many units it sells. If it charges more than £5 per unit, it sells nothing because demanders of the good buy from other suppliers (because they have information about all the other suppliers). The firm could be generous to its customers and charge less than £5 per unit, but it would lose revenue by doing so, because it can sell all that it produces at £5 per unit. A lower price reduces the firm's profit and does not increase its sales, and so a profit-maximizing firm would not charge less than £5 per unit. So although the firm is, in principle, a price-setter that can charge whatever price it chooses, the assumptions of a perfect market economy imply that each firm sells at the market price.

8.2.1 Average and marginal revenue

Suppose that a perfectly competitive firm sells quantity q at price p. Then:

(a) Its **total revenue** is pq.
(b) Its **average revenue** per unit sold is $(pq)/q = p$.
(c) Each additional unit sold adds p to total revenue. This is its **marginal revenue** (see box 3).

Box 3   Note on the word 'marginal'

Marginal is a well used, perhaps overused, word in economics, and it is important to be clear about its meaning. Its use does not always imply a small item; for example, 'marginal cost' does not necessarily mean a small change in cost. Marginal cost is the change in total cost that results from a small change in the output of a good. The change in total cost may itself be large, even though the change in output is small. For example, if it is possible to extract not more than 1,000 litres of water per hour from a well, the marginal cost of increasing output from 1,000 to 1,001 litres of water per hour includes the cost of digging a new well.

We can say the same about any change in one item that is generated by a change in another. When we use the term 'marginal' we refer to a small change in the cause, which may or may not imply a small change in the effect. In mathematical terms, the small change in the cause will lead to a small change in the effect only if the relation between them is continuous; the size of the small change in the effect will be unambiguous only if the relation is differentiable.

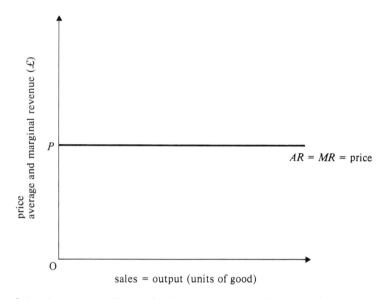

Figure 8.1   Average and marginal revenue curve for a perfectly competitive firm
The firm can sell any amount at the market price P, so average revenue and marginal revenue both equal price.

A firm's marginal revenue is the increase in total revenue when one additional unit is sold.

A perfectly competitive firm can sell one additional unit without affecting the selling price, and so in perfect competition:

$$\text{marginal revenue} = \text{selling price}$$

The selling price p is also the firm's average revenue, so that in perfect competition:

$$\text{marginal revenue} = \text{average revenue}$$

When we examine a firm's decision on how much to produce, it is convenient to represent the relation between average revenue and marginal revenue and the level of sales in a diagram. Figure 8.1 shows this very simple relation: the firm can sell all that it produces at the market price P, and so average revenue AR and marginal revenue MR are the same for all levels of sales. The AR and MR curves are horizontal.

8.2.2 Sales and output

Total revenue depends on the amount of the good that is sold. A firm's sales in a period differ from its output in that period if it sells some goods produced in previous periods, or if it produces goods that it stores to sell later. Most firms have stocks of goods ready for sale, mainly because there may be unforeseen changes in demand (for example, because of changes in tastes), or unforeseen changes in the firm's ability to produce (for example, because there is an interruption in the supply of materials). The assumption of perfect information excludes these unforeseen changes, because a firm knows how much it can sell at each price and what it can produce, both now and in the future. So a perfectly competitive firm does not hold stocks to allow for unforeseen events, and we assume that its sales equal its output. The horizontal axis in all figures in this chapter represents both sales and output.

8.3 Cost

A firm incurs costs by paying for labour, land, materials, equipment and interest on loans. Some costs vary when the firm's output changes, and we should expect that total cost increases when output increases. However, before we can discuss the relation between cost and output in detail, we must specify the **time horizon** that we are considering. If a firm wants to increase its output very quickly, it can do so only by using its equipment more intensively and by asking its employees to work overtime. This may be very expensive, because equipment may wear out rapidly if it is used intensively, and wages for overtime work may be high. On the other hand, if the firm decides now to increase its output next year, it is likely to be able to buy additional equipment and hire more workers. Similarly, a farmer might increase his output of a crop at short notice by using expensive fertilizer; given a longer time horizon, he might rent and cultivate an additional field at a lower additional cost.

So:

(a) In the **short run**, a firm can increase or decrease its output only within the limits of its existing land and equipment. The quantities of some of its factors of production are fixed; these are its **fixed factors**.
(b) In the **long run**, the firm can change the amount of all its factors of production. There is no fixed factor in the long run.

The definitions of the short run and the long run are convenient for analysing firms' decisions. We cannot specify a number of days after which the short run stops and the long run begins because, in reality, several factors may be fixed for a time and the quantity of each can be changed after a different interval. So the movement from the short run, when firms have several fixed factors, to the long run, when there is none, is a gradual process. However, the distinction between the short run and the long run gives a useful framework for examining the behaviour of firms.

8.3.1 Cost in the short run

In the short run, a firm must operate with its existing land and equipment, and it may be unable to employ more workers but it can buy whatever quantities of materials it needs.

We identify three categories of cost:

(a) **Fixed costs** (or **overhead costs**), that are the same for all levels of outputs and are the amounts that the firm must pay for its fixed factors.
(b) Those **variable costs** that are proportional to the level of output. These include the cost of materials and energy, and of labour that is employed as it is needed. The smallness assumption implies that firms cannot influence the price that they pay for any factor of production, and so there are, for example, no discounts for large orders of materials.
(c) Those variable costs that increase more than proportionately when output increases. For example, if a 10 per cent increase in output requires that overtime is worked at wages that exceed basic wages, the cost of labour increases by more than 10 per cent.

A firm's **total cost** is its fixed cost plus the two categories of variable cost.

8.3.2 Average cost

Fixed and variable costs have conflicting effects on average cost (= total cost divided by output) when a firm increases its output:

(a) Fixed cost is spread more widely, so that average fixed cost falls when output increases.
(b) If variable costs increase more than proportionately, then average variable cost increases when output increases.

Table 8.1 gives an example. When output increases from a low level, average cost falls because average fixed cost falls. Variable costs are proportional to output up to 3 units, but the firm must pay overtime wages to increase output beyond 3 units in the short run. So average variable costs increase as output increases beyond 3 units, and eventually average cost increases also. This relationship is illustrated in figure 8.2, where the short-run average cost curve has a U shape.

Table 8.1 Output and costs

1	2	3	4	5	6	7	8
					Total cost	Average cost	
		Average		Average	cost	cost	
	Fixed	fixed	Variable	variable	(col.2 +	(col.3 +	Marginal
Output	cost	cost	cost	cost	col.4)	col.5)	cost
1	180	180	20	20	200	200	
2	180	90	40	20	220	110	20
3	180	60	60	20	240	80	20
4	180	45	88	22	268	67	28
5	180	36	130	26	310	62	42
6	180	30	192	32	372	62	62
7	180	25.7	280	40	460	65.7	88
8	180	22.5	400	50	580	72.5	120
9	180	20	720	80	900	100	320

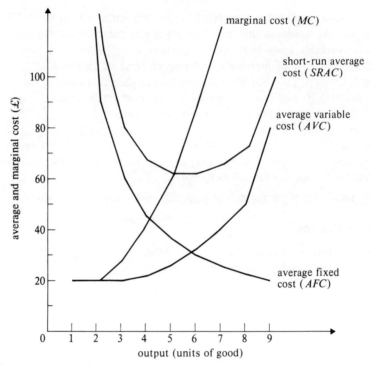

Figure 8.2 Average cost, average variable cost, average fixed cost and marginal cost curves for table 8.1

8.3.3 Marginal cost

A firm's marginal cost is the increase in its total cost when one additional unit is produced.

Column 8 in table 8.1 gives the marginal cost for each level of output in our example, and the marginal cost curve is illustrated in figure 8.2. Fixed costs make no contribution to marginal cost because they do not change when output increases, and so marginal cost is entirely determined by the increase in variable cost as output increases.

8.3.4 Relationship between average cost and marginal cost

Table 8.1 and figure 8.2 show that the marginal cost of increasing output from 5 to 6 units is £62, which is equal to the average cost of producing 5 units and the average cost of producing 6 units. Furthermore, £62 is the minimum average cost in the table. So:

Marginal cost equals average cost at the level of output for which average cost is at its lowest level.

This is reflected in figure 8.2 where the marginal cost curve intersects the average cost curve at the lowest point of the average cost curve.

In addition, figure 8.2 shows that:

(a) Marginal cost is below average cost at those levels of output for which average cost falls as output increases by one unit (outputs 1 to 4).
(b) Marginal cost exceeds average cost at those levels of output for which average cost increases as output increases by one unit (outputs 7 to 11).

These conclusions are in line with common sense:

(a) If the marginal cost of increasing output from 2 to 3 units is less than the average cost of producing 2 units, then the production of the third unit adds less to total cost than the average of the other two, and so the average cost of 3 units is less than the average cost of 2 units.
(b) If the marginal cost of increasing output from 7 to 8 units exceeds the average cost of 7 units, the production of the eighth unit adds more to total cost than the average of the previous 7, and so the average cost of 8 units exceeds the average cost of 7 units.

The relations, that 'average' falls when 'marginal' is less than 'average', and that 'average' increases when 'marginal' exceeds 'average', occur whenever 'marginal' and 'average' appear in other contexts, and can be illustrated by a non-economic example. Suppose that 450 people are in a room, and their average age is 34. One more person – the marginal person – enters; if she is older than 34, the marginal age exceeds the average age of the 450, and the average age of the 451 people exceeds that of the original 450 people. If the age of the newcomer is less than 34, the marginal age is less than the average, and the newcomer reduces the average age.

8.3.5 Cost in the long run

The short-run average cost curve of figure 8.2 shows the average cost of producing various outputs given that some factors are fixed. In figure 8.3, there are three such curves ($SRAC_1$ to $SRAC_3$), each representing the firm's average cost for different quantities of the fixed factors. It is cheaper to produce output Y if the fixed factors are those of $SRAC_2$ than if the fixed factors are those of $SRAC_1$ or $SRAC_3$. In the long run, when the firm can choose the amounts of all factors that it uses, it would prefer to use the factors of $SRAC_2$ to produce output Y. In general in the long run, a firm chooses the combination of all factors that gives the lowest possible total cost and average cost of production for a given output level. So:

The long-run average cost curve follows the lowest of the short-run average cost curves.

Technically the long-run average cost curve is the **lower envelope** of all available short-run average cost curves.

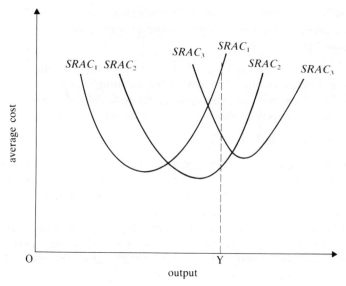

Figure 8.3   Average cost in the short run and the long run
Long-run average cost is the minimum of the short-run average costs for each level of output.

8.4 Profit

Profit is total revenue minus total cost, and is the income of the owners of the firm.

8.4.1 Normal profit

The owners of equipment used by a firm receive **normal profit**, which is the opportunity cost to the owner of using his or her equipment in that way rather than some other. Normal profit is therefore the maximum amount that the owner of the equipment could receive if he or she were to use the equipment in some other way. If the owner of some equipment uses it in a firm but does not make normal profit, material motivation leads him or her to stop using the equipment in that firm and to use it elsewhere to get a higher profit. Thus, if he or she does not receive normal profit, the firm ceases to use the equipment and closes down (or has to operate in some other way).

Normal profit is one of the costs necessary for continuing to produce goods because the firm ceases to operate without it. So we regard normal profit as a part of the costs incurred by the firm in production. It may seem unusual to include a part of profit in cost, but this inclusion can be justified because normal profit is necessary for the continued operation of the firm, just as it is necessary to pay wages to workers and to pay for materials used.

The inclusion of normal profit in total cost allows us to deal in identical ways with two firms that produce the same goods using the same factors, but whose factors are owned by different groups of people. Two firms producing identical goods in identical ways may have a different pattern of ownership but be identical in all other ways. Those who run firm F own the equipment that they use and continue to operate the firm as long as they get normal profits. This normal profit is the amount that the owners of the equipment would get if they used it in some other way or rented it to someone else. So the normal profit equals the market rental for the equipment. Those who run firm G rent the equipment that they use from other people, for which they pay the market rental. Firms F and G produce the same goods in the same way, and their costs will be the same if the normal profit of F is included in its costs at the rental cost of the equipment to G.

8.4.2 Supernormal profit

If the owners of a firm sell the goods produced for more than the costs of the firm (including normal profit), they receive **supernormal** (sometimes **abnormal** or **economic**) **profit**. They receive this profit because they own, and can therefore sell, the goods produced by the firm.

We can separate normal profit from supernormal profit in the manner of the following example. The annual total revenue of firm F is £10,000, and its annual total cost excluding normal profit is £6,000. The firm uses equipment owned by the firm's owners, which it could have rented for £3,000 per year. So the normal profit is £3,000, giving total costs of £9,000 and £1,000 supernormal profit.

Supernormal profit is the income received by people who have set up a firm and who own the goods that it produces. They are motivated to sell the goods for more than the firm's total cost (which includes their normal profit). Supernormal profit is the income that rewards the owners' **enterprise** in setting up and running the firm; those who receive supernormal profit are known as **entrepreneurs**. In market economic systems where there is uncertainty about the future, the entrepreneurs bear the risk that the revenue from selling goods will be less than the cost of production, and supernormal profit may, at least in part, be regarded as the reward for facing this uncertainty. However, this reward is not a part of supernormal profit in a perfect market economy, because there is no uncertainty, and we shall see in section 8.6 that supernormal profit is zero in the long run in a perfectly competitive market.

Note that the words 'normal' and 'supernormal' are descriptive; they involve no value judgement that approves or justifies profit as a source of income. The normal justification (or its opposite) of profit is a separate issue (see section 10.9) from the role of profit in the decisions of firms.

8.5 Profit maximizing

The owners of a perfectly competitive firm are materially motivated, and so they want the largest total profit. Their normal profit is determined by the income that they could get by renting out their factors to others, and the smallness assumption implies that no one can influence the market rent for any type of land or equipment. So the owners of a firm have no influence on the size of normal profit, but their decisions on how much to produce and how to produce it affect supernormal profit, and so a firm maximizes its total profit by maximizing its supernormal profit.

8.5.1 Profit maximizing in the short run

In figure 8.4 we combine the average revenue and marginal revenue curve of figure 8.1 with the average cost and marginal cost curves (that now include normal profit), which are similar in shape to those of figure 8.2. The firm makes a positive supernormal profit at any output between A and B because, for these outputs, average revenue exceeds average cost including normal profit.

The firm can choose its **profit-maximizing output** by using information on its marginal revenue and marginal cost. Suppose that the firm considers increasing its output by one unit. The additional unit gives rise to a marginal revenue and involves a marginal cost. If the marginal revenue exceeds the marginal cost, total revenue increases by more than total cost (including normal profit), and so the increase in output increases supernormal profit. So the firm

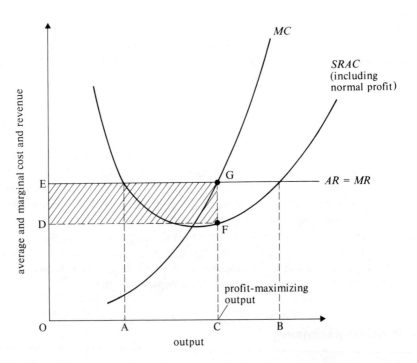

Figure 8.4 Short-run behaviour of a perfectly competitive firm
The firm produces C, where marginal cost equals marginal revenue. Its supernormal profit is DEGF.

has an incentive to expand its output when marginal revenue exceeds marginal cost. In figure 8.4 marginal revenue exceeds marginal cost for all outputs below C, and so the firm produces at least C.

Will the firm go further? If it increases its output beyond C, marginal cost exceeds marginal revenue. The additional unit of output adds more to total cost than to total revenue, and so supernormal profit falls. The firm's profit-maximizing output is therefore C:

> Maximum profit is achieved at the output for which marginal revenue equals marginal cost.

When the firm's output is C average cost is D, and so total cost is given by OC × OD. Average revenue is at E, and so total revenue is OC × OE and the firm's supernormal profit is (OC × OE) − (OC × OD), which is the shaded area DEGF.

Note that the statement that profit is maximized when marginal revenue equals marginal cost is not quite sufficient. In figure 8.5, this occurs at output X and at output Y. If the firm is at X and produces one more unit, its supernormal profit increases because marginal cost is less than marginal revenue. If the firm is at Y and produces one more unit, its supernormal profit falls because marginal cost exceeds marginal revenue. So Y is the output that maximizes profit. So:

> Supernormal profit is maximized when marginal revenue equals marginal cost, and when the marginal cost curve is rising.

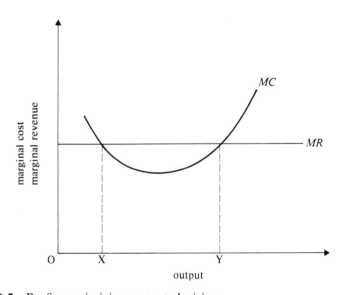

Figure 8.5 Profit-maximizing output decision
When output is X, marginal cost equals marginal revenue, but an increase in output leads to more supernormal profit because MC exceeds MR. Maximum supernormal profit is achieved at Y where MC cuts MR from beneath.

Box 4 Mathematics of profit maximization for a perfectly competitive firm

The firm sells output x at price p:

$$\text{total revenue} = R(x) = px$$
$$\text{average revenue} = p$$

If output increases by Δx, R increases by $\Delta R = p\Delta x$, so that

$$\text{marginal revenue} = \Delta R/\Delta x = p$$

If the increase in output is very small,

$$\text{marginal revenue} = dR/dx = p$$

The firm's fixed costs are F, and its variable costs are $V(x)$. Hence

$$\text{total cost} = C(x) = F + V(x)$$
$$\text{average cost} = C(x)/x = F/x + V(x)/x$$

A very small increase in output gives

$$\text{marginal cost} = dC/dx = dV/dx$$

Profit is $P(x) = R(x) - C(x)$, and the profit-maximizing output (x^*) is found by differentiating P with respect to x and finding the output for which

$$dP/dx = dR/dx - dC/dx = 0$$

So the profit-maximizing output is that for which $dR/dx = dC/dx$; that is, the output for which marginal revenue equals marginal cost.

The second order maximizing condition requires that $d^2P/dx^2 < 0$, so that $d^2R/dx^2 < d^2C/dx^2$. For a perfectly competitive firm $d^2R/dx^2 = 0$, and so the second order condition requires that $d^2C/dx^2 > 0$. This is satisfied if dC/dx increases as x increases, that is, if marginal cost increases as output increases.

8.5.2 Short-run losses and average variable cost

The size of a firm's maximum short-run supernormal profit depends on its average revenue and its average cost. Figure 8.6 illustrates a firm that cannot make a supernormal profit when the price is at X, because average cost (including normal profit) exceeds average revenue at all outputs. At output Z, where marginal revenue equals marginal cost, the firm's loss (= total cost including normal profit minus total revenue, which can be thought of as a negative supernormal profit) is as small as possible. In the short run a firm cannot avoid paying its fixed cost, even if it produces nothing, because it is committed to particular fixed factors. The firm has two alternatives:

(a) It produces nothing, and its loss equals its fixed cost.
(b) It produces output Z, and its loss (XSTU) equals total revenue (OXUZ when the price is X) minus total cost (OSTZ).

The firm chooses the alternative that gives the lower loss, which is the second when the price is X, because its average revenue exceeds its average variable

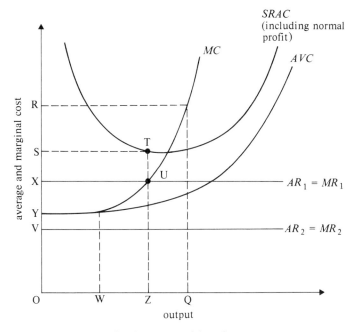

Figure 8.6   Supply by a perfectly competitive firm
The firm supplies nothing if the price is below Y. For prices above Y the firm's supply
curve is its marginal cost curve. The figure assumes that variable cost is proportional
to output up to output W. So $MC = AVC$ for this range of outputs.

cost, and so its loss from producing output Z is less than its fixed cost. It
cannot avoid paying its fixed cost in the short run, and so continues in
production provided that production at least covers its variable costs.

   If the price is V, the average revenue curve is AR_2, and average variable
cost exceeds average revenue for all outputs. The loss exceeds fixed cost at
output Z, the firm chooses to produce nothing, and its loss equals its fixed
cost. So:

   A firm produces a positive output in the short run if it can achieve a
   revenue that exceeds its variable cost.

8.5.3 Supply in the short run

A firm's supply curve shows the amount that it produces at each price. As
long as the price (which equals average revenue) exceeds average variable
cost, a firm produces the output for which marginal revenue equals marginal
cost. If the price is below its minimum average variable cost, the firm produces
nothing. In figure 8.6:

(a) Output is zero when the price is below Y.
(b) Output is Z when the price is X.
(c) Output is Q when the price is R.

So:

> The firm's short-run supply curve is its marginal cost curve for all prices for which it produces a positive output.

The short-run market supply at each price is the sum of the short-run supplies of all firms supplying the market.

8.6 Perfect competition in the long run

Normal profit is the maximum income that the owners of a firm could obtain if they used their factors in some other way. If firms producing good 1 make a positive supernormal profit, then other ways of using the factors needed to produce good 1 would give a smaller income to the owners of these factors. So anyone who owns, or can hire, the factors used to produce good 1 wants to use them to produce that good rather than any other. In the long run, all factors can be transferred from one use to another, and so the number of firms producing good 1 increases. So in the long run the number of firms producing a good increases if firms already producing that good make positive supernormal profit. If, on the other hand, firms producing a good make a loss (total profit less than normal profit), firms cease to produce that good, and so the number of firms producing it decreases. There is no change in the number of firms producing a good if its profits are exactly at the normal level, because there is then no incentive for firms to enter or exit from the market.

8.6.1 Effects of entry and exit of firms

An increase in the number of firms producing a good affects the costs and revenues of all firms producing that good:

(a) The entry of many new firms increases the supply of the good, and so reduces its price. The average revenue and marginal revenue of each firm falls because it now sells at the new, lower price.

(b) The entry of new firms increases the demand for factors of production used to produce the good. The prices of these factors increase, and this increases each firm's total cost.

Note that the entry or exit of one firm has no effect on the prices of the good or the factors, because each firm is small. However, we are now concerned with the entry of many firms whose collective entry or exit affects prices.

The reduction in revenue and the increase in cost reduces each firm's profit, so that the entry of new firms that are attracted by supernormal profit reduces the level of the supernormal profit. The incentive for new firms to produce the good disappears when each firm's supernormal profit falls to zero, and so

> In the long run, the number of firms increases until supernormal profit falls to zero.

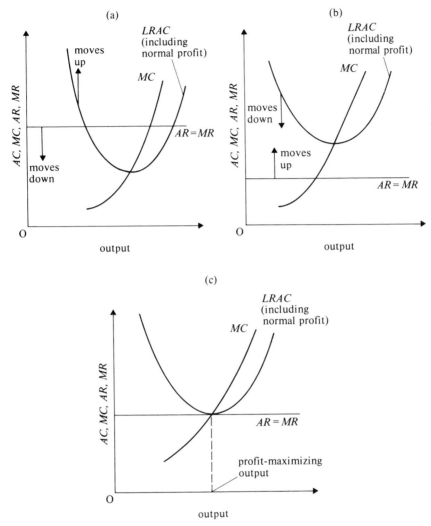

Figure 8.7 Perfectly competitive firm in the long run
(a) short-run supernormal profit positive (firms enter) (b) short-run supernormal profit negative (firms leave) (c) long-run supernormal profit zero (equilibrium).
If firms make positive supernormal profits, the *AR* curve moves down and the *AC* curve moves up as firms enter. If firms make negative supernormal profits, the opposite happens.

These effects on each firm's cost and revenue curves are illustrated in figure 8.7(a).

Firms cease to produce a good if they are unable to achieve a normal profit. The exit of firms from the market affects both costs and revenues in the opposite way to the entry of firms: each firm's revenue increases because the supply of the good falls; each firm's costs fall because the demand for factors is reduced. So the profit of firms that continue to produce the good increases, and firms continue to exit until supernormal profit becomes zero. These effects are illustrated in figure 8.7(b).

8.6.2 Long-run equilibrium

Figure 8.7(c) illustrates the cost and revenue curves for each firm when a perfectly competitive market is in long-run equilibrium. Three conditions hold in this situation:

(a) Each firm produces its output in the least expensive way available to it. Its average cost is given by its long-run average cost curve (see figure 8.3).
(b) Each firm maximizes its supernormal profit by producing the output for which

$$\text{marginal revenue} = \text{marginal cost} \qquad (8.1)$$

(c) Supernormal profit is zero, so that no firm wants to enter or exit, and so:

$$\text{average cost} = \text{average revenue} \qquad (8.2)$$

In addition, for a perfectly competitive firm:

$$\text{average revenue} = \text{marginal revenue} \qquad (8.3)$$

These three equations imply that when a perfectly competitive market is in long-run equilibrium:

$$\text{average cost} = \text{marginal cost} \qquad (8.4)$$

for all firms. Average cost equals marginal cost at the lowest point of the average cost curve (see section 8.3.4), and so equation 8.4 implies that each firm's output is that which gives the minimum average cost, as shown in figure 8.7(c). So:

In long-run equilibrium, each perfectly competitive firm produces at its minimum long-run average cost.

8.7 Perfect competition and efficiency

In section 7.5 we defined an economy to be efficient if all markets are in equilibrium, and if production is at an efficient output level. The first condition is satisfied in a perfect market economy once the rapid movement to equilibrium is complete. The second condition requires that it is not possible to produce more of one good without producing less of another or using more resources. The discovery of a new method of production may permit an increase in the output of one good without a reduction in any other output or the use of more resources, but we are concerned here with the efficiency of a perfect market economy with a given technological knowledge. The following two-stage argument implies that a perfect market economy, including perfectly competitive firms, is efficient when all markets are in long-run equilibrium.

Stage 1

In long-run equilibrium, each firm produces the output that minimizes its long-run average cost. There is no way in which the firm could produce its output at lower cost. Furthermore, there is no other firm that could enter the market and produce at a lower average cost than existing firms: if such a firm could enter, it would achieve a positive supernormal profit, because its average cost is lower than those of existing firms, and its average revenue is the same because the entry of one small firm does not affect the price of the good. So the total output of all firms in the market cannot be produced at lower cost either by existing firms or by new entrants.

Stage 2

Suppose that the economy is not producing at an efficient output level so that it would be possible to rearrange the allocation of resources to produce more of some good without producing less of any other good (and without using more resources). It would be possible to produce the current outputs using fewer resources, thereby reducing the sum of the total costs of producing the current outputs. To reduce this sum of total costs, it must be possible to reduce the total cost of producing the current output of at least one good.

The two stages of the argument imply that:

(a) It is impossible to reduce the cost of producing any good in perfect competition in the long run.
(b) If an economy is not producing at an efficient output level, then the cost of producing some good can be reduced.

Thus when a perfect market economy is in long-run equilibrium, it must be producing an efficient output level. So we can extend the conclusion of section 7.5 to:

A perfect market economy including perfectly competitive firms is efficient in long-run equilibrium.

Once again, this conclusion implies no value judgement on the desirability or otherwise of a perfect market economy. A judgement of such an economy might be based on other issues, including the income distribution.

8.8 Investment decisions: discounting and net present value

A firm's decision to enter a new market to gain supernormal profits is a decision on the profitability of an investment which depends on a wide range of prices, wage rates and interest rates. This decision is principally concerned with activities that occur at different times because the investment must be done now to gain profits in the future. So a major influence on investment decisions is the interest rate, which is the exchange ratio between present and future payments. The firm could borrow £1,000 now to buy a machine if the machine will generate a revenue of £1,100 in one year's time, which can be used to repay the loan and the interest on it.

Investment decisions therefore depend crucially on the interest rate, and in this section we examine this relation in more detail by looking at the technique of **discounting**. This provides a way of comparing present and future costs and revenues that can be used to determine the profitability of an investment project and the relative merits of consuming now and saving for the future.

8.8.1 Discounting: an example

Suppose that a firm is considering spending £2,000 to buy a machine to produce a particular good. The cost of operating the machine (operating cost) is £2,500 per year, and the revenue from selling the good produced is £3,500 per year. So the operating profit is £1,000 in each of the three years of the life of the machine. The firm can borrow or lend money at an interest rate of 10 per cent per year at any time.

The flows of money involved in this project are shown in table 8.2. The operating profit of £1,000 in the first year can be used to pay interest at 10 per cent on a loan of £2,000, and to repay £800 of that loan. This implies that £1,200 of the original loan of £2,000 is carried forward into the second year. The interest on this remaining loan is £120, and this can be paid from the second year of operating profit, and £880 (£1,000 − £120) of the loan can be repaid in the second year, leaving £320 (£1,200 − £880) of the loan remaining in the third year. This, together with the interest (£32) on it, can be repaid at the end of the third year, leaving a surplus of £648 (£1,000 − £320 − £32). The project is profitable when the interest rate is 10 per cent because it is possible to repay the loan, and leave a surplus at the end. Assuming that the interest rate measures normal profit (see section 8.4.1), the project in fact generates a supernormal profit.

The owners of the firm could have obtained £648 after three years if they had lent a sum of £486.85 at 10 per cent interest for three years. Table 8.3

Table 8.2 Cash flows for project (interest rate 10 per cent)

	Start of project	End of year 1	End of year 2	End of year 3
Cost of machine	2,000	—	—	—
Revenue	—	3,500	3,500	3,500
Operating cost	—	2,500	2,500	2,500
Operating profit	—	1,000	1,000	1,000
Interest paid	—	200	120	32
Loan repaid	—	800	880	320
Surplus	—	—	—	648
Loan carried forward	2,000	1,200	320	—

Table 8.3 Accumulation at interest rate 10 per cent

	Start of year 1	End of year 1	End of year 2	End of year 3
Brought forward	—	486.85	535.54	589.09
Interest	—	48.69	53.55	58.91
Carried forward	486.85	535.54	589.09	648.00

shows how £486.85 accumulates to £648 in three years. So £648 in three years' time is equivalent to £486.85 now, or we can say that £486.85 is the **present value** of £648, **discounted** at 10 per cent per year for 3 years.

Any future sum can be discounted to a present value using the formula:

$$\text{present value} = \text{future sum}/(1+d)^n$$

where d is the **discount rate** and n is the number of years of discounting. In our example, d equals the interest rate of 0.1 (10 per cent) and $n = 3$.

The present value of the surplus remaining at the end of the project, after repaying loans, is the **net present value** of the project.

A firm invests in a project if the net present value of the project is positive.

Table 8.2 shows the finances of the project when the discount rate is 10 per cent; after three years, there is a surplus of £648 after repaying the initial loan. Table 8.4 shows the finances of the project when the interest rate is 25 per cent. After three years, £93.75 of the loan remains outstanding and, as the machine has reached the end of its life before the loan can be repaid, the firm does not invest in the project. The example illustrates the principle that:

A higher interest rate implies a lower net present value.

Therefore:

Total investment is reduced if interest rates increase.

Table 8.4 Cash flows for project (interest rate 25 per cent)

	Start of project	End of year 1	End of year 2	End of year 3
Cost of machine	2,000	—	—	—
Revenue	—	3,500	3,500	3,500
Operating cost	—	2,500	2,500	2,500
Operating profit	—	1,000	1,000	1,000
Interest paid	—	500	375	218.75
Loan repaid	—	500	625	781.25
Surplus	—	—	—	—
Loan carried forward	2,000	1,500	875	93.75

8.8.2 Internal rate of return

The firm invests in the project of our example if the interest rate is 10 per cent; it does not invest if the interest rate is 25 per cent. Table 8.5 shows that the project is on the margin of acceptance (the loan is repaid and the surplus is zero) when the interest rate is 23.375 per cent. This interest rate is known as the project's **internal rate of return**:

The internal rate of return of a project is the interest or discount rate for which the net present value is zero.

The internal rate of return is therefore the maximum interest rate at which the firm invests in the project. We have an equivalent investment rule:

A firm invests in a project if the interest rate is less than the internal rate of return of the project.

The formulae for finding the net present value and the internal rate of return for a project are derived in box 5.

Table 8.5 Cash flows for project (interest rate 23.375 per cent)

	Start of project	End of year 1	End of year 2	End of year 3
Cost of machine	2,000	—	—	—
Revenue	—	3,500	3,500	3,500
Operating cost	—	2,500	2,500	2,500
Operating profit	—	1,000	1,000	1,000
Interest paid	—	467.5	343.0	189.5
Loan repaid	—	532.5	657.0	810.5
Surplus	—	—	—	0
Loan carried forward	2,000	1,467.5	810.5	0

8.8.3 Inflation and discounting

If a firm's future costs and revenues rise because of inflation, it will want to use one of two methods:

(a) It can discount the future costs and revenues at the nominal interest rate (see section 6.5.4).
(b) It can eliminate inflation from the future costs and revenues and then discount at the real interest rate.

These two methods give identical answers, given the relation (equation 6.1) between the real and nominal interest rates and the inflation rate. For example, if the firm will have an operating profit of £2,000 in two years' time, there

Box 5   Mathematics of discounting

Consider a project with an initial cost of C that gives future operating profits of $P_1, P_2, \ldots, P_n$. The interest rate (used as the discount rate) is r.

Then, at the end of the first year, the firm pays interest rC, and so it can repay

$$P_1 - rC$$

leaving an outstanding loan of

$$L_1 = C - (P_1 - rC) = (1 + r)C - P_1$$

In the second year, the firm pays interest of rL_1, and repays

$$P_2 - rL_1$$

leaving an outstanding loan of

$$L_2 = L_1 - (P_2 - rL_1) = (1 + r)L_1 - P_2$$
$$= (1 + r)^2 C - (1 + r)P_1 - P_2$$

and so on. At the end of n years, the outstanding loan is

$$L_n = (1 + r)^n C - (1 + r)^{n-1}P_1 - (1 + r)^{n-2}P_2 - \ldots - P_n$$

If the loan has not been fully repaid, L_n is positive. If the loan has been fully repaid, L_n is negative, and represents a surplus, $S = -L_n$.

The net present value of the project is the amount of money that would accumulate in n years to equal the surplus S:

$$NPV(1 + r)^n = S = -L_n$$
$$= -(1 + r)^n C + (1 + r)^{n-1}P_1 + (1 + r)^{n-2}P_2 + \ldots + P_n$$

So that

$$NPV = -C + \frac{P_1}{(1 + r)} + \frac{P_2}{(1 + r)^2} + \ldots + \frac{P_n}{(1 + r)^n}$$

The internal rate of return of the project is the value of r that gives $NPV = 0$. This is an equation involving up to n powers of r, and so it is unlikely that the solution can be found from a simple algebraic formula. In general, the internal rate of return can be found only approximately, using a computer program designed to calculate approximate solutions to equations of degree n.

will be an inflation rate of 12 per cent in each of the next two years and the nominal interest rate is 16 per cent per year, then:

(a) The first method gives a present value of £1,486.33 $(2,000/(1+0.16)^2)$.
(b) The second method uses a real interest rate of 3.57 per cent (because 1.12 = 1.16/1.0357). If £2,000 is reduced by 12 per cent to account for inflation in each of the two years, the operating profit becomes £1,594.39 $(2,000/(1.12)^2)$. The present value of £1,594.39, discounted at 3.57 per cent for two years, is £1,486.33 $(1,594.39/(1.0357)^2)$.

It does not matter which of these methods is used, but it is important to avoid using a combination of them. It is wrong to use the nominal interest rate to discount a sum of money that has already been reduced to account for inflation, and it is wrong to use the real interest rate to discount a sum of money that has not been reduced to account for inflation.

8.9 Summary

Firms in a perfect market economy are perfectly competitive. Each firm is small, so that it has no influence over either its selling price or the prices that it pays for factors of production. Each firm can sell all that it produces at the market price, and so its average revenue and marginal revenue both equal the price.

The average cost curve is U shaped, reflecting the influence of fixed and variable costs. The marginal cost curve intersects the average cost curve at the lowest point of the average cost curve.

It is convenient to separate normal profit (the income from owning factors) from supernormal profit (the income from owning and selling the firm's output). Normal profit is included in total cost. Supernormal profit is maximized at the output where marginal revenue equals marginal cost. A firm produces nothing in the short run if revenue is less than variable cost.

In the long run, firms enter a market if existing firms make a positive supernormal profit. If they make a loss, firms leave the market. This entry and exit leads to a long-run equilibrium in which each firm's supernormal profit is exactly zero. In long-run equilibrium, each firm produces at its minimum long-run average cost. When every market is in long-run equilibrium, a perfect market economy is efficient.

Topics and problems

(1) What markets are supplied by a large number of firms? Is there freedom of entry and exit in these markets?

(2) Do firms maximize their profits? Do they know their marginal revenue and marginal cost curves?

(3) What is the long-run profit of a perfectly competitive firm that does not maximize its supernormal profit? What happens to such a firm?

(4) Draw diagrams to show the response in (a) the short run (b) the long run of a perfectly competitive firm to the introduction of a more efficient method of production.

(5) Draw diagrams to show the effect on a perfectly competitive firm of the introduction of a more efficient method of production of a substitute good in (a) the short run (b) the long run.

(6) A firm's fixed cost is £7, and its variable cost is given in table 8.6 (normal profit is included in cost).

Represent the firm's average cost and marginal cost in a diagram.

What is the firm's profit-maximizing output in the short run if it sells its

Table 8.6 Output and cost for problem 6

Output (units)	Variable cost (£)
0	0
1	5
2	10
3	15
4	21
5	28
6	36
7	45
8	55

product for a price per unit of (a) £4 (b) £6 (c) £10?
In which of these circumstances does the firm make a positive supernormal profit?
What is the firm's short-run supply schedule?

(7) The market demand for a good is 4,000 units at every price. If there are n firms in the industry, each firm's total cost is as in table 8.7.

Table 8.7 Output and cost for problem 7

Output (units)	Total cost (including normal profit) when there are n firms (£)
1	$0.26n$
2	$0.32n$
3	$0.4n$
4	$0.5n$
5	$0.625n$
6	$0.71825n$
7	$0.098125n$

Find each firm's average cost and marginal cost for each level of output when there are n firms.
What is each firm's profit-maximizing output for each of the cases represented in table 8.8?
What is market supply in each case in table 8.8? Which of these cases gives market demand equal to market supply?
What is each firm's supernormal profit in each case in table 8.8?
What is the price and number of firms in long-run equilibrium?

Table 8.8 Data for problem 7

	Number of firms (n)		
Selling price (£)	800	1000	1250
100			
125			

(8) The owner of a firm faces the possibility of investing in the project of table 8.9. Will it do so if it discounts at (a) 3 per cent (b) 5 per cent (c) 10 per cent (d) 25 per cent? What is the internal rate of return?

(9) Governments introduce competition policies to try to increase competition between firms (see chapter 19). Argue the case for or against increased competition in:

Food provision at your school or college.
Rural area bus services.
Non-emergency hospital treatment.
Postal services.

Table 8.9 Cash flows for project in problem 8

	Start of project	End of year 1	End of year 2	End of year 3
Cost of machine	1,000	—	—	—
Revenue	—	2,500	3,200	2,800
Operating cost	—	2,000	2,800	2,500

Chapter Nine

Consumer decisions

Consumption and saving — the influence of income on demand — the influence of prices on demand — choice and preference — utility — consumer's surplus — changes in tastes and consumers' sovereignty

---

9.1 Introduction

The two previous chapters have discussed supplies of goods by specialists and perfectly competitive firms. We now examine demands for goods by looking at how a household's demands for consumer goods depend on its income and on prices. We examine also the extent to which supplies of goods change when households demand different goods.

We refer to the demand for goods by **households** because many decisions on what to buy are taken by groups (particularly families) and not by individuals. The group treats its members' combined incomes as one, and buys most goods jointly. We do not discuss the process of decision-making within a group.

The assumptions of a perfect market system have several implications for households' demands for goods:

(a) Material motivation implies that no household wastes any of its available money: it spends or saves it all.
(b) Freedom of action implies that no one is prohibited from buying any good. The only limit on a household's purchases is determined by what it can afford to buy.
(c) Perfect information implies that each household knows the prices of all the goods that it wants to buy, and need spend no time or money searching for the cheapest suppliers.
(d) Smallness implies that no household can affect the price of any good by demanding more or less of it. There are many buyers for each good, and none is wealthy enough to dominate the market. No group of households combines to gain from bulk-buying. Every household is a price-taker.

9.2 Consumption and saving

In any given period, a household's expenditure on goods is unlikely to equal its income. If it spends less than its income, the household **saves**; if it spends more than its income it either **dissaves** (spends past savings) or **borrows** (and plans to repay from future income).

The decision to save, dissave or borrow depends on the household's future prospects. For example, it may save for retirement, or borrow to buy a house in the expectation that it can repay the loan from its future income. Therefore we need to examine a household's behaviour over a number of years, or perhaps over its whole **life-cycle**, to see how much it spends on consumer goods in one year. A typical life-cycle pattern of income and expenditure is shown in figure 9.1. In this case the household saves, and then dissaves and borrows to buy a house or other goods. In the middle years it repays loans and saves for retirement. In the period of retirement the household consumes more than its income by spending previous savings.

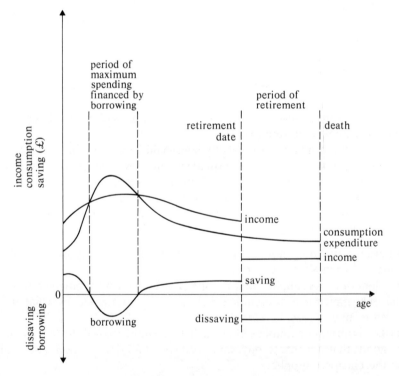

Figure 9.1 Life-cycle income, consumption and saving

9.2.1 Budget line

Each year, a household decides on its saving, dissaving and borrowing, given its intentions for the next few years or for the remainder of its lifetime, and given its outstanding debt from previous borrowings. This decision determines the household's **budget**.

The budget for a period equals income plus dissaving and borrowing minus saving.

The combinations of goods that a household can buy are limited by its budget, and by the prices of the goods that it buys. If it buys only two goods, we can represent these combinations in a diagram. For example if a household spends a budget of £100 on corn (price £4) and milk (price £2), it can buy 25 corn (point A in figure 9.2), or 50 milk (point B), or combinations such as 8 corn and 34 milk (point C). The available combinations are shown by all points on the budget line AB.

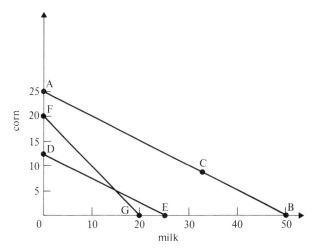

Figure 9.2 Budget lines
AB and DE are generated using the same prices; AB is generated using twice the income used to generate DE.

The slope of the budget line depends on the ratio of the prices of the goods. In the example, the price ratio is 2:1, and so AB shows that the household must give up 2 units of milk to buy one more unit of corn; the opportunity cost of corn in terms of milk is 2. In general a **household's opportunity cost** of good x measured in terms of good y is the number of units of good y that the household must give up in order to buy one more unit of good x.

This opportunity cost equals the ratio of the price of good x to the price of good y.

Figure 9.2 shows the implications of a change in the prices:

(a) The budget line is DE if the prices are £8 and £4. DE is parallel to AB because the price ratio is the same for both budget lines. DE is nearer to the origin than AB because the prices are higher on DE, and so the household can buy less with a given budget.

(b) The budget line is FG if the prices are £5 and £5. The slope of FG is different from that of AB and DE because the price ratio is different.

9.3 Influence of income on demand

A household's budget may differ from its income, but we assume that if its income increases so does it budget. If the prices of the goods that it buys do not change, the budget line moves away from the origin when the household's income increases, but its slope does not change.

A household's income-elasticity of demand for a good is the percentage change in demand caused by a 1 per cent increase in the household's income.

Alternatively, the information that is available may imply that we use the formula:

$$\text{Income-elasticity of demand for good} = \frac{\% \text{ change in demand for good}}{\% \text{ change in the household's income}}$$

If a household buys goods in the same proportions whatever its income, the income-elasticity of demand for every good is 1, because an increase in income leads to an equal percentage increase in the demand for each good. However, most people change the proportion in which they demand goods as their incomes increase, and we categorize goods as follows:

(a) A **luxury** is a good for which the income-elasticity of demand exceeds 1. If its income increases by 1 per cent, a household's demand for a luxury increases by more than 1 per cent. So as its income increases the household spends a larger fraction of its income on luxuries. If the household's income falls by 1 per cent, it reduces its demand for a luxury by more than 1 per cent, and spends a smaller fraction of its income on luxuries. Indeed, it may demand nothing of the good if its income falls far enough.

(b) A **necessity** is a good for which the income-elasticity of demand is between 0 and 1. If the household's income increases by 1 per cent, it buys more of all necessities, but it increases its consumption of each necessity by less than 1 per cent. So as its income increases, a household spends a smaller fraction of its income on necessities. If the household's income falls by 1 per cent, it reduces its demand for necessities by less than 1 per cent, and increases the fraction of its income that it spends on necessities.

(c) A **normal good** is a good for which the income-elasticity of demand is positive. So both luxuries and necessities are normal goods.

(d) An **inferior good** has a negative income-elasticity of demand. A household buys less of an inferior good as its income increases, and more as its income falls.

These definitions often, but not always, conform to the usual uses of the terms. For example, low-quality goods are often inferior, and so also are some goods that are regarded as 'cheap substitutes'. If a household regards sausages as a cheap substitute for beef, it buys fewer sausages and more beef as its income increases, so that sausages are an inferior good for that household. However, the definitions do not always coincide with usual usage. For example, some people regard cigarettes as a luxury, but for many people they are a necessity by our definition, because these people increase their demand for them by less than 1 per cent if their incomes increase by 1 per cent, and reduce their demands by less than 1 per cent if their incomes fall by 1 per cent.

9.4 Influence of prices on demand

In section 4.4 we asserted that the demand for a good falls if its price increases. The extent to which demand falls when the price rises is measured by the price-elasticity of demand. In this section, we examine this assertion and the influences on the price-elasticity of demand.

Our examination is limited to a partial equilibrium analysis in which the price of one good changes and all other prices, and households' budgets, do not change. We look at an example in which a household has a budget of £100 that it spends on corn and milk, and in which the price of milk is £2 throughout. We consider the effects of an increase in the price of corn from £4 to £5. Figure 9.3 shows the budget lines when the price of corn is £4 (line AB) and when the price of corn is £5 (line AC). The price change has two effects on the budget line:

(a) The slope of the line changes, because the price ratio changes (see section 9.2).
(b) The line moves towards the origin (except at point A), so that the household can no longer buy as much as before.

The second effect of the price change is, in some respects, similar to the effect of a reduction in the household's income: both reduce the amounts that the household can buy. It is therefore useful to separate the two effects, and analyse the second using our previous definitions of luxuries, necessities and inferior goods.

9.4.1 Compensating income change

Suppose that, when the price of corn is £4, the household chooses to buy 15 corn and 20 milk (point D in figure 9.3). When the price of corn increases to £5, this combination of goods costss £5 × 15 + £2 × 20 = £115. The household requires an additional £15 of income to enable it to buy the combination represented by D. This £15 is the **compensating income change** needed to offset the effect of the price change.

Budget line EF represents a **compensated situation** in which:

(a) The price of corn is £5 (and the price of milk is £2).
(b) The household's budget is £115.

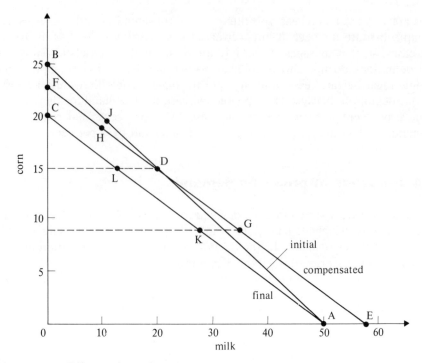

Figure 9.3　Effects of a price change
The compensated budget line EF is parallel to the final budget line AC, and passes
through the initial point of demand D. The axiom of revealed preference rules out
choice on DF. The substitution effect is a move from D to a point on DE, the income
effect from a point on DE to a point on AC.

We use this situation, together with the initial situation (prices £4 and £2,
budget of £100) and the final situation (prices £5 and £2, budget of £100) to
examine the two effects of the price increase listed above.

9.4.2 Substitution effect

In the compensated situation, the household is compensated for the price
change, so that it can, if it wants to, buy combination D. In this sense the
household is as well off in the compensated situation as in the initial situation.
The comparison of the initial and the compensated situations allows us to
examine the extent to which the houshold substitutes one good for another
when the price ratio changes, without a simultaneous reduction in the amounts
that it can buy. This change in demands is the **substitution effect** of the price
increase.

　In the compensated situation, the household can buy D (which it buys in
the initial situation) or any other combination on EF. What does it demand?

(a) It might demand D, in which case there is no substitution of one good for
　　the other, and the substitution effect is zero.

(b) It might demand a combination on DE that includes less corn and more milk than D. For example, if the household demands 9 corn and 35 milk (point G), it demands a combination that would have cost (4×9) + (2×35) = £106 in the initial situation, and so G is not available in the initial situation (G lies outside the budget line AB). If the household demands a combination on DE, the substitution effect reduces its demand for corn when the price of corn increases. In this case the substitution effect on the demand for corn is negative.

(c) It might demand a combination on DF that includes more corn and less milk than D. For example, if the household demands 19 corn and 10 milk (point H) it demands a combination that would have cost (19×4) + (2×10) = £96 in the initial situation, and so H is available in the initial situation (leaving the household with £4 to buy additional goods, or to save). If the household demands a combination on DF, the substitution effect increases the demand for corn when the price of corn increases. In this case the substitution effect on the demand for corn is positive.

9.4.3 Revealed preference

If the substitution effect is positive, there is an inconsistency in the household's behaviour, because:

(a) In the initial situation, it chooses D, although it could have bought H (or even J, which gives more of both goods, and which is therefore better for a materially motivated household). The choice of D rather than H reveals that the household prefers D to H (and also D to J).

(b) In the compensated situation it chooses H even though it could choose D, and this choice reveals that the household prefers H to D.

The **axiom** (or assumption) **of revealed preference** rules out this possibility by assuming that the household does not choose in this inconsistent way. The axiom is:

If a household chooses opportunity x in a situation in which opportunity y is also available, it does not choose y in any situation in which x is also available.

The household reveals that it prefers x to y, and so it does not choose y if x is available.

In our example, the opportunities are combinations of goods and, in the initial situation, the household chooses D when all combinations on DF are available. So the axiom of revealed preference implies that the household does not choose any combination on DF in the compensated situation because D is available. Note that the axiom does not imply that the household chooses D in the compensated situation: it implies only that the household does not choose H or any other combination on DF. So the axiom of revealed preference rules out a positive substitution effect:

The substitution effect reduces, or leaves unchanged, the demand for a good whose price increases.

This conclusion can be demonstrated when there are more than two goods (see box 6).

Box 6   Substitution effect with more than two goods

The household demands quantities $X_1, X_2, X_3, \ldots, X_n$ of goods 1 to n in the initial situation, when their prices are $P_1, P_2, P_3, \ldots, P_n$. The household's budget is then given by

$$Y = P_1 X_1 + P_2 X_2 + P_3 X_3 + \ldots + P_n X_n \qquad (9.1)$$

If the price of good 1 increases to P_1', the compensating income change is Z, where

$$Y + Z = P_1' X_1 + P_2 X_2 + P_3 X_3 + \ldots + P_n X_n \qquad (9.2)$$

Subtracting equation 9.1 from equation 9.2 gives

$$Z = (P_1' - P_1) X_1 \qquad (9.3)$$

We suppose that in the compensated situation the household demands quantities $X_1', X_2', X_3', \ldots, X_n'$. The prices are $P_1', P_2, P_3, \ldots, P_n$ and the household's budget is $Y + Z$, so that:

$$Y + Z = P_1' X_1' + P_2 X_2' + P_3 X_3' + \ldots + P_n X_n' \qquad (9.4)$$

The axiom of revealed preference implies that the combination demanded in the compensated situation is not available in the initial situation (with the initial prices), because the household's budget is insufficient:

$$Y < P_1 X_1' + P_2 X_2' + P_3 X_3' + \ldots + P_n X_n' \qquad (9.5)$$

Subtracting equation 9.4 from inequality 9.5 gives

$$-Z < (P_1 - P_1') X_1' \qquad (9.6)$$

and combining equation 9.3 with inequality 9.6 gives

$$-(P_1' - P_1) X_1 < (P_1 - P_1') X_1' \qquad (9.7)$$

Rearranging inequality 9.7 gives

$$(P_1 - P_1')(X_1' - X_1) > 0 \qquad (9.8)$$

Now $P_1' > P_1$, and so the first parenthesis of the left-hand side of inequality 9.8 is negative. So the second parenthesis is negative, or else the left-hand side would not be greater than zero. Thus $X_1 > X_1'$: the household's demand for good 1 (whose price has increased) is no greater than in the compensated situation than in the initial situation, exactly as we demonstrated in figure 9.3, in which there are only two goods.

9.4.4 Income effect

In the compensated situation, the budget line is EF; in the final situation it is AC. The prices are the same in the two situations, and so from section 9.3 we can conclude that:

(a) The household's demand for normal goods is lower in the final than in the compensated situation.
(b) The household's demand for inferior goods is greater in the final than in the compensated situation.

This change in demand between the compensated and the final situations is the **income effect** of the increase in the price of corn.

In figure 9.3, if the household demands combination G in the compensated situation, then in the final situation:

(a) It demands a combination on KA if corn is a normal good, because any point on KA includes less corn than G, and the demand for a normal good decreases when income falls.
(b) It demands a combination on KC if corn is an inferior good, because any point on KC includes more corn than G, and the demand for an inferior good increases when income falls.

9.4.5 Income and substitution effects combined

The total change in demand is the sum of the income and substitution effects. The substitution effect does not increase the demand for any good whose price has risen, and the income effect reduces the demand for a normal good whose price has risen. So:

A household's demand for a normal good falls if the price of the good increases.

The conclusion is less straightforward for an inferior good, because the substitution effect reduces (or does not increase) demand, and the income effect increases demand. So:

A household's demand for an inferior good falls if the price of the good increases if the substitution effect outweighs the income effect.

If a good is 'very inferior', the income effect may outweigh the substitution effect, so that the demand for the good increases when its price increases. Such goods are known as **Giffen goods** (after the nineteenth-century statistician and economist, Robert Giffen). Alfred Marshall credited Giffen with the observation that the demand for bread by 'the poorer labouring families' increased when its price increased, because the families were forced to reduce their consumption of other foods to maintain their basic nutritional level. So,

A household's demand for a Giffen good increases if the price of the good increases, because the good is inferior and the income effect outweighs the substitution effect.

Corn is a Giffen good in figure 9.3 if the demand in the final situation is on CL (more corn is demanded in the final situation than in the initial situation at D).

A household's demand for a Giffen good increases when the price of the good increases. We would observe this behaviour for a market demand curve only if there were sufficient households for which the good is a Giffen good. So a market demand curve may still have the usual downward slope, even though some households regard the good as a Giffen good, so that their demand curves slope upwards.

9.4.6 Price-elasticity of demand

We have established the *direction* of the change in a household's demand for a good when its price changes, but we cannot establish the size of the change unless we have more information on households' preferences between combinations of goods. However, we can make some remarks about the main influences on the price-elasticity of demand.

The price-elasticity of demand measures the extent to which the demand for a good changes when its price changes. The price-elasticity of demand depends on:

(a) The extent of substitution between the good and other goods. This determines the extent of the change in demand between the compensated and the initial situations. For a given income effect, the price-elasticity of demand for a good is larger if it has many close substitutes than if it has few. If there are many close substitutes for a good, households switch to these substitutes when the price of the good increases.
(b) The income-elasticity of demand, which determines the extent of the change in demand between the compensated and the final situations. For a given size of the substitution effect, the price-elasticity of demand is greater for a luxury than for a necessity. If the price of a luxury good increases, the income effect reduces demand considerably; if the price of a necessity increases, the income effect reduces demand for it by a small amount; if the price of an inferior good increases, the income effect increases the demand, and offsets some of the reduction in demand caused by the substitution effect, so that the price-elasticity of demand is low.

9.4.7 Cross effects

In our example with two goods, the substitution effect of the increase in the price of corn increases (or leaves unchanged) the demand for milk. The income effect reduces the demand for milk unless milk is an inferior good. When there are more than two goods, the substitution effect of an increase in the price of one good may increase or decrease the demand for others. The direction of the income effect on demand depends on whether the goods are normal or inferior. For example:

(a) If there is an increase in the price of oil, the demand for large cars may fall both because of the substitution effect (households substitute small cars in place of large cars because large cars have become relatively even more expensive to run) and because of the income effect (the increase in the price of oil makes households worse off, and large cars are normal goods).
(b) If there is an increase in the price of oil, the demand for bicycles increases because of the substitution effect (households substitute bicycles for cars), and may increase or decrease because of the income effect (depending on whether bicycles are normal or inferior).

If the demand for good 1 increases when the price of good 2 increases, good 1 is a substitute for good 2; if the demand for good 1 falls when the price of good 2 increases, good 1 is a complement to good 2 (see section 4.10.1).

9.5 Choice and preference

The distinction between normal goods and inferior goods implies the direction of the change in demand when a household's income changes, and also implies the direction of the income effect when the price of the good changes. The axiom of revealed preference implies the direction of the substitution effect when the price of the good changes.

If we know the household's **preferences** (or **tastes**) between combinations of goods, we can predict which combination of goods the household will demand if there is a change in its income or in the price of a good. Then we can predict the sizes of changes in demand, and not just the directions. In order to describe its preference between two combinations of goods the household must be able to say one and only one of the following:

(a) That it prefers combination A to combination B.
(b) That it prefers combination B to combination A.
(c) That it is **indifferent** between A and B.

Note that the word 'indifferent' is used to imply that the household does not mind whether it has A or B. Indifference does not imply that the household cannot be bothered to make a statement of preference.

If a household makes one of these statements for all pairs of combinations of goods, we have sufficient information to predict its demands when its income or prices change. To do this, we use the rational choice rule that

A household chooses the combination that it prefers to all other available combinations.

For example, suppose that the household's budget is £16, the price of corn is £4 and the price of milk is £2. It can buy:

A = (4 corn, 0 milk)
B = (3 corn, 2 milk)

$C = (2 \text{ corn}, 4 \text{ milk})$
$D = (1 \text{ corn}, 6 \text{ milk})$
$E = (0 \text{ corn}, 8 \text{ milk})$.

(We assume that it can buy only whole units of the goods.)
The household states the preferences of table 9.1, and so it demands C.

Table 9.1 Consistent prefer-ences

A	preferred to E
B	preferred to A and E
B	indifferent to D
D	preferred to A and E
C	preferred to A, B, D and E

9.5.1 Two difficulties

If the household's preferences were, instead, those of table 9.2, D and C are both preferred to A, B and E. There is no single combination that the household prefers to all others, and it demands either C or D. We cannot predict from its preferences whether the household demands C or D – it might, for example, decide between them by tossing a coin, because it is indifferent between them so that it does not mind which it demands.

Table 9.2 Consistent prefer-ences with ambiguous choice

A	preferred to E
B	preferred to A and E
D	preferred to A, B and E
D	indifferent to C
C	preferred to A, B and E

The second difficulty concerns an assumption made in constructing tables 9.1 and 9.2. In both tables the household prefers C to B and B to A, and it also prefers C to A. Its preferences are **consistent** (or **transitive**). The household's preferences would be **inconsistent** (or **intransitive**) if it preferred A to C, B to A and C to B, as in table 9.3. For these preferences, there is no combination that is preferred to all others and the choice rule does not enable us to predict the household's demands. We can use the choice rule only if preferences are consistent.

Table 9.3 Inconsistent preferences

A	preferred to E and C
B	preferred to A and E
B	indifferent to D
D	preferred to A and E
C	preferred to B, D and E

9.6 Utility

Households demand goods because the members of the household obtain satisfaction from using them. At least since the work of Jeremy Bentham (born London 1748, died 1832), many economists have assumed that this satisfaction can be measured in some way as **utility**. If this is so, a household's demands for goods can be predicted using the choice rule that:

A household chooses the combination that gives it more utility than all other available combinations.

For example, if a household's utilities are those of column 2 in table 9.4, it demands combination C. The utilities of column 2 in table 9.4 can be translated into the preferences of table 9.1 using the rules that:

(a) Greater utility implies preference.
(b) Equal utility implies indifference.

Table 9.4 Utilities consistent with preferences of table 9.1

Combination	2 Utility	3 Utility	4 Utility	5 Utility
A	7	2	20	13
B	10	3	30	14
C	15	4	40	84
D	10	3	30	14
E	5	1	10	7

Similarly, the utilities of table 9.5 can be translated into the preferences of table 9.2 and the household demands either C or D, which give equal utility and which both give more utility than any other combination.

The inconsistent preferences of table 9.3 cannot be translated into utilities such as x is the utility of A, y is the utility of B, z is the utility of C, because these utilities would have to satisfy the following conditions:

x exceeds y
y exceeds z
z exceeds x

which is impossible. So statements of utilities cannot be inconsistent, even though statements of preferences can be inconsistent.

Table 9.5 Utilities consistent with preferences of table 9.2

Combination	Utility
A	15
B	20
C	25
D	25
E	10

9.6.1 Ordinal utility

There are many utilities other than those of column 2 of table 9.4 that translate into the preferences of table 9.1. The utilities given in columns 3, 4 and 5 also translate into the preferences of table 9.1, using the rules that greater utility implies preference and equal utility implies indifference. All the utilities shown in table 9.4 place the opportunities into the same order of preference: C, then B and D, then A, then E. If we want to place the opportunities only into an order of preference, the columns of table 9.4 are equivalent. Each represents the same **ordinal utilities**:

Ordinal utility conveys information only about the order of preferences.

The relative sizes of the utilities imply the order of preference; the absolute sizes of the utilities imply nothing in addition.

Ordinal utilities provide a convenient way to represent preferences, because tables such as 9.1 and 9.4 convey identical information. In table 9.4, the preferences of table 9.1 are described simply by a list of numbers.

9.6.2 Cardinal utility

If satisfaction can be measured as ordinal utility, the statement that a household gets 10 units of utility from opportunity A and 5 from B tells us only that the household prefers A to B. If satisfaction can be measured as **cardinal utility**, the statement tells us also that the household obtains twice as much satisfaction from A as from B:

Cardinal utility conveys information about both the order and the intensity of preferences.

For example, if the utilities of column 2 in table 9.4 are cardinal, then the difference in satisfaction between C and B is the same as that between B and E. The household experiences the same gain in satisfaction when it moves from B to C as when it moves from E to B.

If the utilities of columns 3 to 5 of table 9.4 are cardinal they convey different information from those of column 2. For example, in column 3, the difference between the utilities from B and E is twice as great as the difference between the utilities from C and B, and so column 3 conveys different information on the intensity of preferences (but the same information on the order of preferences) from column 2.

Columns 3 and 4 of table 9.4 are proportional to one another, and so they convey similar information, but in different units. The unit for measuring utility in column 4 is one-tenth the size of the unit in column 3, but this difference in scale is generally unimportant when we use utilities to examine household decisions, just as it is unimportant whether length is measured in metres or centimetres.

9.6.3 Marginal utility

If a household's satisfaction can be measured as cardinal utility, we can define the marginal utility of a good as follows:

the marginal utility is the additional utility obtained from consuming one more unit of the good when the quantities of all other goods are unchanged.

For example, if a household obtains:

140 units of utility from 24 apples and 16 bananas, and
143 units of utility from 25 apples and 16 bananas

then the marginal utility of an apple is 3 units of utility.

The marginal utility of a good is likely to change as the quantities of goods change. For example, if the household in the above example obtains:

165 units of utility from 34 apples and 16 bananas, and
167 units of utility from 35 apples and 16 bananas

then the marginal utility of an apple is 3 when the household has 24 apples, but the marginal utility falls to 2 when the household has 34 apples, given that the household consumes 16 bananas in each case. This example illustrates the principle of **diminishing marginal utility**, which asserts that:

The marginal utility of a good decreases as the quantity of the good increases (keeping the quantities of other goods unchanged).

The total utility increases with each additional unit consumed, but the size of the increase in utility declines as the household consumes more. The first unit of a good confers more additional utility than the second, the second more than the third, and so on. So the first unit consumed gives more satisfaction than the second unit, the second gives more satisfaction than the third, and so on.

The marginal utility of one good may depend on the quantities of other goods. If in our example the household obtains:

90 units of utility from 24 apples and 10 bananas, and
94 units of utility from 25 apples and 10 bananas

then the marginal utility of an apple depends on the number of bananas that the household consumes, because the marginal utility of an apple is 4 when there are 24 apples and 10 bananas and 3 when there are 24 apples and 16 bananas.

9.6.4 Utility maximization

A household chooses the combination of goods that gives the maximum utility of all the available combinations. We use the definition of marginal utility to examine this decision by calculating the marginal utility from spending an additional £1 on each good that the household consumes. For example:

(a) If the price of an apple is £0.5, and the marginal utility of an apple is 6 units of utility, the household gains utility at a rate of 12 units for an additional £1 spent on apples
(b) If the price of a banana is £1, and the marginal utility of a banana is 8 units of utility, the household gains utility at a rate of 8 units for each additional £1 spent on bananas.

What combination of goods does the household demand? In the above example, suppose that the household spends £1 more on apples and £1 less on bananas. It gains 12 units of utility (from the apples) and loses 8 units (from the bananas), a net gain of 4 units. This illustrates the principle that if the additional utility per £1 from good X exceeds the additional utility per £1 spent from good Y, the household can increase its total utility, without spending more, by spending £1 more on good X and £1 less on good Y.

This principle implies that, as long as there are differences between the additional utilities per £1 spent on different goods, the household can increase its total utility without spending more. The only circumstances in which a switch of expenditure from one good to another does not give additional utility are when the additional utility per £1 is the same for all goods. So a household cannot increase its total utility with a given expenditure when the additional utility per £1 is the same for all goods.

We calculate the additional utility per £1 spent on a good by dividing the marginal utility of the good by its price, and so:

A household cannot increase its total utility with a given expenditure when the ratio of the marginal utility of a good to its price is the same for all goods.

So, a household maximizes its total utility when:

$$\frac{MU(X)}{P_X} = \frac{MU(Y)}{P_Y} = \frac{MU(Z)}{P_Z} = \ldots = \frac{MU(N)}{P_N}$$

where $MU(X)$ is the marginal utility of good X, P_X is the price of good X, etc.

This equation implies that

$$\frac{MU(X)}{MU(Y)} = \frac{P_X}{P_Y} \quad \text{and} \quad \frac{MU(X)}{MU(Z)} = \frac{P_X}{P_Z} \quad \text{etc.}$$

So:

A household maximizes its total utility when the ratio of the marginal utilities of any two goods equals the ratio of their prices.

We can illustrate this principle most simply using an example in which a household buys two goods, and its utilities from the two goods are **separable**. This means that the household's total utility is calculated as the sum of the utility gained from each good:

total utility = utility from apples + utility from bananas

The assumption that utilities are separable implies that the marginal utility gained from increasing the number of bananas from 4 to 5 is the same (12 units in table 9.6) whatever the number of apples. This assumption is often unrealistic because, for example, it is unlikely that the marginal utility of butter is independent of the quantity of margarine, and it is unlikely that the marginal utility of petrol is the same for a household when it owns one car as it is when the household owns no car.

Suppose that the household of table 9.6 has an income of £40, the price of an apple is £10 and the price of a banana is £5. The additional utilities per £1 spent are given in columns 4 and 8. The ratio of marginal utility to price is

Table 9.6 Utilities from two goods

Apples @ £10			MU ÷ price	Bananas @ £5			MU ÷ price
(quantity)	Utility	MU		(quantity)	Utility	MU	
0	0			0	0		
1	26	26	2.6	1	50	50	10
2	51	25	2.5	2	70	20	4
3	75	24	2.4	3	86	16	3.2
4	97	22	2.2	4	100	14	2.8
				5	112	12	2.4
				6	123	11	2.2
				7	132	9	1.8
				8	140	8	1.6

2.4 when the household has 2 apples and 4 bananas (which cost a total of £40), and so, by the utility maximizing principle, the household can increase its total utility only by spending more than £40. So the household demands 2 apples and 4 bananas to maximize its total utility, given its budget of £40. Its total utility is then 151.

We can confirm that this is the household's maximum utility by examining the other combinations that it can buy. It could spend £40 on:

(a) 1 apple, 6 bananas, for a total utility of $26 + 123 = 149$.
(b) 3 apples, 2 bananas, for a total utility of 145.
(c) 0 apples, 8 bananas, for a total utility of 140.
(d) 4 apples, 0 bananas, for a total utility of 97.

Note that the ratios of marginal utility to price are also equal when the household buys 3 apples and 5 bananas (both are 2.2). This is not the utility maximizing combination for the household given a budget of £40, because 3 apples and 5 bananas cost £55, and so this combination is not relevant to the household's decision when its budget is £40.

Given that we can find the household's demands if we know the utility that it gains from each combination of goods, we can predict the size of the change in demands when the household's budget or the prices of any goods change.

9.6.5 Is utility theory useful?

The axiom of revealed preference implies only the sign of the substitution effect. If we want to see whether in practice households conform to the axiom, we can observe its behaviour in a number of situations. If we observe that a household chooses combination A when B was available in one situation, and B in another situation even though A is also available, then the household's behaviour does not conform to the axiom. So the relevance of the axiom of revealed preference can be ascertained by observing household behaviour.

We can predict the sizes of changes in a household's demands if we know the household's preferences between combinations of goods, or if we know the household's utilities from the combinations. This information cannot be found by observing what a household does, because actual behaviour tells us only what a household chooses to do, and so tells us only which available combination of goods it prefers to all others, or which available combination gives the most utility. Observation reveals nothing about preferences (or utilities) concerning combinations that have not been chosen previously, but this information is needed to predict the size of the change in the household's demands when circumstances (such as its income, or a price) change.

The information needed to predict the size of the change in a household's demands can be obtained by asking the household a question such as one of the following:

(a) Do you prefer combination A to combination B?
(b) Which of A or B gives you greater utility?
(c) How much utility do you get from A, and how much from B?

If the household can answer the first question for all pairs of combinations of goods (*A* and *B*, *A* and *C*, etc.), we discover the household's preferences. Answers to the second question reveal the household's ordinal utilities, which give exactly the same information as the first question. Answers to the third question reveal the household's cardinal utilities, but it is not clear how a household can answer the third question, because there is no obvious way of measuring satisfaction in the form of cardinal utility.

A household that answers either the first or the second question gives sufficient information to predict the sizes of the changes in its demands when its income or a price changes. The additional information provided by answers to the third question reveals the amount of satisfaction obtained (assuming that the household can measure this) but gives no further information on changes in demands. It is unnecessary to measure the level of satisfaction to predict changes in demands.

The main application of cardinal utility is in making judgements about the outcome of government economic policies. For example, if the government takes £100 by taxing Alan and gives the £100 to Charles as a transfer payment, Alan's satisfaction falls and Charles' satisfaction increases. If we know how much satisfaction each gains and loses, we can assess whether the gain to Charles outweighs the loss to Alan. However, a judgement of this kind requires not only that Alan and Charles can measure their utilities, but also that their utilities are **comparable**. To judge a policy in this way, one unit of one person's utility must be equivalent to one unit of any other person's utility. So we must be able to say that if Charles gains 10 units of utility and Alan loses 9 units of utility, then the gain exceeds the loss because 9 units of Alan's utility are equivalent to 9 units of Charles' utility.

Judgements of policies of this kind are **utilitarian**. We shall compare **utilitarianism** with other ways of judging policies in chapter 22.

9.7 Consumer's surplus

A household's demand schedule for a good shows the quantity that the household would buy at each price assuming that the prices of other goods and the household's income do not change. Alternatively, the demand schedule shows the greatest price that the household would pay for each quantity of the good. For example, the demand schedule of table 9.7 states that the household would pay £4 per unit, but not more, for 10 units. We can use this interpretation of the demand schedule to measure, in money terms, the benefit that a household obtains from buying a good.

Suppose that the actual price of the good is £3, so that the household buys 18 units, paying £54. The demand schedule implies that:

(a) The household would have paid £5 × 4 = £20 for the first four units, although it actually paid £12 for them.
(b) the household would have paid £4 × 6 = £24 for the fifth to tenth units, although it actually paid £18 for them.

(c) the household would have paid £3 × 8 = £24 for the eleventh to eighteenth units, and it actually paid £24 for them.

So the household would have paid £20 + £24 + £24 = £68 for the 18 units, and actually pays £54 because it pays £3 per unit. The household has a **consumer's surplus** of £68 − £54 = £14. In general:

The consumer's surplus equals the total that the household would pay minus the amount that it actually does pay for the quantity bought.

The consumer's surplus is shown in figure 9.4, where points A to F represent the prices and quantities described in table 9.7. The amount actually paid is area OGDI (= £3 × 18); the amounts that the household would pay are OHBJ (= £5 × 4) + JKCL (= £4 × 6) + LMDI (= £3 × 8). The consumer's surplus is:

$$OHBJ + JKCL + LMDI - OGDI = HBNG + KCMN$$

Table 9.7   Demand schedule

Price (£)	Quantity demanded
6	0
5	4
4	10
3	18
2	28
1	40

9.7.1 Consumer's surplus and the demand curve

Our numerical example uses prices at £1 intervals. If we also had information on demands at prices of £5.50, £4.50 and £3.50 we could refine our calculation of consumer's surplus. For example, if the household would buy 2 units when the price is £5.50, then it would pay £11 for units 1 and 2, and £10 for units 3 and 4, so that it would pay a total of £21 for the first four units. This additional information changes the consumer's surplus from these first four units to £21 − £12 = £9, from the £8 calculated previously. In figure 9.4 this recalculation of consumer's surplus from the first four units is GRPS + SQBN, which exceeds the previous measurement (GHBN) by area HRPQ.

If we have yet more detailed information about the demand schedule (for example, demands at prices £6, £5.99, £5.98 and so on), we can refine the measurement of the consumer's surplus further. The consumer's surplus in figure 9.5 is given by the sum of all of the rectangles, such as AFGH, HJKL etc. The total area of these rectangles is almost the whole area bounded by BA, AE and the part of the demand curve between E and B. So, to avoid drawing numerous rectangles:

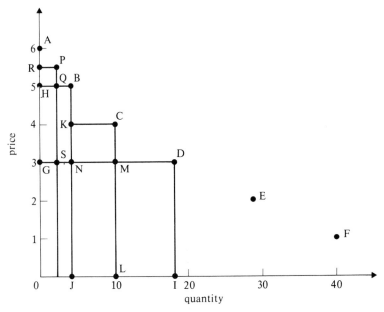

Figure 9.4   Consumer's surplus for the demand schedule of table 9.7
Consumer's surplus from quantity I is represented by areas GRPS + SQBN + NKCM.
Amount paid is area OGDI.

The consumer's surplus derived from a good is measured to be the area between the demand curve, the vertical axis and the line representing the price.

In figure 9.5, this is area EBA.

We can measure the consumer's surplus in this way for a household using the household's own demand curve, of the total consumer's surplus for all households that buy the good using the market demand curve for the good.

9.7.2 Using consumer's surplus

The consumer's surplus measures the benefit to a household (or to all households) that arises from the fact that it is possible to buy goods for less than the total that it (or they) would have paid for it. So the consumer's surplus measures the benefit received from consuming a good in excess of the amount paid for. This measure of the net benefits of consuming a good can be used to decide whether a particular policy is desirable or not. Such a decision generally involves calculating the benefits from the policy, and seeing whether these outweigh the costs of implementing it (including the costs of producing any extra goods demanded because of the policy).

The use of consumer's surplus in this context has one main advantage over, for example, attempts to measure cardinal utility to determine the gains. The advantage of using consumer's surplus is that it is measured in money terms,

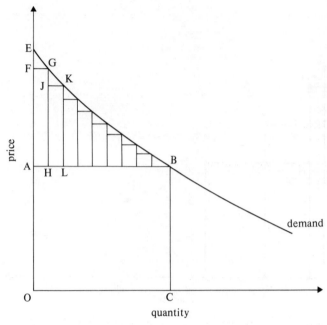

Figure 9.5   Consumer's surplus and the demand curve
Consumer's surplus is area AEB; amount paid is area OABC.

and so is immediately comparable to anything else that can be measured in money terms. However, even using surplus in this way, we must beware comparing one individual's gain with another's loss. If a policy implies that one individual consumes more bread and gains an additional consumer's surplus of £25, and another consumes less bread, losing £20 of consumer's surplus, it might appear that the policy gives a net social gain. However, each individual's surplus measures what he or she would pay for particular goods – which obviously depends on how much he or she can afford. A poor person could not pay as much for a unit of a good as a richer person, and so the poorer person's surplus is likely to be lower. Judgements made using consumer's surplus therefore depend on the existing income distribution, which determines the level of each consumer's surplus.

9.8 Changes in tastes and consumers' sovereignty

We examine now the consequences of changes in demands that do not result from changes in incomes or in prices. We ask how producers in a perfect market economy respond when households' tastes change, because of, for example, a change in fashion. We suppose that a number of households change their demands for goods because, in a perfect market economy, each household is small and so no single household's demands can influence the price of any good. Therefore if one household's tastes change, no price changes, and so there is no effect on any other household or firm.

Suppose that there is a change in tastes away from cigarette smoking and towards chocolate eating. All markets were in equilibrium before the change in tastes and we do not confuse the consequences of the change in tastes with the effects of the responses of households and firms to existing shortages or surpluses or to positive or negative supernormal profits. The change in tastes increases the demand for chocolate and reduces the demand for cigarettes at the existing prices.

9.8.1 Chocolate market

The effects on the chocolate market are shown in figure 9.6. DD is the old (that is, before the change in tastes) demand curve and EE is the new (after the change in tastes) demand curve. The old equilibrium price is P, and the old equilibrium quantity is Q. We can identify three stages:

(a) **The instantaneous effect**. No more chocolate can be produced instantaneously, and so the supply is initially restricted to Q. The price rises towards R, where the new demand equals the supply at Q.

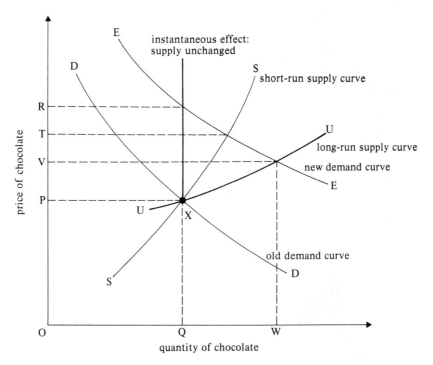

Figure 9.6 Chocolate market (demand increases)
The equilibrium price changes instantaneously from P to R, in the short run to T and in the long run to V.

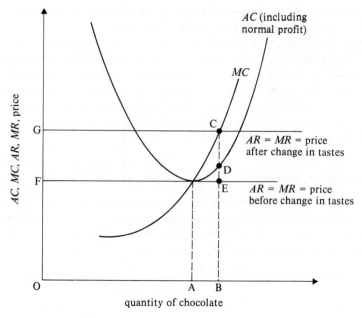

Figure 9.7   Short-run reaction of a chocolate producer
The firm increases output from A to B when the price increases from F to G.

(b) **The short-run effect**. In the short run, a price increase implies that each
    chocolate producer increases its output from its old long-run equilibrium
    (at A in figure 9.7; see section 8.6.2) to its new short-run equilibrium (B),
    and makes a positive supernormal profit (area CEFG). So output increases
    along the short-run supply curve (SS in figure 9.6), and the new demand
    equals the short-run supply at price T.
(c) **The long-run effect**. In the long run, firms enter the industry, the supply
    of chocolate increases and the price falls until profits have returned to the
    normal level. The supply increases on the long-run supply curve (UU in
    figure 9.6), the new long-run equilibrium price is V, and the new long-run
    equilibrium quantity is W. The long-run equilibrium output of chocolate
    increases because firms enter the industry. The long-run equilibrium price
    increases because the new firms add to the demands for the materials and
    factors used to make chocolate, and so the average cost of production
    increases.

9.8.2 Cigarette market

The opposite happens in the cigarette market, as shown in figure 9.8. The old
equilibrium price was A, and:

(a) The immediate consequence of the reduction in smoking is a fall in the

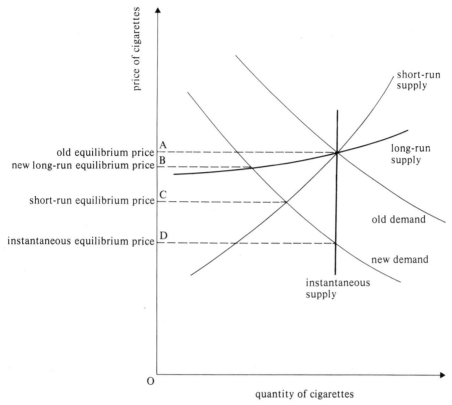

Figure 9.8 Cigarette market (demand falls)
The equilibrium price changes instantaneously from A to D, in the short run to C and
in the long run to B.

price of cigarettes towards the level (D) where the new demand equals
the old equilibrium quantity.
(b) In the short run, firms reduce their outputs in response to the price
reduction, and some (or all) cigarette producers make less than normal
profit. The short-run equilibrium price is C.
(c) In the long run, firms leave the industry until supply has fallen and the
price risen to ensure that remaining firms make exactly normal profit. The
long-run equilibrium output of cigarettes falls because firms leave the
industry. The new long-run equilibrium price (B) is lower than the old
equilibrium price because the demands for the materials and factors used
to make cigarettes are reduced. Their prices fall and so the average cost
of cigarette production falls.

9.8.3 Consumers' sovereignty

The change in tastes causes an increase in demand for one good, and a
reduction in the demand for another. Our example shows that this change in

demands is followed by an increase in the supply of one good and a reduction in the supply of the other. Furthermore, in the long run, firms' profits return to the normal level, so that their owners obtain no long-term benefit from the change in tastes. There is **consumers' sovereignty** in a perfect market economy because, in the long run, the pattern of outputs changes in line with the change in tastes, and firms do not benefit because they do not get long-run supernormal profits.

9.9 Summary

A household's demands for goods depend on its income (which determines its budget), on the prices of goods and on its preferences. A good is a luxury, a necessity, or inferior according to its income-elasticity of demand.

The effect of a price change on a household's demands can be divided into a substitution effect and an income effect. The axiom of revealed preference implies that the substitution effect reduces (or does not increase) the demand for a good when its price increases. The income effect also reduces the demand for a normal good. The demand for a Giffen good increases when its price increases because the income effect increases demand more than the substitution effect reduces it.

We can predict the sizes of changes in demands when prices or incomes change if we know households' preferences or utilities. Ordinal utility indicates only the order of preference; cardinal utility indicates also the intensity of preferences.

Consumer's surplus measures the benefit that a household obtains from consuming a good. It arises because a household would pay more for a good than it actually pays.

Consumers are sovereign in a perfect market economy in the sense that a change in households' tastes leads to increases in the outputs of goods for which demand has increased and reductions in the outputs of goods for which demand has fallen. In the long run, firms' profits return to the normal level.

Topics and problems

(1) Do people take account of their complete life-cycle of expected incomes and expenditures when they make decisions to demand goods?

(2) Can a consumer regard all goods as necessities, or all as luxuries?

(3) Why might a household's behaviour not conform to the axiom of revealed preference? Is such a household inconsistent?

(4) Is it possible to measure the intensity of satisfaction?

(5) Assuming that utility can be measured, is it possible to say that a household would not maximize its utility in some circumstances?

(6) A household demands 6 apples and 4 bananas, given its income, prices and the freedom of action to buy whatever it can afford. Is the household

likely to gain as much satisfaction (ordinal utility is sufficient) if it is forced by the government (or another individual) to take 6 apples and 4 bananas, with no choice? Does freedom of choice matter if you get what you would demand anyway?

(7) A household's budget is 90 per cent of its income. Draw its budget line when its income is £100 and it buys apples (price £0.20) and/or bananas (price £0.50). The household chooses to spend £40 on apples. The household's income increases by £10, and its income-elasticity of demand for apples is 1.5.

How many apples and bananas does it buy after its income increases?
What is the income-elasticity of demand for bananas?
What income-elasticities of demand for apples would be consistent with the statement that bananas are an inferior good?

(8) A household's budget is £100. It demands 150 apples and 80 bananas when the price of an apple is £0.40 and the price of a banana is £0.50. What is the compensating income change when:

The price of an apple rises to £0.50?
The price of a banana falls to £0.40 (with the price of an apple at £0.40)?

Assuming that the household's behaviour conforms to the axiom of revealed preference, which combinations of goods are not demanded in the compensated situations for these two cases?

(9) A household measures its utility according to the formula that its total utility is AB if it consumes A apples and B bananas.

What is its marginal utility of apples when it consumes 8 apples and 4 bananas?
The household's budget is £24, the price of an apple is £3 and the price of a banana is £2. What (whole number) combination of apples and bananas does the household demand?

(10) What is the consumer's surplus when the price is (a) £4, (b) £2 for the household whose demand schedule is that of table 9.8?

Table 9.8   Demand schedule for problem 10

Price (£)	Quantity demanded
1	35
2	27
3	20
4	14
5	9
6	5
7	2
8	0

(11) A university initially sells meals for £1 each; it then introduces a scheme whereby students can pay a flat charge of £20, and then pay 50p per meal. If they do not join the scheme, students can buy better quality meals outside the university for £1.25 each. Draw the budget line for a student who allocates £50 for meals. What happens to the budget line if the university increases the fixed charge from £20 to £30, and reduces the price of a meal from 50p to 30p? To what extent is it in the university's interest to increase the fixed charge and produce meals that are inferior goods?

Chapter Ten

Factor markets and income distribution

Demand for labour by a perfectly competitive firm — supply of labour — labour market — several labour markets — training and education — markets for other factors — income distribution — value judgements of the income distribution

---

10.1 Introduction

Market economic systems include markets for factors of production as well as for goods. In this chapter we examine supply and demand in these markets, the **wages, rents** and **profits** determined in them, and the implications of these factor prices for the income distribution. This chapter examines principles in the context of a perfect market economy. Chapter 6 contains some information on the actual situation in the UK, and in chapter 20 we shall look at the use of government policies to change the income distribution in practice.

The freedom of action assumption (see section 7.2.2) of a perfect market economy ensures that anyone can own any type of land and equipment, up to the limits that he or she can afford, and no one is prevented from supplying any type of labour except by his or her abilities. The smallness assumption rules out trade union activities designed to affect wages by collective action. There is no skill that is exclusive to one individual or small group, because such a person or group could affect the wage paid for that type of labour. For example, if many people want symphonies written, and Mozart is the only person who can do this, then Mozart can influence his own wage as a symphony writer by altering the number of symphonies that he is prepared to write. However, if a large number of other people can write symphonies of a similar quality, then Mozart's output has no effect on his wage per symphony written. If he can write three symphonies in the time that another composer writes one, his income would be greater because of his greater efficiency, but he does not have a unique skill.

10.2 Demand for labour by a perfectly competitive firm

First we examine a factor market using partial equilibrium analysis; thus we assume that the prices and quantities of all goods and all other factors do not change. We begin by looking at the labour market; in later sections we shall divide this market into markets for several types of labour, and we shall consider markets for other factors as well.

The number of man-hours of labour that a firm wants to employ depends on the costs and revenues from doing so. In what circumstances does a firm choose to employ one more man-hour?

10.2.1 Marginal products

The **marginal product of labour** is the additional output that results from the employment of an additional man-hour of labour.

For example, if 40 chairs are produced by 50 man-hours, and 42 chairs by 51 man-hours, the marginal product of the 51st man-hour is 2 chairs.

The marginal product includes changes in the output of the existing labour force as well as the result of the efforts of the additional man-hour. Additional labour may allow for a more efficient division of labour in a factory, so that output increases and the marginal product of labour is positive; alternatively, an additional worker may get in everyone else's way, so that the marginal product is negative.

The **marginal revenue product of labour** is the addition to total revenue obtained by selling the marginal product of labour.

In a perfect market economy, a firm can sell the additional output without affecting the market price, so that:

marginal revenue from employing an additional man-hour	=	marginal revenue product of labour	=	marginal product of labour	×	price of good produced

If the firm in our example sells chairs for £10 each, the marginal revenue product of the 51st hour is £20.

10.2.2 Employment decision

The decision to employ an additional man-hour depends on the difference between the marginal revenue product of that man-hour and the marginal cost of employing it. A firm's decision on whether to employ an additional man-hour does not affect the wage of labour, because firms are small in a perfect market economy. So the marginal cost of employing an additional hour is the wage paid to it. Note that, in reality, there are other costs of employing labour, such as employers' national insurance contributions. These are not considered in the simplified context of a perfect market economy because of the assumption of minimal government.

The firm's decision on whether to employ an additional man-hour is based on the following points:

(a) If the marginal revenue product of the additional hour exceeds the wage, the additional man-hour adds more to the firm's revenue than to its cost, and a profit-maximizing firm employs the additional labour. The firm then examines whether a further additional man-hour again adds to its profits. The firm employs additional labour until the marginal revenue product no longer exceeds the wage.
(b) If the marginal revenue product is less than the wage, the firm reduces the number of man-hours that it employs because, if it employs one fewer man-hour, its cost falls more than its revenue. This reduction in employment continues as long as the wage exceeds the marginal revenue product.

These two points imply that

The firm maximizes its profit when it employs the quantity of labour for which the marginal revenue product equals the wage of labour.

Table 10.1 and figure 10.1 give an example of the relation between the marginal revenue product of labour and the number of workers employed (we assume for simplicity that each worker works for a fixed number of hours). Curve AA has an upward-sloping section (up to employment of 3 workers at B), which allows for the possibility that, for example, two workers can use the firm's equipment more efficiently than one worker (the average output per worker

Table 10.1   Marginal revenue product of labour

Man-hours of labour	Total output	Marginal product	Marginal revenue product when price of goods is £3
0	0	6	18
1	6	8	24
2	14	10	30
3	24	12	36
4	36	12	36
5	48	10	30
6	58	8	24
7	66	6	18
8	72	4	12
9	76	2	6
10	78	0	0
11	78	−2	−6
12	76	−4	−12

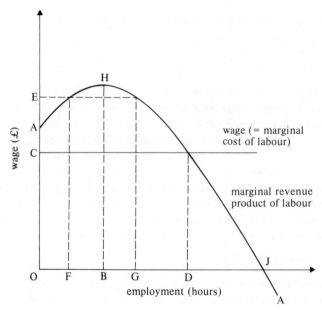

Figure 10.1   Demand for labour by a perfectly competitive firm
The marginal revenue product of labour increases as employment increases from O to
B, and then falls. The firm's labour demand curve is HJ.

rises from 6 to 7 when the second worker is employed) so that the marginal
product of the first worker is less than that of the second. If the firm employs
more labour than B, the marginal product of labour declines. Additional
workers add less and less to total output. The 11th and 12th workers (beyond
J in figure 10.1) actually cause a reduction in output because these workers
hinder the work done by others (remember that the marginal product and
marginal revenue product are calculated for a given amount of equipment and
land, so that additional workers may well hinder others in a fixed area of work
and using a fixed amount of equipment).

   If the wage is C, employment is D. Employment of less than D implies that
the marginal revenue product of labour exceeds the wage, so that additional
employment adds more to the firm's revenue than to its cost. Employment of
more than D implies that the marginal revenue product is less than the wage,
and profit increases if employment is reduced.

   If the wage is E there are two employment levels, F and G, for which the
marginal revenue product equals the wage. However, if employment is F, on
the upward-sloping part of AA, an increase in employment increases the firm's
profit, and so the firm would employ more than F. It would increase
employment to G, and so the profit-maximizing employment is on the
downward-sloping part of AA. So only the downward-sloping part of the curve
is relevant to the firm's employment decision.

   A firm's demand curve for labour is the downward-sloping part of its
   marginal revenue product curve.

The firm's demand curve for labour shows the number of man-hours that the firm wants to employ at each wage. In figure 10.1, this is HJ. If the wage exceeds H, the firm employs no labour and, assuming that its equipment is not fully automatic, it produces nothing. In the short run, the firm's loss equals the cost of any fixed factors; its loss would be even greater if it were to employ labour and produce a positive output (see section 8.5).

10.2.3 Derived demand

A firm's demand for labour increases when the price of the good sold by the firm increases, because this increases the marginal revenue product of labour. Figure 10.2 illustrates the effect of a price increase that shifts the marginal revenue product curve outward from AC to BD, and the demand curve for labour shifts from EC to FD. In particular, if the demand for a good increases, so that its price increases, then the demand for labour to produce that good also increases. The demand for labour (and for other factors of production) is a **derived demand**, because it results from the demand for the goods that are produced by the labour.

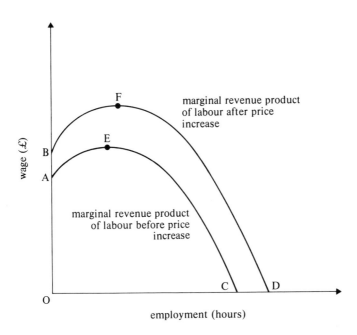

Figure 10.2   Effect on demand for labour of an increase in the price of the good produced
Labour demand is a derived demand. When the price increases, the firm produces more and demands more labour.

10.3 Supply of labour

The assumption of material motivation implies that a person rejects a job if some other job pays a higher income for the same number of hours of work or the same income for fewer hours of work. So labour is supplied by workers who balance the desire for a high income (that is expenditure on goods either now or in the future) against the desire not to work for long hours. Workers choose whether to work more to obtain extra income at the cost of the sacrifice of some leisure time.

Each day, a person has available 24 hours minus essential sleeping time (he or she may choose to spend some of his or her leisure time asleep, but this is not a part of essential sleeping time). Consider an example in which a person has 16 hours for work or for leisure, and in which his wage is £3 per hour. He can choose a daily income between zero with 16 hours leisure, and £48 with no leisure. The available combinations of income and leisure are represented by AB in figure 10.3. Suppose that he chooses an income of £24 and 8 hours leisure (point C), so that he supplies 8 hours labour. We can then ask how his supply of labour changes when the wage increases.

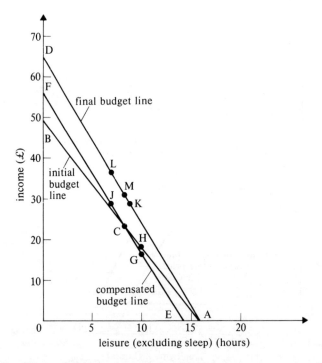

Figure 10.3   Choice between income and leisure
The compensated budget line EF is parallel to the final budget line AD, and passes through initial point C. The axiom of revealed preference rules out choice on CE. The substitution effect is a move from C to a point on CF, the income effect from that point on CF to a point on AD.

If his wage increases to £4, the available combinations of income and leisure are represented by AD: the maximum leisure time remains 16 hours, the maximum income is now £64. The wage increase has two effects:

(a) The **substitution effect**: an hour of leisure has become more expensive, in the sense that he must give up more income for each hour of leisure that he takes.
(b) The **income effect**: his opportunities have increased, because he can have both more income and more leisure than when the wage is £3.

As in section 9.4, we can separate these effects by constructing a compensated situation as follows. Suppose that he were to require 10 hours sleep each day, so that his opportunities (with wage £4) are represented by EF. The income–leisure combinations available range from zero income and 14 hours leisure to zero leisure and an income of £56, and include his original income–leisure combination (£24 income, 8 hours leisure), although in the compensated situation he can earn £24 by working only 6 hours. The two more hours of sleep play the same role as the compensating income change of section 9.4.1. They offset the increase in the opportunities caused by the wage increase, so that we can separate the two effects.

10.3.1 Substitution effect

We use the axiom of revealed preference in the same way as in section 9.4. Consider an income–leisure combination such as G in figure 10.3 (£16 income, 10 hours leisure) that is available in the compensated situation. In the original situation, he could have an income of £18 and 10 hours leisure (H), which is better than G (because it involves a higher income, and no less leisure). However, in the original situation he chooses C rather than H, and so his behaviour reveals that he prefers C to H. The axiom of revealed preference implies that he would not choose H or G in any situation in which C is also available. A similar argument shows that he would not choose any point on CE, and so in the compensated situation he chooses a point on CF, which involves no more leisure than C. So:

The substitution effect of a wage increase causes no increase in leisure time.

10.3.2 Income effect

This is the movement from the compensated situation (represented by EF) to the final situation (AD). The required hours of sleep are reduced from 10 to 8, and the wage remains at £4. He moves from a point on CF (say J) chosen in the compensated situation to a point on AD. If he chooses to have both more income and more leisure when he moves from J to AD, he chooses an income–leisure combination between K and L. Combinations outside KL are perhaps unlikely. A combination on LD (less leisure than at J) implies that he takes less leisure as he becomes better off, implying that leisure is an inferior good. If he chooses a combination on KA, he has less income than at J, and so he chooses to consume less in total as he becomes better off. It seems unlikely that either leisure or consumption-in-general is inferior. Specifically:

> If leisure is a normal good, the income effect of a wage increase causes an increase in leisure time.

10.3.3 The combined effect

Assuming that leisure is a normal good, the income and substitution effects are opposite. Starting from C in the initial situation:

(a) If the substitution effect reduces leisure time more than the income effect increases it, then the individual supplies more labour when his wage increases.
(b) If the income effect increases leisure time more than the substitution effect reduces it, then the wage increase causes a reduction in working hours. The supply of labour falls as the wage increases, and the labour supply curve slopes downwards, contrary to the usual assumption about the shape of a supply curve.

Figure 10.4 shows a **backward-bending labour supply curve**. When the wage is below Z, the individual supplies more labour when the wage increases. When the wage exceeds Z, she supplies less labour as the wage increases. This occurs if the substitution effect dominates the income effect when a person is poor, and if the income effect is dominant when she is richer. A richer person is (perhaps) more likely to be content with a small increase in her income and a substantial increase in her leisure in order to have time to enjoy the benefits of the goods that she can buy. A poorer person might sacrifice some leisure when the wage increases because a little more work, combined with the increased wage, gives her a substantial increase in her total income. The additional work was not worthwhile before the wage increase because the lower wage did not give sufficient compensation for the extra effort. We shall return to this topic in section 20.3, where we discuss the effects of changes in income taxes (which affect take-home wages) on the supply of labour.

10.3.4 Working conditions

We have examined labour supply decisions that result from a choice between combinations of income and leisure. There are other influences on decisions to supply labour: for example, working conditions, location and fringe benefits, such as holidays, pension schemes and company cars. Some of these aspects of a job can be regarded as wages paid other than in the form of money (often to reduce taxes) and, for our purposes, these non-monetary benefits can be included in the wage. Other aspects, such as job location and working

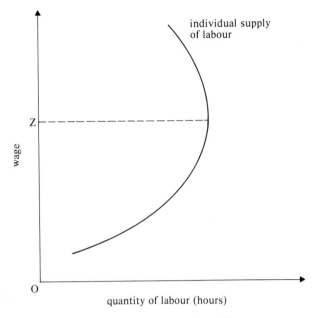

individual supply
of labour

Figure 10.4   Backward-bending supply curve for labour
Above wage Z, households want more leisure when the wage increases, and so supply
less labour. Below wage Z they want less leisure, and supply more labour.

conditions, can affect the outcome of labour supply decisions to the extent
that people in a perfect market economy do not specialize according to their
comparative advantages, so that the economy does not achieve an efficient
output level.

For example, in table 10.2 Alan has a comparative advantage over Bill in
mining compared to farming. If the hourly wage of a miner is £4, and that of
a farmworker is £1, both receive higher incomes as miners. However, if Alan
refuses to work in the mine because of the working conditions, he farms
instead, despite receiving a lower wage. If Bill is willing to work in the mine
he does so because he is paid more as a miner than as a farmworker. So

Table 10.2   Production possibilities for two workers

Person	Output per hour as a miner (tonnes of coal)	Output per hour as a farm-worker (kilograms of corn)
Alan	3	1
Bill	2	2

Alan's refusal to work in the mine implies that they do not specialize according to their comparative advantages.

We can modify the definition of an efficient economic system to take account of this sort of non-material motivation. An economic system is efficient if all markets are in equilibrium, and it is impossible to increase the output of one good without:

(a) Reducing the output of some other good,
(b) Using more resources of labour (if someone's leisure time is reduced), materials, land or equipment, or
(c) Reducing the standard of someone's working conditions, or requiring him or her to take a job in a location that he or she does not like.

If we use this definition, a perfect market economy is efficient even if some people are not entirely materially motivated when they choose their jobs. When the economy is in general equilibrium, each person has the leisure time and the working conditions that he wants, given the wages of all the jobs that he could do, and each person buys the goods that he wants, given prices and his income.

10.4 Labour market

The market demand for labour is found by adding the demands of all firms. Each firm's demand falls when the wage increases, so that the market demand curve (DD in figure 10.5) is downward-sloping. The market supply curve for labour is the sum of all individuals' supplies. The slope of the market supply curve depends on reactions to an increase in the wage. The market supply curve (SS in figure 10.5) bends backwards, representing the possibility that many of the individual labour supply curves bend backwards. This is not a necessary assumption, and none of our conclusions would be affected if the market supply curve sloped upwards at all levels of wages.

The equilibrium wage is Y, and the equilibrium number of man-hours is R. If the actual wage is X, the supply of labour U exceeds the demand V. A firm that advertises a job has many applicants, and the firm reduces its wage offer to increase its profits. The wage therefore falls towards its equilibrium Y. If the wage is T, the demand for labour Q exceeds the supply W, and firms can employ the labour that they want only by offering higher wages to entice workers from other firms. Again the actual wage moves towards the equilibrium, and:

Equilibrium in the labour market is stable.

10.4.1 Real and money wages

We have derived the supply and demand curves for labour in a partial equilibrium analysis which assumes that the prices of goods do not change. If

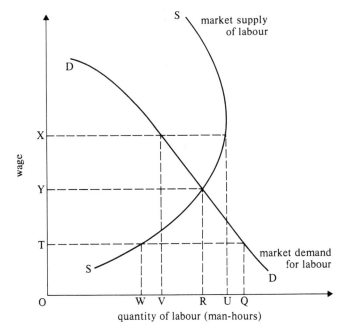

Figure 10.5 Labour market
The equilibrium wage is Y. If the wage exceeds Y, some people who want jobs cannot find them. If the wage is below Y, some firms that want to employ workers cannot do so.

the labour market is not in equilibrium, the money wage changes relative to prices, and so the real wage (money wage ÷ average price level; see section 6.2.4) also changes. In fact, we presume that firms demand and workers supply labour in response to real wages. If all prices and the money wage double simultaneously, the marginal revenue product and the marginal cost of labour change by the same proportion and so firms do not change their demands for labour. Similarly, there is no change in the consumption possibilities from a given number of hours of work, and so there is no change in workers' supply decisions either. So we conclude that (in the absence of money illusion; see section 6.2.4) the demand and supply of labour change only if the real wage changes. Therefore:

The labour market moves to equilibrium through changes in real wages.

10.5 Several labour markets

The analysis of the previous sections ignores differences in abilities and the fact that there are several labour markets, one for each type (or skill) of labour.

It is convenient to distinguish between differences in **abilities** to do different jobs and differences in **efficiencies** of doing the same job. Thus, if Alan can produce 30 food or 60 cloth he has two different abilities. If Bill can produce 20 food or 80 cloth, he also has two abilities. Bill is less efficient than Alan at producing food, and more efficient at producing cloth. If there are different abilities, there are several labour markets.

We do not discuss the extents to which differences in efficiencies and abilities are inborn or are the result of environmental factors and training. The debates of geneticists, psychologists and others on this issue indicate that it is not easy to separate the influences of heredity and environment. We examine the effect of differences in abilities and efficiencies on the income distribution; we do not question the source of these differences.

10.5.1 Different efficiencies

If two people specialize in producing cloth, and one produces 3 metres per hour while the other produces 2 metres per hour, the first receives 50 per cent more by selling an hour's output. So self-employed specialists in a perfect market economy receive incomes in proportion to their efficiencies.

The same conclusion is true when people are employed by perfectly competitive firms, and labour markets are in equilibrium. If Alan takes one hour to do a job that Bill does in two hours, one hour of Alan's labour is worth two of Bill's. If Bill's efficiency is taken as the standard for measurement, Alan contributes twice the standard effort, or two **effective man-hours**, for each actual man-hour worked. We can use effective man-hours to measure the supply and demand for labour in each market, and then calculate each worker's income on the basis of the number of effective man-hours he or she supplies.

When markets are in equilibrium, each effective man-hour of labour of a particular type receives the same wage.

Suppose that some workers ask for a higher wage per effective man-hour than others. All firms demand labour from the lower-wage group, and so the lower-wage group find that they can ask for a higher wage and still find a job. The higher-wage group find that no one wants to employ them, and so they must accept a lower wage to find a job. The wages of the two groups change until everyone is paid the same wage per effective man-hour.

10.5.2 Different abilities

Many people can supply labour of several types because they have several skills, some of which they have acquired by taking training courses. This implies that there is a link between the wages of different types of labour. If people can transfer easily from supplying a poorly paid type of labour to supplying a better paid type, they will do so. The supply of the poorly paid type falls, and its wage increases; the supply of the better paid type increases, and its wage falls. A general equilibrium is reached when no one has an incentive to move from one labour market to another. Differences in wages arise in equilibrium only if it is costly (or impossible) for people to move from supplying one type of labour to supplying another. The costs of moving from one labour market to another are the costs of **training**; we examine these in the next section.

10.6 Training and education

What induces people to train for a particular job? In a perfect market economy, each person is materially motivated, and trains to acquire a different ability if his income from that occupation, minus the costs of training, exceeds his income from his present job. This decision depends on future incomes, and in a perfect market economy people are not uncertain about their potential future earnings. The assumption of freedom of action implies that there is no restriction on the training courses that a person may take up other than his or her ability to follow a course and to pay the fee charged for it.

Suppose that a course in plumbing costs £2,000 in fees, and lasts 1 year. Adam, an economist, has an income of £8,000, which will remain the same in the future. The current and future wage of a plumber is £9,000 per year. In either occupation, Adam will retire in 21 years time. He trains to become a plumber if the additional £1,000 per year for 20 years is sufficient to compensate him for the cost of the course (£2,000) plus the fact that he cannot work as an economist while he is training, so that he has to lose income of £8,000. The cost, including forgone earnings, or becoming a plumber is £10,000.

Adam could spend this £10,000 in some other way. For example, he could buy land with it, and rent it out. If the rent on £10,000 worth of land exceeds £1,000 per year for the next 20 years, he buys the land and remains an economist, because he can obtain a greater total income from being an economist and a landowner than from being a plumber. If the rent is less than £1,000 per year, he trains as a plumber because plumbing gives the higher income. In fact the rent must be sufficiently less than £1,000 per year for 20 years to allow for the fact that, as a landowner, Adam has land that he can sell in 20 years time; as a retired plumber he has no similar asset. If he is to become a plumber, the additional income from plumbing must exceed the rent by an amount that is sufficient to compensate for this difference.

This example shows that, in a perfect market economy:

(a) Decisions to take training courses are taken in a similar way to decisions to buy land or equipment. All such decisions involve buying assets, because knowledge is an asset (known as **human capital**) that can be used to make an income, just as land and equipment are assets. Materially motivated people choose between these assets on the basis of the income that they will achieve.

(b) The difference between the annual wages of two occupations cannot exceed the annual opportunity cost of training from one to the other. This opportunity cost is the annual income from the best alternative use of the money needed for training. If the wage difference exceeds this annual opportunity cost, people train. This increases the supply of the higher-paid type, and reduces the supply of the lower-paid type. So the higher wage falls, and the lower wage increases until there is no further incentive to train.

The wage difference may be less than the annual opportunity cost of training. Then no one has an incentive to train, and the wage of each type of labour is the result of the interaction of the supply and demand for each type of labour. People may train in either direction between two occupations: in our example, we considered an economist deciding whether to train as plumber when the wage of a plumber exceeds that of an economist. If the wage of an economist exceeds that of a plumber, then plumbers might train as economists.

10.6.1 Supply and demand for courses and teachers

As well as demanding courses for training, households may demand education as a consumer good. The effects of changes in prices and incomes on this demand can be analysed in the same way as the effects on any other consumer good (see chapter 9). So there are two groups demanding education: those who want skills for the material benefits, and those who want education as a consumer good. An increase in course fees reduces the demand by both groups: some of those who buy education to obtain a more highly paid skill find that the additional earnings no longer compensate them for the increased fees; consumers buy fewer courses if fees increase, just as they buy less coal when the price of coal increases.

In a perfect market economy, educational courses are supplied by people who are specialist teachers, or by firms that employ teachers. If the ability to teach is itself the result of training, more people train as teachers if the fee that they can charge for a course increases. So an increase in course fees causes an increase in the supply of teachers, and an increase in the supply of courses. There is a supply and demand for each type of course and each market has an equilibrium course fee. There are markets for different types of teachers, and each type has an equilibrium wage. A general equilibrium in a perfect market economy includes equilibrium in all of these markets.

10.6.2 Transfer earnings and economic rent

If a worker can transfer from supplying one type of labour to another without training, she chooses the job where her income is highest given her efficiency at each job. In this case, her opportunity cost of taking that job is the wage in the next most highly paid job.

This opportunity cost is also known as her **transfer earnings**. Any wage that she receives in excess of her transfer earnings is her **economic rent** (a potentially confusing term, because 'rent' is also used to describe income from land and from hiring out equipment). So, if she earns £8,000 per year in job A, and her next most highly paid job would give her an income of £6,000, her transfer earnings are £6,000 per year, and her annual economic rent is £2,000.

If a worker must train to transfer, we have seen that he transfers to another job only if its annual wage exceeds the annual wage that he now receives plus the annual opportunity cost of training. To calculate his transfer earnings, he lists the wage in each occupation minus the annual opportunity cost of training for it. The greatest of these figures is his transfer earnings: the excess of his income above his transfer earnings is his economic rent. For example, suppose that a worker in job A receives a wage of £8,000 per year. Job B pays £8,500, and there is an annual opportunity cost of training of £1,000. Job C pays £9,000 and involves an annual opportunity cost of training of £1,200. His annual wage minus the opportunity cost of training is £7,500 in B, and £7,800 in C. His transfer earnings are the greater of these figures (£7,800), and his economic rent is £200 (£8,000 − £7,800).

10.6.3 Economic rent in the long run

A materially motivated worker transfers to supply a different type of labour if her transfer earnings exceed her wage. So in the long run economic rents are likely to be reduced because better-paid jobs attract workers, so that the supplies of these types increase and their wages fall. The supplies of less well-paid types fall and their wages increase. These changes reduce differences in wages between types of labour. So transfer earnings increase and economic rents fall.

Economic rents do not necessarily fall to zero in a perfect market economy. Suppose that Alan is very efficient in one job, and inefficient (relative to other people) in all other jobs. He works at the job at which he is efficient, his transfer earnings are low and his economic rent is high. Even if other people transfer to supply this type of labour, Alan's wage continues to be much higher than he could receive in other jobs, and so he continues to receive an economic rent in the long run.

10.7 Markets for other factors

The demands for all factors depend on similar profit-maximizing decisions to those that determine the demand for labour:

(a) Firms use a factor up to the point where its marginal revenue product equals the marginal cost of using it. The marginal revenue product is the additional revenue obtained from the sale of the marginal product of the factor. The marginal cost of land or equipment is the rent paid to its owners, or normal profit if a firm uses land or equipment that belongs to the owners of the firm.

(b) The downward-sloping part of a firm's marginal revenue product curve for

a factor is the firm's demand curve for that factor. This curve is drawn assuming that the quantities of other factors used do not change. The market demand is the total of the demands by all firms.
(c) Demands for factors are derived demands that depend on demands for the goods that firms produce.

10.7.1 Supply of land

In many examples the supply of land is fixed. The supply curve is completely inelastic (vertical in our usual diagrams) because there is no change in supply when the rent changes. However, there are markets for several types of land: for example, land suitable for house-building, forest land, grazing land, land that is suitable for airports and so on. The supplies of different types can be varied, even when the total supply of land is fixed: for example, forest land can be cleared for grazing or building; land used as waste dumps can be covered and used for recreation. In a perfect market economy, land is used in the most profitable way, taking into account the cost of changing from one use to another, such as the cost of covering a rubbish dump.

10.7.2 Supply of equipment

In the short run, the supply of equipment is fixed. In the long run, the supply is increased by the production of new equipment. If the price of a type of equipment increases, the profits of firms that sell it increase, and so other firms enter the market and the supply of equipment increases. This increase in supply continues until equipment producers make normal profits. The process whereby the output of a type of equipment increases in a perfect market economy is similar to that used to describe consumers' sovereignty in section 9.8. Indeed, such a process is an extension of consumers' sovereignty through derived demands. If the demand for chocolate increases, then the demand for chocolate-making equipment increases, and so its price increases. This increases the profitability of making this equipment, firms enter the market and supply increases.

10.7.3 Equilibrium prices and profit rates

The supply and demand for each type of equipment and land determine its equilibrium price. Any equipment or land has two prices associated with it:

(a) The market price at which it is bought and sold.
(b) The **gross rent**, which is the amount received by its owner in return for allowing someone else to use the equipment or land for a specified period.

The gross rent received by the owner for a year consists of two parts:

(a) Compensation for any **depreciation** in the market price of the land or equipment during the year. The market price may fall because equipment partly wears out and so becomes less valuable, or for some other reason, such as a change in demand for the goods produced using the land or equipment.

(b) The **net rent** or **net profit**, which is the owner's income given that he or she is compensated for the reduction in the selling price.

The reduction in the market price of land or equipment during 1989 is the market price on 1 January 1989 minus the market price on 1 January 1990, and so

$$\frac{\text{net rent}}{\text{for 1989}} = \frac{\text{gross rent}}{\text{for 1989}} - \left(\frac{\text{market price}}{\text{on 1.1.89}} - \frac{\text{market price}}{\text{on 1.1.90}}\right)$$

10.7.4 Net profit rate

The **net profit rate** on land and equipment is the net rent for the year divided by the market price at the start of the year. For example, if a machine has a market price of £1,000 on 1 January 1990, and net rent of £250 during 1990, the net profit rate on the machine is 25 per cent. We note that the net profit rate falls if the market price increases.

Suppose that two types of machine have different net profit rates. A person who buys a type M machine for £1,000 can obtain a net rent of £300 per year, which is a net profit rate of 30 per cent. If he or she buys a type N machine for £2,000, he or she obtains a net rent of £400, which is a net profit rate of 20 per cent. Materially motivated people prefer to buy two M rather than one N, so that there is no demand for N. The market price of N falls, and so the net profit rate on N increases. This continues until the net profit rates on all types of land and equipment are the same. So:

In a perfect market economy in general equilibrium in the long run, the net profit rate is the same throughout the economy.

10.7.5 Interest rate

Some people lend money to others who use it to buy goods, equipment, land or training. Suppose that a person has £5,000 that she can either lend to someone else in return for interest of £1,000 per year (an annual rate of 20 per cent) or use to buy equipment and receive a net profit of £750 (a net profit rate of 15 per cent). In a perfect market economy no one would buy equipment. The price of equipment falls, because there is no demand for it, and the net profit rate on equipment increases. This continues until the net profit rate is equal to the interest rate. If the net profit rate exceeds the interest rate, no one wants to lend money, and so there is no supply of loans in the loan market. The interest rate increases because the demand for loans exceeds the supply and this continues until all markets, including the loan market, are in equilibrium. Then:

In a perfect market economy in general equilibrium in the long run, the interest rate is equal to the net profit rate.

This conclusion implies that in a perfect market economy it is not possible to make a positive income by borrowing money and using that money to buy equipment. All the net profit on the equipment would be paid as interest on the money borrowed. The net profit rate and the interest rate are the normal profit rate in the economy.

10.8 Income distribution

There are three main categories of income in a market economy:

(a) Incomes from working (including a part of the incomes of self-employed specialists). These incomes differ if people have different efficiencies and different abilities.
(b) Incomes from owning assets, including rent and profit from land and equipment, and interest from lending.
(c) Incomes from owning firms, which are supernormal profit.

In a perfect market economy in long-run equilibrium, the third category of income disappears, and so people's incomes differ because they have different efficiencies and different abilities, and own different assets. The assets, including human capital (see section 10.6), from which a person receives income form his or her **wealth**. So the income distribution depends on:

(a) The distribution of wealth.
(b) The prices, wages, rents, interest and profits determined in markets.

The current distribution of wealth depends on the income distribution in previous years, because wealth is accumulated as the result of past savings, and people with higher incomes in the past are likely to have saved more and so be wealthier now. So the current income distribution is influenced by the income distribution in previous years.

10.8.1 Poverty

People are poor in a perfect market economy because they own little or no land or equipment, have no money to lend and have abilities that are not well paid. Those who are unable to work, perhaps because they are disabled, and who have no other assests have no income. A market economy is one of 'everyone for himself or herself' because there is no government intervention to provide incomes for those who have nothing.

10.8.2 Discrimination

Economic discrimination against a group defined by, for example, race, colour, sex or religious beliefs, is caused by one of the following:

(a) People from a particular group are legally prevented from taking particular jobs, from buying particular goods, or from buying land in particular areas.
(b) Firms prefer to employ people from one particular group.
(c) People from one group are paid less than those from another who do identical work.

The assumption of freedom of action rules out the first form of discrimination from a perfect market economy. The assumption of material motivation rules out the second, because a firm maximizes its profit by employing the most efficient workers regardless of their group. The same assumption also rules out the third form of discrimination, because materially motivated firms want to hire the workers who are paid the least to do a particular job. If women receive £1 per hour less than men who do an identical job, all materially motivated firms want to employ women. There is no demand for male workers, and so their wages fall. This fall in wages continues until the economy is in equilibrium, when both groups receive the same wage for identical work. Discrimination implies a sacrifice of profit, and so it does not occur in a perfect market economy. We can therefore conclude that economic discrimination is the result of imperfections that reduce opportunities available to people from one group and that cause firms to sacrifice profit because they want to discriminate. Firms that discriminate in their employment policy have motives other than or in addition to material motives.

10.9 Value judgements of the income distribution

In a perfect market economy, incomes are received by supplying factors, and this is a positive statement involving no value judgements. However, some people judge the fairness or desirability of the income distribution in part at least on the basis of how it came about. They might also judge it by results (by looking at the Gini coefficient, for example), and we shall discuss questions of government policy on income distribution in chapter 20. In this section we look at value judgements that can be based on the way in which the distribution comes about in a perfect market economy.

10.9.1 Equal treatment of factors

All incomes in a perfect market economy are determined in markets, including markets for labour, land, equipment and loans. All incomes are determined in a similar way by the impersonal market forces of supply and demand. This argument might be used to support the value judgement that all incomes are equally justifiable because they are determined in the same way, so that, for example, profits are no less deserved than wages.

10.9.2 Marginal productivity

In a perfect market economy, a firm uses each factor up to the point where its marginal revenue product is equal to its price. The marginal revenue product is the marginal product of the factor multiplied by the price of the good produced. So:

$$\text{marginal product of factor} = \text{factor price/price of good}$$

The right hand side of this equation is the amount of the good that the owner of the factor (the worker, in the case of labour) can buy with his or her factor income. So, for example, if a worker supplies an hour of labour to a firm, he is paid a wage out of which he can buy the amount of goods that equals the marginal product of labour in that firm. He can buy the goods that would not have been produced if he had not supplied that hour of labour. In this sense, his income equals his contribution to the output of the firm, and a similar argument can be applied to all factors to show that incomes are determined by the marginal productivity of factors that people own. This argument might be used to support the value judgement that the income distribution is fair because incomes are determined by the contribution that each factor makes to production. To make this value judgement requires three statements:

(a) People *should* own the factors that they have accumulated, inherited or learned.
(b) People *should* receive incomes that reflect their contributions to production (and not, for example, incomes that reflect their needs).
(c) The contribution of a factor *should* be measured by its marginal product.

Anyone who makes the judgement that the income distribution in a perfect market economy is not necessarily fair (for example, because extreme poverty is possible) disagrees with at least one of these statements.

10.9.3 Smallness and exploitation

Exploitation, according to the *Oxford English Dictionary*, is 'the action of turning to account: the action of utilizing for selfish purposes'. In a perfect market economy everyone is small, so that no one can 'turn to account, or utilize for selfish purposes' the price in any market, including the markets in which incomes are determined. This argument might be used to support the value judgement that no one is able to exploit anyone else in a perfect market economy.

10.9.4 Exploitation as a fact of capitalism

Marxist economists regard exploitation as an integral part of capitalist economic systems, because those who receive incomes from owning assets (who together form the **capitalist class**) exploit those who receive incomes by working (who together form the **working class**). This view stems from the writings of Karl Marx (born 1818 at Trier in Germany, died 1883; lived and worked in London from 1849 to his death, supported by financial contributions from Friedrich Engels), and in particular from his major economic work *Das Kapital* (which was completed by Engels after Marx died).

The Marxist view is derived from the value judgements that:

(a) Labour is the factor that is the source of all value, because it is ultimately responsible for all output.
(b) Land is a gift of nature whose owners have taken it over (**appropriated** it) for their own gain.
(c) Equipment is produced by labour, but the owners of the firms that produce equipment appropriate it, and sell it to gain an income for themselves.

This view leads to a **labour theory of value**, which states that the value of a good is measured by the number of man-hours taken to produce it and not by its market price. The man-hours needed to produce a good include those needed to produce the materials used in its production and those needed to make the equipment that wears out as the good is produced. Workers supply this labour and receive wages, with which they can buy goods. However, workers supply more man-hours in total than are needed to produce the goods that workers can buy with their wages. The remainder of their working time is spent producing goods that will be bought by the capitalist class. The working time that is spent by the working class making goods for the capitalist class measures the extent of the exploitation of the working class.

For example, if 100 workers each supply 40 hours per week, and buy goods with their wages that are produced in 3,000 hours, then the capitalist class buy goods that are produced in 1,000 hours. The rate of exploitation is 1,000/3,000 = 33 per cent (time spent making goods for capitalists/time spent making goods for workers).

The value judgement that workers are exploited because they are deprived of a part of the product of their labour is based on two statements:

(a) Labour is the source of all value.
(b) The owners of other factors have appropriated them.

Anyone who takes the view that exploitation is not a fact of capitalism must disagree with one of these statements.

10.10 Summary

The demand for a factor is determined by the profit-maximizing rule that the marginal revenue product equals the price (wage, rent or profit) paid to use one unit of the factor. The supply of labour is the result of individual choices between income, leisure and working conditions. The supply of a type of labour may be increased by training. The supply of a type of land may be increased by clearing, reclamation etc. The supply of equipment is the result of decisions made by equipment-producing firms. Factor markets reach equilibrium through changes in real factor prices. In particular, real wages change to bring labour markets to equilibrium.

Wage differences result from differences in efficiencies and abilities. Workers train if the additional income obtained by acquiring a skill exceeds the opportunity cost of training. This opportunity cost is the highest income that could be obtained from land or equipment bought with the money spent on training.

The net profit rate on all assets is the same, and equal to the interest rate when a perfect market economy is in long-run equilibrium.

The income distribution is determined by the wealth distribution and by factor prices and is the result of market forces of supply and demand. Each factor owner receives an income equal to the marginal product of his or her factor. In the Marxist view, workers are exploited because incomes other than wages can be used to buy goods produced by labour.

Topics and problems

(1) Do you expect that you will be compensated by sufficient additional income for the cost of your current training course? Would your answer change if you had to pay all the costs of the course (assuming that you receive some grant or subsidy towards your tuition fees and/or living expenses)?

(2) The author of this book was at school with someone who is now a famous pop star. What is the explanation for the fact that, despite better examination results, the author has a much lower income than the pop star?

(3) Does a person who succeeds in a training course deserve a higher income than someone who fails?

(4) Do you disagree with any of the value judgements that support the view that the income distribution in a perfect market economy is fair because people are rewarded according to their contribution?

(5) Do you think that it is right that people receive incomes other than wages?

(6) Is society divided into classes of capitalists and workers? Can people move easily from one class to another?

(7) Table 10.3 shows how a firm's output depends on the amount of labour that it employs (with the quantities of other factors fixed). The firm sells its

Table 10.3 Output and employment for problem 7

Employment (man-hours)	Output (units)
1	4
2	10
3	18
4	24
5	28
6	31
7	33
8	34

output for £5 per unit. List the firm's marginal revenue product at each level of employment. How much labour does the firm demand when the wage is (a) £15 per hour (b) £30 per hour?

(8) A person has 18 hours per day to divide between work and leisure. She receives a wage of £5 per hour. Draw a diagram to represent her opportunities for income and leisure. How do her opportunities change when the wage increases to £6 per hour? When the wage is £5 per hour, she chooses 10 hours of leisure. Construct a compensated situation to separate the income and substitution effects of the wage increase.

(9) A person who is 45 years old receives a wage of £8,000 per year. He can buy machines for £500 each that will last for 20 years, and each machine gives an annual income of £50 per year for 20 years (after which the machine is worn out). Alternatively, he can spend one year training and receive a wage of £9,000 per year until he retires at age 65.

What is the maximum that he will pay for the training course, given that he receives no wages during the year of training?

What is the maximum that he would pay to train for a job that pays £8,800 per year?

Chapter Eleven

Macroeconomic aspects of a perfect market economy

Investment and saving — unemployment — economic growth — price level and inflation — inflation and the quantity theory of money — perfect market economies and the real world

---

11.1 Introduction

We have reached several conclusions on the outcome of a perfect market economy, including:

(a) A perfect market economy is efficient (see sections 7.5 and 8.7).
(b) There is consumers' sovereignty (see section 9.8).
(c) The income distribution is the outcome of the interaction of supply and demand in markets for factors, goods and loans (see section 10.8).

These conclusions concern the structure of the economy. Efficiency and consumers' sovereignty are concerned with the relative sizes of outputs of goods; the income distribution describes the relative sizes of incomes. In this chapter we discuss macroeconomic aspects of the economy: investment, saving, unemployment, economic growth and inflation. We end this chapter with a section that shows the extent to which the analysis of the very much simplified perfect market economy has implications for more realistic economies in which there are imperfections and government intervention.

11.2 Investment and saving

In a perfect market economy the government is small, so that there are no taxes. A household receives money from:

(a) Factor incomes (wages, rent, profits) and interest.
(b) Loans from other households.
(c) Revenue from selling land and used equipment.

A household spends money on:

(d) Consumer goods.
(e) Loans to other households (including loans to the owners of firms).
(f) New equipment and training courses sold by firms.
(g) Purchases of land and used equipment.

If we take all households together, the total of money lent is the same as the total borrowed, because there must be a borrower and a lender for each loan. So:

$$\text{total of (b)} = \text{total of (e)} \qquad (11.1)$$

Similarly, total sales of land and used equipment equal total purchases of land and used equipment. So:

$$\text{total of (c)} = \text{total of (g)} \qquad (11.2)$$

A materially motivated household will spend all its income in one of the ways listed as (d) to (g). It has no need to hold reserves against unforeseen contingencies since it has sufficient information to plan without uncertainties. So the total of the incomes for all households equals the total of the expenditures of all households:

$$\text{totals of (a) + (b) + (c)} = \text{totals of (d) + (e) + (f) + (g)} \qquad (11.3)$$

Using equations 11.1 and 11.2:

$$\text{total of (a)} = \text{totals of (d) + (f)} \qquad (11.4)$$

or

$$\text{total factor incomes} = \text{total consumption} + \text{total purchases of new equipment and training}$$

Newly produced equipment and training courses are the investment goods that permit an increase in outputs in the future. By definition, saving is that part of income not spent on consumer goods (given that there are no taxes), so:

$$\text{total saving} = \text{total factor incomes} - \text{total consumption}$$

Putting these together, we see that

$$\text{total saving} = \text{total investment}$$

as the national incomes equation 5.17 requires. (Note: where it is clear from the context that we are referring to all households together, we drop the word 'total'.)

The saving of a single household does not necessarily equal that household's contribution to total investment because a household may borrow or lend, and may buy or sell used land and equipment. A household may invest more than it saves (by borrowing from others) or less than it saves (by lending). In addition, a household or firm might buy or sell used equipment, which changes its own stock of investment goods but does not change the total stock in the economy.

11.2.1 Macroeconomic equilibrium

A market economy (in which the government is small, and there is no foreign trade) is in **macroeconomic equilibrium** when desired saving equals desired investment.

Desired saving is the amount that households want to save, given their incomes, the prices (including prices of equipment and training courses) and the interest rate on loans. The decision on the level of desired saving is reached simultaneously with the decision on desired consumption. **Desired investment** is the amounts of newly produced equipment and training that are wanted, given the incomes that will be generated using them, and given the costs of obtaining them. These costs involve the prices of equipment and training, and the interest rate that must be paid on money borrowed to buy them.

When desired saving equals desired investment, the demands and supplies for land, equipment, skilled labour and loans are all in equilibrium. Thus macroeconomic equilibrium occurs as a part of the general equilibrium of a perfect market economy, in which all markets clear rapidly. So:

In a perfect market economy, macroeconomic equilibrium is established by the changes in prices of goods and of factors and in the interest rate.

In other economic systems, macroeconomic equilibrium can occur even if there is no general equilibrium: in particular, we shall see that when there are imperfections it is possible that desired saving and desired investment can be equal, even though markets for labour are not in equilibrium, and some people who want a job at the existing real wage cannot find one (see chapter 15). So its is useful later to distinguish macroeconomic equilibrium from general equilibrium, even though they do not occur separately in a perfect market economy.

11.2.2 Movement to equilibrium

If the economy is not in macroeconomic equilibrium, desired saving and desired investment are not equal. Suppose that desired saving exceeds desired investment. Households have money to lend for which they can find no borrower, or have assets (land, equipment or skill) which no firm wants to use. In a perfect market economy, the interest rate would fall, thus increasing the demand for loans and reducing the number of households that want to lend. The cost of using (the rent of equipment or land; the wage differential for skilled labour) the unused assets would fall, so that firms would want to use more of them. Markets would move towards equilibrium, and the whole economy would move towards macroeconomic equilibrium. The opposite process would occur if desired investment exceeded desired saving.

11.2.3 Net and gross saving and investment

We have not specified whether we are discussing net or gross investment (see section 5.6). Gross investment includes the replacement of worn-out equipment;

net investment does not. We can define a household's gross income to include money spent on replacing the worn-out equipment that it owns (including that which it owns because it owns shares in firms), and its net income as its gross income minus spending on replacements. Then a household's gross income is the total income that it receives; its net income is the amount that it has available to spend once it has replaced worn-out equipment. Then, gross saving is the part of gross income that is not spent on consumer goods including money saved to make replacements; net saving is the part of net income that is not spent on consumer goods excluding money saved to make replacements. When a market economy is in macroeconomic equilibrium desired gross saving equals desired gross investment, and desired net saving equals desired net investment.

11.3 Unemployment

When labour markets are in equilibrium, everyone who wants a job at the equilibrium wage can find one. So unemployment in a perfect market economy is one of the following:

(a) **Voluntary**, because some people do not want a job at the equilibrium wage. They have some other source of income, and the wage does not compensate them for loss of leisure, poor working conditions, or the need to move home to get a job.
(b) **Frictional** as people change jobs when the outputs of goods change. Frictional unemployment is very temporary in a perfect market economy because markets clear rapidly. It arises because of the effects of changes in tastes, the introduction of new methods of production and changes in skills as young workers enter the labour force and older workers retire from it. These changes imply that some firms in less profitable industries go out of business, and new firms enter more profitable industries (see section 8.6). It is improbable that workers who leave one firm can immediately take up a job elsewhere, but the information available in a perfect market economy implies that the delay is not long, because unemployed workers do not need to make a lengthy search for a job. Frictional unemployment is therefore the result of the fact that markets do not clear instantaneously, but it does not persist because they clear quickly. In other types of economy, changes in tastes, methods of production and skills can cause much longer-lasting structural unemployment (see section 6.2.5) because markets move slowly to equilibrium.

11.3.1 The movement to equilibrium

If the real wage of some type of labour is below its equilibrium level, the demand for that type exceeds the supply. Firms compete with each other to employ the available labour, the wage increases and the labour market moves towards equilibrium.

If the real wage of some type of labour exceeds its equilibrium level, the supply exceeds the demand, and some people who would like a job at that wage cannot find one. There is involuntary unemployment but in a perfect market economy this is eliminated by reductions in real wages. These occur because firms can employ workers even if they offer lower money wages, and firms do this to increase their profits. The wage reductions affect both new recruits and those who are already employed. If a worker who has a job does not agree to work for a lower wage, the firm can dismiss him or her, and employ one of the unemployed instead. This is possible in a perfect market economy, because there is no government legislation that limits the possibility of dismissals, or that requires redundancy payments to those who are dismissed. Also, there are no trades unions to resist wage reductions by collective action. It is difficult for most UK firms to reduce their workers' wages because of union activities and legislation.

Markets are interrelated, and the reductions in wages that remove involuntary unemployment have two other major effects:

(a) The incomes of workers fall, and this affects their demands for goods. Their demands for luxuries fall considerably; their demands for necessities fall by a smaller percentage than their incomes have fallen; their demands for inferior goods increase (see section 9.3). These changes in demands affect the prices of these goods. In addition, households are likely to save less. This increases the interest rate and reduces the demands for investment goods, so that the prices of these goods fall also.

(b) Profits increase when firms' costs fall, and so new firms enter industries. This increases the demand for factors of production. The incomes of the owners of land and equipment rise, and there are changes in the demands for goods bought by these people. If those who receive incomes from rent and profit save a greater proportion of their incomes than wage-earners (as seems to be the case in fact), the supply of loans and the demands for investment goods increase. The interest rate falls, and prices of investment goods increase.

These changes lead to further changes in demands and supplies, but although there are many consequences of a change in wages these changes occur rapidly in a perfect market economy, and the economy reaches a general equilibrium. We can conclude that:

In a perfect market economy involuntary unemployment is eliminated by movements of the prices of goods and factors and of the interest rate to their general equilibrium levels.

11.4 Economic growth

The major influences on the rate of economic growth were listed in section 6.4: here we discuss three of them in the context of a perfect market economy.

11.4.1 Investment in new equipment

An increase in desired saving increases:

(a) The demand for land, equipment and training courses by those who save by buying investment goods.
(b) The supply of factors available to firms.
(c) The supply of loans.

The increase in the supply of loans reduces interest rates and so it is cheaper to borrow to buy more equipment. This increase in the demand for equipment leads to an increase in the price of new equipment, and the increase in saving reduces the demand for, and the price of, consumer goods. So it becomes relatively more profitable to produce investment goods than to produce consumer goods, and new firms enter investment goods industries. So:

> The output of investment goods and the rate of economic growth increase in a perfect market economy if households decide to save more.

This argument is similar to that which established consumers' sovereignty when people demand more of one consumer good and less of another. The pattern of production changes in response to a change in tastes. The increase in saving is a change in tastes that involves a desire to consume less now and more at some time in the future, and the additional investment implies that it is possible to produce more consumer goods in the future to meet this increased demand. So consumers are sovereign in that the pattern of production reflects their preferences about when goods are consumed, as well as their preferences about which goods they consume.

11.4.2 Education

People retrain in order to take a higher-paying job (see section 10.6). The amount of retraining increases if workers reduce their demands for consumer goods and save more. When the demand for training courses increases, the fee charged for a course increases, and so the profits of schools and colleges that provide training courses increase. This attracts others to set up schools and colleges and so the output of training courses increases in response to the increase in demand. This argument is similar to that on the increase in the demand for equipment: if households want higher incomes in the future, and are prepared to consume less now, the demand for training increases. The labour force becomes better trained, and so it is possible to increase outputs in the future.

11.4.3 Spread of new technology

There is freedom of action and perfect information in a perfect market economy. No one is prevented from copying another person's invention either by law (such as a patent or copyright) or by lack of information. Anyone who has the necessary ability can use any method of production. This freedom to copy helps to ensure that people specialize according to their comparative advantages. If an inventor can prevent others from using his invention, he may prevent specialization by those who have a comparative advantage in using the invention.

The use of a more efficient method of production reduces a firm's costs, and attracts new firms into the industry. Any firm that does not use the new method makes a lower profit than its competitors because its costs are higher. In the long run, those that do not use the new method of production make less than normal profit and leave the industry. So, the rate of **diffusion** of new inventions (that is, the rate at which the use of a new invention spreads throughout an industry) is increased because firms must introduce the new method to survive.

The preceding arguments appear to imply that patents reduce the rate of economic growth because they prevent firms from introducing a new method. However, this ignores the incentive to invent: people may be more inclined to become inventors if they can benefit from their inventions by limiting the use of the more efficient technology to their own firm to prevent other firms from entering the industry to compete away the supernormal profits that arise from the use of the new method. The lack of this incentive to invent in a perfect market economy may reduce the rate of economic growth, and it may offset some or all of the advantages of the rapid diffusion of inventions.

11.5 Price level and inflation

Inflation is an increase in the **price level** (which is the average level of prices), and so any discussion of the causes of inflation requires a discussion of the determinants of the price level. In a market economy, prices are determined by supply and demand and, assuming that no one experiences money illusion (see section 6.2.4), the following are true:

(a) Each household's demands for goods depend only on prices relative to its income. If the prices of all goods double, and the household's money income doubles, its demands do not change.
(b) Each household's labour supply decision depends on real wages. Again, if the prices of all goods double, and the money wage doubles, the household's labour supply decision is unchanged.
(c) Each firm's decisions to supply goods depend on the relative profitability of different industries. If the prices of all goods and factors double, the relative profitability of different industries is unchanged, and firms' decisions to produce, to enter markets or to exit from them are unchanged.
(d) Each firm's demands for factors depend on real factor prices (including the real wage for labour). If all prices and all factor prices double, demands for factors are unchanged.

These points imply that an analysis of demands and supplies for goods and factors does not determine the average price level: it determines only relative prices of goods and factors.

11.5.1 Supply and demand for money

In a perfect market economy the price level is determined by the interaction between the amount of money available for use, which is the **supply of money**, and the amount that people and firms want, which is the **demand for money**.

The factors influencing the supply of money depend on whether money is privately produced (for example, by firms that produce gold: see section 3.5) or is supplied by the government. If money is privately produced, the supply depends on the profitability of producing it. If (as is the case in the UK) money is supplied by the government, the amount supplied depends on the reasons that the government has for supplying it. These reasons are, in practice, closely related to government policies that are designed to affect the outcome of the economy, and we shall discuss these in part IV. Until then we do not discuss the determinants of the supply of money by the government, or even what the supply of money really is (which is a matter of great controversy in practice).

11.5.2 Transactions demand for money

Households do not buy all the goods that they want immediately they receive their incomes, and firms do not pay for factors immediately they receive revenues from selling goods. So households and firms hold money to make their day-to-day transactions: this is known as the **transactions demand for money**. The transactions demand depends on:

(a) The quantities of goods that people want to buy. If there is economic growth, so that more goods are produced, households need more money to finance the additional purchases.
(b) The prices of those goods. If the price level increases, households need more money to finance a given number of purchases.

There are other reasons for holding money in practice, particularly when people are uncertain about the future, so that they hold money in case there is an emergency or an unforeseen opportunity to buy something at a low price. The assumption of perfect information eliminates these other reasons from a perfect market economy. We return to them in chapter 14.7.

11.5.3 Price level and the supply of money

When all markets are in general equilibrium, the supply and demand for all goods are equal, and all households and firms hold the amounts of money that they need to finance their transactions. The equality of the demand and supply of money is achieved as follows:

(a) If households have more money than they want, the supply of money exceeds the demand, and households get rid of the surplus money by demanding goods. The demands for some goods increase, and their prices rise, so that the price level increases. This increase in the price level increases the demand for money. Prices continue to increase until the demand for money equals the supply of money.

(b) If households have less money than they want, the demand for money exceeds the supply, and households increase the amount of money that they hold by reducing their purchases of goods. So the prices of goods fall, which reduces the demand for money, and this continues until the demand for money is reduced to equal the supply.

So:

In a perfect market economy, the equilibrium price level is achieved by changes in the prices of goods and factors that make the demand for money equal to the supply.

11.5.4 Quantity equation

We can represent this relation between the price level and the supply of money using the **quantity equation**. This relates the total value of transactions in the economy to the supply of money, allowing for the possibility that each unit of money in the economy may be used several times in a year. The quantity equation is:

$$MV = PT \qquad\qquad (11.5)$$

where M is the supply of money, V is the **velocity of circulation of money** (which is the average number of times that a unit of money is used in a period), P is the price level and T is the number of transactions in the period.

The velocity of circulation of money (V) depends on:

(a) The average time that households hold a unit of money between receiving it and spending it on goods or lending it. This time may be measured roughly by the average amounts that households keep in their bank cheque (or current) accounts. If these amounts increase, households are, on average, holding more money and delaying buying (or at least delaying paying for) goods, and so the velocity of circulation falls.

(b) The average time that firms hold money between receiving it as revenue and paying it as an income or for materials.

If either of these average times increases, the velocity of circulation falls, because each unit of money is used, on average, less often.

The number of transactions that occur depends on the ways in which goods are produced and sold. If partly finished goods are sold from one firm to another, and if finished goods are sold by the producer to a wholesaler, and from the wholesaler to a retailer, the number of transactions (and the amount of money needed to finance them) is greater than if one firm produces and sells the good. However, it is generally true that if more goods are produced more transactions occur.

The quantity equation, as we have stated it, is always true in any economy (it is a tautology). If money is used for other purposes, each unit of money may be used infrequently to finance a transaction, but this is reflected in the velocity of circulation. So, if 25 million transactions occur (T) in a year, at an average price (P) of £6, and if the supply of money (M) is £30 million, then

$$V = \frac{PT}{M} = \frac{6 \times 25{,}000{,}000}{30{,}000{,}000} = 5$$

Each unit of money is used, on average, five times in the year to finance transactions.

11.6 Inflation and the quantity theory of money

The quantity equation has been used for many years (at least since the sixteenth century) to explain the price level and the inflation rate, which is the change in the price level. The equation is used in the **quantity theory of money**. The simplest form of this theory explains the inflation rate by making the following assumptions:

(a) The average number of times that a unit of money is used to make transactions does not change, so that V is constant.
(b) The number of transactions is proportional to the quantity of goods produced, so that T increases at the rate of economic growth.

Given these assumptions, changes in P are explained by changes in M and by the rate of economic growth. If the supply of money increases, MV rises and so there must be a corresponding increase in PT to maintain the quantity equation. The increase in PT is partly due to economic growth, which increases T, and partly due to inflation, which increases P. Then, at the start of a period (say a year):

$$MV = PT \qquad\qquad\qquad (11.5)$$

and at the end of the year:

$$[M(1 + m)]V = [P(1 + i)][T(1 + g)] \qquad\qquad\qquad (11.6)$$

where $m \times 100$ is the percentage increase in the supply of money in the year (so that, for example, $m = 0.1$ implies a 10 per cent increase), $g \times 100$ is the percentage rate of economic growth in the year (and percentage rate of increase of T) and $i \times 100$ is the percentage inflation rate in the year.
   Dividing equation 11.6 by equation 11.5 gives:

$$(1 + m) = (1 + i)(1 + g) \qquad\qquad\qquad (11.7)$$

and

$$i = (m - g)/(1 + g) \qquad\qquad\qquad (11.8)$$

When the annual rate of economic growth (g) is within the range usually experienced (the UK annual rate of economic growth has not exceeded 8 per cent, and has averaged 2.3 per cent in the period since 1951; see figure 6.5), equation 11.4 implies that i is almost equal to $(m - g)$, so that, according to the quantity theory of money:

> The annual inflation rate is approximately equal to the annual rate of increase of the supply of money minus the annual rate of economic growth.

This conclusion can be stated in two other ways:

(a) If there is no economic growth, the inflation rate equals the rate of increase of the supply of money.
(b) If there is to be no change in the price level, the supply of money must increase at the rate of economic growth.

The two assumptions of the quantity theory of money may be open to question in various ways. For example:

(a) V may not be constant because the income distribution changes. If Alan spends his income as soon as it is paid, whereas Bill delays many of his purchases, V increases if Alan's income rises and Bill's falls because, on average, each unit of money is held for a shorter period between transactions.
(b) T may not change in proportion to outputs because some industries involve more transactions than others. In some industries there are many transactions of intermediate goods, and transactions between producers, wholesalers and retailers. In others there are fewer transactions because the good is produced by a single firm and sold by that firm direct to households. For example, the production of beef may involve the sale of calves from one farmer to another, the sale of cows to an abattoir, the sale of meat to a wholesale butcher, then to a retailer, and from the retailer to households. The production of oil, on the other hand, may involve few transactions, because a single firm extracts and refines the crude oil, and sells the refined products to households. If the economic growth occurs because the output of beef increases, the number of transactions increases by more than if economic growth occurs because the output of oil increases.

The quantity theory of money is open to further objections when we consider uncertainty and other imperfections, because people may hold money for purposes other than making predictable day-to-day transactions. However, the quantity theory of money is often used as an approximate guide to the inflation rate, given the increase in the supply of money and the rate of economic growth – and it has been very influential on some policy-makers, as we shall see in chapter 21.

11.7 Perfect market economies and the real world

Why have we studied a perfect market economy in detail, given that it involves many unrealistic assumptions? There are several answers to this question:

(a) A perfect market economy is an aid to understanding because the assumptions of the system simplify the discussion of the ways in which individual decisions interrelate. Without these simplifications, it would be difficult to build up the analysis of more complex, and more realistic, market and mixed economies.
(b) A perfect market economy is a point of comparison that we can use to discuss the effects of imperfections knowing that a perfect market economy is efficient and that there is no involuntary unemployment. The income distribution in a perfect market economy may be just or unjust, according to the value judgement that we make. So we can discuss the extent to which imperfections can lead to inefficiency and unemployment, and improve or make worse the income distribution compared with a perfect system.
(c) Some government policies are based on the assumption that the conclusions of this chapter on macroeconomic aspects of a perfect market economy remain valid even when there are imperfections. These policies are supported by the method of market analysis that we discuss below.
(d) The efficiency of a perfect market economy justifies some government policies. In chapter 19, in particular, we shall discuss policies that are designed to remove or reduce imperfections to gain some of the advantages of the efficiency of a perfect market economy.

11.7.1 Method of market analysis

The main contribution of the analysis of a perfect market economy to the analysis of macroeconomic aspects of other economic systems is **market analysis**. Whenever we use it:

> Market analysis assumes that markets clear rapidly after a change that affects supply or demand in any market.

Using market analysis, any change in supply or demand (such as a change in households' tastes, in methods of production, in government policy, or in the demands for exports) leads to changes in the prices of goods, in wages, in rents and in interest rates that restore a general equilibrium. Firms respond to changes in the profitability of industries by leaving those that have become less profitable and entering those that have become more profitable, until there is no further incentive for entry or exit. When we use market analysis later in this book, we retain the conclusions derived in this chapter, even though we are no longer examining perfect market economies:

(a) Macroeconomic equilibrium is brought about by changes in prices and interest rates. If households decide to save more, the supply of loans increases and interest rates fall, which causes an increase in investment, and an increase in the rate of economic growth.
(b) Involuntary unemployment is temporary, and is reduced when real wages fall. This reduction in involuntary unemployment is the result of market forces: the presence of unemployment permits employers to offer lower wages, and this increases the demand for labour. Markets clear rapidly, and so government policy is not needed to reduce unemployment, except perhaps temporarily.
(c) The inflation rate is related to increases in the supply of money (at least approximately) according to the quantity theory of money. So the government can reduce the inflation rate by reducing the rate of increase of the supply of money.
(d) Firms enter and leave industries easily according to the relative profitability of different opportunities open to them, and so there is consumers' sovereignty when tastes change.

11.7.2 Perfect market economies and government policies

Market analysis based on a perfect market economy supports the use of some policies, including:

(a) Control of the supply of money, to control inflation.
(b) Intervention to reduce imperfections as far as possible, particularly to increase freedom of action by removing government and other restrictions, and to reduce the influence of some firms and trades unions that are not small.

The analysis of a perfect market economy may also lead to support for measures to change the income distribution if it is felt that, without intervention, the system would lead to unacceptable poverty.

One difficulty with the use of policies to control imperfections, and/or to change an unacceptable income distribution, is that the use of the policies requires that the government is not small, which is itself an imperfection. If the government employs a significant number of civil servants to control imperfections and/or to redistribute incomes, the government has an important influence on wages. If the government levies taxes on goods and on people's incomes, it can affect the combinations of goods that people want to buy and the number of hours that they want to work (see section 20.3). If it makes transfer payments to change the income distribution, the government may affect decisions on work and leisure, because some people choose not to work but to receive transfer payments instead (see section 20.3.1). So government policies may themselves cause inefficiency, because they make the economic system less perfect.

11.8 Summary

In a perfect market economy, macroeconomic equilibrium is established by changes in prices that establish market equilibrium and by changes in the interest rate that clear the market for loans.

Any unemployment that is not voluntary is quickly removed by changes in real wages that clear labour markets.

The rate of economic growth is determined by the amounts that households want to save. This saving leads to an equal volume of investment in equipment and training, and the additional investment increases the potential to produce goods in the future.

The price level is determined by the volume of transactions, the velocity of circulation and the supply of money, as described by the quantity equation. If the velocity of circulation is approximately constant, and the volume of transactions increases approximately at the rate of economic growth, then the inflation rate is approximately equal to the rate of increase of the supply of money minus the rate of economic growth.

The outcome of a perfect market economy provides a justification for the use of policies to remove or reduce imperfections. The analysis of a perfect market economy is the basis of the use of market analysis of macroeconomic aspects of other economic systems.

Topics and problems

(1) Is any existing unemployment in the UK voluntary or frictional? What might prevent real wages from changing to reduce the amount of unemployment?
(2) Is it desirable for inventors to hold patents on goods? Is it desirable for authors (or publishers) to have copyrights on books and other material? How would the abolition of patents and copyrights affect the UK economy?
(3) How, if at all, can the government remove or reduce the imperfections that arise from imperfect information?
(4) How is the velocity of circulation likely to be affected by:

A change from weekly to monthly payment of wages
The introduction of electronic banking from the home, using computers and telecommunications equipment
The increased use of credit cards?

Part III

Imperfections and macroeconomic analysis

The model of the perfect market that we developed in part II is useful because it allows us to isolate important features of supplies, demands and their interactions. However, many of its assumptions appear to be highly unrealistic. In this part we examine market economies in which firms and trades unions have market influence, in which households and firms react to uncertainty, and in which markets do not necessarily move rapidly to equilibrium. We shall continue to ignore the activities of the government until part IV.

We see in this part that a number of conclusions from part II may not hold when there are imperfections: in particular, we develop different theories (based on the existence of imperfections) of macroeconomic equilibrium, unemployment and inflation from those of chapter 11. These alternative theories (together with those of chapter 11) form an important foundation for the analysis in part IV of government policies designed to reduce unemployment or inflation.

Chapter Twelve

Monopoly and market influence

Sources of monopoly power — pricing and output decisions of a monopolist — monopoly and resource allocation — distribution and discrimination — monopolistic competition — market influence and wages

12.1 Introduction

Many industries in the UK and elsewhere do not have a perfectly competitive market structure because one or other of the following imperfections occurs:

(a) Some firms are large enough to influence the prices at which they sell their outputs.
(b) There are restrictions on the entry of new firms to an industry.

The extent of these two imperfections defines the extent to which the market structure differs from perfect competition. In this chapter and in chapter 14 we consider three alternative market structures to add to the perfectly competitive market structure discussed in chapter 8:

(a) **Monopoly.** There is a single supplier of the good who has no actual or threatening rivals. Firms are not free to enter the market, and the single firm can influence the price in the market.
(b) **Monopolistic competition.** Each firm can influence its selling price, the entry of new firms is not restricted, and each firm makes its decisions on pricing and output assuming that its competitors do not change their prices or outputs in response to its own actions.
(c) **Oligopoly.** There is more than one firm, and the pricing and output decisions of each firm are greatly influenced by the decisions of other firms in the market. Each firm believes that its competitors may change their prices and/or outputs in response to its own decision, and in turn may want to respond to these reactions of its rivals. New firms can attempt to enter an oligopolistic market, and existing firms may try to prevent them.

We examine monopoly and monopolistic competition in this chapter; we shall look at oligopoly in the next.

12.2 Sources of monopoly power

The first market structure that we investigate is monopoly. A single firm produces all of a particular good, and so its supply is equal to the market supply. Such a firm has no competitors within its market, and the only restriction on its sales is the extent of market demand for its product. If the firm wants to sell more, it must cut its price, but does not need to worry about what any rival might do. In practice, there are substitutes for all goods, and so no firm can act as a completely isolated monopolist, but we can discuss the effects of market influence and of restrictions on the entry of new firms most simply in a market where there is a single producer.

Monopolies can arise and be maintained in the face of other firms that would like to enter the industry in a variety of ways:

(a) Some goods can be produced only in a single place. For example, a person may own the only land suitable for building a port, the only known source of some useful mineral, or every access route to a tourist attraction.

(b) Many firms produce goods for which they have legally enforcable patents, or they produce under licence, paying a fee or royalty to the patent holder. Composers, writers and painters (or their publishers) have monopolies over their products that are protected by copyright law. So you should not be reading this from a photocopy! Patents and copyrights are not necessarily easy to maintain: they can be defended in court actions, but this takes time. In the USA, for example, there have been many years of legal argument between Polaroid and Kodak over patents used in the production of cameras that produce instant pictures.

(c) A **natural monopoly** arises if it is possible to produce a good only in a complex factory, or after the installation of a large amount of equipment (a telephone network or electricity grid, for example). It would be very wasteful of the nation's resources to have more than one firm supplying such a good. For example, water, gas and electricity supply are often regarded as natural monopolies because it would be very wasteful to have two or more sets of pipes or cables in every street in the country. Many natural monopolies were nationalized in the UK after the Second World War, and some have recently been privatized again (see section 19.3.3).

(d) A private firm may be able to preserve a monopoly, particularly if a large amount of equipment is necessary in production, by threatening a price-cutting war if another firm enters the market. The existing firm can increase production quite cheaply because it has already bought the necessary equipment, and so it can reduce the price to a level at which the new entrant would make a loss. The existing firm can increase the costs of entry further if it advertises, so that the new entrant must advertise to establish its brand name.

12.3 Pricing and output decision of a monopolist

A firm maximizes its profit when its output is at the level where marginal
revenue equals marginal cost. The argument for this is the same as in section
8.5.

12.3.1 Revenues of a monopolist

The major differences between the diagram representing the costs and revenues
of a perfectly competitive firm (figure 8.4) and that representing those of a
monopolist are the revenue curves:

(a) A monopolist can affect its selling price by changing the quantity that it
    offers for sale. It faces a downward-sloping demand curve (which is the
    market demand curve) because it can sell more only if it reduces the price.
(b) A firm in perfect competition can sell any amount that it can produce
    without affecting the market price, and so its average revenue and marginal
    revenue curves coincide and are horizontal.

The definitions of total, average and marginal revenue are the same as in
section 8.2:

(a) Total revenue is the quantity sold $\times$ the selling price.
(b) Average revenue is the selling price. The average revenue from quantity
    X is the price at which consumers demand X.
(c) Marginal revenue is the addition to total revenue from the sale of one
    more unit.

Table 12.1 gives a monopolist's demand schedule. The demand curve (which
is the same as the average revenue curve) and the marginal revenue curve are
shown in figure 12.1. (Note that marginal revenue is below average revenue,
and that average revenue falls as output increases exactly as in the discussion
of the relation between average cost and marginal cost in section 8.3.4.)

Table 12.1 Demand schedule for a monopolist

Sales	Price	Total revenue	Marginal revenue
1	40	40	38
2	39	78	33
3	37	111	25
4	34	136	14
5	30	150	0
6	25	150	−17
7	19	133	−37
8	12	96	−60
9	4	36	

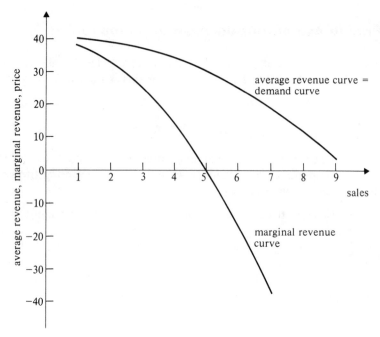

Figure 12.1   Average and marginal revenue curves for the monopolist of table 12.1

The marginal revenue is less than the average revenue because the sale of an extra unit requires a reduction in the price of all units sold.

12.3.2 Marginal revenue and price-elasticity of demand

The extent to which a firm must reduce its price to sell more depends on the price-elasticity of demand for the good:

(a) If the price-elasticity of demand is 1, a 1 per cent increase in price leads to a 1 per cent fall in demand, so that there is no change in total revenue and marginal revenue is zero. This is illustrated in table 12.1 by the increase in price from 25 to 30 (a 20 per cent rise) and the fall in sales from 6 to 5 (a 20 per cent fall, in that 1 is 20 per cent of 5).

(b) If the price-elasticity of demand exceeds 1, a 1 per cent price fall causes an increase of more than 1 per cent in demand. So consumers spend more on the good and total revenue increases when additional goods are sold, and marginal revenue is positive. This is illustrated by sales of less than 5 units in table 12.1.

(c) If the price-elasticity of demand is less than 1, a 1 per cent price fall causes an increase of less than 1 per cent in demand. So consumers spend less on the good and total revenue falls when additional goods are sold, and marginal revenue is negative. This is illustrated by sales of more than 5 units in table 12.1.

So:

Marginal revenue is positive if price-elasticity of demand exceeds 1.

Box 7 shows the mathematical derivation of this conclusion.

12.3.3 Cost for a monopolist

The reasoning that led to a U-shaped short-run average cost curve for a perfectly competitive firm remains plausible when firms are not small. At low levels of output, the production of an additional unit spreads the fixed costs more widely, but further increases in output eventually involve variable costs that increase more rapidly than output. A large firm may dominate the market for some of its materials and factors, so that it can buy in bulk, and this contributes to a reduction in its average cost when output increases.

Box 7   Marginal revenue and price-elasticity of demand

Suppose that a firm can sell Q units at price P', and $Q + 1$ units at price P. If it sells Q

$$\text{total revenue} = P'Q$$

If it sells $Q + 1$

$$\text{total revenue} = P(Q + 1)$$

So

$$\text{marginal revenue, } MR = [P(Q + 1)] - (P'Q)$$

and so

$$MR = P - (P' - P)Q \tag{12.1}$$

If the price rises from P to P', demand falls from $Q + 1$ to Q. The percentage change in price is $100(P' - P)/P$, and the percentage change in demand is $-100(1/Q)$, (this has a minus sign, because demand falls when the price increases from P to P'), so that

$$\text{price-elasticity of demand, } E = -(1/Q)/[(P' - P)/P]$$
$$= -P/[Q(P' - P)]$$

Therefore

$$(P' - P)Q = P/E \tag{12.2}$$

Combining equations 12.1 and 12.2 gives

$$MR = P - P/E = P(1 - 1/E).$$

So if E is large, $1/E$ is small, and marginal revenue is almost equal to the price. If E is small, $1/E$ is large, and so marginal revenue is considerably less than the price, and is negative if the price-elasticity of demand is less than 1.

12.3.4 Profit maximizing

A firm maximizes its profit when its marginal cost equals its marginal revenue (see section 8.5). In figure 12.2, the firm maximizes supernormal profit at output X because marginal revenue equals marginal cost. The monopolist sells this quantity at price Y (which equals average revenue), and its average cost including normal profit is Z. Its total supernormal profit is YZ × OX, which is area ZYVW.

In the long run, other firms want to enter the market to share in this supernormal profit, but the monopoly restriction prevents them from doing so. Therefore, in contrast with a perfectly competitive firm whose short-run supernormal profit is competed away (see section 8.6.2):

A monopolist can make a positive supernormal profit in the long run.

A monopolist's long-run average cost may be less than his short-run average cost because, in the long run, he can change the amount of all of his factors, including those (such as land and equipment) that are fixed in the short run.

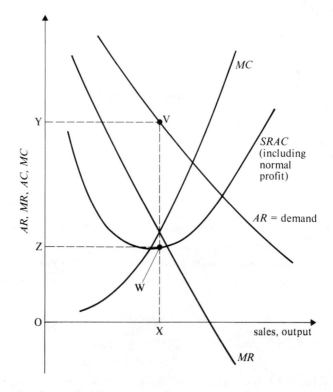

Figure 12.2   Profit-maximizing output for a monopolist
The monopolist produces output X where marginal cost equals marginal revenue. Supernormal profit is ZYVW.

The monopolist does this if he increases his profit by doing so, and so he may make more supernormal profit in the long run than in the short run.

12.4 Monopoly and resource allocation

A monopolist does not produce the output that minimizes his average cost unless, by coincidence, the marginal revenue curve passes through the lowest point of the average cost curve (at R in figure 12.3(a)). In figure 12.3(b), the profit-maximizing output S exceeds Q, which minimizes average cost. In figure 12.3(c), the profit-maximizing output Z is less than P, which minimizes average cost. In figure 12.3(b), it is technically possible for two firms each to produce output V, which is half of the monopolist's profit-maximizing output S. If two firms each produce V, the average cost is W, which is less than the monopolist's average cost X. However, the technical possibility of reducing average cost is prevented by the monopoly restriction, and this diagram illustrates the possibility that:

A monopolist may use more resources than are technically necessary to produce its output.

In figure 12.3(c), average cost is lower if output is Y, where the firm makes no supernormal profit, than if output is at the profit-maximizing level Z. This diagram illustrates the possibility that:

A monopolist may produce at a higher average cost than would arise if it produced the output that gives zero supernormal profit.

12.4.1 Monopoly and consumers' sovereignty

In a perfect market system consumers are sovereign in that output levels respond to a change in demand, and firms gain no long-run benefit from the change in tastes. Firms enter industries producing goods for which demand has increased, firms leave industries producing goods for which demand has fallen, and this process continues until supernormal profits have been eliminated.

This does not occur when there is a monopoly producer of a good. Figure 12.4 shows the effects of an increase in the demand for the good produced by a monopolist. The demand curve shifts from DD to D'D', and this increases total revenue and marginal revenue at each output. The marginal revenue curve shifts from EE to E'E', and the profit-maximizing output increases from Q to Q'. The selling price increases from S to S', the average cost changes from T to T' and supernormal profit changes from TSUV to T'S'U'V'. The following argument shows that the firm makes more supernormal profit.

(a) The firm could sell the output Q at price W after the increase in demand and, if it were to do this, its supernormal profit would be TWXV. W exceeds S, and so

TWXV exceeds TSUV

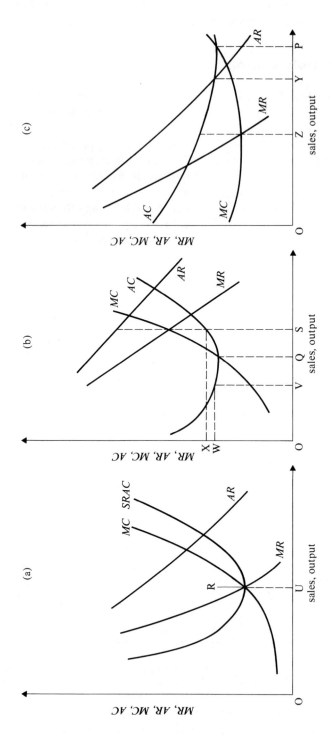

Figure 12.3 Monopoly and average cost

(a) coincidental case of minimized average cost (b) case in which two producers, each producing V (where OV = VS), could have a lower average cost than the monopolist producing at S (c) case in which average cost would be lower if there were no supernormal profit (output P compared to profit maximizing output Z).

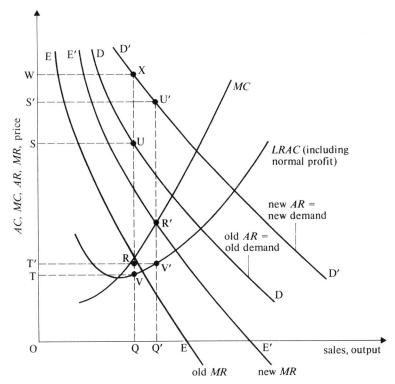

Figure 12.4 Monopolist's response to an increase in demand
The demand curve shifts from DD to D'D', so that the marginal revenue curve shifts
from EE to E'E'. Profit-maximizing output increases from Q to Q', and supernormal
profit increases from TSUV to T'S'U'V'.

(b) The maximum supernormal profit after the increase in demand is T'S'U'V',
     and this exceeds the possible profit TWXV, so that

$$\text{T'S'U'V' exceeds TWXV}$$

Therefore

$$\text{T'S'U'V' exceeds TSUV}$$

and so the firm's supernormal profit increases. A monopolist can limit the
extent to which output increases, and so restrict consumers' sovereignty, by
increasing the price of the good to gain more supernormal profit. So:

An economic system that includes firms with monopoly power is not as
responsive to changes in demand as is a perfect market system.

12.5 Distribution and discrimination

A monopolist is plainly able to influence the income distribution in its own
favour by using its monopoly power to make a positive supernormal profit in

the long run. The ability to exclude other firms is a valuable asset that gives the monopolist an income. Figure 12.5 shows the extent to which the monopolist gains and consumers lose, compared to a situation in which output is A where average revenue equals average cost (including normal profit), so that there is no supernormal profit:

(a) The firm's supernormal profit is area CDEF when output is B, and zero when output is A.
(b) The consumer's surplus (see section 9.9) is area DEP when output is B and is area GHP when output is A.

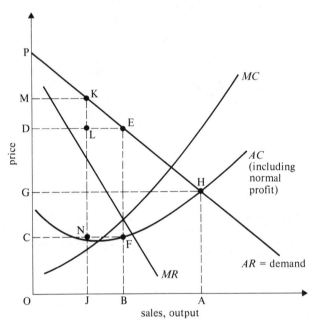

Figure 12.5 Gains from price discrimination
If the monopolist does not discriminate, consumer's surplus is DPE, supernormal profit is CDEF. If it discriminates, consumer's surplus is reduced by DMKL, and supernormal profit is increased by DMKL.

12.5.1 Price discrimination

A firm **discriminates** between customers if it sells to some at a higher price than to others, even though the cost of producing the good is the same whoever consumes it. For example, in figure 12.5, if the monopolist can sell quantity J at price M, and the remainder of quantity B at price D, its revenue is OMKJ + JLEB. Its supernormal profit in this case is CMKN + NLEF, which exceeds the maximum supernormal profit CDEF that it can achieve if it does not discriminate between customers. The gain in supernormal profit is DMKL. The consumers' surplus is reduced by DMKL, because the price discrimination implies that consumers pay this amount extra to buy the total quantity B. So:

Price discrimination implies greater supernormal profit and lower consumers' surplus.

A firm can discriminate between customers if it is not possible for one customer to resell the good to another. So, for example, British Gas can charge its domestic customers a different price from its industrial customers because it is (virtually) impossible (and also illegal) for industrial customers to supply gas to houses. Similarly, British Rail can sell tickets more cheaply to an identifiable group, such as pensioners, who cannot resell the tickets to younger people because pensioners can be identified, if necessary, by their birth certificates. However, a bookshop cannot sell copies of this book more cheaply to pensioners than to other people, because any other buyer could persuade a pensioner to buy the book for him or her at the lower price. So booksellers cannot discriminate between customers by selling to different groups at different prices.

12.5.2 Profit maximizing by a discriminating monopolist

Figure 12.5 illustrates a possible output and pricing scheme for a firm that discriminates between two groups (those who pay M and those who pay D), but it does not necessarily represent the firm's profit-maximizing output and pricing decisions. In general, if a firm can divide its market into several submarkets, it achieves the maximum supernormal profit when the marginal revenue in each submarket equals the marginal cost of production. The firm sells the same good in each submarket, and the cost of producing an additional unit is the same wherever that unit is sold. Marginal cost is the same in all submarkets, so that:

A discriminating monopolist achieves maximum supernormal profit when marginal revenue is the same in all submarkets, and is equal to marginal cost.

The output and pricing decisions for a discriminating monopolist are illustrated in figure 12.6. The demand curves and the marginal revenue curves in the two submarkets are shown in figure 12.6(a) and (b). Curve AA in figure 12.6(c) is constructed by adding the sales in the two submarkets for each marginal revenue, given that marginal revenue is the same in the two submarkets. For example, when marginal revenue is $O_cB = O_aU = O_bT$, the firm sells D in submarket 1 and C in submarket 2. Total sales for this marginal revenue are E, where

$$O_cE = O_aD + O_bC$$

If the firm produces output H in figure 12.6(c), and sells F in submarket 1 and G in submarket 2 (where $O_cH = O_aF + O_bG$), then marginal revenue is the same in the two submarkets and marginal revenue in each submarket equals marginal cost.

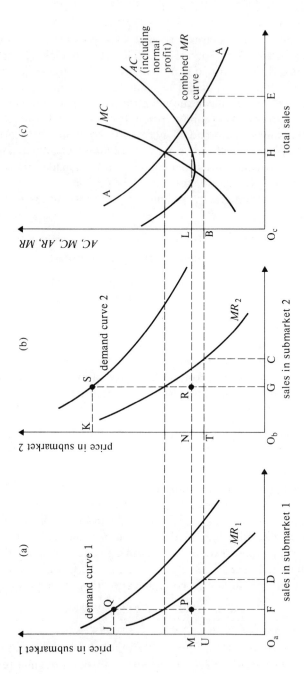

Figure 12.6 Profit-maximizing decisions of a discriminating monopolist

Curve AA is the sum of the sales in the two submarkets at each marginal revenue. The profit-maximizing output is H, selling F in submarket 1 and G in submarket 2. Total supernormal profit is MJQP + NKSR.

The demand curves in figures 12.6(a) and 12.6(b) show that the firm can sell F at price J in submarket 1, G at price K in submarket 2. So the price in submarket 1 is lower than that in submarket 2.

The average cost of production (including normal profit) is L, and so the supernormal profit per unit sold in submarket 1 is JM. The total supernormal profit in that submarket is JM $\times$ O_aF = MJQP and, similarly, in submarket 2 total supernormal profit is NKSR.

Box 8 derives the inverse elasticity rule for a discriminating monopolist, which shows that the profit-maximizing policy involves charging a higher price in a submarket with a lower price-elasticity of demand. This is intuitively reasonable, because a higher price will discourage many buyers if the price-elasticity of demand is high. The rule also implies that price discrimination is profitable only if the price-elasticity of demand at a given price is different in two (or more) submarkets.

Box 8   Inverse elasticity rule for a discriminating monopolist

We saw in box 7 that

$$MR = P(1 - 1/E)$$

A discriminating monopolist who charges two prices, P_1 and P_2, in two submarkets maximizes profits when

$$MR_1 = MR_2$$

so that

$$P_1(1 - 1/E_1) = P_2(1 - 1/E_2)$$

where E_1 and E_2 are the price-elasticities of demand in the two submarkets. So if E_1 exceeds E_2, P_2 exceeds P_1, and:

The customers in the submarket with the higher price-elasticity of demand pay the lower price.

For example, if $E_1 = 3$ and $E_2 = 2$, $P_1 = (3/4)P_2$.

12.6 Monopolistic competition

In a monopolistically competitive industry:

(a) There are many firms, each of which has some market influence, but none of which is very much larger than the average firm.
(b) New firms are free to enter the market, and existing firms are free to leave the market.

For example, the market for private education in the UK satisfies these conditions: there are many schools and the barriers to the entry of new schools to the market are not significant. Monopolistic competition generally involves firms that produce similar but not identical products. Firms **differentiate** their products from one another by producing their own brands or by operating in different places. A firm may advertise its brand to try to establish **brand loyalty** so that it does not lose all its customers if other firms reduce their selling prices. Consumers remain loyal if they believe that the difference between brands justifies paying a higher price.

To simplify the analysis of a monopolistically competitive firm, we make an assumption about the way in which firms behave:

> Each firm makes its pricing and output decision assuming that other firms do not change their prices.

So each firm has an **assumed demand curve**, such as DD in figure 12.7, and the price-elasticity of demand of this curve depends on the extent of brand loyalty. If customers are very loyal, few buy other brands if the firm increases its price, and so the curve DD is inelastic. If they are not very loyal, the firm's demand falls considerably if it increases its price, and curve DD is elastic.

Although there are some differences between their brands, all firms are likely to behave in similar ways if there is a change in market demand or in conditions of supply (such as the prices of materials and factors) that affect all firms. So if one firm has an incentive to reduce or increase its price, all firms

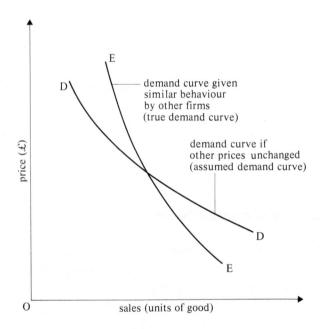

Figure 12.7 Two demand curves for a monopolistic competitor
The assumed demand curve DD reflects the firm's assumption that other firms do not change their prices. The actual demand curve EE reflects the fact that all firms behave similarly.

have a similar incentive. If all firms change their prices, the assumption used to draw the assumed demand curve DD for a firm is untrue. If many firms change their price when one does, then:

(a) The gain in sales from a price reduction is less than the firm assumes, because all other firms reduce their prices.
(b) The loss of sales from a price increase is less than the firm assumes, because all other firms increase their prices.

Curve EE in figure 12.7 represents the **actual demand curve** faced by a firm, given that all other firms change their prices in the same proportion. This represents the firm's share of the market demand. For example, if the firm supplies 2 per cent of the total in the market as long as price differences between brands do not change, the curve EE represents 2 per cent of the market demand.

12.6.1 Short-run behaviour

The assumption used in monopolistic competition is that a firm chooses its output according to its assumed demand curve. This assumed demand curve gives an assumed total revenue for each output level and, in figure 12.8, the assumed marginal revenue curve is FF. In figure 12.8(a), the firm chooses output Y, and it assumes that other firms do not change their prices, and so it can sell output Y at price Z. In fact, all other firms make similar decisions and the firm's actual demand at price Z is X, so that it cannot sell all that it assumed. The firm has unsold goods, and so is not in equilibrium. It therefore reduces its output.

Figure 12.8(b) illustrates the alternative possibility. The firm assumes that it can sell output U (for which the assumed marginal revenue equals marginal cost) at price S. At that price, demand is actually T, and so there is a shortage of its product. The firm therefore increases its output.

These changes in outputs continue until the market is in short-run equilibrium, in which each firm's actual demand equals its assumed demand. This equilibrium is shown in figure 12.9, where the two demand curves (DD and EE) intersect at the profit-maximizing output T. The firm assumes it can sell T at price U (point Q is on DD), and in equilibrium this assumption is correct (because Q is also on EE). At this output level, the firm's average revenue is U, and its average cost (including normal profit) is R. Total supernormal profit is OT × RU = area RUQS.

12.6.2 Entry and exit

In the long run, new firms enter the industry if existing firms make supernormal profits. The entry of new firms affects the revenues and costs of existing firms as follows:

(a) Each firm sells less at each price as new brands are introduced, so that average revenue falls.

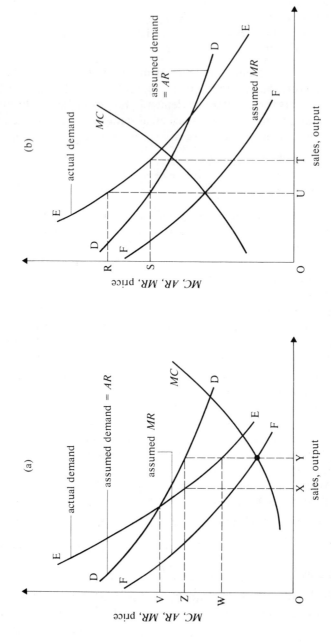

Figure 12.8 Short-run disequilibrium for a monopolistic competitor
(a) marginal cost equals assumed marginal revenue at output Y, for which the assumed price Z exceeds the actual price W (b) marginal cost equals marginal revenue at output U, for which the assumed price S is less than the actual price R.

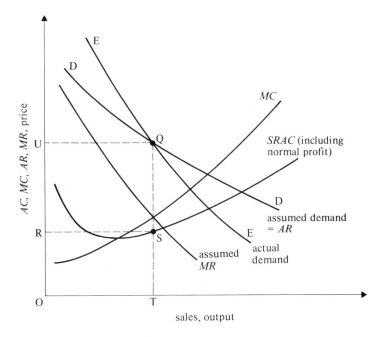

Figure 12.9 Short-run equilibrium for a monopolistic competitor
The firm's profit-maximizing output is T for which the assumed price equals the actual price (both U). Supernormal profit is RUQS.

(b) New firms add to the demand for factors and materials so that average cost increases.

Therefore supernormal profit is reduced by the entry of new firms and, as in a perfectly competitive industry, the reduction in profit continues until supernormal profit is eliminated. If profit falls below the normal level, some firms leave the industry, the average revenue of remaining firms increases, their average cost falls and their profits increase until supernormal profit reaches zero in the long run.

12.6.3 Long-run equilibrium

A long-run equilibrium is established when:

(a) Each firm maximizes its profit on the basis of its assumed demand and marginal revenue (as in the short run).
(b) Assumed demand equals actual demand (as in short-run equilibrium).
(c) The number of firms in the industry has changed to ensure that each firm's profit is at the normal level.

This equilibrium is illustrated in Figure 12.10. The profit-maximizing output is X, where assumed marginal revenue equals marginal cost. At that output, assumed demand equals actual demand (DD and EE intersect at Y), and

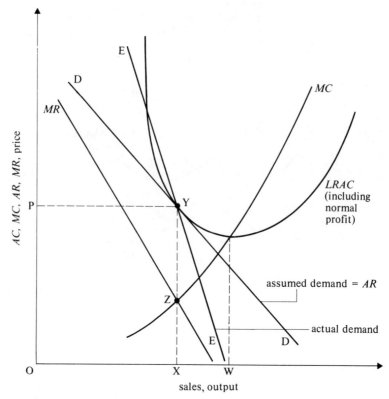

Figure 12.10   Long-run equilibrium for a monopolistic competitor
The firm's profit-maximizing output is X, for which the assumed price equals the actual
price (both P). Supernormal profit is zero because average cost (including normal
profit) equals average revenue (both assumed and actual) at output X.

assumed and actual average revenue (given by the demand curves DD and
EE) both equal average cost. At all other output levels average cost exceeds
actual average revenue. So point Y, where average cost equals average revenue,
must lie above the point Z, where marginal cost equals marginal revenue,
because both of these points indicate that supernormal profit is maximized.

12.6.4 Efficiency

Resources may not be used efficiently in a monopolistically competitive
industry, even in long-run equilibrium, because firms do not produce at their
minimum average costs. In figure 12.10, output X is less than output W. So
the average cost would be lower if the total market supply were produced by
fewer firms, each of which produces W. So

It is technically possible for fewer firms to produce the market supply at
lower total cost, therefore using fewer resources.

For example, if 24 firms in a monopolistically competitive industry each produce 100 units (X in figure 12.10) at an average cost of £5, the total cost of supplying the 2,400 units is £12,000. If each firm could produce 120 units at the minimum average cost of £4 (point W), it is technically possible to produce the 2,400 units at a total cost of £9,600.

In practice, firms need not all produce the same quantity, and they may have different costs of production (which are matched by lower prices for brands that are cheaper to produce), but it remains true that the total output of a monopolistically competitive industry could be produced more cheaply by fewer firms. Monopolistic competitors do not minimize average cost because it is profitable for each firm to limit output in order to charge a higher price.

12.6.5 Three market structures compared

A perfectly competitive market involves no imperfections, uses resources efficiently and gives no long-run supernormal profit. A monopolistically competitive industry involves one imperfection (firms have market influence, because each can affect its price by changing the amount that it sells), does not use resources efficiently and gives no long-run supernormal profit. An industry that is supplied by a monopolist involves two imperfections (a monopolist has market influence and other firms are not free to enter the market) does not use resources efficiently and gives long-run supernormal profit.

So the analysis of these three market structures shows that:

(a) Market influence causes inefficient use of resources.
(b) Entry restrictions lead to supernormal profit.

12.7 Market influence and wages

A firm maximizes its profit by choosing the output level where marginal revenue equals marginal cost, and so it demands labour up to the point where the marginal revenue product of labour equals the additional wage cost of employing one more unit of labour (see section 10.2). This rule applies whether or not a firm is small, but its application is more complex when a firm has market influence. The smallness assumption of a perfect market system allows two simplifications:

(a) The selling price of the good produced does not change if the firm increases its output by employing one more unit of labour.
(b) The wage is unchanged if one firm employs one more unit of labour.

In an imperfect market system, a firm may have influence in the market for its good, or in factor markets. We examine the implications of these possibilities for the demand for labour.

12.7.1 Labour demand by a monopoly producer

If a firm has monopoly power in the market for its good, the price of the good falls when it increases its output. Table 12.2 and figure 12.11 show an example of a firm's marginal revenue product of labour when the firm has influence in the market for its good. Table 12.2 and figure 12.11 also show the marginal revenue product curve that would arise if the firm had no market influence and sold its good at a price of £10. If the firm has market influence, and the wage is £30 (point C), the firm demands 3 hours of labour (point A) and produces 25 units. If it has no market influence, it demands 8 hours (point B) and produces 55 units. This reflects the conclusion that a monopolist restricts output in order to obtain supernormal profit. The restriction on output implies a reduced derived demand for labour. In the absence of other imperfections, the reduced demand for labour implies that the wage is lower. Wages are reduced and the firm makes supernormal profit.

Table 12.2   Marginal revenue product of labour

Employ-ment (hours)	Output	Marginal product of labour	Firm with market influence			Firm without market influence
			Price	Total revenue	Marginal revenue product of labour	Marginal revenue product of labour, price = 10
0	0	6	—	0	96	60
1	6	10	16	96	128	100
2	16	9	14	224	76	90
3	25	8	12	300	30	80
4	33	7	10	330	−10	70
5	40	6	8	320	−44	60
6	46	5	6	276	−72	50
7	51	4	4	204	−94	40
8	55	3	2	110	—	—

12.7.2 Labour demand by a monopsony buyer

A sole supplier is a monopolist. A sole demander in a market is a **monopsonist**. A firm that is a major employer in an area has monopsony power in the labour market, particularly for some types of labour that have few opportunities even in other areas. Table 12.3 and figure 12.12 show a monopsonist's demand for labour. If the firm wants to employ more people it must increase the wage to entice workers from other firms or to persuade them to take less leisure. The labour supply curve SS is derived from columns 1 and 4, and shows the wage that the firm must pay at each level of employment. Curve TT is derived from

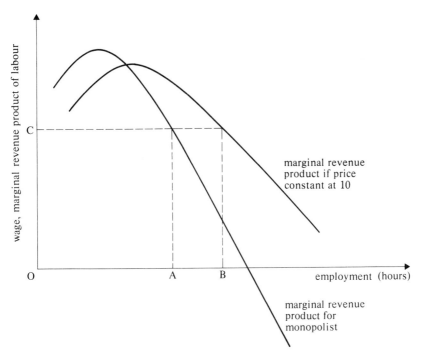

Figure 12.11 Marginal revenue products for a monopolist and for a firm without market influence
The monopolist must reduce its selling price to sell more, and so its marginal revenue product is lower (over most of the range) than that of a firm that can sell all it wants at a fixed price.

Table 12.3 Marginal revenue product for a monopsonist

1	2	3	4	5
		Marginal revenue product		
Employment	Output	if price = 10	Wage	Marginal cost
0	0	60	—	20
1	6	100	20	22
2	16	90	21	27
3	25	80	23	35
4	33	70	26	46
5	40	60	30	60
6	46	50	35	77
7	51	40	41	97
8	55	30	48	120
9	58	—	56	—

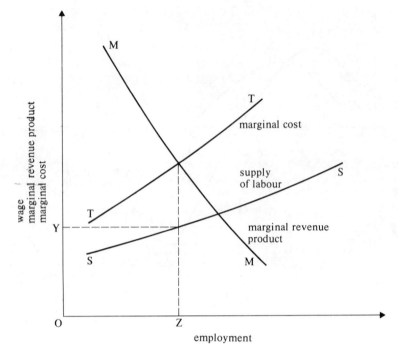

Figure 12.12 Labour market with a monopsony seller
The wage increases as labour supply increases, so that the marginal cost of labour
exceeds the wage. Marginal cost equals marginal revenue product (profit-maximizing
level) at employment Z and wage Y.

columns 1 and 5 and shows the marginal wage cost, which is the increase in
total wage payments when the firm employs one more unit.

MM is the firm's marginal revenue product curve, which may include the
effects of monopoly power in the market for its good. The firm employs Z,
where the marginal revenue product equals the marginal wage cost. To employ
Z, the firm must pay a wage of Y.

12.7.3 Trades unions

Trades unions have market influence because collective action by a group of
workers can affect, or threaten to affect, the supply of labour. Few individual
workers have sufficient influence in the labour market to affect their wage by
refusing to work, because a firm can employ someone else if one person refuses
to work. However, if most workers and potential workers are members of a
trade union, a firm may be unable, or unwilling, to employ others when the
union takes collective action. This collective action can take a number of forms,
of which the strike or threat to strike, is the most important. Some of a trade
union's ability to affect wages may be the result of previous negotiations with
a firm. For example:

(a) a firm may agree to employ only members of a particular union. This is a **closed shop** agreement.
(b) A firm may agree to reserve particular tasks for members of a union, so that it cannot replace skilled workers with cheaper, less skilled workers.
(c) A firm may agree to limit the employment of inexperienced workers so that union members are not replaced by younger workers who can be paid lower wages.

In figure 12.13, the equilibrium wage is F in the absence of a trades union. The union can influence the wages of those who work if it can ensure that the wage is, say, G. Then the demand for labour is H, and the supply would be J, but the union is able to prevent the excess supply from reducing the wage. So, assuming that the excess workers cannot find jobs elsewhere, the union can establish a wage of G and create unemployment equal to HJ. If the union increases the wage to M, unemployment changes to KL.

If unions prevent the movement of wages to equilibrium, there is unemployment in the labour markets where unions are strong. This causes either an increase in the national level of unemployment or an increase in the supply of labour in non-unionized labour markets, as those who cannot find jobs in the unionized sector seek jobs elsewhere. So wages in the non-unionized labour markets fall.

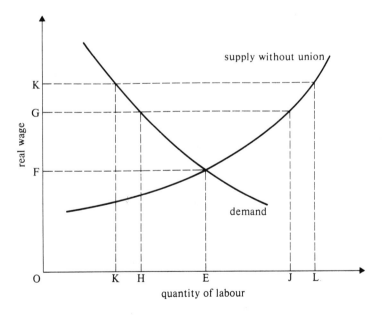

Figure 12.13   Effect of a trade union on wages and employment
The equilibrium real wage is F. If the union can maintain a real wage G, the supply of labour exceeds the demand by JH.

12.7.4 Labour market

The market demand for labour is the total of the demands of all firms (the firm's demand is the market demand if it has a complete monopsony over one type of labour). The supply of labour is affected by individual decisions and by the actions of trades unions. It is difficult to reach firm conclusions on the effect of market influence on the wage paid to each type of labour for at least two reasons:

(a) The influence of a large firm in the labour market may be offset by that of a trades union. The wage is established by bargaining between them in a situation known as **bilateral monopoly** (monopoly plus monopsony in the same market).
(b) There are interactions between markets. In particular, wages and the level of employment affect demands for goods, which in turn affect the derived demand for labour. So, for example, if unemployment occurs or wages fall, fewer goods are demanded, and so producers demand less labour causing a further rise in unemployment or a fall in wages. This cumulative effect is one of the bases of the multiplier, which we shall discuss further in chapter 15.

12.7.5 Other factor markets

Monopoly and monopsony can occur in other factor markets. If all of the supply of a particular type of land or equipment is owned by a single individual, he or she has monopoly power. Some types of land, specialized equipment and raw materials may be demanded by only one or a few firms, which then have monopsony power. Some of these market influences may offset, and lead to a bilateral monopoly. For example, large firms bargain over the prices of materials or equipment sold by one to the other.

12.8 Summary

Both monopoly and monopolistic competition involve market influence, and cause the inefficient use of resources. A monopolist can prevent the entry of new firms and achieve supernormal profit in the long run. A discriminating monopolist can increase its supernormal profit and reduce consumers' surplus by setting the marginal revenue in each submarket equal to marginal cost and charging different prices to different customers.

A monopolist restricts the demand for labour as a result of its restriction on output that gives supernormal profit. Unions and large firms bargain over wages that may be above the equilibrium level so that there is unemployment in the economy or reduced wages in the non-unionized parts of the economy.

The ability of unions to prevent wage reductions is an important element in our discussion of unemployment in chapter 16 and, in addition, it is an important element in our discussion of the persistence of inflation.

Topics and problems

(1) 'Large scale production is efficient, but monopolies are inefficient.' Is it possible to reconcile these opposing views of large firms?
(2) Should patents be abolished?
(3) The market price of a painting that is found to be a forgery usually falls. Does this mean that artists need not be protected by copyright laws?
(4) What industries are monopolistically competitive? Do they behave in the manner described in this chapter?
(5) 'Trades unions cause unemployment and depress other people's wages, and should therefore be abolished.' 'Trades unions are the only defence for workers against exploiting employers.' Discuss these two claims.
(6) A monopolist faces demand schedules from two submarkets and total cost curve as in tables 12.4 and 12.5.

Table 12.4   Demands for use in problem 6

Price	Demand in submarket 1	Demand in submarket 2
5	9	13
6	8	12
7	7	11
8	6	10
9	5	9
10	4	8
11	3	7
12	2	6
13	1	5
14	0	4
15	0	3

Table 12.5   Costs for use in problem 6

Output	Total cost
7	45
8	50
9	55
10	60
11	65
12	71
13	78
14	86

Table 12.6 Labour market data for problem 7

	Market 1		Market 2	
Wage	Demand	Supply	Demand	Supply
4	100	30	70	10
5	90	50	60	30
6	80	62	55	40
7	70	70	52	45
8	60	75	50	50
9	50	70	49	55
10	40	65	48	57

What is its profit-maximizing output if it charges the same price in each submarket?

What output minimizes average cost?

What prices does it charge if it maximizes profits and discriminates between the two submarkets?

(7) Demands and supplies in two non-unionized labour markets are as in table 12.6. In market 1, workers in market 1 then organize a trade union that can maintain the wage £1 above the equilibrium level. All the workers who would like a job at that wage, but cannot find one, supply labour in market 2. How far does the equilibrium wage in market 2 decline? Is the assumption that all the workers unemployed in market 1 would move to market 2 realistic?

Chapter Thirteen

Oligopoly and market uncertainty

Oligopoly as a game — entry and exit — competition, collusion and efficiency — price and output changes — motivation: security, profits and growth

13.1 Introduction

We have examined three market structures: perfect competition, monopoly and monopolistic competition. In perfect competition each firm knows that it can sell all that it can produce at the given market price, and that it can buy all the factors and materials that it needs at given prices. So a perfect competitor does not face any **market uncertainty**. Similarly, a monopoly firm knows the demand curve for its good (it is the same as the market demand curve), so that it can calculate its marginal revenue. We assumed also that it knows the costs of materials and factors, and so a monopolist is able to make a profit-maximizing decision that is not affected by market uncertainty. A monopolistic competitor acts as though it knows its demand curve (because it assumes that other firms do not change their prices) and it too can make a profit-maximizing decision on the basis of its assumed demand and marginal revenue curves. The theory of monopolistic competition has an awkward feature, because firms continue to assume that other firms do not change their prices, even when they have had a long period of experience that this assumption is not true. This expectation is not rational, because firms persistently make predictions that are repeatedly shown to be wrong.

This problem with the assumption of monopolistic competition leads us to look for a better way of analysing the interactions between firms. The main feature of **oligopoly** is that firms are uncertain about the pricing and output decisions that their rivals will take, and so no firm knows how much it can sell at each price. In these circumstances, demand and marginal revenue curves are unknown, and it is important to develop a theory that does not rely on them.

An oligopoly arises when more than one firm supplies a market, but each firm is large enough for its actions to have significant effects on its rivals' sales and profits. In such a market structure, a firm can affect the amount that its rivals sell by changing its price or by advertising, and so each firm tries to forecast its rivals' pricing and advertising decisions when it makes its own decision. In addition, a firm must allow for the possibility that its forecasts are wrong, and attempt to take decisions that will not be disastrous whatever its rivals may do.

Economists have developed a variety of methods of analysing oligopoly, making a variety of assumptions on the reaction of each firm to its rivals' decisions. One such model, that of A.A. Cournot (born 1801 in Haute-Saône, France, died 1877; one of the first economists to use mathematical methods in the analysis of economic problems), assumes that each firm makes its output decision assuming that other firms do not change their output levels. Although this model has some interesting features, it fails to capture the market uncertainty that characterizes oligopoly, because it makes an assumption about firms' reactions that does not allow for their attitudes to uncertainty.

13.2 Oligopoly as a game

We examine a model of oligopoly that does allow for reactions to uncertainty, and for firms' guesses about the actions of their rivals. The model uses game theory, originally developed by John von Neumann to represent mathematically the actions of players in games. It is used by economists to analyse oligopoly, and by strategists to examine international relations, because oligopoly and the arms race, like bridge and football, involve the reactions of players (firms, nations) to each others' actions. (Von Neumann was born in Budapest in 1903 and died in 1957, and was professor of mathematics at Princeton University, USA, from 1931 to 1957. He was a leading figure in twentieth-century pure and applied mathematics, and made major contributions to quantum mechanics, mathematical logic and the operation of computers. As a member of the US Atomic Energy Commission, he was closely involved in the development of the hydrogen bomb.)

We shall illustrate the general approach using a simple example. This example supposes that there are two shops in a town, selling a similar range of goods, that are deciding on whether to open on Sundays.

13.2.1 Strategies

The main strategies that are open to an oligopolist can be divided into:

(a) **Price competition**. A firm attracts customers by selling at a lower price than its rivals. We should not assume that a firm necessarily wants to sell at a lower price than all of its rivals, because it may be able to sell a sufficient quantity at a higher, more profitable price, particularly if it has established some brand loyalty.

(b) **Non-price competition**. A firm attracts customers by introducing new brands, by advertising, and on the basis of its reputation for quality or after-sales service. The decision to open on Sundays is a form of non-price competition.

A firm may use price and non-price competition at the same time by, for example, introducing a new brand at an initial low price, in the hope of establishing brand loyalty that will remain even after a price increase.

13.2.2 Outcomes

The amount that each firm sells depends on the strategies pursued by every firm. If only one firm increases its price, it is likely to lose some of its market share (which is the firm's percentage of total sales in the market). If all firms increase their prices by similar amounts, fewer goods are sold in total (because market demand is reduced), but each firm's market share may remain approximately unchanged. A firm may change its market share if it alone advertises, but competing advertisements may offset each other if all firms in the market advertise.

For a materially motivated firm, the outcome is measured by profitability, which depends on its price, its market share and its costs. In our example of Sunday opening, each firm has two basic strategies: to open on Sundays and not to open on Sundays (although each firm might in practice combine one of these strategies with some other policy such as a decision to cut prices). The profits of each firm for each combination of strategies are listed in table 13.1, where we see that:

(a) If both firms open, each firm's profit is lower than if neither opens. This arises because the example assumes that Sunday opening does not generate many additional sales in total, and that Sunday opening requires the payment of overtime wages to staff, additional heating and lighting bills and so on.

Table 13.1 Profits for two firms

	Strategy for firm F	
	Open	Not open
Strategy for firm G		
Open	(10,12)	(6,14)
Not open	(13,7)	(18,15)

Each pair of figures represents first F's profit and second G's profit for the given combination of strategies. So, for example, if F opens and G does not, F's profit is 13 and G's profit is 7. The units of measurement are unimportant (they could be hundreds of pounds per week, for example).

(b) If only one firm opens, its additional revenue is not sufficient to offset its additional cost. The other firm loses profit because it loses trade on other days.

13.2.3 Information

An oligopolist has imperfect information because, although he knows the strategies available to his rivals, he does not know the strategies that they will choose. This uncertainty results in activities such as industrial spying, as firms try to find out whether rivals have new brands or intend to launch a major advertising campaign. The lack of information may also result in collusion between the firms, so that they agree to exchange information to reduce uncertainty.

13.2.4 Motivation

An oligopolist cannot choose a strategy that is guaranteed to maximize its profit, because it does not know what its rivals will do. In the Sunday opening example, F makes the greatest profit if it does not open, provided that its rival does not open either. However, if F does not open and G opens, F loses many customers to G, and this loss of revenue exceeds the saving in costs from not opening on Sundays. So if F chooses not to open, it may make a profit of 18, which is the largest available, but it may make only 6. If it chooses to open, it makes either 10 or 13. Opening is therefore, in a sense, a safer strategy than not opening: the maximum gains are less, but the worse outcome from opening is not as bad as the worse outcome from not opening. Similarly, G makes its highest profit (15) if neither opens, but if G does not open and F opens, G's profit is only 7. If G opens, its profit is either 12 or 14.

   If a firm can estimate probabilities to represent the likelihood of each combination of its rivals' strategies, it may choose its strategy according to the likelihood of the outcomes. However, if a firm chooses its strategy on the basis of the probabilities of the other firm's choice of strategy, it must have a view of the sizes of those probabilities. The use of game theory to analyse oligopoly has traditionally assumed that each firm is so uncertain of its rivals' decisions that it is unable to estimate these probabilities. So traditionally game theory has concentrated on the motivation that firms want to avoid choosing strategies that may have poor outcomes. This is the **maximin motivation**, and it involves a two-stage choice of strategy:

(a) For each of its strategies, a firm works out the worst possible strategies that its rivals could use. The firm judges each of its own strategies on the minimum profit that it could achieve.
(b) The firm chooses the strategy whose worst outcome is least bad.

So each firm maximizes its minimum profit – hence the name maximin. In our example, firm F goes through the following process to find its maximin strategy:

(a) If F opens, its minimum profit is 10, which occurs if G opens too.
(b) If F does not open, its minimum profit is 6, which occurs if G opens.
(c) The larger of these minimum profits is 10, and so F's maximin strategy is to open.

Similarly, for G:

(a) If G opens, its minimum profit is 12, which occurs if F opens too.
(b) If G does not open, its minimum profit is 7, which occurs if F opens.
(c) The larger of these minimum profits is 12, and so G's maximin strategy is to open.

So if both firms use the maximin strategy, both open. F's profit is 10 and G's profit is 12. By adopting this cautious maximin strategy, the firms each end up with less profit than they could have achieved if both had decided not to open. Neither is willing to take the risk of not opening for fear of the consequences if the rival chooses to open.

Even if a firm cannot estimate the probabilities of its rivals' strategies, it may not be motivated to choose the maximin strategy. For example, there may be several strategies that allow it to make normal profit, and it may be prepared to choose the one of these that gives it a chance of a large supernormal profit, even if there is some strategy that has a better outcome if the firms' rivals do their worst. If F's normal profit is less than 6 in our example, it may be prepared not to open, in the hope that G will not open either, so that F can achieve a profit of 18. Even if G opens, F makes more than its normal profit.

13.3 Entry and exit

13.3.1 Entry

Oligopolists have the potential to make supernormal profits (up to the level of profit of a monopoly if they collude), and so other firms may be tempted to enter the market. The cost of entry may be high if the good is produced using much expensive equipment, and firms that are already in the market can reduce the profitability of entry by:

(a) Reducing their prices, or threatening to do so, when the new entrant appears. The existing firms may be well placed to do this because the marginal cost of production is low once the equipment is installed, and so they can produce quite cheaply the additional goods that they will sell if they cut their prices.
(b) By advertising, so that the new entrant must advertise too to establish its brand.

These barriers to entry may be increased if existing firms have patents that they are prepared to defend in expensive and lengthy court cases (see section 12.2).

13.3.2 Exit

An oligopolist that persistently makes less than normal profit is likely to cease to produce. However, unlike in perfect competition and monopolistic competition where the decision to cease to produce is the result of impersonal market forces, an oligopolist may be forced to leave the market by the actions of other firms. One firm may be able to force another to cease to produce by cutting its price to such an extent that the other firm is unable to operate profitably. This is possible if one firm introduces a new, cheaper method of production protected by patents so that its rivals cannot copy it, or if a firm produces more than one good, so that it can offset the losses on one good by making profits on other goods.

If a firm is able to force its rivals to cease to produce, it can establish a monopoly and increase its prices to gain the supernormal profit of a monopolist. This supernormal profit may attract other firms to the industry, but the monopolist may be able to protect its position by threatening a price war or by extensive advertising. However, a strategy of attempting to force rivals to cease to produce by cutting prices may not be successful, and all the firms, including the 'aggressor', may end up with unchanged market shares and much reduced profits. This appears to happen periodically in the petrol market, where firms engage in price cutting wars that eventually lead them to sell at a price that is less than their average cost. When this happens, the firms either agree to increase prices simultaneously, or a few of the larger firms announce price increases, which is a signal for other firms to follow.

13.4 Competition, collusion and efficiency

Each firm chooses its strategy (its selling price, its output and any aspect of non-price competition) according to its motivation and the information that it has. The **competitive outcome** is the outcome that arises if each firm chooses its strategy independently of other firms. In the example in table 13.1, the competitive outcome that arises if both firms have the maximin motivation is a profit of 10 for F and 12 for G. The **collusive outcome** is the outcome that arises if the firms agree on their choice of strategy. In the example, F's profit is 18 and G's profit is 15 if they agree that neither opens. In this case, the collusive outcome is better for both firms than the competitive outcome, and so they have an incentive to collude. This is not necessarily the case: table 13.2 shows an example in which collusion cannot improve on the competitive (maximin) outcome. Table 13.2 differs from table 13.1 in that Sunday opening generates considerable additional trade and involves little additional cost, so that profits are higher if both open than if neither opens. F's maximin strategy is to open, because the minimum profit from opening is 20 (if G opens too), and from not opening is 6 (if G opens). Similarly, G's maximin strategy is to open, and they can do no better by collusion.

A further possibility arises if Sunday opening generates some additional trade, and involves some additional cost, so that the total profit of the two

Table 13.2 Profits for two firms: no advantage from collusion

	Strategy for firm F	
	Open	Not open
Strategy for firm G		
Open	(20,18)	(6,25)
Not open	(28,7)	(14,15)

Each pair of figures represents first F's profit and second G's profit for the given combination of strategies.

firms would be greatest if one opens (to take advantage of the additional trade) and the other does not open (to avoid the additional cost). Such a situation is shown in table 13.3, where each firm's maximin strategy is to open, so that the competitive outcome from the maximin motivation is profit of 12 for F and 16 for G. The firms could agree not to open, and each would make more profit, but the greatest total profit of 35 is achieved if F opens and G does not. This can arise only if the firms agree, and F pays G not to open. If F makes a payment of 10 to G, and F opens and G does not, F has $28 - 10 = 18$ and G has $7 + 10 = 17$, and both of them have more than if they do not co-operate. There is scope for bargaining on the size of this payment because both firms would be better off than in the competitive outcome if the payment is 15, so that F has 13 and G has 20.

If firms co-operate, and are prepared to make agreements involving side-payments, they can maximize their joint profits and act as a single monopolist. The only difference between this collusion and a monopolistic market structure is that the oligopolists must decide on the distribution of the total profit between them by agreeing on the size of the payment from one firm to the other.

Table 13.3 Profits for two firms: advantage from collusion with payment

	Strategy for firm F	
	Open	Not open
Strategy for firm G		
Open	(12,16)	(6,27)
Not open	(28,7)	(14,19)

Each pair of figures represents first F's profit and second G's profit for the given combination of strategies.

As we shall discuss in section 19.2, the UK government attempts to outlaw collusive agreements between oligopolists because they involve similar inefficiencies to monopoly. However, even if open agreements are illegal, firms may collude secretly. It is impossible to prevent meetings and telephone calls between the senior managers of firms that provide each other with information on likely strategies, and form the basis for agreements not to use mutually unfavourable strategies (such as the strategy of opening by both firms in table 13.1). These private collusive agreements can include payments only if these are in some way hidden in the firms' published accounts, and so secret agreements may fail because some firms find that it is profitable to break the agreement. In our example the first firm that breaks the agreement not to open on Sundays may gain profit at least temporarily, and may in fact establish sufficient brand loyalty that it loses few Sunday customers when its rival also opens.

13.4.1 Efficiency

If oligopolists collude, they may act as if they were a single monopolist and restrict output in order to maximize the total supernormal profit. So colluding oligopolists are likely to use resources inefficiently for similar reasons to those discussed in section 12.4. Competing oligopolists are not perfect competitors, and so they too may not use resources efficiently.

A major reason for the inefficient use of resources by oligopolists is that firms have excess capacity (the capacity to produce more than is actually produced) for strategic reasons. If a firm fears that a rival firm may reduce its price, or that a new firm may enter the market, it wants to keep open the option to respond by reducing its own price and increasing its sales. To respond effectively in these circumstances, a firm must be able to increase its sales rapidly when it reduces its price, and so an oligopolist is likely to have excess capacity and stocks of materials ready for use.

If no rival firm reduces its price and if no firm enters the market, the excess capacity is unused. The excess capacity could be used to produce more goods but is not, and so some resources are left unused. The parallel between this situation and deterrence theories of national defence is close, because the firm hopes that its 'readiness' – that is, its ability to retaliate – will deter others from 'surprise attacks' of price cutting.

13.4.2 Consumers' sovereignty

The extent of consumers' sovereignty in an economy is shown by the extent to which an increase in the demand for a good leads to an increase in supply. In a monopolistic market, an increase in demand may lead to little increase in supply: instead the producer increases its supernormal profit. A similar conclusion is likely if oligopolists collude. If, on the other hand, firms compete and it is easy for new firms to enter the market, it is likely that an increase in demand leads to an increase in supply, with little increase in supernormal profit.

This general point is subject to an important qualification. Consumers' sovereignty refers to the response of an economic system to a change in demands caused by a change in consumers' tastes. In a perfect market system, firms have no influence on consumers' tastes, because there is no interrelation between firms and households other than through market prices (this is the assumption of no external effects). However, all forms of non-price competition are attempts to change tastes, because they are attempts to change consumers' demands given their budgets and prices. In particular, a successful advertising campaign implies that firms can affect consumers' tastes, and so if advertising is successful firms influence the demands for and outputs of goods, and consumers cannot be said to be sovereign.

13.5 Price and output changes

In a perfect market system, prices change rapidly to reach their equilibrium levels. This assumption is unrealistic when firms face the uncertainties of oligopoly. There are several reasons why an oligopolist may be slow to change its price even if there is a permanent change in the demand for its good:

(a) An oligopolist is accustomed to variation in its sales, because it is affected by the strategies of other firms. A firm is unlikely to change its price every time demand changes (if only for the administrative reasons that lists, labels and advertisements must be changed). Initially, a permanent expansion of demand is indistinguishable from a temporary fluctuation, and a firm is unlikely to respond to the change in demand until its stock of unsold goods has fallen to an unusually low level, or until it is buying from its suppliers unusually frequently. Correspondingly, a firm does not respond to a reduction in demand until it has an unusually large stock of unsold goods.

(b) A firm that has spare capacity (some of which may be kept to allow it to fight or to deter a price-cutting war) is likely to view an increase in demand as an opportunity to increase its sales rather than its prices, and to reduce its average costs of production by spreading its fixed costs over a larger output.

(c) An oligopolist may be reluctant to be the first to increase its price. The firm that is first to increase its price suffers a double disadvantage, because the price increase reduces its sales as long as other firms do not increase their prices, and because the other firms can respond by announcing somewhat smaller price increases. The firm that is first to increase its price loses sales permanently unless it is willing to change its price again in response to its rivals' actions.

(d) If demand falls, a firm that reduces its price before it reduces its cost of production is likely to suffer a considerable reduction in its profit, and perhaps even face a cash flow problem. If the suppliers of materials do not reduce their prices, and if the firm has employed labour, rented land or hired equipment on long-term contracts, it may be unable to reduce its average costs of production quickly, and it is then reluctant to reduce its average revenue by reducing its price.

If a firm is slow to change its price in response to a change in demand, it must change its output instead. If demand increases but the firm does not increase its price, it must produce more, and this is likely to increase its employment of labour and of other factors. If demand falls, the firm must produce less (or find that its stocks of unsold goods increase, and it may be costly to store these). If a firm produces less, it reduces its demand for labour and for other factors. So:

If firms are slow to change their prices, outputs and employment levels change instead.

13.5.1 Cost increases

If one firm faces an increase in its costs when its rivals do not, it is likely to have to accept a reduction in its profit (or cease production), because it would lose sales if it increased its price. However, if a firm knows that all its rivals are experiencing similar changes in costs, because there is a general increase in wages or in the costs of materials, it is likely to be less reluctant to increase its price. It knows that its rivals must increase their prices too, or suffer much reduced profits. A firm that delays a price reduction when its costs increase may increase its market share, but only at the cost of a considerable reduction in profit.

The incentive to increase prices in line with costs is increased if firms recognize that their costs rise because of a general increase in money wages. The increases in money wages imply that their customers' incomes increase, so that they are able to afford to pay the higher prices. The price increase is unlikely to lead to any reduction in the market demand for the good.

13.5.2 Macroeconomic implications

We use two conclusions from this section in our examination of macroeconomic aspects of an imperfect market economy (see chapters 15 and 16) and of government policies to reduce unemployment and the inflation rate. These conclusions are:

(a) Firms may respond to changes in demand by changing their outputs and employment of labour and not their prices.
(b) Firms may respond to cost increases that affect all firms in similar ways by increasing their prices.

The first conclusion is clearly relevant to the analysis of unemployment, and the second is relevant to the analysis of inflation, because the price increases cause further inflation, which may lead to further increases in costs and so to a perpetuation of inflation (see section 16.4).

13.6 Motivation: security, profits and growth

Important decisions in large firms are often made by managers who are not shareholders in the firm, and whose interests may not coincide with those of the shareholders. Managers are likely to be interested in increasing their own incomes and maintaining their job security. There are several aims that are likely to motivate their decisions on the firm's choice of strategy, and that imply that the firm may not maximize its profit:

(a) To maintain sales to avoid bankruptcy and cash flow problems.
(b) To increase the firm's revenue and employment and, with these, their own power and prestige from association with a growing firm.
(c) To retain the confidence of shareholders who may dismiss the senior managers at a general meeting.

The last of these aims implies that the managers cannot ignore profit, but the other aims imply that managers may not make decisions that would maximize the firm's profit.

13.6.1 Advertising

One way in which a firm might maintain and increase its sales is by advertising. A profit-maximizing firm uses advertising in the same way that it uses other inputs: it advertises if the gains from doing so outweigh the costs. An additional advertisement generates additional sales and additional revenue, and:

> A profit-maximizing firm advertises up to the point where the marginal revenue (from the additional sales generated by one more advertisement) equals the marginal cost (of that advertisement).

A firm whose managers do not maximize profits may advertise more than this principle implies, because additional advertising generates some additional sales (although not enough to cover the cost of the additional advertising), and so helps to ensure a flow of revenue into the firm that is sufficient to avoid cash-flow problems and the possibility of bankruptcy.

13.6.2 The growth of firms

A firm can increase its output and employment (and hence its managers' prestige and their incomes if they are paid bonuses on the basis of increased sales) by investing in new equipment. This investment can be paid for by selling shares or by borrowing from banks. Share sales can be expensive to run and bank borrowing may be subject to interest rate changes, and so it is often easier to finance investment projects from undistributed profits. So, for this reason at least, managers are likely to favour high profits, but not their distribution to shareholders. To some extent, this may not worry shareholders (whose incomes are reduced if profits are not distributed), because the value of the firm that they own is increased if the firm buys more equipment, and so the value of their shares may increase. However, share prices are affected in many ways, not just by the value of the firm's assets. Share prices depend on the interest rate on bonds and on speculative activity in markets for shares (see section 14.5.1), so that shareholders are likely to favour distributions of profit as an assured form of income, compared to the uncertain prospects of changes in share prices. So there is likely to be some conflict between the shareholders and the managers.

13.6.3 Sufficient profit

There is a limit to the extent to which the managers of a firm are likely to reduce distributed profits, because:

(a) As noted, shareholders may use their votes at a general meeting to dismiss managers if the shareholders are unhappy at the size of distributed profits.
(b) If distributed profits are very low, the demand for the firm's shares is likely to be low, and so the share price is low. At the same time, the accumulation of undistributed profits permits the firm to buy more equipment so that the value of the firm's assets increases. The low share price invites a take-over bid: a bidder tries to buy the shares to take control of the firm and, when the share price is low but the firm has valuable assets, a successful bidder can obtain control of valuable assets cheaply. This is unlikely to be in the managers' interests, because a successful bidder is likely to dismiss the senior managers.

So we can conclude that the managers of a firm strike a balance between:

(a) Distributing profit to avoid antagonizing shareholders and to avoid take-over bids.
(b) Keeping profits that can be used for investment projects to expand the firm.

13.7 Summary

The analysis of oligopoly as a game shows how each firm's profit depends on the decisions taken by all firms in the market. Oligopolists may be able to make more profit if they collude than if they compete, but agreements to collude may require payments by one firm to another. An agreement may fail if some firms believe that they can make more profit by competing than by colluding. Oligopolists are likely to keep excess capacity in order to fight, or deter others from starting, price-cutting wars, and in order to be able to expand output when a new firm wants to enter the market.

An oligopolist may not change its price rapidly when the demand for its good changes. Instead, it may change its output and the amount of labour that it employs. Oligopolists may contribute to the persistence of inflation by increasing their prices when their costs of production increase.

The decision-makers of large firms may not take decisions that maximize the incomes of shareholders, because it is in their interests to follow a more cautious strategy or to build reserves of undistributed profits so that the firm can invest and grow.

Topics and problems

(1) Does advertising cause people to switch from one brand to another? Does advertising increase the market demand for a good at each price? Does negative advertising (such as anti-smoking campaigns) work? Are advertising campaigns an infringement on the liberty of individuals to choose without undue influence?

(2) In parts of Ontario, in the spring of 1983, the price of petrol fell from approximately 40 cents per litre to approximately 18 cents. At 3 p.m. on a particular day, all sellers increased their price to approximately 43 cents. Can you explain the price reduction and subsequent increase?

(3) Can you explain the phenomenon of cut-price sales by firms? In what circumstances are these likely to occur?

(4) The shareholders of a firm are devising an incentive scheme for paying the managers of their firm. What would you advise them to do? Should workers be given similar incentives?

(5) Two firms sell in a market. Each has annual sales of 1,000 at a price of £1. An advertising campaign costs £100. Both firms maintain a price of £1, and both prefer more profit to less. If both firms advertise, neither sells any more; if one firm advertises, they receive the same combined total revenue, but the advertising firm receives three times as much as the non-advertising firm. Their production costs (which exclude advertising costs) are as in table 13.4.

What do both firms do if they do not collude?
What do the firms do if they collude?

Table 13.4 Costs for use in problem 5

Output	Total production cost (each firm)
500	400
1,000	600
1,500	900

Table 13.5 Profits for two firms, for use in problem 6

	Strategy for firm F	
	Open	Not open
Strategy for firm G		
Open	(15,10)	(−2,38)
Not open	(30,3)	(14,16)

Each pair of figures represents first F's profit and second
G's profit for the given combination of strategies.

The advertising agencies increase their charges (without changing the effectiveness of the advertisements). How much can they charge before they price
themselves out of business (assuming that the firms do not collude)?

(6) A 'Sunday opening game' has the outcomes given in table 13.5. What do
the firms do if each has the maximin motivation? What do they do if they
collude?

Chapter Fourteen

Uncertainty: investment, saving and liquidity

Uncertainty and expectations — attitudes to uncertainty — insurance and gambling — financial assets: bonds and shares — uncertain exchange rates — liquidity preference: demand for money — investment

14.1 Introduction

Apart from the market uncertainties associated with oligopoly, many decisions of households and firms are affected by uncertainty about the future and by a lack of relevant information. For example:

(a) Firms' investment decisions are affected by their views of possible future profits and losses that depend on the prices of goods and factors that cannot be predicted with certainty when the investment is made.
(b) Households' saving decisions are affected by the possibility of unforeseen events. They are likely to want to hold money or other assets so that they can meet an emergency, buy a good when an unexpected bargain appears or have a source of income if a household member becomes unemployed.
(c) Households and firms pay for insurance cover against possible future events.

In this chapter we examine the consequences of uncertainty for insurance, investment, saving and the supply and demand for money and other assets. We begin by examining ways of analysing uncertain prospects.

14.2 Uncertainty and expectations

An event is uncertain if it has several possible outcomes. Households and firms have **expectations** of the range of possible outcomes of the event, and of the **probability** (or likelihood) that a particular outcome will occur. The formation of these expectations involves making predictions, and this can be done in two ways:

(a) On the basis of experience of similar events. For example, if a firm wants to predict changes in the price of the good that it sells, it may base its expectation on recent price changes. It may predict that if the price has risen by 10 per cent over the past year, then the price will rise by 10 per cent over the next year. Alternatively, it can use a formula based on price changes over several previous years, or it may predict a range of possible prices based on the ranges of prices in previous years. Whatever the exact formula, the firm's expectations of future prices are based on prices observed in the past.

(b) On the basis of a model of the major influences on the event. A firm that is attempting to predict its price may build a model of the major influences on demand and supply, and base its prediction of the price on this model. Among other items, the firm needs to know the income-elasticity of demand for the good if it expects that its customers' incomes will increase in the future. The firm may estimate the income-elasticity of demand using past evidence of changes in income and changes in demand. If, for example, the firm estimates that the income-elasticity of demand is between 1.4 and 1.6, and that it expects that its customers' incomes will increase by an average of between 2 per cent and 2.5 per cent over the next year, then the firm expects an increase in demand from this source of between 2.8 per cent (1.4 × 2 per cent) and 4 per cent (1.6 × 2.5 per cent). Other influences, such as changes in the prices of substitute or complementary goods, may add to or subtract from this expectation of an increase in demand.

14.2.1 Systematic errors

If a household or firm discovers that its method of forming expectations consistently over-predicts or consistently under-predicts some important figure, it is likely to change its method of forecasting to try to eliminate the systematic error. Indeed, it would be irrational to persist in forming predictions if it is clear that the method has some systematic bias. If a firm consistently under-predicts its price by 10 per cent, it is rational to add 10 per cent to predictions made using that method. A firm or household that is successful in making forecasts that have no systematic error forms **rational** (or unbiased) **expectations**, and its forecasts are no more likely to under-predict than to over-predict.

Expectations can be made rational only after the method has been used for some time so that systematic biases can be detected. Some forecasts cannot be adjusted on the basis of past evidence. For example, a firm that wants to predict the price at which it can sell a newly invented good has no past evidence to examine to see whether the predicted price usually exceeds or is usually less than the actual price. A systematic error can be eliminated only after it has been revealed by comparing a number of predictions with actual outcomes.

14.2.2 Expected value

A household or firm can make a variety of predictions of an event, some of which may involve only the *direction* of change (such as the prediction that unemployment will rise over a period) and not the *size* of the change. It may predict the range of likely outcomes or the most likely outcome, and many predictions involve the calculation of the expected value of some magnitude (such as a price, an output level or national income).

For example, suppose that a firm predicts that the price of its product next year will be between £28 and £34, and that the most likely price is £32. In addition, it may make a prediction of the probability of various outcomes as in table 14.1. The list contains all the prices that the firm believes to be possible, so that the total of the probabilities is 100 per cent. From the table, the firm can calculate the expected value using the formula:

$$EP = q_1 P_1 + q_2 P_2 + q_3 P_3 + \ldots + q_n P_n$$

where EP is the expected value of the price, P_1, P_2, P_3, $\ldots$, P_n are the possible prices, and q_1 is the firm's view of the probability that the actual price will be P_1, etc.

Table 14.1 Expected value of an uncertain prospect

Price (£)	Probability (%)	Probability × price (£)
28	5	1.4
29	10	2.9
30	15	4.5
31	20	6.2
32	25	8.0
33	15	4.95
34	10	3.4
Total	100	
		Expected value 31.35

So, from table 14.1, the expected value of the price is:

$$(5\% \times £28) + (10\% \times £29) + (25\% \times £30) + (20\% \times £31)$$
$$+ (25\% \times £32) + (15\% \times £33) + (10\% \times £34) = £31.35$$

The expected value of the price is sometimes known as the expected price: this is a convenient abbreviation, as long as it does not lead to the mistaken view that the firm in our example confidently expects a price of £31.35, rather than that £31.35 is the average of a number of possible outcomes.

14.3 Attitudes to uncertainty

How does a household or firm act once it has formed its expectations? One way of analysing the attitude to an uncertain prospect is to find its **certainty equivalent**.

In the example of table 14.1, we can find the firm's certainty equivalent by asking the firm which of the following it prefers:

(a) The uncertain prospect with the possible outcomes and probabilities listed in table 14.1.
(b) The prospect that the price is certain to be some fixed amount P.

If the firm prefers the uncertain prospect to the certain prospect when $P =$ £30, then the certainty equivalent exceeds £30, and we can ask the question again using a higher value of P. If the firm prefers the certain £30 to the uncertain prospect, then the certainty equivalent is less than £30, and we can ask the question again with lower value of P. The certainty equivalent of the uncertain prospect of table 14.1 is the value of P for which the firm is indifferent (see section 9.5) between the uncertain prospect of the table and the certain prospect of receiving price P. In general,

> If a household or firm is indifferent between a certain prospect and an uncertain prospect, then that certain prospect is the certainty equivalent of the uncertain prospect.

The **risk premium** of an uncertain prospect is the expected value of the prospect minus its certainty equivalent.

14.3.1 Risk-averse, risk-neutral and risk-preferring behaviour

We can use the certainty equivalent and the expected value of an uncertain prospect to classify attitudes to uncertainty.

(a) A household or firm is **risk-averse** towards an uncertain prospect if its **risk premium is positive** because its certainty equivalent is less than its expected value.
(b) A household or firm is **risk-neutral** towards an uncertain prospect if its **risk premium is zero** because its certainty equivalent equals its expected value.
(c) A household or firm is **risk-preferring** towards an uncertain prospect if its **risk premium is negative** because its certainty equivalent exceeds its expected value.

In our example, the firm is risk-averse if the certainty equivalent is less than £31.35; it is risk-neutral if the certainty equivalent is £31.35; it is risk-preferring if the certainty equivalent exceeds £31.35.

14.4 Insurance and gambling

14.4.1 Insurance

Households and firms buy insurance to avoid facing uncertainty. For example, suppose that a firm has a factory worth £250,000 and believes that there is a probability of 1 per cent that the factory will burn down. If it does not insure, it faces an uncertain prospect with a 99 per cent probability that it will lose nothing, and a 1 per cent prospect of losing £250,000. The expected value of this prospect is

$$(99\% \times £0) + (1\% \times -£250,000) = -£2,500$$

(Note that we use a minus sign because the prospect involves a loss.) If the firm is willing to pay up to £3,750 for insurance, it is indifferent between the uncertain prospect and the certain prospect of paying £3,750. The certainty equivalent of the uncertain prospect is −£3,750, which is less than the certainty equivalent (−3,750 is less than −2,500 because it is a larger negative number), and so the firm is risk-averse. The risk premium is £1,250 (£3,750 − £2,500).

The insurance company sells fire insurance to many households and firms, and it is very likely that only a few of these will involve any payment by the insurance company each year. If it insures property worth £50 million, all of which has a 1 per cent probability of being destroyed by fire in a year, then it faces the prospect of paying out any sum from zero (if there are no fires) to £50 million (if all the property is destroyed). However, assuming that the property is not all in one place, so that fires do not spread through it, the insurance company pays out an annual average of 1 per cent of £50 million which is £500,000. So if it insures £50 million of property, the expected value of the annual payout by the insurance company is £500,000.

If the insurance company receives £500,000 for insuring the £50 million of property, its revenue equals the expected value of its payout and (ignoring its operating costs) the expected value of its profit is zero. The expected value of the insurance company's profit is zero if it charges annual insurance premiums equal to 1 per cent of the value of the insured property.

In fact, the insurance company wants an annual revenue that exceeds £500,000, both because it wants to make a profit and because it must pay out more than £500,000 in a year when more than 1 per cent of the property is destroyed. To meet such a 'bad year' the insurance company needs reserves, which it builds up in good and average years. So it will charge an annual premium of more than 1 per cent of the value of the insured property. In our example, the firm is willing to pay £3,750, which is 1.5 per cent of the value of the insured property. If all those who want insurance are willing to pay 1.5 per cent, then the insurance company receives £750,000 to insure the £50 million of property. The insurance company can only operate if those who insure are risk-averse, so that they are willing to pay more than 1 per cent. This example illustrates the principle that:

Anyone who insures behaves in a risk-averse way.

14.4.2 Moral hazard

Insurance provides households and firms with a way of reducing the effects of some uncertainties, but it is not possible to insure against all uncertain prospects. It is simplest to insure against events that are outside the control of the insured, such as the financial effect of being struck by lightning. In other cases, the insurance company attempts to avoid the possibility that the presence of insurance increases the chance that the specified event will occur. For example, a firm that insures against the effects of fire damage is likely to be required by the insurance company to install some fire-prevention equipment. Otherwise, the firm suffers no loss in the event of a fire, and it has a much reduced incentive to prevent fires.

The problem that the presence of insurance may increase the probability that the insured event will occur is known as **moral hazard**, and implies that it is not possible to buy insurance against some events. For example, a firm cannot insure against the effects of its own bankruptcy, because such insurance would remove the incentive for the firm's owners to operate the firm in an efficient way. If the firm could insure against all the effects of bankruptcy, its profit would be the same however it operates, and it would be likely to choose to be inefficient, because this is the easier option. Then it would be very likely to become bankrupt, and the insurance company would face the almost certain prospect of paying out to the insured.

14.4.3 Futures and forward markets

It is not usually possible for a firm to insure against increases in the prices of materials, against the possibility that the selling price of its good may fall, or against changes in exchange rates if it exports its products or imports its raw materials. If it could so insure, the insurance company would have no guarantee that the insured firm would attempt to buy at the lowest possible price or sell at the highest possible price (moral hazard again). Instead, it is possible to buy and sell futures (or forward) contracts for some goods and for foreign currencies that specify:

(a) The delivery of a quantity of the good or currency at a specified date.
(b) A price (which is an exchange rate for a foreign currency) that is agreed at the time when the contract is made.

This price is the **futures** (or **forward**) **price**; it is generally different from the **spot price**, which is the price paid for immediate delivery of the good or currency. It is important to distinguish the current futures price for a contract to buy and sell at a future date, and the spot price at that future date. The futures price is determined now; the spot price is unknown until the relevant date.

In London, there are futures markets in cocoa, coffee, sugar, rubber (on the London commodity market), many metals (on the London metal exchange), grains (on the London grain futures market) and for many foreign currencies.

There are also other futures markets internationally in goods such as oil, frozen orange juice and meat. On these markets, it is possible to make futures contracts for a variety of periods, up to at least one year ahead. Firms can therefore make contracts to buy materials in the future which remove some uncertainty about the future costs. Some firms can enter contracts to sell goods in the future, and this reduces uncertainty about future revenues.

To see how a futures price is determined, it is simplest to examine futures markets first in an economic system where there is no uncertainty. We shall then examine the effects of uncertainty on the price. Suppose that a buyer wants to make a contract to buy a tonne of corn in one year's time. There is no uncertainty, and the buyer knows that the spot price of a tonne of corn in one year's time will be £110. The interest rate is 10 per cent per year. If the futures price exceeds £100, the buyer can lend the money, have more than £110 at the end of the year, buy the corn at the end of the year and have some money left over. So if the futures price exceeds £100, the buyer prefers not to buy the futures contract.

If the futures price is less than £100, the seller prefers to sell next year at next year's spot price of £110, rather than to sell a futures contract for say £95 and have £104.5 (= £95 + £9.5 interest) next year. So if the futures price is less than £100, the seller prefers not to sell the futures contract.

Therefore, the only price at which both buyer and seller are willing to enter into the futures contract is £100.

If the price of a tonne of corn in one year's time is uncertain, the price paid for the futures contract depends on the buyer's and seller's expectations of the price in one year's time. Both buyer and seller have a certainty equivalent of the uncertain price and:

(a) The buyer is prepared to buy the futures contract as long as the futures price does not exceed his or her certainty equivalent of the uncertain prospect of waiting to buy at next year's spot price. If the futures price exceeds this certainty equivalent, the buyer prefers to wait and buy at the uncertain spot price in one year's time.

(b) The seller is prepared to sell the futures contract as long as the price is not less than his or her certainty equivalent of the uncertain prospect of waiting to sell at next year's spot price. If the price is less than this certainty equivalent, he or she prefers to wait and sell at the uncertain spot price in the future.

These conclusions imply that:

(a) If the buyer and seller have the same certainty equivalent, the only possible futures price equals their certainty equivalents.

(b) If the buyer's certainty equivalent exceeds the seller's certainty equivalent they will enter a futures contract at a price between the seller's and the buyer's certainty equivalents.

(c) If the seller's certainty equivalent exceeds the buyer's certainty equivalent, they will not enter a futures contract, because there is no price that exceeds the buyer's certainty equivalent and is less than the seller's certainty equivalent.

The principles that determine futures prices are influenced by the possibility that the buyer pays only a fraction of the price (known as the **margin** required) at the time when the contract is made, and the remainder when the goods are delivered. This affects the interest that the buyer or seller can obtain on the money paid in advance of delivery of the goods. In the previous example of corn futures, if 30 per cent of the price is to be paid in advance, and the remaining 70 per cent on delivery, then the price when there is no uncertainty (or when the buyer and the seller agree that the certainty equivalent is £110), is £106.80. Of this, 30 per cent (£32.04) is paid in advance, and can be lent by the seller for £3.20 in interest. The remainder of the price (£74.76) is paid when the tonne of corn is delivered. At the time of delivery, the seller has £74.76 + £32.04 + £3.20 = £110, and both buyer and seller are willing to enter the futures contract.

We have examined the price (or the range of prices when there is uncertainty) at which individual buyers and sellers are willing to enter into futures contracts. In practice, buyers and sellers need not establish a mutual coincidence of wants, because futures contracts are traded on markets. The principles established for the uncertain case imply that:

(a) The supply of futures contracts at each price is determined by the number of sellers whose certainty equivalents are less than the price.
(b) The demand for futures contracts at each price is determined by the number of buyers whose certainty equivalents exceed the price.

The market price of a futures contract is then the result of the interaction of this supply and demand. A firm that buys a futures contract has eliminated uncertainty about the price of a material in the future and so has reduced the uncertainty of its costs. A firm that sells a futures contract has eliminated uncertainty about the price of its product in the future and so has reduced the uncertainty of its revenues. There is no moral hazard, because firms are motivated to buy at the lowest price and sell at the highest price.

14.4.4 Gambling

A gambler pays to face uncertainty. If a person buys a lottery ticket for £10 that gives him a 1 per cent probability of winning £500, he has a 99 per cent chance of losing £10, and a 1 per cent chance of winning £490 (the prize minus the price of the ticket). The expected value of the uncertain prospect is

$$(99\% \times -£10) + (1\% \times £490) = -£9.9 + £4.9 = -£5$$

He buys the ticket if he prefers the uncertain prospect to the certain prospect of paying and receiving nothing if he does not enter the lottery. The certainty equivalent of the prospect of buying the lottery ticket must exceed zero if he buys it, and so the certainty equivalent (more than zero) exceeds the expected value (-£5). So:

Anyone who gambles behaves in a risk-preferring way.

14.4.5 Are people risk-averse?

Many people both insure and gamble. This does not imply that they are inconsistent, but that they are risk-averse towards some uncertain prospects (those that might involve a potentially disastrous loss), and risk-preferring towards other uncertain prospects (that involve a probable small loss and a possible large gain). As we shall see, most aspects of economic behaviour are risk-averse, and involve a positive risk premium. For example, savers usually want the expected value of the dividend from a risky share to exceed the certain income that they could obtain by using their money in some other way; firms usually want a higher expected value of profit from a project in which profit is subject to great uncertainties than from a project that gives a relatively certain profit.

14.5 Financial assets: bonds and shares

A risk-averse individual does not avoid all uncertain prospects, but expects an uncertain prospect to have a greater expected value than a certain prospect. In financial terms, an individual is willing to pay more for a financial asset that gives a certain income of £X per year than for an asset that gives an uncertain income with an expected value of £X. In general, individuals who save are likely to want to hold a **portfolio** of assets ranging from those that give an absolutely certain return and a low income to those with an uncertain return and a higher expected return.

14.5.1 Bonds and shares

To correspond to risk-averse savers' willingness to hold assets of varying degrees of uncertainty (with greater uncertainty compensated by higher expected returns), firms can issue various forms of security. In fact, firms raise money in two main ways to allow for these different preferences of savers:

(a) Firms sell **bonds**. A **bondholder** lends money to the firm, and is entitled to receive a specified amount of interest each year until the **redemption date**, when the bondholder receives the **redemption value** (or **principal** or **face value**) of the bond and the life of the bond is ended.
(b) Firms sell **shares**. A firm's **shareholders** are its owners: a share (or **common stock** or **equity**) is an entitlement to the ownership of the firm. Shareholders receive a **dividend**, whose size depends on the size of the firm's profit after it has paid interest to bondholders. If no profit remains shareholders receive nothing; if the firm makes a very large profit, the dividend may be very large, although the firm's directors may decide to retain some undistributed profit for financing investment projects and as a reserve that can be used in the event that future profits are lower.

Some firms issue more than one type of share. A **preference share** includes an agreement that the firm will pay a specified dividend provided that it makes sufficient profit to do so. The payment of the dividend on the preference shares take precedence over the payment of any dividend to owners of **ordinary shares**. An ordinary shareholder receives a dividend only if the firm's operating profit is sufficient to pay interest to bondholders and dividends on preference shares. The ordinary shareholder faces a greater chance that he or she will receive no dividend, but the maximum income that he or she can receive is not limited, as is the maximum income from a preference share. Ordinary shareholders are (usually, although some firms issue non-voting ordinary shares) entitled to vote at **general meetings** of the firm on the appointment of directors and on other aspects of the operation of the firm. Usually, preference shareholders have no such vote.

When a firm issues new shares to finance an investment project, each existing share represents a smaller fraction of the ownership of the firm. If the new shares are bought by people who are not already shareholders, the fraction of the firm that is owned by each existing shareholder is reduced. Each shareholder receives a smaller fraction of the total profit, and those who can vote have less influence in general meetings. To prevent this, a firm may make a **rights issue**: existing shareholders are given the right to buy newly issued shares in proportion to their existing holdings of shares so that they can continue to own the same fraction of the firm.

14.5.2 Stock market

Bonds and shares are bought and sold on the stock market. Firms sell bonds and shares on the stock market to raise money to finance new investment. These assets are demanded by savers who can combine the more certain return from bonds with the less certain return from shares. A very risk-averse saver demands few shares, because he or she prefers the certainty of bonds; a risk-preferring saver demands mainly shares, and may concentrate on shares sold by firms whose profits are highly uncertain (such as firms that prospect for minerals in an area of unknown potential).

As well as demanding bonds and shares, households can supply bonds and shares that they already own. It is convenient to distinguish **new bonds and shares** that are supplied by firms raising money for investment, from **old** (that is, previously issued) **bonds and shares** that are supplied by households who have previously bought the assets and now want to sell them.

These demands and supplies determine the equilibrium prices of new and old bonds and shares. The expected rate of return on a financial asset can be derived from the price using the formula:

$$\text{expected rate of return} = \frac{\text{expected value of income from the asset}}{\text{price of the asset}}$$

So:

The expected rate of return on an asset falls if the price of that asset increases.

14.5.3 Bond prices

We discuss bonds assuming that people expect that the interest on them will be paid, and that the redemption value will be repaid as promised at the end of the life of the bond. If there is uncertainty about the income from, or eventual redemption of, a bond then it takes on some of the characteristics of a share, whose prices are discussed below.

When bond markets are in equilibrium, the prices of bonds are the same if they give identical incomes and have identical redemption values on the same date. If these prices are not the same, all savers demand the bond that has the lower price, and the price of that bond rises. The price of the other bond falls because there is no demand for it. The prices change until they are equal.

The following example shows how the prices of bonds that yield different incomes are related. Suppose that a firm issues a new bond that pays interest of £10 per year for a specified period and has a redemption value of £100. If the firm can sell this bond for £100, the annual interest rate is 10 per cent. An old bond, that was originally sold for £100 with an interest rate of 6 per cent, gives an interest income of £6 per year. Savers will not pay £100 for the old bond, given that they can obtain 10 per cent interest on the new bond. If the interest payments were the only influence on the price of the old bond, savers would pay £60 for the old bond, so that it too gives an annual interest rate of 10 per cent.

However, the interest payment is not the only influence on the price of the old bond, because the old bond will be redeemed at the end of its life. If the redemption value of the old bond is £100, the buyer of the old bond receives £6 per year and £100 at the end of its life. Suppose that, for example, the old bond has one more year of life, so that the buyer of an old bond receives £106 after one year. If she pays only £60 for the old bond, she receives a return of £46 for her expenditure of £60, which is an expected rate of return (including the difference between the price and the redemption value) of 76.7 per cent ($100 \times 46/60$). The expected rate of return on the new bond is 10 per cent (there is no difference between the current price and the redemption value of the new bond, and so the only income is from interest). The price of the old bond would be approximately £96.36 because the buyer then receives £106 after one year, which is her payment of £96.36 plus 10 per cent interest on £96.36 (£106 almost exactly equals £96.36 + £9.636). Then the expected rate of return on the old bond and the expected rate of return on the new bond are equal.

If the interest rate on the new bond was 15 per cent, the price of the old bond would be lower (£92.2, so that £106 = £92.2 + (15% × £92.2)). This example illustrates the principle that:

If the interest rate on new bonds increases, the prices of old bonds fall.

14.5.4 Share prices

The same considerations affect the prices of shares:

The price of a share falls if the expected rate of return on it falls relative to the expected rate of return on other assets.

The dividend from a share is uncertain and the price of a share, compared to the price of a bond that has the same expected rate of return but with no uncertainty, reflects attitudes to uncertainty. A saver compares the certain opportunity of buying a bond with the uncertain opportunity of buying the share. If the redemption yield on bonds is 10 per cent per year, and the expected value of the income from the share is £10 per year, then a saver is prepared to pay:

(a) £100 for the share if he is risk-neutral, because he is indifferent between the certain opportunity and the uncertain opportunity when each has the same expected rate of return.
(b) Less than £100 for the share if he is risk-averse, so that the expected rate of return on the share is higher, to compensate for the uncertainty.
(c) More than £100 for the share if he is risk-preferring, so that the expected rate of return on the bond is higher, to compensate for its lack of uncertainty.

So the demand for a firm's shares at each price depends on savers' expectations of the firm's profits, and on the extent to which savers are risk-averse, risk-neutral and risk-preferring. If, as seems likely, most savers are risk-averse the prices of shares are lower than if most savers are risk-preferrers.

14.5.5 Expectations and speculation

This analysis of the prices of shares ignores the fact that people buy shares in a firm when they expect that the price of those shares will increase, and sell shares when they expect the price to fall. These demands and supplies are **speculative**, because they are based on expectations of changes in the prices of shares, and not on expectations of the firm's profits, although these may be related. If people expect that the price of a share will increase, and buy it for that reason, the expectation is likely to be **self-fulfilling**, because the speculators add to the demand for the share and so the price increases as they expect. Similarly, if people expect that the price of a share will soon fall, speculators supply shares that they hold and this brings about the price reduction that they expect.

If speculation causes the price of a share to rise, some people may expect that it will continue to rise, because they base their expectations of the future change in price on that recently experienced. So speculative pressure may lead to a boom in the price of a share, and if the prices of many shares are affected in similar ways to a general increase in the price of shares (and an increase in the average price quoted in the **Financial Times Index** for the London Stock Exchange and the **Dow Jones Index** for the New York Exchange). Similarly, speculation can cause a slump in prices of shares if expectations of further price falls follow from recent price falls. The speed of a slump may be increased if speculators have previously bought shares with borrowed money. If the prices of their shares fall, their wealth is reduced and those who have lent to them may be unwilling to renew the loans when they become due for repayment. The speculators must then sell shares to repay the loans, and this selling adds to the downward pressure on prices. The rapid reductions of prices on all major stock markets in October 1987 was partly due to these self-fulfilling expectations. It is likely that the price reductions were also accelerated by automatic selling programmed into computers: when the price of a share falls, the computer initiates sales of the share so that those who own it are not left holding an asset with a reduced value. These sales, of course, add to supply in the market and further depress the price of the share, thus triggering more sales.

14.5.6 Bankruptcy

Bondholders have financial priority over shareholders. If the firm is unable to pay interest on bonds, bondholders can declare the firm bankrupt and force it to sell assets to pay its debts. In the event that the firm ceases to operate, the firm's debts, including wages, payments for materials, rented land, hired equipment and the redemption value of bonds, are repaid before any money is paid to shareholders.

Bondholders are not the only group who can initiate bankruptcy proceedings. Any creditor (including suppliers of materials, workers or landlords) has the right to force the firm into bankruptcy. It must then sell some or all of its assets to pay its debts. Any money remaining is paid to shareholders. If the firm cannot sell its assets for a sufficient amount to pay all its debts, its creditors receive only part of the money that they are owed, and the shareholders receive nothing.

In the UK shareholders in most large firms are protected by **limited liability** (denoted in the name of a firm by Ltd or by PLC, for Public Limited Company). The shareholders in these firms are not required to pay the debts that remain after the firm has sold its assets. Shareholders without limited liability are responsible for its debts and may have to sell their personal possessions to repay creditors. Limited liability status is valuable to a firm's shareholders because it transfers the risks of bankruptcy from shareholders to creditors, and is granted only after the firm has demonstrated some financial soundness. Despite this, major bankruptcies occur in which creditors receive only a fraction of the money that they are owed. An example is that of Laker Airlines in 1982.

14.5.7 Gearing and survival

A firm's **gearing ratio** is the ratio of its borrowing (by selling bonds) to the total of money raised by selling shares and by borrowing.

So a firm's gearing ratio is between zero (no borrowing; all money raised by selling shares) and one (all borrowing; no money raised by selling shares). This ratio affects the firm's ability to avoid bankruptcy and hence the uncertainties faced by its shareholders, as the following example shows.

Consider two firms that operate in identical ways, and both buy equipment for £10,000 at the beginning of 1989. Each sells goods for £2,500 in 1989 and £1,500 in 1990. In both years, the operating cost of each firm (total cost excluding normal profit and interest payments) is £1,000. So the operating profit of each firm is £1,500 in 1989 and £500 in 1990.

The firms differ in that:

(a) Firm F sells shares to raise the £10,000 needed to buy the equipment.
(b) Firm G sells £2,000 worth of shares and borrows £8,000 at an interest rate of 8 per cent per year to buy the equipment.

Firm F can pay its shareholders dividends totalling £1,500 in 1989 and £500 in 1990. So F has no cash-flow problem, because all its creditors (who supply materials, labour and land) can be paid in each year. Firm G must pay £640 interest in each year. It can do this, and pay a dividend of £860 (£1500 − £640) in 1989. However, in 1990 its interest payments exceed its operating profit, and if it has no reserves of cash and cannot borrow, it must sell assets to pay its creditors. Firm F has the lower gearing ratio, and is better able to survive when its operating profits are low.

The advantage of the higher gearing ratio to the shareholders of firm G is that, in 1989, they could receive a dividend of £860 on their £2,000 of shares (a rate of return for the year of 43 per cent). The shareholders of F, on the other hand, can receive dividends of £1,500 and £500 on their £10,000 of shares, which are rates of return of 15 per cent in 1989 and 5 per cent in 1990. So the shareholders of a firm with a higher gearing ratio obtain a higher rate of return when operating profits exceed interest payments, and are more likely to face bankruptcy when operating profits are lower.

If a firm has a year of low operating profits and borrows to avoid bankruptcy, its gearing ratio is increased and so its chances of survival in future years of low operating profit are reduced. So during a period when firms' sales are low, they may accumulate debts that eventually force them into bankruptcy unless they are able to issue shares from time to time, and use the revenue from selling shares to repay bonds, so that the gearing ratio is reduced. This conclusion plays a role in explaining why increases in interest rates can be so damaging to firms at times when sales are low.

14.6 Uncertain exchange rates

Households and firms also face uncertainty in foreign exchange markets. If they expect that exchange rates will change, exporters are not certain of the amount that they will receive when they sell their goods abroad. Similarly, importers face uncertainty if they plan to buy goods abroad in the future. The methods for reducing this uncertainty include futures markets in foreign exchanges, where an exporter can make a contract now that guarantees the exchange rate for his or her export earnings at a specified future date. Similarly, importers can make futures contracts to guarantee the exchange rate that they will face when they want foreign currency to buy imports. The principles of these futures markets are similar to those outlined in section 14.4.3.

14.6.1 International borrowing and lending

If a household or firm buys a bond in its own country and holds it until it is redeemed, the return consists of the interest plus the difference between the redemption value and the price paid for the bond (see section 14.5.1). The only uncertainty concerns the price at which the bond could be sold before the redemption date if the bondholder needs to sell early.

Additional uncertainty is introduced when a resident of one country (say the UK) buys a bond issued by a firm or government in another country (say the USA). The UK resident must use pounds to buy dollars in order to buy the bond, and the interest payments and repayment of the principal are made in dollars. The UK resident is likely to want to exchange the dollars paid in interest and as repayment for pounds. The cost of buying the bond depends on the current exchange rate between the pound and the dollar, and the future return depends on the future exchange rate. The future exchange rate is not known with certainty, unless countries agree to preserve exchange rates at announced levels and the UK resident is confident that the agreement will not be broken while he owns the US bond. Then the UK resident either faces the uncertainty himself, or must use a futures contract to guarantee the exchange rate. In general, futures transactions are possible for only a limited period in advance (a year, typically) and so this form of insurance against exchange rate changes does not apply to bonds with a longer life.

For example, suppose that a UK resident buys a US government bond for $300 at the start of 1989 when the exchange rate is £1 = $1.5. He must pay £200 for the $300. The bond matures in one year, when the $300 is repaid together with interest of $30 for the year. If the exchange rate has not changed, he obtains £220 with his $330 at the end of 1989, and his return is £20, or 10 per cent for the year. However, if the exchange rate changes to £1 = $1.375 (the pound depreciates against the dollar), he obtains £240 with his $330, and his return increases to £40, or 20 per cent. If the exchange rate changes to £1 = $1.571 (the pound appreciates against the dollar), he can exchange $330 for £210, and his return is £10, or 5 per cent. This example illustrates the principle that:

(a) The return on a foreign bond **increases** if the buyer's currency **depreciates** against the currency in which the bond is issued.
(b) The return on a foreign bond **decreases** if the buyer's currency **appreciates** against the currency in which the bond is issued.

This principle arises because the depreciation of a currency implies that it is worth less in terms of other currencies, and it is profitable to sell a currency before it depreciates and to buy it again after it depreciates when it exchanges for less foreign currency. So, in our example, the UK resident gains if he sells pounds when he can get $1.5 for £1 and buys pounds when he has to pay less than $1.5 for £1.

14.6.2 Expectations and international borrowing

The demand for foreign bonds depends on people's expectations of future exchange rate changes, as well as on the interest rate. In the example, the UK resident buys a US bond that pays an annual interest rate of 10 per cent in any of the following circumstances (we are ignoring bonds issued in countries other than the USA and the UK for simplicity):

(a) He expects no change in the exchange rate, and bonds issued in the UK pay interest at less than 10 per cent per year.
(b) He expects that the pound will depreciate by the end of the year to £1 = $1.375, and bonds issued in the UK pay less than 20 per cent per year.
(c) He expects that the pound will appreciate by the end of the year to £1 = $1.571, and bonds issued in the UK pay less than 5 per cent per year.

Similar arguments apply to the demand for shares issued by foreign firms, except that shares involve the additional uncertainty that future dividends depend on the profitability of the firm.

Influences on borrowing and lending work in both directions: the demand by US residents for bonds and shares issued in the UK also depends on the exchange rate between the pound and the dollar. US residents are likely to buy UK bonds and shares if they expect that the dollar will depreciate against the pound – that is, if they expect that the pound will appreciate against the dollar. So assuming that most potential lenders in the two countries have similar expectations of changes in the exchange rate, that the interest rates on bonds issued in the two countries are equal and that no other countries are involved:

(a) If the pound is expected to depreciate against the dollar, UK residents demand bonds issued in the USA. This increases the supply of pounds as dollars are demanded on the foreign exchange market. Also, US residents do not demand bonds issued in the UK, so that they also demand bonds issued in the USA, and this reduces the demand for pounds. So there is pressure for the pound to depreciate against the dollar.
(b) If the pound is expected to appreciate against the dollar, US residents demand bonds issued in the UK. UK residents do not demand bonds issued in the USA, so that they also demand bonds issued in the UK. This causes pressure for the pound to appreciate against the dollar.

So widely held expectations of exchange rate changes are likely to be self-fulfilling:

(a) If expectations change from a generally expected depreciation of the pound against the dollar to a generally expected appreciation, residents of both countries change their demands in similar ways, and the pound is likely to appreciate, as expected.
(b) If expectations change from a generally expected appreciation of the pound against the dollar to a generally expected depreciation, the pound is likely to depreciate, as expected.

In reality, international lending involves many countries, and depends on expectations of changes in many exchange rates. In addition, bonds issued in different countries pay different interest rates and are subject to different rates of tax, both in the country where the bond is issued and in the country where the bondholder lives. The demands for bonds therefore depend on interest rates and taxation systems as well as on the expected changes in exchange rates. However, the conclusion that generally expected appreciations and depreciations actually occur remains.

These conclusions concern the effects of expectations of changes in exchange rates on the demand for UK and foreign bonds. It is less easy to predict the effects of an actual (rather than an expected) change in exchange rates. A depreciation of the pound may lead to the expectation of a further depreciation, so that the demand for UK bonds falls and that for foreign bonds increases. On the other hand, if the depreciation was expected to be smaller than it actually is, it may be thought that the pound will soon appreciate again, because it has overshot the expected level. In this case, the demand for UK bonds increases as households and firms want to hold their assets in an appreciating currency.

14.6.3 Foreign currency bonds

Governments and firms do not necessarily issue bonds for sale in the currencies of their own country. For example, many Third World countries issue bonds denominated in dollars, and Ireland has issued bonds denominated in German marks. If the Irish government wants to borrow, it may find that lenders in other countries are unwilling to buy bonds denominated in the Irish punt because they expect a depreciation of the punt against their own currencies. If the Irish government issues a bond denominated in marks, and promises to pay interest and repay the principal in marks, then lenders do not need to worry about the possibility that the punt will depreciate while they hold the bond. The Irish government faces uncertainty about the exchange rate between the punt and the mark, and the buyers of the bonds do not face that uncertainty:

(a) If the punt depreciates, the Irish government must pay more punts to buy the marks necessary to pay interest on, and to repay, the bonds.
(b) If the punt appreciates, the Irish government pays fewer punts to buy the marks necessary to pay interest on, and to repay, the bonds.

By selling bonds to foreigners, the government helps to finance its own budget deficit and the balance of trade deficit at the same time. By issuing bonds in a foreign currency, it is more likely that foreigners rather than domestic residents will buy the bonds, helping the simultaneous funding of both deficits.

14.6.4 Hot money

Many firms and banks have large amounts of liquid funds (or **hot money**) that they can convert rapidly from one currency to another. In particular, multinational firms (firms that operate in more than one country) transfer money from one currency to another because they receive revenues and pay production costs, taxes, interest and dividends in several currencies. The timing of these transfers can have significant effects on exchange rates.

These firms transfer their liquid assets in order to hold currencies that appreciate, and to try to avoid holding currencies that depreciate. These transfers are often of very short duration: the money is lent for very short periods (overnight or a few days) to banks, and may then be used to meet the firm's costs, taxes, interest or dividends, or it may be converted into another currency. Hot money can have significant effects on exchange rates because the amounts involved can be very large in comparison with the transfers of currency by importers and exporters.

For example, if a firm has liquid funds in pounds, but it believes that the pound will depreciate soon relative to the dollar, the firm buys dollars and sells pounds. This increases the supply of pounds, so that the pound depreciates relative to the dollar. The firm's action has helped to bring about the depreciation that it expected. Similarly, if the firm holds dollars, and expects that the pound will appreciate, it demands pounds, and the expected appreciation occurs. So movements of hot money help to make expectations self-fulfilling. They also make it possible for a small change in interest rates (which make lending in one country more attractive relative to lending in another) to lead a very large transfer of funds, and perhaps to a large effect on exchange rates as firms try to move large amounts of money from one currency to another.

14.7 Liquidity preference: demand for money

One form of certainty that an individual is likely to want is the knowledge that he or she can spend money immediately. Cash and some forms of bank and building society accounts are highly **liquid** (see section 3.4.3) because they can be used immediately or almost immediately to buy goods. The cost of this liquidity is that cash yields no return (or a negative real return on cash held at times of inflation) while the interest rate on these bank or building society accounts is less than that on other accounts from which money cannot be drawn so quickly, and certainly less than the interest or profit rate on bonds and shares.

The advantages of liquidity imply that savers generally include cash or other very liquid assets in their portfolios: in short, they demand money.

14.7.1 The demand for money

Households and firms demand money for at least three reasons:

(a) To finance expected purchases of goods, materials, factors, bonds and shares (this is the **transactions demand for money**: see section 11.5.1).
(b) To finance unexpected purchases in emergencies, or when an unexpected opportunity to buy goods cheaply occurs. This is known as the **precautionary demand for money**. To some extent, households and firms may hold bonds and shares that they sell when an emergency or an unexpected opportunity arises, but it may not be possible to sell them immediately or, if they are sold, the price may have fallen (see section 14.5.3). So some money is held because of its liquidity.
(c) To finance speculative purchases of bonds and shares. If a household expects that the price of bonds or shares will soon fall it delays buying until the price fall has occurred. In the meantime, it holds money, so that it is ready to buy at the most advantageous moment. This is the **speculative demand for money**.

14.7.2 The demand for money and national income

An increase in national income increases the transactions demand for money. If national income increases because more goods are produced, there are more transactions; if national income increases because of inflation, each transaction requires more money.

14.7.3 The demand for money and interest rates

The cost of holding money as a liquid asset is the loss of the interest or dividends that could have been obtained if the household owned bonds or shares instead. This loss increases if the rate of return on bonds and shares increases. So:

> The cost of holding money as a liquid form of saving increases when interest rates increase.

This implies that a household is likely to hold less money and more bonds when interest rates increase. In so far as households can reduce their transactions demand for money, they are likely to do so when interest rates increase. They may also reduce the money held for precautionary purposes, which increases the chance of not being able to meet an emergency or take advantage of an unexpected bargain. The household accepts this greater risk as a cost of obtaining more interest.

The speculative demand for money is also reduced when interest rates increase, but in another way. If interest rates increase, the prices of old bonds fall (see section 14.5.3). If the increase in interest rates is regarded as temporary, people expect that they will soon fall and that bond prices will increase. So, when interest rates increase, households buy bonds to benefit from the expected price increase, and the speculative demand for money is low. The speculative demand for bonds increases the prices of bonds, and so the speculation is self-fulfilling. Similarly, if interest rates fall, and are expected to rise again, bond prices rise and people expect that they will soon fall. Households sell bonds in order to avoid the expected loss in value, and they hold money instead. So the speculative demand for money increases when interest rates fall.

This argument, that the speculative demand for money increases when interest rates fall, depends on the assumption that people regard the change in interest rates as temporary. If, on the other hand, people base their expectations on the recent trend, they expect a further fall in interest rates when interest rates have recently fallen. So they expect further increases in bond prices, and they want to hold bonds and not money for speculative purposes. However, it is unlikely that people expect that a decrease in interest rates will persist until interest rates reach unusually low levels, and so a decrease in interest rates eventually leads to the expectation that they will rise again. This expectation causes a speculative demand for money. Similarly, a continued increase in interest rates eventually leads to the expectation that they will fall again, so that speculators reduce their holdings of money and buy bonds to benefit from the expected price increase.

14.7.4 Liquidity preference curve

Figure 14.1 illustrates **liquidity preference curve** that shows the relation between the demand for money and the interest rate for a fixed level of national income. The higher curve (MM) shows the liquidity preference for a higher level of national income than the lower curve (LL). We shall use these curves to examine the effects of government policies that involve changes in the supply of money.

The slope of the curve can be described using the **interest-elasticity of the demand for money**, which is:

> The percentage decrease in the demand for money caused by a 1 per cent increase in the interest rate.

(Note that a 1 per cent increase in the interest rate occurs, for example, when the interest rate increases from 8 per cent to 8.08 per cent, and not when it increases from 8 per cent to 9 per cent, which is a 12.5 per cent increase.)

14.7.5 LM curve

In later analysis of macroeconomic equilibrium and policy issues, we use **LM curves**. An LM curve shows the combinations of the interest rate and national income that give rise to a demand for money equal to a fixed supply. The demand for money increases as national income increases, because the transactions demand rises. The demand for money falls as the interest rate

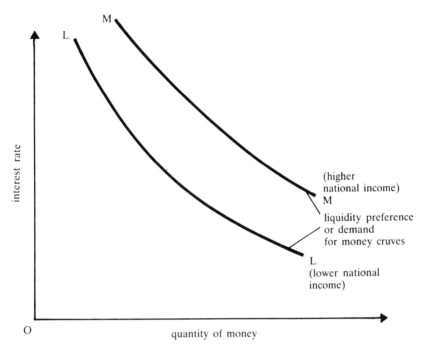

M

L

interest rate

(higher
national income)
M

liquidity preference
or demand
for money cruves

L
(lower national
income)

O   quantity of money

Figure 14.1 Liquidity preference curve
The liquidity preference curve shows the relation between the demand for money and
the interest rate. If national income rises, transactions demand for money rises and so
the curve moves upwards.

increases as shown by a liquidity preference curve. So if national income rises
(so that the demand for money rises), the interest rate must also rise to reduce
the demand for money to keep the demand equal to the fixed supply. Hence:

The LM curve slopes upwards.

This can be seen in figure 14.2. If we consider a higher supply of money, the
LM curve is further to the right: so LM_1 is drawn for a lower supply of money
than LM_2.

In pure monetarist theory, the demand for money depends only on the level
of national income, as described in the quantity theory of money (see section
11.6). So:

The monetarist LM curve is vertical.

This is because a given supply of money is consistent with only one level of
national income, as in figure 14.3.

Note the difference between an LM curve and a liquidity preference curve:
an LM curve shows the combinations of interest rate and national income that
give a particular demand for money; a liquidity preference curve shows the
demand for money for each interest rate at a given level of national income.

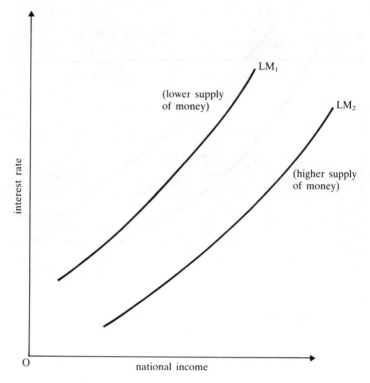

Figure 14.2 LM curves
The LM curve shows the combinations of national income and the interest rate that
keep the demand for money equal to a fixed supply. If the supply of money increases,
the LM curve shifts downwards.

14.8 Investment

A firm buys new equipment if it expects to make a profit by using it in the
future. We saw in section 8.8 how investment decisions depend on the net
present value of the project: in an uncertain environment, we must examine
the expected net present value; if this is positive, then the project has a positive
expected profit. However, the investment still may not occur, because the
shareholders (or potential shareholders) may be risk-averse, and the expected
net present value may not be large enough to compensate for the uncertainty
because the certainty equivalent of the uncertain profit is negative.

The expected profit depends on the costs of the investment and on the
revenue that the firm expects to receive from selling the output made using
equipment. So a firm's decision to invest depends on:

(a) The price of the necessary equipment and the cost of obtaining the money
needed to buy it. If the project had an entirely certain future return it
could be financed by issuing bonds at the current market interest rate. In

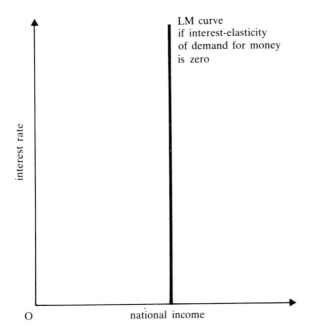

Figure 14.3   Monetarist LM curve
The demand for money depends on the level of national income but not on the interest rate (using the quantity equation).

an uncertain environment, the firm must issue shares and sell them to those who are willing to take on the uncertainty. It may be very difficult to finance a highly risky investment because risk-averse savers will not pay much for shares with a very uncertain return.

(b) The firm's expectations of its future costs and revenues. Investment increases if firms' expectations of their future sales and profits become more optimistic. This is particularly likely if many firms expect an increase in national income, because they are then likely to expect an increase in their sales.

So total investment depends on prices of investment goods, on the cost of borrowing (which rises when the interest rate rises) and on expectations of changes in national income. Economists differ in their views of the relative importance of these causes – and particularly on the **interest-elasticity of investment**, which is the percentage fall in total investment caused by a 1 per cent rise in the interest rate. Those who believe that the interest-elasticity of investment is low argue that investment is most strongly influenced by the optimism of firms' expectations.

14.9 Summary

People react to an uncertain prospect according to whether they are risk-averse, risk-neutral or risk-preferring towards the prospect. People insure against an outcome of an uncertain event if they are risk-averse towards the event. It is impossible to insure against some outcomes because the presence of insurance makes it more likely that the outcome will occur (moral hazard). People gamble on the outcome of an event if they are risk-preferring towards the event. It is not inconsistent to insure against some eventualities and also to gamble, because people have different views on different uncertain prospects. Firms can reduce some uncertainties on prices by entering futures contracts. The futures price depends on the attitudes of buyers and sellers to uncertainty.

Firms issue bonds (on which the return is relatively certain) and shares (on which the return is relatively uncertain). This mixture of financial assets allows a household to buy a portfolio involving whatever degree of risk it wants. The prices of old bonds increase if interest rates fall. The expected rate of return on shares exceeds that on bonds if most savers are risk-averse. Speculation occurs when people buy assets whose price is expected to increase, and sell assets whose price is expected to fall. Speculation in markets for bonds and shares is likely to be self-fulfilling, and may lead to cumulative increases or decreases in prices.

A firm's ability to survive bankruptcy depends on its ratio of bonds to shares (its gearing ratio). If a firm has a high gearing ratio, it is more likely to face bankruptcy in years of low operating profits than a firm with a lower ratio. A firm that borrows to avoid bankruptcy increases its gearing ratio, and may therefore face greater problems in future when its operating profit is low.

The uncertainty of exchange rates can also be offset to some extent through futures contracts. Remaining uncertainty affects the relative incomes from domestic and foreign bonds. Large amounts of hot money can be moved rapidly from one currency to another, causing large fluctuations in exchange rates.

Households include money in their portfolios to finance day-to-day transactions, to meet emergencies and to have money readily available to profit from speculative ventures. Households demand less money if interest rates are high, both because they do not want to sacrifice the high income and because high interest rates imply low bond prices. So households buy bonds to benefit from anticipated price rises.

Topics and problems

(1) What is the basis of your expectations of future employment prospects and future inflation rates?

(2) Does a risk-averse household insure against every possible eventuality?

(3) You are going abroad for a year. You are offered the choice between buying a round trip airline ticket now at price £300, or buying a one-way ticket for £170, and leaving the purchase of the ticket for the return journey until the time of your return. Assuming that you could afford to buy the round trip ticket now, how would you decide which option to choose? How does your decision relate to the analysis of futures markets?

(4) You have £1,000 that you want to lend for two years. You can either lend for one year at an interest rate of 10 per cent for the year and relend at the end of the year at the interest rate at that time, or lend for two years at 11 per cent for each of the years. In what circumstances would you not lend now for the two-year period? How might your answer change if you were unsure when you would need your money to spend on goods?

(5) Should the government guarantee to pay the debts of bankrupt firms? How would such a guarantee affect firms' behaviour?

(6) Table 14.2 shows the cost of a machine and the expected revenue from operating it. There is a probability of 60 per cent that the revenues are as in line (A) and a probability of 40 per cent that the revenues are as in line (B). What is the expected present value of the project, using discount rates of (a) 3 (b) 5 (c) 10 (d) 25 per cent?

Table 14.2 Costs and revenues for problem 6

	Start of project	End of year 1	End of year 2	End of year 3
Cost of machine	1,000	—	—	—
Operating cost	—	2,000	2,800	2,500
Expected revenue (A)	—	2,500	3,200	2,800
Expected revenue (B)	—	2,600	3,300	2,900

Chapter Fifteen

Macroeconomic analysis and the multiplier

Price, output and employment changes — consumption function and the saving function — macroeconomic equilibrium — investment multiplier — multiplier process — market analysis and macroeconomic analysis — reduction in real wages — market economies and ineffective demands

---

15.1 Introduction

In chapter 11 we examined macroeconomic aspects of a perfect market economy and introduced the method of market analysis. This assumes that after any change in demands for goods, general equilibrium is re-established and unemployment (apart from voluntary unemployment) is eliminated by rapid changes in the prices of goods and factors and in interest rates. However, as we shall see in the next section, it is possible that imperfections prevent markets from reaching equilibrium, or at least slow down the movement to equilibrium. In particular, the real wage may remain above its equilibrium levels, so that there is an excess supply of labour: some people who want a job at the current wage are unable to find one. If this is so, market analysis may not be the only useful method for analysing macroeconomic aspects of an imperfect market economy. In this chapter we develop an alternative method.

15.2 Price, output and employment changes

An economy is in macroeconomic equilibrium when desired saving equals desired investment (see section 11.2.1). Market analysis assumes that macroeconomic equilibrium occurs as a part of the general equilibrium of all markets. For example, if households decide to save more, market analysis implies that:

(a) The demands for and the prices of bonds and shares increase, so that the interest rate on bonds and the expected rate of return on shares fall (see section 14.5). So firms can afford to finance more investment projects and the demand for investment goods rises.

(b) The demands for and prices of consumer goods fall, so that some firms cease to produce consumer goods and begin to produce investment goods, whose prices increase because of the increased demand.

(c) The demands for and wages of the types of labour needed in consumer goods industries fall, and the demands for and wages of the types needed in investment goods industries increase. So workers have an incentive to move from jobs producing consumer goods to jobs producing investment goods.

Therefore, an increase in desired saving leads to an increase in desired investment, and to an increase in the outputs of investment goods. This process continues until macroeconomic equilibrium is established, and the supply of each type of labour equals the demand.

15.2.1 Unchanging prices and wages

The adjustment to macroeconomic equilibrium predicted by market analysis can occur only if prices and wages can move freely to re-establish the general equilibrium. This movement may be prevented or slowed down by imperfections. In particular:

(a) Workers and trades unions resist reductions in their money wages.

(b) If money wages do not fall, any firm that reduces its prices faces a reduction in revenue with little or no reduction in its costs. So a price reduction implies a reduction in profit, and the need not to make a loss places a limit on the extent to which price cuts are possible if money wages do not fall.

(c) Oligopolists may be slow to change prices (see section 13.5).

(d) Monopoly restrictions may prevent firms from entering a market when demand for a good increases.

15.2.2 Output changes

The possibility that prices and money wages do not change or change only slowly when demands change alters the sequence of events that follows an increase in desired saving. If households want to save more, they reduce their demands for consumers goods, and firms increase their stocks of unsold goods and reduce production, so that the outputs of goods fall. This shifts the labour demand curve from DD to D'D' in figure 15.1 and, if money wages do not fall and prices do not rise, real wages do not fall. Even if money wages do fall, firms' costs of production fall, and so they may cut their prices. Then real wages do not fall, and the labour market moves no nearer to equilibrium (we shall develop this theme further in section 16.4.6). So if the labour market was previously in equilibrium at real wage A, the reduction in the demand for labour causes unemployment BC. The incomes of the newly unemployed are reduced, so that national income falls. The initial increase in saving leads to:

(a) Unemployment that does not disappear, because real wages do not change to bring labour markets to equilibrium.
(b) A reduction in national income.
(c) In addition, it is likely that total investment falls because firms become less optimistic about future sales and profits as their sales fall when national income falls. So the outcome may contradict the prediction of market analysis that the increase in desired saving leads to an increase in desired investment.

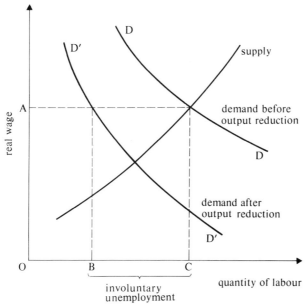

Figure 15.1   Effect of a reduction in the demand for labour
When outputs fall, the derived demand curve for labour shifts from DD to D'D', causing unemployment BC if the real wage does not change.

15.2.3 Reduction in desired saving

If households reduce their saving they buy more consumer goods. If firms invest more they buy more equipment, and firms that produce the equipment increase their outputs to meet the increased demand without changing their price. As outputs increase, so does the demand for labour, so employment increases, either because firms employ more people or because people work more hours. So households' incomes increase and this increases desired saving.

Once again, this sequence of events differs from that predicted by market analysis, in which the reduction in desired saving causes an increase in interest rates and the expected return on shares, so that investment falls to match the reduction in desired saving.

15.2.4 Increase in desired investment

If firms become more optimistic about their future prospects, they are likely to carry out more investment projects. This has a similar effect to a reduction in desired saving, because firms producing equipment sell more, and increase their outputs, their demand for labour and the incomes that they pay. Households save more out of these higher incomes, and so desired saving increases to equal the new level of desired investment.

This sequence of events also differs from the prediction of market analysis that the increase in desired investment increases interest rates and the expected return on shares, which causes an increase in saving.

15.2.5 Reduction in desired investment

If investment falls, firms that produce equipment sell less, but may not reduce their prices immediately in response to this reduction in sales. So the stocks of equipment held by producers of equipment increase and they reduce their outputs. They employ fewer workers or reduce working hours, so that households' incomes fall. Households save less from their reduced incomes, and so desired saving falls in response to the reduction in desired investment.

This sequence of events differs from that predicted by market analysis, in which saving falls because interest rates and the expected return on shares falls.

15.2.6 Macroeconomic analysis

The sequences of events that involve changes in firms' outputs and employment levels, rather than changes in their prices, are an example of the method of **macroeconomic analysis**. The simplest way of developing this method of examining macroeconomic aspects of market and mixed economies further is to use the assumption that:

> Prices and money wages do not change, and firms respond to a change in demand by changing their outputs and employment

We modify this assumption to allow for conditions of general inflation in most or all prices and money wages in section 16.4. Until then, for simplicity, we base macroeconomic analysis on the assumption that prices and money wages do not change at all.

15.3 Consumption function and saving function

If firms produce less and employ fewer people, households' incomes and national income are reduced. This reduction in national income causes a reduction in consumers' expenditure. Basic elements of macroeconomic analysis are the **consumption function** and the associated **saving function**.

> The consumption function describes the total expenditure on consumer goods that households want to make (desired consumption) out of each

level of national income. The saving function describes total desired saving out of each level of national income.

In a market economy with minimal government and no foreign transactions, income equals consumption plus saving, and so the saving function is easily derived from the consumption function.

Table 15.1 gives an example of a consumption function and a saving function, and these are illustrated in figure 15.2.

Table 15.1 Consumption and saving functions

National income (£ million)	Desired consumption (£ million)	Desired saving (£ million)	APC	MPC	APS	MPS
1,200	1,040	160	0.867	0.8	0.133	0.2
1,300	1,120	180	0.862	0.7	0.138	0.3
1,400	1,190	210	0.85	0.6	0.15	0.4
1,500	1,250	250	0.833	0.5	0.167	0.5
1,600	1,300	300	0.813	0.4	0.187	0.6
1,700	1,340	360	0.788	0.3	0.212	0.7
1,800	1,370	430	0.761	—	0.239	—

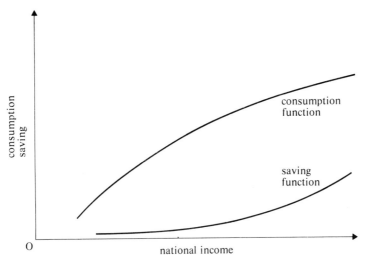

Figure 15.2 Consumption and saving functions
Desired consumption and desired saving at each level of national income.

15.3.1 Propensities to consume and to save

The consumption function and the saving function can be described in terms of:

(a) The **average propensity to consume** (*APC*), which is the fraction of national income that households want to consume.

(b) The **average propensity to save** (*APS*), which is the fraction of national income that households want to save.
(c) The **marginal propensity to consume** (*MPC*), which is the fraction of an increase in national income that households want to spend on consumer goods.
(d) The **marginal propensity to save** (*MPS*), which is the fraction of an increase in national income that households want to save.

So:

$$APC = C^*/Y \qquad APS = S^*/Y \qquad MPC = \Delta C^*/\Delta Y \qquad MPS = \Delta S^*/\Delta Y$$

where C^* is desired consumption, Y is national income, S^* is desired saving and the symbol Δ (delta) means 'change in'.

The assumptions of minimal government and no foreign transactions imply that

$$C + S = Y$$

and that

$$\Delta C + \Delta S = \Delta Y$$

so that

$$\frac{C}{Y} + \frac{S}{Y} = 1$$

and

$$\frac{\Delta C}{\Delta Y} + \frac{\Delta S}{\Delta Y} = 1$$

or

$$APC + APS = 1$$
$$MPC + MPS = 1$$

The four propensities for the example are listed in table 15.1: the marginal propensities are calculated by considering an increase of £100 million in national income. For example, if national income increases from £1,400 million to £1,500 million, households want to spend 60 per cent of the increase on consumer goods, and to save 40 per cent, so that when national income is £1,400 million the *MPC* is 0.6 and the *MPS* is 0.4.

Table 15.1 reveals that:

(a) If *MPC* is less than *APC*, then *APC* falls as national income increases.
(b) If *MPS* exceeds *APS*, then *APS* rises as national income increases.

These relations between marginal and average propensities are the same as the relations between marginal and average costs discussed in section 8.3.4.

The marginal propensities to consume and to save equal the slopes of the consumption function and the saving function. As national income increases, the slope of the consumption function falls because successive increases in national income are accompanied by smaller additions to desired consumption. The slope of the saving function increases as national income increases, because the marginal propensity to save increases.

15.3.2 Shifts in the consumption function and the saving function

The consumption function and the saving function shift if there is a change in desired consumption and desired saving out of each national income. Shifts of this kind are likely to occur if the expected rates of return on financial assets change, although the directions of the changes in desired consumption and desired saving are not clear cut. For example, if expected rates of return increase:

(a) A household can achieve a target future income with a lower total of assets, so that it may save less.
(b) The reward for saving (or the compensation for delaying consumption) is increased, so that a household may save more.

The combination of these opposing effects may shift the saving function in either direction.

15.3.3 Income distribution and the consumption function

The consumption function describes a relation between desired consumption and national income assuming that the average and marginal propensities to consume out of each level of national income do not change if the distribution of that national income changes. This may not be true if, for example, we compare the additional desired consumption when national income increases by £1 million because: (a) some previously unemployed people become employed; (b) the wages of people with jobs increase; (c) firms become more profitable, and increase shareholders' dividends. Poor people generally want to spend a larger fraction of their additional incomes on consumer goods than richer people so that the marginal propensity to consume (for the society as a whole) is likely to be greater in case (a) than in cases (b) or (c).

When we use consumption and saving functions, we assume that increases or decreases in national income affect households at all levels of income to a similar extent and we ignore distributional effects. This is a simplifying assumption that allows us to concentrate on changes in the level of national income without concern for the distribution.

15.4 Macroeconomic equilibrium

In an economy where there is minimal government intervention and no foreign trade, the national accounts imply that total saving equals total investment. Furthermore, the economy is in macroeconomic equilibrium when desired saving equals desired investment.

Macroeconomic analysis assumes that:

(a) Desired saving is given by the saving function.
(b) Desired investment depends on firms' expectations of future profits, and on interest rates that determine the cost of financing investment.

In particular, macroeconomic analysis assumes that desired investment does not depend on the level of national income. When we use macroeconomic analysis in later sections, we shall allow for the possibility that changes in national income affect firms' expectations of future sales and future profits, because they expect to sell more if national income is increasing, so that they invest more. However, at this stage, we assume for simplicity that desired investment is unaffected by national income. Indeed, to begin our examination of macroeconomic analysis, we suppose that firms' expectations and interest rates are unchanged, so that desired investment is given.

We can use the saving function to determine the **macroeconomic equilibrium national income** for a given desired investment.

The macroeconomic equilibrium national income is the national income for which desired saving equals desired investment.

In the example of table 15.1, the macroeconomic equilibrium national income is £1,600 million if desired investment is £300 million. Figure 15.3 shows a saving function and a level of desired investment (B). The macroeconomic equilibrium national income is C.

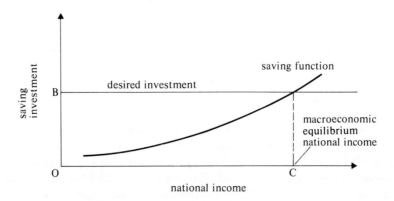

Figure 15.3 Macroeconomic equilibrium
Desired saving is given by the saving function, and when desired investment is B macroeconomic equilibrium national income is C.

15.4.1 Aggregate demand

There is an alternative method of calculating the macroeconomic equilibrium national income. Goods are demanded by consumers and by firms, and:

Aggregate demand equals desired consumption plus desired investment.

Table 15.2 shows how aggregate demand depends on national income in the example of table 15.1 when desired investment is £300 million. Figure 15.4 illustrates this relation as an aggregate demand function. Curve CC is the consumption function, and desired investment is OF. The height of any point, such as H, on EE equals desired consumption (KJ) out of national income (K) plus desired investment (HJ = OF). So KH = KJ + OF. With minimal

Table 15.2 Aggregate demand function

National income (£ million)	Desired consumption (£ million)	Desired investment (£ million)	Aggregate demand (£ million)
1,200	1,040	300	1,340
1,300	1,120	300	1,420
1,400	1,190	300	1,490
1,500	1,250	300	1,550
1,600	1,300	300	1,600
1,700	1,340	300	1,640
1,800	1,370	300	1,670

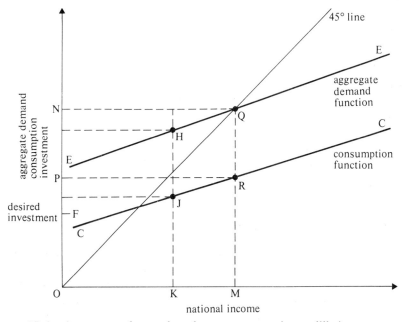

Figure 15.4 Aggregate demand and macroeconomic equilibrium
The aggregate demand function shows desired consumption plus desired investment for each level of national income. Aggregate demand equals national income on the 45° line. Macroeconomic equilibrium national income is M.

government and no foreign trade, national income equals consumption plus investment. So:

> National income is at its macroeconomic equilibrium level when aggregate demand equals national income.

Table 15.2 shows that this occurs when national income is £1,600 million as before.

In figure 15.4 national income is measured horizontally and aggregate demand is measured vertically. The only points in the figure at which national income equals aggregate demand are those that are equal distances from the two axes. These points lie on the 45 degree line. So the macroeconomic equilibrium national income is at M, where aggregate demand (N) out of national income (M) equals national income (M). Desired consumption is P, and desired saving is the remainder of the income, which is distance RQ. Desired saving equals desired investment (RQ = OF) and so the economy is in macroeconomic equilibrium.

The decision whether to use the method illustrated in figure 15.3 or that illustrated in figure 15.4 is not important. Both methods give the same macroeconomic equilibrium national income, because the saving function used in one can be derived from the consumption function used in the other.

15.5 Investment multiplier

The calculation of macroeconomic equilibrium national income using macro-economic analysis leads to two important questions:

(a) To what extent does macroeconomic equilibrium national income change if there is a change in firms' expectations or in interest rates that changes desired investment, or if there is a shift in the consumption and saving functions caused by a change in the rates of return on financial assets?
(b) Does national income move towards its macroeconomic equilibrium level when one of these changes occurs? In other words, does macroeconomic analysis imply that the macroeconomic equilibrium is stable?

We examine the first of these questions in this section, the second in the next.

15.5.1 Change in desired investment

Figure 15.5 shows the effects of a change in desired investment using each of the two methods developed in the previous section. In figure 15.5(a), an increase in desired investment from A to B increases the macroeconomic equilibrium national income from C to D. In figure 15.5(b), the increase in desired investment increases aggregate demand at each level of national income, so that the aggregate demand function shifts upwards. The macroeconomic equilibrium national income increases from E to F.

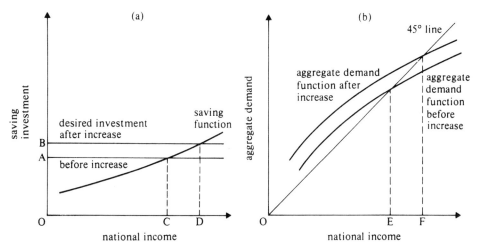

Figure 15.5   Effect of an increase in desired investment
(a) using saving function: macroeconomic equilibrium national income increases from C to D when desired investment increases from A to B (b) using aggregate demand function: macroeconomic equilibrium national income increases from E to F when aggregate demand increases.

When macroeconomic equilibrium national income increases, desired saving increases by an amount given by the marginal propensity to save:

$$\Delta S^* = MPS \times \Delta Y^*$$

where Y^* = macroeconomic equilibrium national income.

When desired investment increases, desired saving must increase by the same amount to restore macroeconomic equilibrium:

$$\Delta S^* = \Delta I^*$$

where I^* = desired investment.

Hence

$$\Delta I^* = MPS \times \Delta Y^*$$

or

$$\Delta Y^*/\Delta I^* = 1/MPS \qquad (15.1)$$

This equation determines the size of the **investment multiplier.**

The investment multiplier is the change in macroeconomic equilibrium national income divided by the change in desired investment.

From equation 15.1, we see that:

The investment multiplier equals the inverse of the marginal propensity to save.

The marginal propensity to save is less than 1, because households want to save only a part of an increase in national income, and so the inverse of the marginal propensity to save exceeds 1. So:

The investment multiplier exceeds 1, and macroeconomic equilibrium national income increases by more than the increase in desired investment.

As we see in detail in the next section, this additional increase in macroeconomic equilibrium national income occurs because additional demand for investment goods causes an additional derived demand for labour. This leads to an increase in employment, and the newly employed workers demand additional consumer goods, thereby causing a further increase in national income.

In the example of table 15.1, macroeconomic equilibrium national income increases from £1,600 million to £1,700 million when desired investment increases from £300 million to £360 million. So the multiplier is

$$(£1,700 - £1,600)/(£360 - £300) = 5/3 = 1.67$$

This is confirmed by equation 15.1, because the marginal propensity to save is 3/5 when national income is £1,600 million.

15.5.2 Shift in the saving function

If the saving function and the consumption function shift because of, for example, a change in expected rates of return on financial assets, the macroeconomic equilibrium national income changes. Figure 15.6(a) shows the effect of an increase in the average propensity to save at each level of national

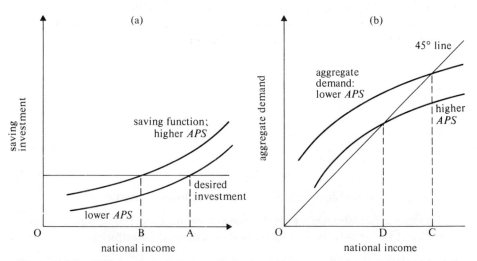

Figure 15.6 Effect of an increase in desired saving
(a) using saving function: the function shifts up, and macroeconomic equilibrium national falls from A to B, so that there is no change in total saving (b) using aggregate demand function: the curve shifts down, because higher saving implies lower consumption. Macroeconomic equilibrium national income falls from C to D.

income. The macroeconomic equilibrium national income falls from A to B. Figure 15.6(b) shows the equivalent effect of a decrease in the average propensity to consume on aggregate demand. The macroeconomic equilibrium national income falls from C to D which is the same fall as from A to B in figure 15.6(a). In each case, the macroeconomic equilibrium national income falls, because the necessary desired saving is generated out of a lower national income. **Total saving out of the macroeconomic equilibrium national income does not change** because it remains equal to the unchanging desired investment, so that the increase in the average propensity to save leads to no increase in the total amount saved when national income is at its macroeconomic equilibrium level.

Suppose that, in the example of table 15.1, the average propensity to save from each level of national income increases by 25 per cent. The new saving, consumption and aggregate demand functions (with desired investment of £300 million) are given in table 15.3. The macroeconomic equilibrium national income falls from £1,600 million to £1,500 million, so that desired saving is unchanged at £300 million.

Table 15.3 Consumption, saving and aggregate demand

National income (£ million)	Desired consumption (£ million)	Desired saving (£ million)	Desired investment (£ million)	Aggregate demand (£ million)
1,200	1,008	192	300	1,308
1,300	1,084	216	300	1,384
1,400	1,148	252	300	1,448
1,500	1,200	300	300	1,500
1,600	1,240	360	300	1,540
1,700	1,268	432	300	1,568
1,800	1,284	516	300	1,584

15.5.3 Paradox of thrift

The prediction of macroeconomic analysis that an increase in the desire to save leads to no increase in total saving is known as the **paradox of thrift** (or the paradox of saving). The paradox emphasizes how, in macroeconomic analysis, the changes in the outcome of the economy that result from changes in individuals' behaviour may not be in line with the intentions of the individuals. So macroeconomic analysis denies that consumers are sovereign, at least when they decide to save more, because this decision may lead to no increase in total saving.

15.5.4 IS curve

We saw in section 14.8 that total investment depends on the interest rate (as well as on the optimism of firms' expectations). We have argued in this chapter that the main cause of changes in saving is changes in national income. So, given firms' expectations, if the interest rate increases, investment falls. Macroeconomic analysis then argues that national income must fall to restore macroeconomic equilibrium. If the increase in the interest rate increases the average propensity to save – because saving is now more attractive and buying consumer goods on credit is less attractive – there must be a greater fall in national income to restore macroeconomic equilibrium.

The macroeconomic equilibrium relation between the interest rate and national income implied by this analysis can be represented as an **IS curve**. Figure 15.7 shows an IS curve, which slopes down because a higher interest rate implies a lower macroeconomic equilibrium national income. We use the IS curve (with the LM curve of section 14.7.5) in section 21.6 in discussions of economic policy.

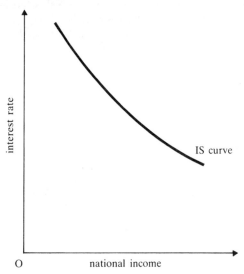

Figure 15.7   IS curve
The IS curve shows the combinations of national income and the interest rate that keep saving equal to investment.

15.6 Multiplier process

The investment multiplier tells us the extent to which macroeconomic equilibrium national income changes when desired investment changes: the **multiplier process** tells us how national income moves to the new macroeconomic equilibrium level.

We divide the multiplier process into a series of stages. In each stage some firms receive additional revenue, and so they pay additional incomes to workers, to the suppliers of other factors and as profit. The additional income generated equals the additional revenues of firms that sell additional final goods, which (see section 5.3) equal the additional value added of all firms, including those that sell additional intermediate goods. We assume that there is no undistributed profit, so that each firm pays all of its value added as incomes to households.

Undistributed profit can be regarded as a part of saving (see section 5.10), and so this assumption is made only to simplify the discussion.

The following example describes the multiplier process that occurs when firms become more optimistic about their future profits, so that desired investment increases by £1,000. The marginal propensity to consume is 0.8, and so the marginal propensity to save is 0.2. From equation 15.1, the investment multiplier is 5(1/0.2). So the macroeconomic equilibrium national income increases by £5,000. The multiplier process describes how this increase occurs, and its various stages are shown in table 15.4. We suppose that national income is at its macroeconomic equilibrium level before the increase in desired investment.

Table 15.4   Stages of the multiplier process

Stage	Additional investment (£)	Additional national income (£)	Additional consumption (MPC = 0.8) (£)	Additional saving (MPS = 0.2) (£)
1	1,000	1,000	800	200
2	—	800	640	160
3	—	640	512	128
4	—	512	409.6	102.4
5	—	409.6	372.68	81.92
6	—	327.68	262.14	65.54
.		.	.	.
.		.	.	.
.		.	.	.
20	—	14.41	11.53	2.88
Sum of first 20 stages	1,000	4,942.35	3,953.88	988.47
.		.	.	.
.		.	.	.
.		.	.	.
50	—	0.018	0.014	0.004
Sum of first 50 stages	1,000	4,999.93	3,999.94	999.99

The stages of the multiplier process in which actual national income increases by £5,000 from its previous macroeconomic equilibrium level are as follows.

Stage 1

The additional £1,000 investment expenditure is received as revenue by firms that sell equipment, so that £1,000 additional income is paid to households. Of this additional income, £800 is spent on consumer goods (because the MPS is 0.8) and £200 is saved.

Stage 2

The additional £800 consumption expenditure is received as revenue by firms that sell consumer goods, so that £800 additional income is paid to households.

Of this additional income, £640 (0.8 × £800) is spent on consumer goods and £160 is saved.

Stage 3

The additional £640 consumption expenditure is received as revenue by firms that sell consumer goods, so that £640 additional income is paid to households. Of this additional income, £512 (0.8 × £640) is spent on consumer goods and £128 is saved.

Stage 4

The additional £512 consumption expenditure is received as revenue by firms that sell consumer goods, so that £512 additional income is paid to households. Of this additional income, £409.60 (0.8 × £512) is spent on consumer goods and £102.40 is saved.

The process continues with smaller additions to national income at each stage.

In each stage after the first, additional income is paid as a result of additional consumption expenditure in the previous stage, and this additional income generates further additional consumption expenditure. So, in principle, the stages continue indefinitely, and less additional income is paid at each stage. More of the stages in our example are shown in table 15.4, where we see that by the fiftieth stage the additional income is very small.

The total of the additional incomes generated in the first 20 stages is £4942.35 and as we take more stages the additional income generated grows ever closer to £5,000, but never exceeds £5,000. The additional income generated converges to the £5,000 needed to bring national income to its new macroeconomic equilibrium level. Households want to save one-fifth of this additional income so that the additional desired saving equals the additional desired investment that began the process.

Box 9 shows the multiplier process in mathematical form.

15.6.1 Reduction in investment

We can trace a similar series of stages if desired investment falls. At each stage, the revenues of firms are reduced, and so they pay less income. So household's consumption expenditure is reduced and this causes a reduction in incomes paid in the next stage. So macroeconomic analysis implies that national income moves towards its new macroeconomic equilibrium level after a change in desired investment. The macroeconomic equilibrium is stable.

15.6.2 Shift in the saving function

If the average propensity to save increases and the average propensity to consume falls, firms that sell consumer goods receive less revenue, and so they

Box 9   Mathematics of the multiplier process

If there is an increase of ΔI^* in desired investment, the stages of the multiplier process give additional income, consumption and saving as follows:

Stage	Additional income	Additional consumption	Additional saving
1	$\Delta Y_1 = \Delta I^*$	$\Delta C_1 = MPC \times \Delta Y_1$	$\Delta S_1 = MPS \times \Delta Y_1$
2	$\Delta Y_2 = \Delta C_1$	$\Delta C_2 = MPC \times \Delta Y_2$	$\Delta S_2 = MPS \times \Delta Y_2$
3	$\Delta Y_3 = \Delta C_2$	$\Delta C_3 = MPC \times \Delta Y_3$	$\Delta S_3 = MPS \times \Delta Y_3$

and so on.

So
$$\Delta Y^* = \Delta Y_1 + \Delta Y_2 + \Delta Y_3 + \Delta Y_4 + \ldots$$
$$= \Delta I^* + (MPC \times \Delta I^*) + (MPC^2 \times \Delta I^*) + (MPC^3 \times \Delta I^*) + \ldots$$
$$= \Delta I^* \times (1 + MPC + MPC^2 + MPC^3 + \ldots)$$

The geometric series $(1 + MPC + MPC^2 + MPC^3 + \ldots)$ has a sum of $1/(1 - MPC)$, because $MPC < 1$, and so

$$\Delta Y^* = \Delta I^*/(1 - MPC) = \Delta I^*/MPS$$

as given by the multiplier equation 15.1.
    Also

$$\Delta S^* = \Delta S_1 + \Delta S_2 + \Delta S_3 + \ldots$$
$$= MPS \times \Delta I^* + MPS \times MPC \times \Delta I^* + MPS \times MPC^2 \times \Delta I^* + \ldots$$
$$= MPS \times \Delta I^* \times (1 + MPC + MPC^2 + MPC^3 + \ldots)$$
$$= MPS \times \Delta Y^* = \Delta I^*$$

confirming that the multiplier process restores macroeconomic equilibrium.

pay out less income. This reduction in income implies that there is less consumption expenditure, and so less income is paid out at the next stage. National income falls and so desired saving falls to equal the unchanging desired investment.

15.6.3 National accounts during the multiplier process

The process describes how national income moves towards its macroeconomic equilibrium level, but desired investment and desired saving are not equal until the process is complete. However, the national accounts tell us that (with no government activity and no overseas trade) actual saving equals actual investment at all times. So during the multiplier process:

(a) Either actual saving is not equal to desired saving.
(b) Or actual investment is not equal to desired investment.

If, in our example, we interrupt the first stage of the multiplier process at the point where firms have received £1,000 in additional investment expenditure, but have not yet paid the money as incomes, the £1,000 is unspent. So at that point additional actual saving (in the sense of incomes as yet unspent) is £1,000, equal to the additional investment. Then, as the process continues, £200 is saved out of the £1,000 additional income and £800 is spent on consumer goods. If we interrupt the process in the second stage, this £800 is as yet unspent, and so the additional actual saving at that point equals the £200 that households want to save from the additional £1,000 income of the first stage, plus £800 actual saving in the form of incomes as yet unspent. Again, the total of these additional savings is £1,000, equal to the additional investment.

A more detailed examination of the multiplier process reveals that actual investment may not always equal desired investment. Consider the first stage in the example. Firms buy £1,000 in additional equipment and, at least initially, some of this additional equipment is supplied from stocks held by firms. Suppose that 40 per cent of the additional equipment is supplied initially from firms' stocks and 60 per cent is supplied from additional production. Increases in stocks are a part of investment (see section 5.10), and so additional investment is initially £1,000 − £400 = £600. Actual investment increases towards the desired level when goods are produced to rebuild the stocks back to their previous level. If these goods are not replaced, because firms want to reduce their stocks, desired investment is reduced by the extent of the desired reduction in stocks.

15.6.4 Duration of the multiplier process

Each stage of the multiplier process takes time to complete, for at least two reasons:

(a) Firms do not immediately pay additional revenue as additional incomes: wages may be paid monthly, dividends yearly, and so on.
(b) Households do not make all of their intended purchases immediately they receive their incomes.

These delays in the process are offset to some extent by the fact that, in reality, the second stage begins before the first stage is complete. Some of the additional consumption expenditure from stage 1 is made soon after the additional income is received (some, indeed, may be made before the income is received if households know that their incomes will increase), and this additional expenditure generates additional income in stage 2. Some of the additional expenditure in stage 1 occurs after this part of stage 2 has occurred.

15.7 Market analysis and macroeconomic analysis

We now have two methods of analysing how macroeconomic equilibrium is established after a change in desired saving and desired investment:

(a) Market analysis assumes that prices, wages and interest rates change, that macroeconomic equilibrium is re-established as a part of the general equilibrium of all markets, and that there is no persistent unemployment (apart from those who do not want a job at the equilibrium wage).

(b) Macroeconomic analysis assumes that prices do not change, and that macroeconomic equilibrium is re-established by changes in the outputs of goods, in employment and in national income that bring desired saving into equality with desired investment. Macroeconomic analysis allows that there may be persistent unemployment.

Table 15.5 compares the predictions of the two methods when households decide to increase the average propensity to save. Market analysis predicts that an increase in the average propensity to save causes an increase in the demand for bonds and shares, and a reduction in the demands for consumer goods. Interest rates and the expected return on shares fall, so that the cost of financing investment falls, and the demand for investment goods increases. Firms are attracted to the production of investment goods and away from producing less profitable consumer goods. Involuntary unemployment is eliminated as workers shift from jobs in consumer goods industries to jobs in investment goods industries. National income is unlikely to change greatly because the reduced output of consumer goods is likely to be offset by the increased output of investment goods. Consumers are sovereign, in that the decision to save more is reflected in the outcome of the economy because total saving and total investment increase.

Table 15.5 Effects of an increase in the marginal propensity to save

	Market analysis	Macroeconomic analysis
National income	little change	down
Saving	up	unchanged*
Investment	up	unchanged*
Consumption	down	down
Interest rates	down	no discussion
Persistent unemployment	unchanged at zero	up
Economic growth	up	unchanged*

*Unless the reduction in national income makes firms less optimistic about future sales and profits so that investment falls. In this case, saving and economic growth are reduced also.

Macroeconomic analysis predicts that an increase in the average propensity to save shifts the saving function (see figure 15.6(a)), and the macroeconomic equilibrium national income falls. So the increase in the average propensity to save leads to a reduction in employment and in national income that ensures that desired saving remains equal to desired investment. If desired investment does not change, the change in national income is sufficient to ensure that desired saving does not change even though the average propensity to save has increased.

Even though the two methods agree that consumption falls, market analysis predicts a smaller fall. If prices change as market analysis assumes, the effect of the reduction in the average propensity to consume is offset, at least in part, by the effect of the reduction in the prices of consumer goods as the demand for them is reduced. Macroeconomic analysis predicts that consumption falls both because the average propensity to consume has fallen and because national income falls.

15.7.1 Economic growth

Market analysis predicts that an increase in the average propensity to save leads to additional investment. This increases the potential to produce goods in the future, and so the rate of economic growth increases. Macroeconomic analysis, in its most simple form, assumes that desired investment does not change when national income falls, so that the potential for future increases in production is unchanged. However, this conclusion is modified if the reduction in national income makes firms less optimistic about their future sales, so that they invest less. In addition, a considerable amount of investment is financed from undistributed profits, and the reduction in firms' revenues caused by the reduction in national income is likely to imply a reduction in profits. So firms can finance less investment from their own resources, and the rate of economic growth is reduced.

15.7.2 Mixed analysis

Market analysis is built on the assumption that prices and money wages change rapidly to re-establish a general equilibrium; macroeconomic analysis is based on the assumption that prices and money wages do not change at all. These are both extreme assumptions that are useful for establishing some basic principles, but it is likely that in practice some prices change rapidly and others change much more slowly. So we use a **mixed analysis**, which is based on the assumption that when the demands for goods change prices change rapidly towards equilibrium in some markets, but in others prices move slowly (or not at all) and so outputs and employment levels change as macroeconomic analysis describes. In mixed analysis the extent and speed of price changes towards equilibrium are limited by imperfections.

Firms may be slow to change their prices because they are unsure whether the change in demand is temporary or permanent, and because they are unsure of the possible reactions of other firms (see section 13.5). There is a delay in changing prices during which firms change their output levels, but eventually some of the price changes needed to bring markets towards equilibrium occur.

As well as using this mixed analysis in later chapters, we shall continue to examine and to compare the implications of market and macroeconomic methods of analysis. This is useful, partly for simplicity and partly because there is scope for disagreement on the speed of price changes. Those who believe that prices change relatively quickly put more weight on the conclusions of market analysis than those who believe that prices change only very slowly. This disagreement on the choice of method leads to some fundamental disagreements on the effectiveness of some government policies, and we can outline the scope of these disagreements by contrasting the predictions of the two extreme methods.

15.8 Reduction in real wages

Macroeconomic analysis allows for the possibility of persistent unemployment, because prices and money wages do not change, or they change in similar proportions so that real wages do not change. Market analysis assumes that real wages fall when there is an excess supply of labour at the existing real wage, and that the reduction in real wages from Y to Z in figure 15.8(a) increases the demand for labour and reduces unemployment from AB to CD.

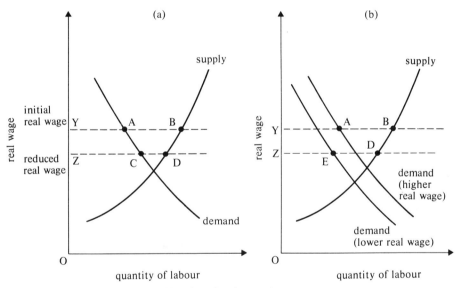

Figure 15.8   Effect of a reduction in the real wage
(a) market analysis: the excess supply of labour falls from AB to CD so that unemployment is reduced (b) macroeconomic analysis: the derived demand curve for labour shifts as people with lower wages demand fewer goods. The excess supply changes from AB to ED, which may or may not reduce unemployment, depending on the shapes of the curves and the extent of the shift in the derived demand curve.

Macroeconomic analysis disagrees, because it concentrates on the effects of the reduction in real wages on aggregate demand. If real wages fall, workers' incomes are reduced and they demand fewer consumer goods. At the same time, the reduction in real wages occurs because money wages fall relative to the prices of goods, so that firms' costs fall relative to their revenues, and therefore profits increase. Shareholders' incomes increase, and they spend more on consumer goods.

The increase in consumption by shareholders is unlikely to offset the reduction in consumption by workers, because those who receive dividends generally consume a lower fraction of their incomes than those who receive wages, because most workers have lower incomes than most shareholders. So when real wages fall and profits increase, the average propensity to consume for society as a whole falls. This effect is reinforced by the fact that many shares are owned by financial institutions (such as pension funds) that do not distribute all of the dividends that they receive to households. These undistributed dividends are not spent on consumer goods, and so total consumption is reduced.

The reduction in real wages and increase in profits causes a reduction in aggregate demand for goods, and reduces the derived demand for labour. The labour demand curve shifts in figure 15.8(b), and unemployment changes from AB to ED when the real wage falls from Y to Z. So macroeconomic analysis predicts that a reduction in real wages reduces the demand for labour, and that this may increase unemployment. The direction of the change in unemployment when the real wage falls depends on the shapes of the supply and demand curves, and on the extent to which the demand curve shifts.

15.9 Market economies and ineffective demands

Market and macroeconomic methods differ radically in their predictions concerning unemployment:

(a) Market analysis assumes that unemployment (other than voluntary unemployment) is eliminated by changes in real wages that make it profitable for firms to employ more workers. So market forces ensure that involuntary unemployment is eliminated.

(b) Macroeconomic analysis allows for persistent involuntary unemployment that is reduced if firms produce more goods. If firms produce more, the previously unemployed have higher incomes, demands for goods increase, and so firms can sell the additional goods that they produce.

So macroeconomic analysis implies that involuntary unemployment could be reduced if firms would employ more people to produce more goods, because the increase in employment increases households' incomes, so that they buy the additional goods produced.

In a market economy, firms do not have the information needed to make decisions that would increase employment in this way. The difficulty is that no single firm has an incentive to increase its output and its demand for labour on these grounds. If a firm increases its output and demands more labour, the newly employed have higher incomes, but they spend only a small fraction of this increased income on the good produced by the firm that employs them.

Additional goods produced by a single firm are demanded only if many firms employ additional workers, because each newly employed worker spends only a small fraction of his or her income on the goods produced by any one firm.

This argument implies that the additional goods that people would demand if they were employed are **ineffective** in persuading firms to produce more and to demand more labour. Firms base their decisions on how much to produce only on **effective demands**, that is, on the demands out of incomes that they expect people to have. Unless most firms believe that most other firms will expand their employment, all firms presume that unemployment will continue, so that the demands for their products will be lower than if there were no involuntary unemployment. In a market economy there is no way in which firms can indicate to one another that each is willing to expand its output and its employment provided that most others are willing to do the same. There is a 'vicious circle': the ineffective demands become effective only if most firms believe that employment will increase substantially, but firms increase employment only in response to effective demands. So ineffective demands for goods do not become effective, there is no increase in the demand for labour and employment is not increased.

The possibility of ineffective demands arises from a fundamental feature of market economic systems. Ineffective demands cannot become effective unless firms make *co-ordinated* decisions to increase their outputs and employment, so that each firm knows that other firms will also increase their outputs and employment. The outcome of a market economy is based on the interaction of *unco-ordinated* decisions that are determined by the prices of goods and factors and by interest rates. These prices give firms no information on the employment intentions of other firms.

15.9.1 Implications for government policy

Market analysis predicts that if prices and real wages change the unco-ordinated decisions of firms and workers result in the elimination of involuntary unemployment. The problem of ineffective demands shows that if prices and wages do not change in this way, unco-ordinated decisions may not eliminate involuntary unemployment, even though co-ordinated decisions might do so. This conclusion gives support to the use of government policies to reduce unemployment that:

(a) Co-ordinate the actions of firms using some form of planning.
(b) Increase aggregate demands for goods (by, for example reducing income taxes, so that households have more money to spend) in ways that are 'public knowledge', so that firms can increase their outputs and employment and be confident that the additional goods will be sold.

We shall discuss these policy implications of macroeconomic analysis in part IV, but we can see from even this short discussion that the use of market analysis does not support the use of these policies, because it does not allow for ineffective demands. There is scope for considerable disagreement on the effectiveness of economic policies. This disagreement can be traced back to the assumption made on the speed at which prices change when there is a change in demands for goods.

15.10 Summary

Macroeconomic analysis and market analysis differ in their assumption about firms' reactions to changes in demand. Macroeconomic analysis assumes that prices and money wages do not change (or that they change in proportion to each other so that real wages do not change), and that firms change their outputs and demands for labour instead. Market analysis assumes that prices change, and that these changes rapidly re-establish a general equilibrium.

Macroeconomic analysis is based on the consumption and saving functions that relate desired consumption expenditure and desired saving to national income. The economy is in macroeconomic equilibrium when desired saving equals desired investment. Macroeconomic analysis predicts that national income changes to bring the economy to macroeconomic equilibrium.

Macroeconomic analysis predicts that macroeconomic equilibrium national income increases through the multiplier process when desired investment increases. The ratio of the increase in macroeconomic equilibrium national income to the increase in desired investment is the investment multiplier. Macroeconomic analysis predicts that national income falls when desired saving increases, and that if desired investment is unchanged an increase in the average propensity to save causes no increase in total saving.

Macroeconomic analysis predicts that unemployment may persist, and that reductions in real wages may not reduce unemployment. Unemployment can be reduced if many firms increase their outputs, but a market economic system provides no signal that each firm would increase its output if they were sure that other firms would do so too.

Topics and problems

(1) 'Unemployment persists only because workers refuse to allow wage reductions.' Do you agree?

(2) Could the government get around the problem of ineffective demands by making and publicizing 'planning agreements' with large firms that indicate their investment intentions?

(3) What would be the likely multiplier effects of a complete closure of all UK car-producing factories?

(4) The average propensity to consume in an economy is 0.75 and the marginal propensity to consume is 0.6 when national income is £150 billion.

What is total consumption when national income is £150 billion and when national income is £151 billion?

What level of investment ensures that the macroeconomic equilibrium national income is £150 billion?

What increase in investment increases macroeconomic equilibrium national income to £151 billion?

Describe the first three stages of the multiplier process that follows this increase in investment.

(5) Firms pay out 96 per cent of all revenues in incomes, retaining the remainder as undistributed profits. Households save 25 per cent of all income that they receive, and spend the remainder on consumer goods. What is the increase in macroeconomic equilibrium national income that follows an increase of £1,000 in desired investment? Describe the first three stages of the multiplier process.

(6) Describe the first three stages of the multiplier process that follow a reduction in the average propensity to save from 25 per cent to 20 per cent in an economy where desired investment is £1,500. What is the size of the change in macroeconomic equilibrium national income?

Chapter Sixteen

Unemployment and inflation

Full employment national income — Phillips curve — inflationary spiral — market analysis and inflation — mixed analysis — implications for government policy

---

16.1 Introduction

Macroeconomic analysis predicts that the level of national income changes if there is a change in desired investment or in desired saving. Macroeconomic analysis assumes that this change occurs through changes in outputs, and that prices and money wages do not change. An increase in outputs increases the derived demand for labour and reduces unemployment. However, the available supply of labour limits the possible increase in outputs and employment, and it may not be possible for outputs to increase far enough to bring about macroeconomic equilibrium if desired investment increases or the average propensity to save falls. This leads to two questions:

(a) How far can outputs and employment increase without any change in prices and money wages?
(b) What does macroeconomic analysis predict if there is insufficient labour to produce the additional goods needed to restore macroeconomic equilibrium through the multiplier process described in section 15.6?

16.2 Full employment national income

If the real wage does not change (because neither prices nor money wages change, or they change in the same proportions), the derived demand for labour increases as the demands for goods increase. Then:

> Full employment national income for given real wages and a given price level is the national income that equates the demand for labour to the supply of labour at that real wage.

For each level of national income, there is a different demand curve for labour, such as LD_1, LD_2 and LD_3 in figure 16.1. Full employment is point Z, and so the full employment national income for real wage X is that which gives labour demand curve LD_2. If prices and money wages were different, so that the real wage is Y, then the full employment national income is that which gives curve LD_1.

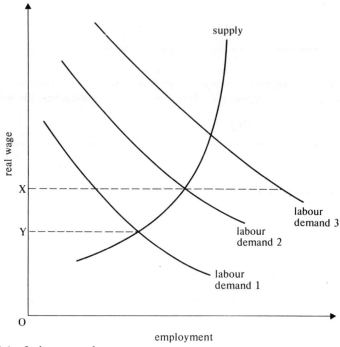

Figure 16.1   Labour market
The labour demand curve when there is full employment Z at real wage X is LD_2. If national income falls to give LD_1, national income is at V if the real wage remains at X. If national income increases to give LD_3, national income is at W if the real wage remains at X.

Note that full employment national income depends on the level of prices as well as on real wages. A 10 per cent increase in all prices and money wages does not change real wages, so that there is no change in the output levels needed to ensure full employment, but the full employment national income increases by 10 per cent because national income equals the total of outputs multiplied by prices.

We use the term 'full employment' to denote the absence of all unemployment, except for people who do not want a job at the existing real wage and those who are unemployable because no one would, in any circumstances, be willing to employ them at the existing real wage. Full employment implies the absence of involuntary unemployment. If there were full employment in this sense, there would still be some people registered as unemployed in the UK (see section 6.2.6), because some people who are not actively seeking work are included in the published figures. In addition, full employment in the sense used here includes the employment of some people (such as married women) who are currently unemployed, but who do not appear in the official statistics because they do not register as unemployed.

16.2.1 Deflationary gap

Desired savings and desired investment determine the macroeconomic equilib-rium national income (see section 15.4). If the macroeconomic equilibrium national income is below the full employment national income for the given real wage and price level, there is unemployment and:

The deflationary gap equals the full employment national income minus the macroeconomic equilibrium national income.

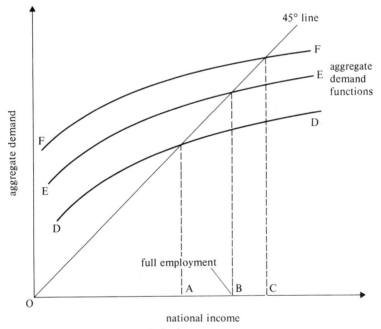

Figure 16.2 Inflationary and deflationary gaps
Full employment national income is B. If the aggregate demand function is DD, macroeconomic equilibrium occurs at A below full employment (deflationary gap). If the aggregate demand curve is FF, macroeconomic equilibrium occurs at C above full employment (inflationary gap).

Figure 16.2 shows a deflationary gap of AB between the full employment national income (B) and the macroeconomic equilibrium national income (A). In this case, the economy is in **underemployment equilibrium**. The macroeconomic equilibrium national income increases towards the full employment national income if there is an increase in aggregate demand. In figure 16.2, the deflationary gap is eliminated if the aggregate demand curve shifts from DD to EE, and if real wages and prices do not change, so that the full employment national income remains at B.

16.2.2 Inflationary gap

If the aggregate demand function shifts beyond EE in figure 16.2, the aggregate demand for goods exceeds the total supply (or aggregate supply) that can be achieved even at full employment. Firms cannot increase their outputs because they cannot obtain more labour, and so it is no longer reasonable to suppose that prices do not change. Furthermore, employers are competing for the limited supply of labour, and so they are likely to offer higher money wages. So if the aggregate demand function shifts beyond EE there is inflation. Then:

> The inflationary gap equals the macroeconomic equilibrium national income minus the full employment national income.

If the aggregate demand function is FF in figure 16.2, the **inflationary gap** is distance CB. The inflation that arises when aggregate demand increases is known as **demand-pull inflation**.

16.3 Phillips curve

Macroeconomic analysis predicts that:

(a) When the macroeconomic equilibrium national income is below the full employment national income, there is involuntary unemployment.
(b) When the macroeconomic equilibrium national income exceeds the full employment national income, there is inflation.

It would appear that the outcome of a change in aggregate demand is either unemployment or inflation (but not both), depending on whether there is a deflationary or an inflationary gap. However, this clear-cut division is unlikely because if aggregate demand increases some prices and money wages are likely to increase before full employment is achieved. This happens because:

(a) Some types of labour may become fully employed before others. The money wage of that type then increases as demand for it increases further, even though people with other skills remain involuntarily unemployed.
(b) Wages are not the only cost of production. If aggregate demand increases, so does the derived demand for land, equipment and materials. The prices of some of these other factors and materials increase; this increases firms' costs, and this is likely to cause firms to increase their prices.

As unemployment falls, more shortages of labour, other factors and materials occur, and price increases become more common. So macroeconomic analysis predicts that:

The inflation rate increases as involuntary unemployment falls.

This conclusion is reflected in the **Phillips curve** of figure 16.3. The original curve was derived using evidence for the UK from 1861 to 1957 by A.W.H. Phillips (born in New Zealand, 1914, died 1975; professor of economic science and statistics at the London School of Economics, 1958–67). The curve derived by Phillips indicated that the rate of increase of money wages would be zero if approximately 5 per cent of the workforce were unemployed. If unemployment exceeds 5 per cent, the Phillips' curve gives a negative inflation rate: money wages and prices fall, but only slowly, because the curve never falls far below the horizontal axis.

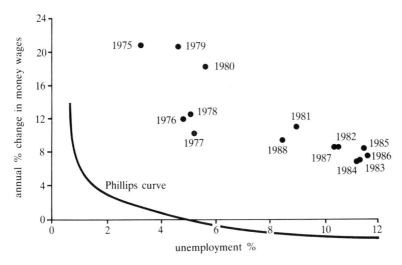

Figure 16.3   The Phillips curve for the UK and more recent evidence
The measure of inflation used by Phillips is the change in money wages, which exceeds the change in prices by the extent to which real wages are increased by economic growth. The Phillips curve was fitted as close to each annual unemployment/inflation point as possible. Evidence since 1975 shows consistently a higher inflation rate for each level of unemployment (or higher unemployment for each level of inflation).

More recent evidence on UK unemployment and inflation (see section 6.5.2) does not support the use of the Phillips curve of figure 16.3. In recent years, unemployment has far exceeded 5 per cent, even in years when there has been considerable inflation. Furthermore, over the past decade or so both the inflation rate and the unemployment rate have increased (for example, from 2.17 per cent unemployment and 9.2 per cent inflation in 1973 to 5.67 per cent unemployment and 18 per cent inflation in 1980). So we must look further for an explanation of the relationship between unemployment and inflation.

16.4 Inflationary spiral

A major reason for the failure of the Phillips Curve to describe recent UK inflation and unemployment is that **inflation is persistent** (at least in the 1970s and 1980s). The Phillips curve and the macroeconomic analysis from which it is derived assume that inflation occurs if unemployment is low, but if unemployment increases then the rate of price increases is reduced. According to the Phillips curve of figure 16.3, the inflation rate increases from 0.5 per cent to 2.8 per cent if unemployment falls from 4 per cent to 2 per cent. Then if aggregate demand falls, so that unemployment rises back to 4 per cent, inflation returns to 0.5 per cent.

In practice, a reduction in inflation is likely to occur much more slowly than an increase in inflation. The two-way relationship between changes in money wages and changes in prices causes inflation to persist in an **inflationary spiral**, in which prices and money wages continue to increase at approximately the same rate. This spiral arises because:

(a) The rate of change of money wages often depends on the recently experienced rate of change of prices.
(b) The rate of change of prices often depends on the recently experienced rate of change of money wages.

16.4.1 Influence of money wages on prices

Wages are a very large part of the value added of firms (approximately 74 per cent in the UK in 1987), so that a firm's profits are likely to be considerably reduced if it does not increase its prices to cover wage increases. Furthermore, firms know that if there is a general increase in money wages their customers' incomes have increased, and so they are likely to lose few sales because households can afford to pay the higher prices. So money wage increases are likely to cause price increases (and then there is **wage-push inflation** or **cost-push inflation**).

16.4.2 Influence of price increases on money wages

A wage agreement specifies the money wage, and the real wage falls if prices increase more rapidly than the money wage. The agreement maintains the real wage if it contains an **escalation** (or **index-linking**) **clause**, whereby the money wage is increased at the same rate as the prices of consumer goods.

Even if a wage agreement does not contain an escalation clause, a worker or a union may be able to negotiate an increase in the money wage that equals:

(a) Either its expectation of the future inflation rate so that the real wage is maintained if the actual inflation rate equals the expected rate.
(b) Or the inflation rate since the previous agreement so that the real wage is maintained if the future inflation rate is the same as the rate in the past.

In practice, expectations of future inflation are likely to be based on the rate experienced in the recent past, and so in either case the increase in money wages is based on the recent increase in prices.

16.4.3 Inflation and expectations

If inflation persists at an approximately constant rate, households and firms are likely to expect that it will continue, and so they make decisions on the basis of that expected inflation rate. Future real incomes are broadly unchanged, and so the demands for consumer goods are unlikely to change greatly. If the inflation rate is predictable, households and firms can be confident of the future real interest rate (equals normal interest rate minus the inflation rate, see section 6.5.4), and so decisions to supply and demand bonds and shares are likely to be based on that real interest rate. Similarly, firms making investment decisions can be confident of their expectation of the inflation rate, and so they can confidently allow for the effects of inflation when they calculate their expected future costs and revenues (see section 8.8.3). A firm's decision to invest is affected by expectations of the level of sales, but in an inflationary spiral which is expected to continue, inflation does not add to the firm's uncertainty.

16.4.4 Unexpected inflation and unemployment

The conclusion that expected inflation does not affect decisions ignores the fact that a confidently predicted inflation rate is an average of price changes. If all prices and money wages change at the same rate (a pure inflation) then no household or firm has reason to worry that it will be adversely affected by inflation, and no reason to expect that it will be favoured by inflation. However, if there is uncertainty about the changes in particular prices and wages (even though the average rate is confidently predicted), decisions are affected. For example:

(a) A household may save more to accumulate more financial assets if it is possible that its money income will increase at a lower rate than the average price of the goods that it buys. Even if there is also a chance that the household's money income will increase faster than prices, a risk-averse household is more concerned with the pessimistic possibility than with the optimistic possibility, and this risk-aversion is likely to lead to increased saving.
(b) A firm is likely to reduce its investment if it is possible that its costs will rise more rapidly than its revenues. Even if there is also a chance that its revenues will increase more than its costs, a risk-averse firm is more concerned with the pessimistic possibility than with the optimistic possibility, and this risk-aversion is likely to lead to reduced investment.

We can therefore conclude that if an increase in inflation leads to an increase in the range of rates of change in individual prices and money wages, and if most households and firms are risk-averse, then an increase in the inflation rate increases total saving and reduces total investment.

If an increase in the inflation rate leads to increased saving and reduced investment, the real level of aggregate demand falls and macroeconomic analysis predicts that unemployment increases. This is one explanation of the simultaneous increase in the inflation rate and in the level of unemployment that is not allowed for by the Phillips curve.

16.4.5 Ratchet effect

The imperfections that give rise to the inflationary spiral imply that the inflation rate is unlikely to fall rapidly. If inflation has been 10 per cent per year for several years, workers and firms are likely to predict a continuing 10 per cent annual inflation. If for some reason aggregate demand does not increase by 10 per cent, prices and wages are likely to continue to increase at 10 per cent per year for some time. Workers and their unions resist smaller increases in money wages, and firms continue to increase prices to cover the increased wage costs. The smaller rise in aggregate demand can occur only if some outputs fall and unemployment rises. The rate of inflation is slow to fall, and so employment must fall instead.

There is no such constraint on increases in inflation, because workers and unions do not resist increases in money wages. So it is likely that increases in aggregate demand lead to increases in the inflation rate, whereas reductions in aggregate demand lead to little reduction in the inflation rate. This implies

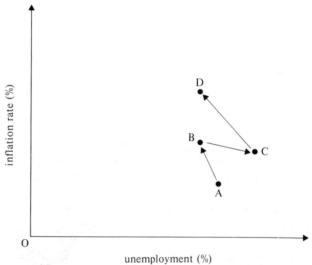

Figure 16.4   Ratchet effect in macroeconomic analysis
If there are alternate increases and decreases in aggregate demand, inflation rises and unemployment falls (A to B), then inflation falls and unemployment rises (B to C), and so on. In each cycle, inflation rises by more than it falls.

that if there are periodic increases and decreases in aggregate demand, the inflation rate and the level of unemployment are related as in figure 16.4. An increase in aggregate demand increases the inflation rate, with little reduction in unemployment (movement from A to B); a reduction in aggregate demand causes an increase in unemployment and little reduction in the inflation rate (B to C). A further increase in aggregate demand then leads to higher inflation (C to D), and so on. There is a **ratchet effect**: the inflation rate tends to rise without the reduction in unemployment that the Phillips curve would indicate.

16.4.6 Inflation and the foundations of macroeconomic analysis

Macroeconomic analysis rests on the assumption that unemployment persists because real wages do not change to clear labour markets. In chapter 15 we introduced macroeconomic analysis using the assumption that prices and money wages do not change. We have seen that prices and money wages may change, but they change by similar proportions in an inflationary spiral. If money wages and prices change at the same rate, the real wage is unchanged and involuntary unemployment persists. So the imperfections that give rise to an inflationary spiral help to explain *both* the persistence of inflation *and* the persistence of unemployment.

16.5 Market analysis and inflation

Market analysis of macroeconomic aspects of a perfect market economy involves the quantity theory of money, which predicts that the inflation rate (i) is approximately equal to the rate of increase of the supply of money (m) minus the rate of economic growth (g) (see section 11.6):

$$i = m - g \qquad (16.1)$$

If there is an inflationary spiral, this equation must be reinterpreted because the inflation rate in any year is largely determined by its previous level. So we can rewrite equation 16.1 as:

$$g = m - i \qquad (16.2)$$

so that the rate of growth of outputs is determined by the rate of increase of the supply of money and the persistent rate of inflation. So, if m falls below i and i does not fall because there is an inflationary spiral, g is negative: outputs are reduced, the derived demand for labour falls, and so unemployment increases.

Market analysis would challenge this conclusion, at least as a long-run prediction, because it predicts that in the long run real wages change to ensure full employment, and so outputs cannot fall in the way assumed above. The rate of economic growth is determined by the rate of introduction of new technology and by the level of investment, and so, at least in the long run, the inflation rate must change so that it equals $m - g$. If, in the short run, outputs and employment fall, market analysis predicts that workers are unable to maintain their previous rate of increase in money wages, and that firms increase their prices at more than the rate of increase of money wages, so that real wages fall and full employment is restored. The long-run rate of inflation then adjusts to equal $m - g$, so that in the long run the inflation rate does not persist at a fixed rate as the inflationary spiral supposes.

16.5.1 Natural rate of unemployment

As we have used it so far, market analysis assumes that markets move rapidly to equilibrium despite the presence of imperfections. It is possible to modify market analysis to take account of the effects of important imperfections, including those that give rise to a persistent inflationary spiral. **Modified market analysis** allows for the possibility that imperfections prevent full movement to equilibrium of labour markets: real wages may fall if there is unemployment, but not far or fast enough to give the rapid equilibrium of market analysis. So real wages can remain above their equilibrium levels and there is persistent involuntary unemployment.

Modified market analysis allows that markets operate in an economy that is not perfect in the sense used in part II. In particular, governments intervene in ways that affect labour markets by giving unemployment benefits that reduce individuals' incentives to take up jobs as soon as they are offered (see section 20.3.1). Even without government intervention, trades unions prevent reductions in money wages, and may be able to slow down the reductions in real wages that are needed to bring about equilibrium in labour markets. Other market imperfections may also slow down the rapid move to equilibrium assumed in a perfect market economy. Despite these imperfections, markets operate and, after a change in economic conditions, prices and money wages change to bring real wages as near to equilibrium as imperfections permit. The resulting unemployment is the **natural rate of unemployment**:

> The natural rate of unemployment is the minimum unemployment consistent with the market forces given the imperfections of the economic system.

16.5.2 Stability of the natural rate

Suppose that the economy is in macroeconomic equilibrium and unemployment is at the natural rate. Then aggregate demand increases (because desired investment rises or desired saving falls). The increase in demands for goods causes prices to increase more rapidly than previously, so that there is an increase in the inflation rate. The rate of increase of money wages does not adjust instantly to the higher rate of increase in prices (if only because many wages are set in annual agreements), and so, for a while, the real wage is reduced. This reduction in real wages causes a temporary increase in the demand for labour, and so unemployment falls temporarily below the natural rate. After a time, workers and unions negotiate money wage increases that restore real wages to their previous level. The demand for labour falls, and unemployment increases back to the natural rate. So modified market analysis predicts that an increase in aggregate demand leads to:

(a) A temporary reduction in unemployment.
(b) An increase in the inflation rate.
(c) A long-run return to the natural rate of unemployment.

A reduction in aggregate demand leads to a reduction in the rate of increase of prices as firms find that they have excess supplies. The rate of increase of money wages does not adjust immediately and so there is a temporary increase in real wages. This reduces the demand for labour, and so there is a temporary increase in unemployment. However, firms want to restore their profitability and so they resist permanent increases in real wages. Real wages return to their previous level, the demand for labour increases and unemployment returns to the natural rate.

Modified market analysis implies that unemployment is at the natural rate, except temporarily. Curve VV in figure 16.5 is sometimes known as a **vertical Phillips curve**. An increase in aggregate demand increases the inflation rate and temporarily reduces unemployment (A to B), but unemployment soon

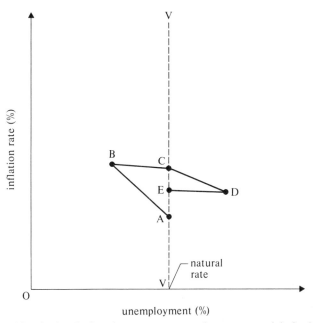

Figure 16.5 Vertical relation between unemployment and inflation
In the long run unemployment is at the natural rate. A short-run decrease in unemployment can be achieved if inflation increases (A to B), but inflation does not fall as unemployment returns to the natural rate (B to C). Inflation can be reduced if there is a movement from C to D (a reduction in aggregate demand) and then from D to E as unemployment returns to the natural rate.

returns to the natural rate without any reduction in inflation (B to C). A reduction in aggregate demand temporarily increases unemployment and may reduce inflation (C to D). Then unemployment returns to its natural rate (D to E). If inflation increases more readily than it decreases (as the inflationary spiral indicates), it is likely that periodic increases and decreases in aggregate demand cause an increase in the inflation rate, with no permanent reduction in unemployment.

16.5.3 Changes in the natural rate

The definition of the natural rate and the prediction that the economy returns to it imply that the level of unemployment in the economy can be permanently reduced only if there is a reduction in the force of the imperfections that prevent the economy from reaching full employment. In section 21.3.1 we shall discuss government policies that might reduce these imperfections – obvious candidates are policies to reduce the powers of trades unions (by, for example, limiting the right to strike) and powers to reduce the market influence of firms.

16.6 Mixed analysis

Because there are forces that are likely to make inflation persist we have seen how inflation can increase even though unemployment does not fall – contrary to the analysis of the Phillips curve. In developing a mixed analysis (see section 15.7.3), we assumed that:

(a) The initial response of most firms to a change in demands is to change their outputs and derived demands for labour as macroeconomic analysis assumes.
(b) Later, prices begin to change as market analysis (and modified market analysis) assumes.
(c) Inflation persists as in the analysis of the inflationary spiral, and the inflation rate increases more readily than it decreases.

Given these assumptions, what are the effects of a decrease in aggregate demand?

We can trace three stages which correspond to the three assumptions above:

(a) The initial reduction in outputs causes a reduction in the derived demand for labour and involuntary unemployment increases. The inflation rate persists at its previous level.
(b) In the second stage, the rate of increase of prices slows in the face of the reduction in demands. This leads to a temporary increase in real wages, because money wages continue to increase at their previous rate. The demand for labour is further reduced, and involuntary unemployment increases further. The inflation rate is reduced to some extent.
(c) The reduction in the rate of increase of prices is later matched by a reduction in the rate of increase of money wages, so that the real wage is

reduced. This increases the demand for labour, and so reduces involuntary unemployment. The reduced rate of money wage increases helps to maintain the lower inflation rate.

The overall increase in unemployment depends on the extent to which the inflation rate falls. If inflation is very persistent, unemployment may rise considerably because there is little change in the rates of change of prices and money wages in the second and third stages, and so there is little change in real wages.

The eventual outcome also depends on the extent to which workers and their unions can maintain real wages. If real wages return to their initial level, involuntary unemployment increases because the reduced output levels reduce the derived demand for labour at each real wage. If workers and unions cannot restore real wages, some of the reduction in the demand for labour caused by the reduction in aggregate demand is offset by an increase in the demand for labour caused by a permanent reduction in real wages.

16.6.1 Effect on expectations

The three stages outlined above affect households' and firms' expectations in two ways which have different effects on aggregate demand:

(a) If the inflation rate falls, there may be an eventual reduction in the uncertainties faced by households and firms. Therefore households may save more and firms may invest more, so that aggregate demand increases and involuntary unemployment is reduced.
(b) As unemployment increases firms sell less, and this is likely to make them less optimistic about their future sales and profits. This causes them to invest less, and so aggregate demand and employment fall.

16.6.2 Increase in aggregate demand

We have considered so far the effects of a reduction in aggregate demand. There are also three stages to consider if there is an increase in aggregate demand, although it is not necessarily true that the effects of an increase are equal and opposite to those of an equal sized decrease in aggregate demand.

When there is an increase in aggregate demand, the macroeconomic equilibrium national income increases, so that unemployment is reduced and the inflation rate increases. If there is little unemployment, inflation is likely to increase considerably. If there is much existing unemployment, workers fear that they will price themselves out of a job, and so the inflation rate is likely to increase less.

In the second stage, prices increase more rapidly than money wages, so that real wages fall temporarily. This causes a temporary increase in the demand for labour, and reduces unemployment.

In the third stage, the rate of increase in money wages rises to match the rate of increase of prices. The real wage increases (but not necessarily to its initial level) so that unemployment increases. In addition, the increased inflation rate makes firms and households more cautious; the increase in sales makes firms more optimistic.

16.7 Implications for government policy

Our analysis in this chapter begins from a change in aggregate demand. In a market economy, aggregate demand equals the demand for consumer goods by households plus the demand for investment goods by firms. These demands can change because households' tastes change, because firms' expectations become more or less optimistic, or because interest rate changes affect saving and/or investment. However, a major source of changes in aggregate demand in the UK economy is government policy, which affects consumption, investment and the government's own demands for goods. In part IV we shall examine the implications of government policies for aggregate demand and we can use the conclusions of this chapter to examine the effects of aggregate demand policies on unemployment and inflation. We can also trace the effects of changes in total imports and exports – which are likely to occur if there are substantial changes in exchange rates. These variations in aggregate demand also have implications for inflation and unemployment that we shall consider in part IV.

A very persistent inflationary spiral implies that a very large reduction in aggregate demand is needed to reduce the inflation rate by 1 per cent. Such a reduction in aggregate demand would cause a very large increase in unemployment, and this has obvious implications for government policies that attempt to reduce inflation by reducing aggregate demand. Most governments look for policies that reduce the persistence of inflation by breaking the links between prices and money wages.

The conclusions of this chapter also concern other aspects of government policies:

(a) The government controls the supply of money, and so we must examine more closely the role of the quantity theory of money. We shall see that the effects of changes in the supply of money are closely related to other aspects of government policies, including attempts to change aggregate demand.

(b) Government policies may cause or reduce imperfections, and this may influence the persistence of an inflationary spiral and the size of the natural rate of unemployment.

16.8 Summary

If there is no inflationary spiral, macroeconomic analysis predicts that the relationship between unemployment and inflation is that described by the Phillips curve. When there is an inflationary spiral, macroeconomic analysis predicts that a 1 per cent decrease in aggregate demand is likely to lead to an increase in unemployment and a reduction in the inflation rate. A 1 per cent increase in aggregate demand reduces unemployment and increases the inflation rate. However, a 1 per cent decrease in aggregate demand causes a larger change in unemployment and a smaller change in inflation than does a 1 per cent increase in aggregate demand. Therefore, over a period both inflation and unemployment may increase.

Market analysis predicts that full employment is restored in the long run and that the inflation rate is determined by the quantity theory of money. Modified market analysis assumes that changes in prices and wages are restricted by imperfections so that unemployment returns to the natural rate. If aggregate demand falls, modified market analysis predicts a temporary increase in the real wage. This temporary increase becomes permanent if workers and unions are powerful enough to prevent reductions in real wages. If this occurs, the natural rate of unemployment increases.

A mixed analysis predicts that unemployment first increases and later falls (but not necessarily to the initial level) when aggregate demand falls. The reduction in aggregate demand causes a reduction in the inflation rate. The size of this reduction depends on the extent of the imperfections that give rise to the inflationary spiral.

Topics and problems

(1) 'Trades unions cause inflation, reduce employment and reduce the incomes of non-unionized workers.' 'Trades unions protect workers from the excessive power of large firms.' To what extent can and should the government legislate to limit union power?

(2) 'Large firms cause inflation, reduce employment and reduce workers' incomes.' 'Large firms are often more efficient than small firms.' To what extent can and should the government legislate to limit the power of large firms?

(3) 'We can live with inflation, but unemployment is a waste of resources.' Does this imply that high inflation is a price worth paying for the efficient use of resources?

(4) In times of inflation, people are likely to spend money as soon as they receive it. Does this imply that inflation increases the demands for goods? If it does, what are the macroeconomic consequences of an increase in the inflation rate?

(5) What are the consequences for the velocity of circulation of the fact that people do not want to hold large stocks of money for long periods in a time of inflation?

Part IV

Government policy and the open economy

The economic analysis that we have met in parts II and III has been built with two major omissions: we have ignored the activities of the government and largely ignored issues related to international trade and the balance of payments. The first omission has enabled us to see how a market economy might work – with more than one view of the outcomes that are possible. Now, having seen how markets work on their own, we can examine whether government policies can change various aspects of the outcome of the economy.

For the UK and other developed economies, it is difficult to examine the consequences of government policies without giving explicit attention to the problems of international trade, the balance of payments and currency exchange rates. So in this part we consider an open economy with imports and exports, and international movements of financial capital.

In the first four chapters of the part we consider the consequences of various government policies for some measures of the performance of the economy (particularly the level of unemployment, the inflation rate and the distribution of income). In chapter 21, we consider the two main strands of thought on the operation of the economy (market analysis, developed in part II, and macroeconomic analysis, developed in part III) in the context of potential objectives for government policy. Finally, in chapter 22, we examine ways in which it may be possible to judge whether policies actually do cause an improvement by examining more closely the role of value judgements in economics that was discussed in chapter 1.

Chapter Seventeen

Fiscal and monetary policies

Aggregate demand — multipliers — monetary policy, interest rates and exchange
rates — pure monetary policy — fiscal and monetary policies

17.1 Introduction

Our examination of macroeconomic aspects of perfect and imperfect market
economies gives us several conclusions that form the basis of government
policies that are designed to influence employment and inflation. These
conclusions include:

(a) Using macroeconomic analysis, the inflation rate and the level of
    employment are affected by aggregate demand (see chapter 16).
(b) Inflation may persist in an inflationary spiral that prevents real wages from
    changing so that unemployment persists (see section 16.4).
(c) Market analysis implies that markets return rapidly to equilibrium, so that
    unemployment consists of those who do not want a job and those who are
    unemployable. The inflation rate is approximately equal to the rate of
    increase of the supply of money (which the government controls) minus
    the rate of economic growth (see section 11.6).
(d) Modified market analysis argues that, in the long run, unemployment is
    at the natural rate, which is the minimum consistent with the imperfections
    in the economy (see section 16.5). The government may be able to affect
    some imperfections.

These conclusions are not all consistent with one another because they rest on
different foundations. Those that come from market analysis and modified
market analysis are based on an assumption that firms change prices in response
to changes in demands. Those that come from macroeconomic analysis are
based on an assumption that prices and money wages do not change, or that
they change in proportion to one another so that real wages do not change.

   In this chapter we examine the ways in which the government can affect
national income by influencing aggregate demand, and also at some of the
consequences of changes in the supply of money. In the next chapter we extend

our examination of the supply of money to a more realistic situation, which takes account of important interrelations between banks and government policies. In chapter 21 we examine the consequences of these and other policies for employment and inflation.

As well as introducing government policies, we recognize the influence of transactions abroad, including imports and exports and foreign borrowing and lending. This **open economy** context is particularly (but by no means exclusively) relevant to the UK economy, where the interrelations between aggregate demand and the balance of trade and between interest rates, exchange rates and international payments are crucial.

17.2 Aggregate demand

The introduction of both government policy and international transactions implies that we use the national accounting equation (see section 5.10):

$$I + G + X = S + T + M \tag{17.1}$$

where I is private investment, G is government expenditure, X is exports, S is saving, T is tax payments to the government and M is imports. Total investment in the economy includes both private investment (by privately owned firms) and investment by the government, which is here included in government expenditure.

The difference $G-T$ between government expenditure and its tax receipts is the **government's budget deficit** (the government has a **surplus** if T exceeds G). The difference $X-M$ between exports and imports is the balance of **trade surplus** (**deficit** if M exceeds X). The difference $S-I$ is the **private sector balance**. From equation 17.1, we see that

$$(G - T) + (X - M) = (S - I) \tag{17.2}$$

so that:

Budget deficit plus balance of trade surplus equals private sector balance.

17.2.1 Macroeconomic equilibrium

In the simple models of parts II and III, macroeconomic equilibrium occurs when aggregate demand (desired consumption plus desired investment) equals national income. Allowing for government activity and international trade, aggregate demand consists of:

(a) Desired consumption.
(b) Desired private investment.
(c) Government expenditure.
(d) Demand for exports by people in other countries.

Note that tax policies affect aggregate demand through consumption and investment decisions. If the government cuts income taxes, people have higher

disposable incomes and so they are likely to demand more consumer goods; if taxes paid by firms are reduced, they may spend more on investment goods.

Aggregate demand can be met in two ways: by domestically produced goods and by imported goods. Together these form **aggregate supply**. In an open economy:

Macroeconomic equilibrium occurs when aggregate demand equals aggregate supply.

17.2.2 Government expenditure and taxation

The government can affect aggregate demand by changing its expenditure and the tax revenue that it collects, and:

the government's **fiscal policy** consists of its decisions on its expenditures and taxation.

Government expenditures include purchases of consumer and investment goods, payments of wages to civil servants and other employees, transfer payments such as pensions and unemployment benefits, subsidies to firms and the payment of interest to those who have lent to the government. Taxes are generally divided between **direct taxes** (mainly taxes on incomes, such as income tax, corporation tax, national insurance charges, capital gains tax and the UK community charge), **indirect taxes** (taxes on goods, such as value-added tax, duties on petrol, alcohol, tobacco and cars, road fund licences, taxes or rates on property) and **capital taxes** (including taxes on gifts and bequests). The analysis of fiscal policy is generally concerned only with total government expenditure and total tax payments; we shall discuss other aspects of government expenditure and the tax system, including the effects of particular taxes, in chapter 20.

17.2.3 Tax function

Total payments of taxes increase when national income increases. For a given set of tax policies (determined by the government when it sets the rates of VAT, income tax and other taxes), we can derive a **tax function** that relates tax payments to national income. We use the following definitions:

The **average tax rate** (ATR) is the fraction of national income that is paid in tax.

The **marginal tax rate** (MTR) is the fraction of an increase in national income that is paid in tax.

17.2.4 Disposable income

Disposable income is national income minus tax payments. Disposable income is divided between consumption and saving, and the consumption and saving functions (see section 15.3) now relate consumption and saving to disposable income. So:

The **average propensity to consume** is the fraction of disposable income that is spent on consumer goods.

The **marginal propensity to consume** is the fraction of an increase in disposable income that is spent on consumer goods.

The **average propensity to save** is the fraction of disposable income that is saved.

The **marginal propensity to save** is the fraction of an increase in disposable income that is saved.

17.2.5 Import function

All aspects of aggregate demand are likely to include demand for imported goods: private individuals, firms and the government all demand goods from abroad for consumption and investment. Even demand for exports is likely to generate a demand for imports because the production of most goods involves imported raw materials or components. So as national output (and hence national income) increases, so also does the demand for imports. We can derive an **import function** that relates the demand for imports to national income.

The **average propensity to import** (APM) is the ratio of imports to national income.

The **marginal propensity to import** (MPM) is the ratio of an increase in imports to the increase in national income that causes the increase in imports.

17.2.6 Macroeconomic analysis

The simplest version of the macroeconomic analysis of government expenditure and taxation in an open economy makes the following assumptions:

(a) Desired private investment does not change when national income changes.
(b) Government expenditure does not change when national income changes.
(c) Exports do not change when national income changes.

These assumptions imply that total desired injections to the circular flow do not change when national income changes. This is a simplifying assumption which makes the basic analysis very much clearer.

We used assumption (a) in the simplest version of the macroeconomic analysis of a market economy (see section 15.4). In practice, changes in national income do affect private investment because firms are likely to become more optimistic about their future sales and profits if national income increases.

In practice, government expenditure also changes when national income changes because a part of government expenditure is on transfer payments, including those paid to the unemployed. If national income increases, and unemployment is reduced, government expenditure falls. On the other hand, if national income increases because of inflation, government expenditure on some items (including index-linked pensions and other benefits) increases. Of course, the government may change its expenditure in response to changes in national income, particularly if it believes that changes in government expenditure can influence unemployment or the inflation rate. However, the cause of such a change in government expenditure is a change in government policy, and here we examine the effects of a given policy.

We analyse later how changes in national income may coincide with changes in exchange rates between currencies. These latter are likely to affect exports, but here we make assumption (c), that export demand depends on national incomes in other countries but not on domestic national income.

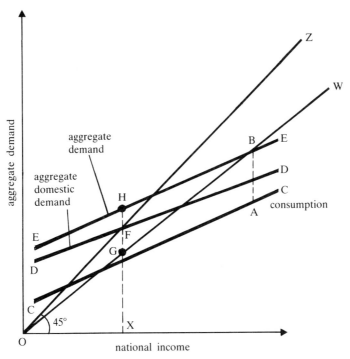

Figure 17.1   Aggregate demand in a mixed, open economy
CC shows consumption, EE aggregate demand and DD aggregate domestic demand.
OW is the tax function.

Figure 17.1 shows an **aggregate domestic demand function** DD. For any level of national income, aggregate domestic demand is calculated as follows:

(a) Subtract tax paid on national income (as given by the tax function) from national income. This gives disposable income. The disposable income for each level of national income is given by OW, and tax payments at each level of national income are given by the vertical difference between the 45 degree line OZ (which represents disposable income if there are no taxes) and OW.

(b) From the consumption function, find consumption given disposable income. This gives the line CC. Note that consumption can exceed disposable income if people spend their previous savings.

(c) Add the sum of private investment, government expenditure and exports to consumption. This gives aggregate demand EE, which is parallel to CC. Distance AB is equal to the sum of private investment, government expenditure and exports which do not depend on national income given the assumptions made above.

(d) For the given level of national income, subtract imports (as given by the import function) from aggregate demand. This gives DD, which is the aggregate domestic demand function. The vertical distance between EE and DD represents the import function. This distance increases as national income increases because imports rise as national income rises.

Macroeconomic equilibrium national income is then found at the intersection F of the aggregate domestic demand function DD with the 45 degree line OZ (compare figure 15.4), and equilibrium national income is at X. Disposable income is G, taxes paid are FG and imports are FH.

17.3 Multipliers

Figure 17.2 shows the effect on the macroeconomic equilibrium national income of an increase in aggregate domestic demand (DD to D'D') and aggregate demand (EE to E'E') caused by an increase in any of investment, government expenditure or exports by BB' from AB to AB'. The macroeconomic equilibrium national income increases from X to X'.

(a) If the increase in national income is caused by an increase in private investment, the ratio of the distances X'X to B'B is the **investment multiplier**.

(b) If the increase in national income is caused by an increase in government expenditure, the ratio of the distances X'X to B'B is the **government expenditure multiplier**.

(c) If the increase in national income is caused by an increase in exports, the ratio of the distances X'X to B'B is the **export multiplier**.

An increase in any of the three injections (investment, government expenditure or exports) to the circular flow of national income must be matched by an increase in withdrawals (saving, taxation and imports) if macroeconomic equilibrium is to be restored. An increase in withdrawals occurs when national income increases. The increase in tax payments depends on the marginal tax rate; the increase in saving depends on the marginal propensity to save; the increase in imports depends on the marginal propensity to import. Together,

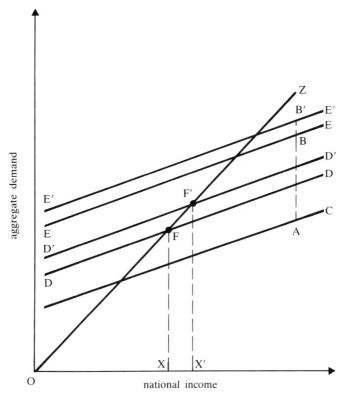

Figure 17.2   A shift in aggregate demand
Investment, government expenditure or exports increase, aggregate demand increases
from EE to E'E' and aggregate domestic demand from DD to D'D'.

these determine the fraction of any increase in national income that is not
spent on domestically produced goods.

For the examples of this section, we suppose an initial situation in which:

(a) The average and marginal tax rates are 0.25.
(b) The average and marginal propensities to save out of disposable income
    are 0.2.
(c) The average and marginal propensities to import are 0.3.
(d) Private investment is £93,400, government expenditure is £120,000 and
    exports are £110,000; the sum of these is £323,400.

The first column of table 17.1 shows that national income is £462,000, that the
government has a budget deficit of £4,500 and that there is a balance of trade
deficit of £28,600. Total withdrawals are £323,400, equalling the sum of private
investment, government expenditure and exports.

Suppose that the government increases its expenditure on roads by £23,100.
The second column of table 17.1 shows that macroeconomic equilibrium
national income increases by £33,000, taxation increases by £8,250, saving by
£4,950 and imports by £9,900. The increase in total withdrawals equals the

Table 17.1   National accounts in multiplier example

	Column 1	Column 2	Difference (col.2 − col.1)
National income	462,000	495,000	33,000
Tax (at 25%)	115,500	123,750	8,250
Disposable income	346,500	371,250	24,750
Saving (at 20% of disposable income)	69,300	74,250	4,950
Imports (at 30% of national income)	138,600	148,500	9,900
Total withdrawals	323,400	346,500	23,100
Private investment	93,400	93,400	—
Government expenditure	120,000	143,100	23,100
Exports	110,000	110,000	—
Total injections	323,400	346,500	23,100
Government budget deficit	4,500	19,350	14,850
Balance of trade deficit	28,600	38,500	9,900

increase in government expenditure; the government's budget deficit increases by £14,850 and the balance of trade deficit increases by £9,900. The government expenditure multiplier is 33,000/23,100 = 10/7 = 1.43. The increase in national income would be the same if the additional expenditure were private investment or exports, so that the three multipliers are the same.

The somewhat complicated formulae for these multipliers are derived in box 10.

17.3.1 Multiplier process

An increase in private investment, government expenditure or exports generates a multiplier process similar to that described for a market economy in section 15.6. In the example given above, the increase of £33,000 in national income occurs in a multiplier process whose stages are as follows:

Stage 1

The additional government expenditure generates £23,100 additional revenue for road-building firms, and so an additional £23,100 national income. Twenty-five per cent (£5,775) is paid in taxes, £3,465 (20 per cent of the extra disposable income) is saved and £6,930 is spent on imports. The remainder (£6,930) is spent on domestically produced goods.

Stage 2

The additional expenditure on domestically produced goods in stage 1 generates an additional £6,930 national income. From this 25 per cent (£1,732.5) is paid

---

Box 10   Multipliers in an open economy

The average tax rate is $ATR = T/Y$; the marginal tax rate is $MTR = \Delta T/\Delta Y$, where Y is national income, T is tax revenue and the symbol Δ means 'change in'. Disposable income is $Y_{dis} = Y - T$. The average and marginal propensities to consume out of disposable income are respectively $APCD = C/Y_{dis}$ and $MPCD = \Delta C/\Delta Y_{dis}$, where C is consumption. The average and marginal propensities to save (out of disposable income) are respectively $APSD = S/Y_{dis}$ and $MPSD = \Delta S/\Delta Y_{dis}$, where S is saving. The average and marginal propensities to import are respectively $APM = M/Y$ and $MPM = \Delta M/\Delta Y$.

If there is an increase ΔY in national income, then

$$\Delta T = MTR \times \Delta Y$$
$$\Delta S = MPSD \times \Delta Y_{dis} = MPSD(\Delta Y - \Delta T) = MPSD(\Delta Y - MTR \times \Delta Y)$$
$$= MPSD(1 - MTR)\Delta Y$$
$$\Delta M = MPM \times \Delta Y$$

The total increase in withdrawals from the circular flow is therefore

$$\Delta T + \Delta S + \Delta M = (MTR + (MPSD(1 - MTR)) + MPM) \times \Delta Y$$

If there is a change ΔI in private investment, then macroeconomic equilibrium is restored by a change ΔY where

$$\Delta I = (MTR + (MPSD(1 - MTR)) + MPM) \times \Delta Y$$

and so the investment multiplier is

$$\Delta Y/\Delta I = 1/(MTR + (MPSD(1 - MTR)) + MPM)$$

The government expenditure and export multipliers are the same as the investment multiplier.

Table 17.2   Multiplier process following an increase in government expenditure

Stage	Additional national income	Additional taxation	Additional disposable income	Additional saving	Additional imports	Additional aggregate domestic demand
Initial						23,100
1	23,100	5,775	17,225	3,465	6,930	6,930
2	6,930	1,732.5	5,197.5	1,039.5	2,079	2,079
3	2,079	519.75	1,559.25	311.85	623.7	623.7
.	.	.	.	.	.	.
.	.	.	.	.	.	.
.	.	.	.	.	.	.
10	0.455	0.114	0.341	0.068	0.136	0.136
Sum of first 10 stages	32,999.35	8,249.84	24,749.51	4,949.9	9,899.8	32,999.8
.	.	.	.	.	.	.
.	.	.	.	.	.	.
Eventual total	33,000	8,250	24,750	4,950	9,900	33,000

in taxes, £1,039.5 (20 per cent of the extra disposable income) is saved and £2,079 is spent on imports. The remainder (£2,079) is spent on domestically produced goods. And so on.

Table 17.2 lists more of these stages, and shows that the total additional national income after 10 stages is close to the £33,000 needed to restore macroeconomic equilibrium.

17.3.2 Taxation multiplier

A reduction in the average tax rate at each level of national income affects both the government's total receipts from taxation and consumers' disposable incomes. So a change in tax policy can also generate successive stages similar to the multiplier process described above. The **taxation multiplier** caused by a change in tax rates is the change in national income divided by the change in tax revenue that would have occurred if national income had not changed. This definition is used because it is easier to see the initial effect of the change in tax payments (assuming that national income is unchanged) than the eventual change in tax payments allowing for the subsequent changes in national income.

For example, suppose that the average tax rate in our example is reduced from 25 per cent to 20 per cent. Before the change in the tax rate, national income is £462,000 and total tax payments are £115,500, saving is £69,300 and imports are £138,600. After the change in the tax rate, national income increases to £490,000, total tax payments are £98,000, saving is £78,400 and imports are £147,000. Both before and after the change in the tax rate, total withdrawals are £323,400. If national income were to remain at £462,000 when the tax rate falls to 20 per cent, total tax payments would be £92,400, and the taxation multiplier is therefore $(490,000 - 462,000)/(115,500 - 92,400) = 28,000/23,100 = 1.21$. Note that the reduction in tax payments out of the initial level of macroeconomic equilibrium (£23,100) exceeds the eventual reduction in tax payments £17,500) because macroeconomic equilibrium national income increases.

This taxation multiplier process occurs in stages as follows:

Stage 1

Given the original national income of £462,000, the reduction in tax rates increases disposable income by £23,100, so that saving increases by £4,620 and demand for domestically produced goods increases by £18,480. Note that imports do not increase at this stage since increases in these are related to national income (and not to disposable income).

Stage 2

The additional expenditure on domestically produced goods from stage 1 increases national income by £18,480, of which £3,696 is paid in tax (at 20 per cent), imports increase by £5,544 and saving increases by £2,956.8. Demand for domestically produced goods increases by £6,283.2. And so on.

Table 17.3 lists further stages, and shows that the increase in national income becomes ever closer to £28,000 (no additional national income is generated in stage 1, because firms' revenues do not increase until stage 2). There is no change in private investment, government expenditure or exports, and so the additional saving plus the additional imports exactly equals the eventual reduction in taxation of £17,500.

Table 17.3 The multiplier process following a reduction in taxation

Stage	Additional national income	Additional taxation	Additional disposable income	Additional saving	Additional imports	Additional aggregate domestic demand
1	—	−23,100	23,100	4,620	—	18,480
2	18,480	3,696	14,784	2,956.8	5,544	6,283.2
3	6,283.2	1,256.64	5,026.56	1,053.12	1,884.96	2,136.29
.	.	.	.	.	.	.
.	.	.	.	.	.	.
10	3.3	0.66	2.64	0.53	0.99	1.12
Sum of first 10 stages	27,995	−17,501	45,496	9,099	8,398	27,998
.	.	.	.	.	.	.
.	.	.	.	.	.	.
Eventual total	28,000	−17,500	45,500	9,100	8,400	28,000

The two examples of tables 17.2 and 17.3 are comparable in that the initial reduction in taxation in table 17.3 is the same size as the increase in government expenditure in table 17.2. However:

The effect on macroeconomic equilibrium national income of an increase in government expenditure is greater than the effect of an equal-sized tax reduction.

In table 17.2, the increase in government expenditure of £23,100 generates a total increase of £33,000 in macroeconomic equilibrium national income. In table 17.3, an initial reduction of £23,100 in taxes generates an increase of £28,000 in macroeconomic equilibrium national income. This difference arises because the increase in government expenditure has a greater effect on aggregate domestic demand than does the reduction in taxation. The initial increase in aggregate domestic demand in table 17.2 equals the whole of the increase in government expenditure, whereas a tax reduction increases disposable income, and aggregate domestic demand increases only by the amount of additional demand for domestically produced goods out of this additional disposable income. Some of the additional disposable income is saved, and this offsets some of the effect of the tax reduction.

17.3.3 A target deficit

Changes in the government's budget deficit have implications other than those implied by the multiplier. In particular, a government must find the money to cover a deficit or in some way dispose of any surplus that it has. These financial arrangements themselves have implications for the economy and, in some circumstances, a government may have a target deficit that it wants to maintain even though it also wants to increase its expenditure. Suppose that, in our example, the government wants to increase its expenditure by £23,100 but wants to maintain its deficit at £4,500. It must therefore increase the average tax rate.

It might be thought that national income will not change if the government increases its expenditure and taxation by the same amount, so that injections to and withdrawals from national income increase by equal amounts. However, if the government increases the tax rate with no change in national income, disposable income falls and so saving falls. Imports remain the same (at 30 per cent of national income in our example), and so total withdrawals fall. This is shown in column 1 of table 17.4, where the government increases the average tax rate to 30 per cent. If national income remains at £462,000, taxes rise by £23,100 to match the extra expenditure, but saving falls to £64,680 (20

Table 17.4 National accounts in example with target government budget deficit of £4,500

	Column 1	Column 2
National income	462,000	471,240
Tax	(at 30%)	(at 29.41%)
	138,600	138,600
Disposable income	323,400	332,640
Saving (at 20% of disposable income)	64,680	66,528
Imports (at 30% of national income)	138,600	141,372
Total withdrawals	341,880	346,500
Private investment	93,400	93,400
Government expenditure	143,100	143,100
Exports	110,000	110,000
Total injections	346,500	346,500
Government budget deficit	4,500	4,500
Balance of trade deficit	28,600	31,372

per cent of disposable income) and total withdrawals are £341,880, which is £4,620 less than total injections. So national income must rise to restore macroeconomic equilibrium. The true picture is shown in column 2 of table 17.4. The average tax rate is increased to 29.41 per cent, and national income rises to £471,240. Taxes increase by £23,100 and total withdrawals equal total injections so that macroeconomic equilibrium is restored.

Even though the government deficit is unchanged, national income has risen by £9,240. The target deficit is maintained at a higher national income. A similar example can be used to establish that macroeconomic equilibrium national income increases when government expenditure increases even though the government changes the average tax rate to maintain a balanced budget. Thus fiscal policy (changes in expenditure and taxation) may still be used to change national income even if the government aims at a balanced budget or at a target surplus or deficit.

17.3.4 The national debt

If government expenditure is less than its tax revenues, the government must decide what to do with the surplus. Given that there are reasons why it may want to issue more money, or continue to sell shares in privatized companies, the government will be able to repay some previous loans and reduce the **national debt**, which is the sum of all outstanding loans to the government.

Economists and politicians sometimes make the value judgement that the government should balance its expenditure with receipts from taxation or even that it must run a surplus to reduce the national debt. There are several possible reasons why this value judgement is made, including:

(a) A political belief that the government must ensure good housekeeping by not spending beyond its income. This may not be consistent with other views that people have on the rights and wrongs of government actions. For example, a person may believe that it is desirable for the government to provide a health service or to control a natural monopoly (see section 12.2) such as the supply of water, so that the government buys investment goods (for example, hospitals and water pipes). Is it then consistent to argue that the government should not borrow to finance these investment projects (a balanced budget would require that they are financed from taxation), given that they would be financed by borrowing if the projects were the actions of privately owned firms. A more consistent value judgement might be that the government may borrow to finance investment projects, but not to finance current expenditure, such as purchases of consumer goods, the wages of civil servants, pensions or unemployment benefit.
(b) A deficit has undesirable consequences for interest rates and other aspects of the economy. We discuss these consequences in this and subsequent chapters.
(c) Money borrowed now must be repaid in the future, and this is a burden on people in the future. This has been the subject of considerable debate

between economists for several centuries. We shall discuss in section 23.5 the problems that countries have in repaying money that they have borrowed from other countries, and see that this can indeed be a burden. However, if the government borrows from its own residents, interest payments and eventual repayment of bonds involve payments to one group out of taxes paid by another. The two groups are likely to overlap, because almost everyone pays some taxes, but the major effect of these payments is on the income distribution.

The interest and repayments due in a year make up the cost of **servicing** the national debt. If this cost becomes large, the government may find that it cannot raise sufficient tax revenue or borrow enough to finance all of its desired expenditure and to service the national debt. So the major burden of a large national debt is that it may reduce the scope for increases in government expenditure or for tax cuts. Table 17.5 shows how the UK national debt has increased since 1938. In 1988, the interest on the debt was £18,027 million, which was 10 per cent of total UK government expenditure.

Table 17.5 UK national debt 1938–88

Year	£ million
1938	7,111
1943	15,933
1948	25,722
1953	26,142
1958	27,232
1963	29,848
1968	34,194
1973	36,884
1978	79,180
1983	127,072
1988	197,295

Source: *Annual Abstract of Statistics, Financial Statistics*

17.4 Monetary policy, interest rates and exchange rates

The national accounts allow for the possibility that the government has a budget deficit (government expenditure exceeds tax revenue) or a budget surplus (tax revenue exceeds government expenditure). The government finances a budget deficit by supplying a variety of financial assets that domestic and foreign households and firms (including in particular firms that operate pension funds and insurance companies) add to their portfolios. The main categories of financial assets that the government uses to finance its deficit are:

(a) **Bonds**. The government borrows by selling interest-bearing bonds;
(b) **Money**. The government prints notes and coins, and allows the banking system to create additional money that households and firms use to make transactions and for other purposes (discussed in detail in chapter 18).
(c) **Shares**. The government obtains money by selling shares in previously nationalized industries (or other public sector organizations). The extent of these share sales is a consequence of the government's **privatization policy** (discussed in detail in chapter 19).

The government's monetary policy is its decision on the mixture of assets issued to finance its deficit.

17.4.1 Basic monetary policy

Monetary policy is in fact very complex, mainly because of the interrelations between the government and the banking section. We reserve discussion of these complexities until chapter 18 because it is possible to examine the main principles of monetary and fiscal policy in a simpler context. So in this chapter we make three simplifying assumptions:

(a) All borrowing is in the form of bonds sold to the non-bank private sector (households and firms, including insurance and pension firms) and to foreign lenders.
(b) All money is notes and coins.
(c) Share sales by the government are unchanged.

In fact, the government also borrows from the banking sector, and households and firms use a variety of methods for making payments (including cheques drawn on bank accounts) and so they hold money in a variety of forms, of which notes and coins are one. We discuss these other financial assets and the relation between banks and the government's monetary policy in chapter 18.

17.4.2 Borrowing from the non-bank private sector

The government sells two main types of bonds:

(a) **Non-marketable bonds** (sold through National Savings in the UK). These include Savings Certificates, Save-As-You-Earn schemes and Premium Bonds (on which the interest is paid as randomly distributed prizes). The main feature of these bonds is that they cannot be sold by one person to another. The lender can obtain repayment of his or her money only by reselling the bond to the government, and this may not be possible (or may be possible on very unfavourable terms) before a set period has elapsed.
(b) **Marketable bonds (gilt-edged securities)** that are bought and sold on the Stock Market. These bonds resemble those issued by firms, with the additional security that the government will not go bankrupt, if only

because the government controls the issue of new money and can repay its debts by printing banknotes if it cannot do so from tax revenues or by additional borrowing.

Table 17.6 shows the extent of these two forms of borrowing from the non-bank private sector in the UK in recent years. Over the period covered by the table, government borrowing from the non-bank private sector financed an average of 80 per cent of the deficit, including one year (1988) in which the government repaid debts to the banking sector.

Table 17.6 UK central government borrowing from the non-bank private sector 1984–8

Year	National Savings (£ million)	Marketable bonds (£ million)	Total (£ million)	% of total government deficit
1984	3,390	7,484	10,874	107
1985	2,491	6,363	8,854	75
1986	2,617	3,329	5,946	71
1987	2,547	1,673	4,220	103
1988	1,488	−3,458	−1,970	—

In 1988, there was a government surplus, and a net repayment to the non-bank private sector of £1,970 million.

Source: *Financial Statistics*

17.4.3 Bonds and inflation

The **real rate of return** on a bond differs from the **nominal rate of return** if there is inflation. Equation 6.1 tells us that if a household expects that the inflation rate over the next year will be i and if the interest rate on a bond is n, then the expected real rate of return on the bond is r, where:

$$(1 + r) = (1 + n)/(1 + i)$$

For example, if the expected inflation rate is 10 per cent (i.e. 0.1), and a bond pays a nominal interest rate of 14 per cent, the expected real rate of return is 3.63 per cent ($1.0363 = 1.14/1.1$).

In recent years the UK government has issued **index-linked bonds** (both marketable and non-marketable), whose redemption value and interest payments increase at the same rate as the Retail Prices Index. When the expected inflation rate is 10 per cent, a risk-averse household prefers an index-linked bond paying (as in our example) 3.63 per cent, to a non-index-linked bond that pays 14 per cent, because the real rate of return on the index-linked bond is always 3.63 per cent, whatever the inflation rate, whereas the real rate of return on the non-index-linked bond is uncertain, because the inflation rate cannot be predicted with complete certainty. If the inflation rate is actually 12 per cent, the real rate of return on the non-index-linked bond is 1.79 per cent. If the inflation rate is actually 8 per cent, the real rate of return is 5.56 per cent. A risk-averse household views the pessimistic possibility more seriously than the optimisitic possibility and so it is prepared to buy a non-index-linked bond only if the expected rate of return is higher than the certain return on an index-linked bond. So if most households are risk-averse when they make their saving decisions, the government can borrow at a lower expected real rate of return (and hence with a lower total expected value of interest payments) by issuing index-linked bonds.

17.4.4 Interest rates and exchange rates

Foreigners are attracted to buy bonds or shares in the UK if the rate of return (interest on bonds, expected dividends and capital appreciation on shares) on UK assets exceeds that available in other countries *and* if the pound is not expected to depreciate sufficiently against other countries to offset the higher rate of return. Plainly, the demand for UK bonds increases *ceteris paribus* if interest rates in the UK rise relative to interest rates in other countries. Foreigners can buy UK bonds in pounds, and so an increased foreign demand for UK bonds implies an increased demand for pounds. *Ceteris paribus* an increase in the demand for pounds leads to a rise in the value of the pound. So:

> The pound appreciates against other currencies if UK interest rates increase relative to interest rates paid in other countries.

In section 14.6 we discussed speculation in foreign currencies and the movement of 'hot money'. The large sums of money involved, and the potential for their rapid transfer between currencies, imply that a small change in interest rates may lead to a rapid increase in the demand for pounds and hence a rapid appreciation of the pound against other currencies. A similar rapid depreciation following a reduction in the demand for pounds following a fall in UK interest rates is, of course, equally possible.

17.4.5 Government deficit and balance of payments

The national accounts allow for the possibility that the country has a foreign trade deficit (imports exceed exports) or a trade surplus (exports exceed imports). A trade deficit must be financed; importers demand foreign currency to buy goods; foreign currency is supplied by exporters who have received it by selling abroad (and who need domestic currency to pay their workers and other costs at home). A deficit implies that exporters are not receiving enough foreign currency to meet this demand from importers. Additional foreign currency is supplied to the UK by those foreigners who want to buy bonds or shares issued in the UK; additional foreign currency is demanded by UK residents who want to buy bonds and shares issued abroad. So a trade deficit could be financed if foreign purchases of bonds and shares in the UK exceed by a sufficient amount the purchases of bonds and shares abroad by UK residents. Otherwise, foreign currencies must be supplied from reserves held by the government or by official government borrowing from abroad (see section 5.9.3). Any surplus of foreign currency (if supply exceeds demand) can be used to repay previous official borrowing or to increase the reserves.

So if the government has a deficit which it finances by borrowing, and some of its bonds are sold to foreigners, the financing of the government's deficit also leads to a supply of foreign currency which can be used to help to finance a deficit on the balance of trade.

17.5 Pure monetary policy

The government uses a **pure monetary policy** if it changes the ratio of borrowing (by selling bonds) to money creation which it uses to finance its budget deficit, but does not change its total expenditure, tax rates or proceeds from privatization. We compare two policies:

Policy A: a large proportion of the deficit is financed by borrowing, and a small proportion by issuing new money.

Policy B: a large proportion of the deficit is financed by issuing new n.oney, and a small proportion by borrowing.

The analysis of the demand for money and liquidity preference in section 14.7 implies that policy A causes higher interest rates than B. The interest rate must be higher in A to persuade people to buy the extra bonds and to reduce their demand for money.

The higher interest rates in A are likely to:

(a) Reduce private investment because firms are less willing to borrow.
(b) Reduce consumption because people are less willing to buy on credit.
(c) Increase saving because people are likely to change their saving behaviour in the light of the higher interest rates.
(d) Appreciate the exchange rate as domestic interest rates increase relative to foreign interest rates, thus attracting more people to buy bonds issued by domestic government and firms. The appreciation implies that imports are likely to rise and exports fall as domestic goods become more expensive relative to foreign goods.

Howevever, there is a major difference of opinion on the overall effects of a pure monetary policy between two groups of economists: **Keynesians** and **monetarists**.

17.5.1 Keynesian view

This view is based mainly on the analysis of macroeconomic aspects of a mixed economy of John Maynard Keynes. In *The General Theory of Employment, Interest and Money* (1936), Keynes responded to the prolonged unemployment of the great depression of the 1930s by introducing many of the ideas that are incorporated into macroeconomic analysis. The Keynesian view is based on the assumptions that:

(a) The interest-elasticity of the demand for money is large, so that the liquidity preference curve is nearly horizontal. A large change in the supply of money requires only a small change in interest rates to re-establish equilibrium between the demand and supply of money. This implies that if policy B is used interest rates are only a little lower than if policy A is used.
(b) The main influence on private investment is firms' optimism about future sales, and the somewhat lower interest rates if B is used have little effect on private investment.

The small effect on interest rates is also presumed to have little effect on consumption and saving. Keynes himself did not consider the effect on the exchange rate in his *General Theory*, and it is certainly true that even small changes in interest rates can trigger significant changes in the exchange rate as hot money moves rapidly from one currency to another. However, macroeconomic analysis assumes that the prices of goods do not change rapidly, and many Keynesians would argue that changes in exchange rates have a slow, and quite possibly small, effect on imports and exports.

Therefore the small change in interest rates has a very small effect on aggregate domestic demand, and so:

> The Keynesian view is that pure monetary policy has little effect on national income (and so can have little effect on unemployment or inflation).

(Keynes was born in 1883 in Cambridge, and died in 1946. He was a fellow of King's College, Cambridge, a successful operator in financial markets, and a senior government economic adviser during both world wars. He had wide-ranging interests in the arts, and was a founder member of the Arts Council and a member of the 'Bloomsbury Group' of authors, artists and intellectuals that flourished in the period before and after the First World War.)

17.5.2 Monetarist view

The modern form of this view is associated with Milton Friedman (born in New York, 1912; now senior research fellow at the Hoover Institute, Stanford University, California, and professor of economics at the University of Chicago from 1948; Nobel prizewinner in economics, 1976). Monetarism is based on the assumptions that the transactions demand is the most important source of demand for money and that the most important reason for changes in national income is changes in the money supply, as predicted by the quantity equation, with the velocity of circulation constant (see section 11.6).

Therefore national income is greater if policy B is used, since it involves a larger supply of money. The larger national income arises because households spend the additional money on goods to reduce their holdings of money to the desired level, and this additional demand increases outputs and/or prices. The higher demand for goods increases imports and higher prices are likely to reduce exports and increase imports, as domestic goods become more expensive relative to those from abroad. However, this increase in imports does not completely offset the rise in national income implied by the quantity equation. So:

> The monetarist view is that pure monetary policy can have a considerable effect on national income (and so can have a considerable effect on unemployment or inflation).

In practice, monetarist economists often support the use of market analysis rather than macroeconomic analysis (because they believe that prices change to bring markets to equilibrium), and so they predict that involuntary unemployment is eliminated, or reduced to its natural rate (the idea of which was first introduced by Friedman). Therefore the main effect of an increase in the money supply is higher prices.

17.5.3 Monetarists, Keynesians and the velocity of circulation

The monetarist conclusion concerning pure monetary policy is based on the assumption that the velocity of circulation is approximately constant. So in the quantity equation $MV = PT$, M is higher if policy B is used, so that PT is higher and national income is higher. The Keynesian view implies that V is lower if policy B is used, because national income is little higher and so PT is little higher, despite the greater supply of money. The velocity of circulation falls, in the Keynesian view, because the additional money is held in portfolios of financial assets, and so each unit of money is used, on average, less frequently if policy B is used than if policy A is used.

17.6 Fiscal and monetary policies

The government can change its monetary policy without changing its expenditure or tax rates (this is a pure monetary policy), but any fiscal policy affects the size of the government deficit, and so requires that the government chooses a monetary policy to finance the increased or the reduced deficit.

We compare two policies, in both of which the government increases its expenditure and leaves tax rates unchanged. This increases the government deficit (or reduces it surplus). The two policies differ in the way in which the increased deficit is financed:

Policy C: the government finances the additional deficit by additional borrowing.

Policy D: the government finances the additional deficit by creating additional money.

The analysis of section 14.5 implies that policy C causes higher interest rates than D to ensure equilibrium in the bond market and equality of the supply and demand for money. Once again, there is a major difference of opinion on the relative effects of the two policies between Keynesian and monetarist economists.

17.6.1 Keynesian view

The Keynesian view of the outcome of the policies is based on the macroeconomic analysis of the fiscal policy, together with the assumption that the interest-elasticity of the demand for money is high, so that only a very small reduction in interest rates follows a large increase in the supply of money. The small reduction in interest rates leads to only a very small rise in investment (if any), and so aggregate demand does not change greatly as a result of monetary policy.

The macroeconomic analysis of the fiscal policy predicts that national income increases, and that the size of the increase is determined by the size of the change in government expenditure and by the government expenditure multiplier (see section 17.3). This increase in national income occurs whichever of the two policies is used, and the Keynesian assumptions imply that the monetary policy used to finance the additional deficit has little further effect on aggregate domestic demand or national income. Policy C leads to somewhat higher interest rates than policy D, but this has little effect. So:

> The Keynesian view of fiscal policy is that national income changes according to the government expenditure multiplier (or the taxation multiplier if tax rates are changed), and that the method of financing the additional deficit is unimportant.

The increase in national income predicted for both policies leads to an increase in saving, and so to an increase in the demand for bonds. This increase in demand increases the price of bonds and reduces interest rates on bonds. This offsets some of the effect of an increase in the supply of bonds that occurs if the additional deficit is financed by borrowing. Keynesian economists use this as an additional support for the view that there is little change in interest rates or in private investment following an increase in government expenditure or a reduction in taxation.

17.6.2 Monetarist view

In the monetarist view, the most important source of changes in national income is changes in the supply of money. So policy D leads to a larger increase in national income than does policy C, because policy D involves the greater increase in the money supply. The question remains of how it is possible that national income does not increase (or increases only a little) if policy C is used.

If the government uses policy C, interest rates increase, and this reduces private investment and consumption. The increase in the interest rate causes the exchange rate to appreciate and this reduces exports and increases imports. According to market analysis these price changes occur fairly quickly and restore macroeconomic equilibrium. In the monetarist view, the effect of policy C is that the increase in government expenditure **crowds out** an almost equal amount of consumption, investment and exports, leaving only a small increase (if any) in aggregate demand. This small increase is met by an increase in imports rather than an increase in domestic output. So there is no change in national income. In the monetarist view, this is consistent with the fact that policy C involves no increase in the supply of money.

If the government uses policy D, national income increases. There is no change in interest rates and so private investment is not reduced. The increase in national income is given by the quantity equation, in which the velocity of circulation is assumed to be constant. So:

> The monetarist view is that the effect of fiscal policy depends on the method of financing the resulting government deficit. If the government borrows, national income is unchanged; if the government creates additional money, the increase in national income is proportional to the increase in the supply of money.

Once again, the monetarist use of market analysis implies that the main effects of policy D are on the price level, since an increase in the supply of money leads to inflation.

17.6.3 Privatization

In principle, the government could finance an increased deficit by selling more shares by privatizing more state-owned firms. The macroeconomic effects of this depend on the way in which sales of shares affect interest rates. There are three possibilities:

(a) The demand for the new shares reduces the demands for other shares, whose prices fall. Private firms are less able to raise money for new investment by issuing shares, and so private investment falls. If the total demand for shares does not increase at all, much of the increase in government expenditure will be offset by the reduction in private investment.

(b) Those who buy the shares reduce their holdings of other financial assets. They sell bonds and reduce their accounts with banks and building societies to buy the shares. In effect, this reduces the demand for bonds and the availability of loans to those who borrow from banks and building societies. Thus interest rates on bonds and on these loans increase, so that the sale of shares has a similar effect to the sale of additional government bonds.

(c) Shares are a different form of financial asset from bonds. People within the country may reduce their consumption to buy shares, and foreigners who would not buy bonds or other UK shares buy shares in privatized firms. This is perhaps particularly likely if the shares are widely thought to be underpriced. Then the government succeeds in funding its increased deficit without affecting interest rates, although the decline in consumption will, to some extent, offset the effects of the additional government expenditure.

There is likely to be a mixture of all of these effects if the government sells more shares, so that the overall reduction in other components of aggregate demand is likely to be significant, but less than the full crowding out implied by the monetarist analysis of section 17.6.2.

17.6.4 Supply-side effects

Privatization, reductions in government expenditure and tax cuts are all ways of reducing the extent of government influence on the economy. Market analysis implies that the economy operates efficiently when there is very little government intervention (see part II), and therefore national income is likely to increase as government intervention is reduced. These **supply-side effects** are very important in the modern market analysis of an economy and in the justification of many aspects of UK government policy in the late 1980s.

Government policies that are designed to make the economy more like the market economy described in part II have effects on various parts of the economy. For example, privatization of state monopolies leads to questions on the control of monopoly power; income tax reductions lead to questions on incentives to people to supply more labour. We shall discuss these issues in later chapters; for this chapter, we note that these policies may have an overall effect on national income that is different from (or perhaps in addition to) the effects of changes in aggregate demand and the effects of monetary and fiscal policy as we have described them here.

If national income increases because the supply-side effects are significant, there may be an additional multiplier effect on national income. As national income increases, tax revenues will increase to offset (at least to some extent) the effects of reductions in tax rates. Thus the government will need to reassess its monetary policy, perhaps changing interest rates and the supply of money, and therefore generating other changes in aggregate demand and national income.

17.7 Summary

The use of macroeconomic analysis and the concepts of aggregate demand and macroeconomic equilibrium can be extended to include government activity and foreign trade. An increase in any of private investment, government expenditure and exports leads to a multiplier process and an increase in national income. A reduction in tax rates also leads to a multiplier increase in national income, but the taxation multiplier is less than the government expenditure multiplier because, in the first stage of the multiplier process, households save some of the increased disposable income that results from a tax cut.

The government's budget deficit can be financed by borrowing or by creating money. Increased borrowing implies higher interest rates, and is also likely to lead to an appreciation of the exchange rate. Borrowing from abroad may serve two purposes: financing the government's budget deficit and supplying foreign currencies to finance a deficit on the balance of trade.

Keynesian economists stress the role of fiscal policy and argue that pure monetary policy has little effect on national income. Free market economists argue that changes in fiscal policy are offset by crowding out, and that monetary policy alone can affect national income in the long term. The implications of these differences in view for inflation, unemployment and other aspects of the economy will be discussed further in chapter 21.

Topics and problems

(1) Is the government expenditure multiplier the same as the investment multiplier if the additional government expenditure is:

(a) Wages of additional civil servants who save a part of their incomes
(b) Pensions paid to people who do not save
(c) Additional child benefit paid to households with a high marginal propensity to save
(d) The cost of building a nuclear power station
(e) Increased defence expenditure?

(2) Should the government aim to have a budget surplus, so that it can pay back a part of the national debt each year?

(3) A government allows a deficit only to finance investment. Should it finance expenditure on retraining as a part of its deficit? How should it regard social security payments to those who are retraining?

(4) Why does the government borrow through National Savings as well as by selling marketable bonds?

(5) 'Fiscal policy may expand national income, but the associated monetary policy contracts it again.' Discuss.

(6) Provide a script for a debate between Keynes and Friedman on the effectiveness of monetary and fiscal policy.

(7) In an economy with no international trade, private investment is £3,000, government expenditure is £2,000, the average propensity to save out of disposable income is 10 per cent and the average tax rate is 25 per cent.

What is the macroeconomic equilibrium national income?
What is the government's budget deficit or surplus?

(8) How large is the change in the macroeconomic equilibrium national income in the economy of problem 7 if the marginal propensity to save equals the average propensity to save and the marginal tax rate equals the average tax rate, and:

Government expenditure is increased by 10 per cent
Private investment falls by 10 per cent
The average and marginal tax rates are reduced to 20 per cent?

What is the change in the budget deficit or surplus in each case?
(9) In the example of problem 7, the government increases the average tax rate to 30 per cent. What is the macroeconomic equilibrium national income if:

(a) Each £1 reduction in national income increases government expenditure by £0.25 (perhaps because the reduction in national income increases unemployment so that transfer payments are higher)
(b) Each £1 reduction in national income reduces private investment by £0.25 (perhaps because firms become less optimistic as national income falls)
(c) Both (a) and (b) occur
(d) Neither (a) nor (b) occurs?

Comment on the implications of (a) for government attempts to change its deficit or surplus by changing tax rates.
(10) Recalculate answers to problems 7 to 9 assuming that the marginal propensity to import is 0.1 and exports are fixed at £1,500. What is the surplus or deficit on the balance of trade in each case?

Chapter Eighteen

Banks and monetary policy

Measuring the supply of money — central bank — banks' assets and liabilities — cash and liquidity — credit creation — credit creation and pure monetary policy — monetary and fiscal policy — credit creation and the control of the supply of money — other aspects of monetary policy

---

18.1 Introduction

Our discussion of monetary policy in chapter 17 was based on two simplifying assumptions:

(a) The only form of money is notes and coins.
(b) The government finances its deficit by creating additional money, by borrowing from the **non-banking private sector** (households and firms other than banks) and from abroad and by selling shares by privatizing firms.

Effectively in chapter 17 we ignored the activities of **banks**. The **banking sector** (or **monetary sector**) includes:

(a) **Clearing banks** (or commercial or high-street banks), that are so called because they operate the clearing house system for dealing with cheques drawn by a customer of one bank and paid to a customer of another.
(b) A variety of other financial institutions, which in the UK form a part of 'the City'.

18.2 Measuring the supply of money

The banking sector provides households and firms with a variety of means of payment other than notes and coins, including cheques, bank transfers, the Giro system, credit cards and the electronic movement of funds from one bank account to another. These other methods of payment are a part of the money supply that is available to finance transactions: households and firms hold a variety of accounts at banks and building societies (these are non-profit-making firms in the UK that borrow households' savings and lend these to others to buy houses), which they use to make transactions or to meet emergencies. So the activities of the banking sector complicate the definition of the supply of money.

In the UK, the government uses several definitions of the supply of money that is available to meet the demand for making transactions and for precautionary and speculative purposes. These include:

(a) **M0**, which is notes and coins in circulation and in banks' tills and banks' deposits at the Bank of England.
(b) **M1**, which is notes and coins in circulation plus private sector (i.e. privately owned firms and households) sight deposits (these are bank accounts from which money can be drawn without notice).
(c) **M2**, which is M1 plus sight accounts with building societies and National Savings accounts.
(d) **M3**, which is M1 plus time bank deposits (i.e. those for which the holder must give notice of withdrawal); note that M3 is not necessarily bigger than M2.
(e) **M4**, which is M3 plus time deposits at building societies.
(f) **M5**, which is M4 plus private sector bills.

Table 18.1 shows the sizes of these various measures of the money supply in the UK.

In this chapter we examine the relation between the banking sector and the government, with particular reference to changes in the supply of money. In the next chapter we shall examine how policies that affect the supply of money may be used to influence inflation and employment. When we discuss the supply of money in this way, we want to include all the items that households and firms regard as money available for financing transactions (not all this money need be used, because some may be held for precautionary purposes). Each of the above definitions of the supply of money includes different items, and it is difficult to say which measure corresponds most closely to the supply of money as we generally use the term. The financial system of the economy develops (particularly as changes involving the electronic transfer of funds

Table 18.1   Measures of the UK money supply 1983 to 1988 (figures are for the end of June in each year and are measured in £ billion)

	1985	1986	1987	1988	1989
M0	13.7	14.3	14.8	15.6	16.7
M1	53.5	64.2	79.2	95.8	108.9
M2	136.5	151.5	171.0	192.7	221.0
M3	114.1	133.4	159.6	193.0	233.6
M4	205.6	235.8	270.3	315.6	372.5
M5	219.5	249.5	284.3	331.4	387.8

Source: *Financial Statistics*

occur), and it is likely that useful definitions of the supply of money will change (as they have in the past). This affects the way in which the government can control the supply of money, but may not affect the principles that lie behind the analysis of the effects of changes in the supply of money on employment and inflation (see sections 17.5 and 17.6).

18.2.1 Financing the government's budget deficit

We can now distinguish four methods of financing the government's budget deficit:

(a) The creation of cash.
(b) Borrowing from the non-banking private sector and from abroad.
(c) Borrowing from the banking sector.
(d) Selling shares by privatization.

The deficit that is financed in the first three ways (that is, the total deficit minus the part financed through privatization issues) is known as the **public sector borrowing requirement (PSBR)**. This term includes the creation of cash, because technically the creation of cash occurs when the government borrows from the **central bank** (the Bank of England in the UK, the Federal Reserve in the USA). The fact that the UK government owns and controls the Bank of England implies that borrowing to create cash has different effects from borrowing from the non-banking private sector and from the banking sector. Table 18.2 shows how the UK government has financed the PSBR in recent years (note that the PSBR is negative in 1988, implying that the government had a surplus and repaid past loans to the various sectors).

Table 18.2 Financing the UK public sector borrowing requirement 1978–88 (figures are in £ million)

	1978	1983	1988
PSBR	8,348	11,536	−11,668
Non-bank private sector	7,299	12,197	−6,366
Banking sector	−343	−2,043	−3,922
Overseas	1,392	1,382	−1,380

Source: *Financial Statistics*

18.3 Central bank

The central bank plays a major role in the operation of the government's monetary policy. The central bank acts as banker to the government and to the banking sector, whose accounts at the central bank have four main functions:

(a) A bank can withdraw cash from its account at the central bank if it needs notes and coins to meet the needs of its account holders.

(b) If Alan, who has an account at bank M, writes a cheque to Bill, who has an account at bank N, then M must transfer money to N, so that N can credit the money to Bill's account. This transfer is made by a reduction in M's account and an increase in N's account at the central bank.

(c) If a household or firm pays a cheque drawn on an account at bank M to the government (for example, to pay taxes, to buy a government bond or a share in a newly privatized firm), the money is tranferred to the government by reducing M's account and increasing the government's account at the central bank. The opposite process occurs if the government pays a cheque to a household or firm (for example, to pay a pension, a civil servant's salary or for a new hospital) that has an account at M.

(d) The banking sector lends money to the government. This lending is achieved by a transfer from banks' accounts at the central bank to the government's account at the central bank.

The third and fourth functions of banks' accounts at the central bank show how money lent by the non-banking private sector and by the banking sector reaches the government: the government's account at the central bank is increased and banks' accounts at the central bank are reduced by the amount borrowed.

18.3.1 Creation of cash

The government's account at the central bank is increased whenever it decides to increase the amount of cash as a way of financing its deficit. When it creates cash, the central bank lends to the government by crediting the government's account with the amount of cash created – effectively, the central bank allows the government to overdraw on its account up to the extent of the cash created.

Note that, in practice, the government's account at the central bank is kept to a very low level in comparison with the total of government expenditure, taxation and borrowing. This is done by using any surplus in the account to buy back government bonds, which reduces the amount of interest that the government must pay to bondholders.

The total amount of cash created differs from the total of notes and coins in circulation. Cash is created when the government's account at the central bank is increased by borrowing from the central bank. Some of this may be withdrawn by the government in the form of notes and coins, particularly to make transfer payments through post offices and social security offices. However, most government expenditure is by cheque or other bank transfer, and this involves an increase in banks' accounts at the central bank and a reduction in the government's account. The central bank needs to supply notes and coins only when the banks require them to meet the needs of their customers. If banks do not withdraw notes and coins, the cash remains in the form of a book-keeping entry recording the size of banks' accounts at the central bank. It is included in the measure of money M0 and in all measures that include M0.

18.4 Banks' assets and liabilities

A bank's **assets** (apart from buildings and equipment that it owns) are:

(a) Notes and coins held by the bank.
(b) The bank's account at the central bank on which it can draw at any time.
(c) Loans made to other firms in the banking sector to the non-banking private sector, to the government or to people abroad. These are assets because the bank holds a bond, a mortgage deed or another financial asset that indicates that the borrower owes money to the bank.

A bank's **liabilities** are its accounts (or deposits). These are a liability to the bank because its account-holders can withdraw money from their accounts (not necessarily immediately).

Table 18.3 shows the major components of the assets and liabilities of UK banks in 1989. In this table, the banks' total assets equal their total liabilities. This equality is maintained in the manner indicated by the following examples:

(a) If an account-holder pays £100 cash into a bank, the bank receives an additional asset (the £100 cash) and has an equal additional liability (an account has increased by the £100 paid in).
(b) If an account holder pays the £100 in the form of a cheque paid by another account-holder at the same bank, the bank's total assets and liabilities are unchanged: one account increases by £100, the other account falls by £100.
(c) If Alan (who holds an account at bank M) receives a cheque for £100 from Bill (who holds an account at bank N), then M's assets rise and N's assets fall because £100 is transferred from M's account to N's account at the central bank. M's liabilities increase by £100 (because Alan's account at M increases); N's liabilities fall (because Bill's account at N is reduced).
(d) If M lends £200 to Alan, the bank's assets increase by £200 because Alan owes it £200. M's liabilities increase by £200 because the loan is made by increasing the amount that Alan can withdraw from its account by £200. If Alan withdraws the £200 in cash, the bank's assets fall because it has £200 less in notes; its liabilities fall because Alan's account is reduced by £200.
(e) If bank M lends £1 million to the government, its assets are unchanged. M's assets fall by £1 million because M transfers £1 million to the government from M's account at the central bank; M's assets rise by £1 million because it acquires government bonds.

18.4.1 Bills

Banks' assets include bonds of the kind bought by the non-banking private sector, and **bills** (which represent short-term loans of a few months) that the banking sector buys from firms, the government and local authorities. Bills sold by the government are known as Treasury bills. These are loans to the government for three months (sometimes for six months).

Table 18.3 Assets and liabilities of UK banks, 31 March 1989

	£ million	% of total
Assets		
Notes and coins	2,755	0.9
Balances at Bank of England including cash ratio deposits	909	0.3
Market loans (mainly to other firms in banking system)	33,442	10.8
Bills and government bonds	12,129	3.9
Other loans and advances	162,905	52.8
Loans in currencies other than sterling	59,195	19.2
Miscellaneous	37,205	12.1
Total	308,540	100
Liabilities		
Sterling deposits		
Private sector	142,711	46.3
Public sector	4,451	1.4
Monetary sector	21,119	6.8
Overseas sector	19,402	6.3
Non-sterling deposits	52,283	16.9
Miscellaneous (including items in transit)	68,754	22.3
Total	308,450	100

Source: *Bank of England Quarterly Bulletin*

The main practical difference between Treasury bills and government bonds is that the holder of a bond receives interest plus the redemption value of the bond when it matures (see section 14.5.1). The only repayment on a Treasury bill is the redemption value. The lending bank receives interest because it buys the bill at a **discount** – that is, for less than £100. If a bank buys a bill for £96, and the bill is repaid three months later for £100, the bank receives £4 as interest on its £96. This gives an annual interest rate of approximately 17.7 per cent (4/96 = 4.16 per cent for three months; if this is compounded four times for the year, the resulting interest rate is approximately 17.7 per cent, because $1.0416 \times 1.0416 \times 1.0416 \times 1.0416 = 1.177$).

The government issues Treasury bills because they provide it with flexibility in the amount that it borrows. In some weeks, the government sells more new Treasury bills than it redeems, and so it borrows; in other weeks the government redeems more Treasury bills (issued three months earlier) than it sells, so that total government borrowing is reduced. The government needs this flexibility because its inflows of tax revenues do not match its outflows of expenditures. Most expenditures, particularly transfer payments and wages, are made regularly, whereas some taxes are not received in a steady stream. For example, firms pay VAT at quarterly intervals, and a considerable fraction of income taxes (particularly of the self-employed) is received in June and December of each year.

18.5 Cash and liquidity

A bank's reserves of cash are the notes and coins that it holds plus its account at the central bank from which it can withdraw notes and coins. (Note that UK banks are, from time to time, required by the government to maintain minimum deposits at the Bank of England, and these deposits are not a part of the banking system's reserves of cash; see section 18.10.) A bank needs cash to meet its account holders' demands for notes and coins, and to make payments from its account at the central bank to other banks and to the government. However, its reserves of cash need not equal the whole of its liabilities (that is, the total of all accounts at the bank), because:

(a) Few account-holders withdraw everything from their account in the form of notes and coins at any time, and many outpayments of notes and coins by a bank are offset by inpayments of notes and coins by customers (particularly by shops and other firms that receive large amounts of notes and coins from households).
(b) On any day, a bank pays to and receives from other banks and the government. Its account at the central bank falls by the difference between these outflows and inflows (the account increases if the inflows exceed the outflows), and it is very unlikely that the difference between outflows and inflows on any day will exceed a small fraction of the bank's total liabilities.

Therefore a bank's **net cash requirement** on any day is its:

	outflow of notes and coins
plus	payments from its account at the central bank
minus	inflow of notes and coins
minus	payments to its account at the central bank.

A bank needs to have sufficient cash to meet its net cash requirement, but the maximum amount that is likely to be needed is a fraction of the bank's total liabilities. So a basic principle of banking is that a bank needs to hold only a fraction of its total assets in the form of cash reserves.

A bank's **cash ratio** is the ratio of its reserves of cash to its total assets.

In the UK the government requires that banks hold a certain amount of their assets in the form of cash. This requirement is reflected in the **cash ratio deposits** in table 18.3. This requirement is partly aimed at ensuring that banks do not fail to meet their cash requirements (in 1972–3 there was a banking crisis in the UK, in which certain banking institutions – not the familiar high street banks – had extreme difficulties in meeting their cash requirements and had to be 'rescued' by the central bank), and is partly a way in which the government attempts to control the supply of money (see section 18.9). The size of cash ratio deposits must be maintained: therefore a bank cannot use them to meet an unexpectedly large demand for cash, and banks keep additional deposits at the central bank to meet their day-to-day needs.

18.5.1 Liquid assets

All a bank's assets, except its holdings of cash, are loans on which the bank receives interest. So if its cash ratio increases the bank receives less interest. On the other hand, if its cash ratio falls it becomes more likely that the bank will not be able to meet its customers' demands for notes and coins, or its payments from its account at the central bank. No bank can afford to turn away account holders who are demanding cash, because people would rapidly lose confidence in the bank, and more and more would want to withdraw notes and coins from it to avoid the risk that it would not pay them later. The bank's cash requirement would increase, and the run on the bank might eventually destroy it.

To avoid the possibility that it would be unable to meet its cash requirement, and also to avoid having a large cash ratio, a bank keeps some of its assets in the form of loans that are liquid but that pay some interest. These assets are either:

(a) **Market loans** made to other firms in the banking sector (including other banks, merchant banks and discount houses), who agreed to repay the loans immediately in the form of cash if the bank has a large cash requirement.
(b) Loans made to reputable borrowers (large firms and the government) in the form of bonds or bills that can be sold if the bank needs cash. These bonds or bills must be from reputable borrowers or it may be impossible to find a buyer quickly, thus reducing the liquidity of the asset and its usefulness in meeting a cash crisis.

> A bank's **liquidity ratio** is its ratio of liquid assets (including cash, which is the most liquid asset of all) to its total assets.

A bank wants to have sufficient cash and liquid assets to meet its cash requirements, but it is likely to be flexible on the exact sizes of the cash and liquidity ratios. A bank is likely to be prepared to allow its cash ratio to fall (within the limits that the government will allow) as long as its liquidity ratio does not fall as well. It may want an increase in its liquidity ratio if its cash ratio falls, because the future selling prices of bonds and bills are uncertain, and so it may need to sell at less than the current price if it has an unexpected need for cash in the future. So a bank has a range of desired cash and liquidity ratios and, if the cash ratio falls, it is likely that the desired liquidity ratio increases.

18.5.2 Last resort

An asset is liquid only if the bank can sell it. If the demand is low, the bank receives a very low price, and this revenue may be insufficient to meet an unexpectedly large cash requirement. In these circumstances the government acts as a **last resort** supplier of cash to prevent banks from reaching a situation in which they are unable to meet their customers' demands for cash. The government can operate a last resort facility either by lending to banks or by buying assets from them.

If the government acts as **lender of last resort** it lends to a bank using the bank's liquid loans as security. For example, if a bank holds a £100 Treasury bill that matures in one month, the government may lend £100 to the bank for the month. The repayment of the bill is then offset against the repayment of the emergency loan to the bank. Of course, the government charges interest to lend to banks in this way. This interest rate is the **minimum lending rate** (MLR, formerly the **Bank Rate**).

The minimum lending rate must exceed the interest rate paid by the government on Treasury bills so that a bank faces a positive cost for emergency borrowing. If the minimum lending rate were less than the interest rate on Treasury bills, a bank could make a profit by borrowing from the government and then lending the borrowed money back to the government by buying Treasury bills. The government does not want this to happen (because the interest that it receives would be less than the interest that it pays) but in the days when changes in the Bank Rate were considered to be of major political significance (particularly before 1971), the government was at times so reluctant to change the Bank Rate that the interest rate on Treasury bills exceeded the Bank Rate. Since then, the minimum lending rate has been set by a formula that prevents it from falling below the interest rate on Treasury bills.

The second form of last resort arises when the government buys **eligible securities** from a bank. These include Treasury bills, local authority bills and bills issued by reputable private firms from the banking sector. As a last resort facility, the government buys bills at a price that implies that the bank makes a loss on the transaction. For example, if a bank holds a Treasury bill for which it will receive £100 in one month's time, the government may pay £97 for the bill. Assuming that the bank cannot obtain £3 by lending £97 for one month, it is worse off if it sells to the government than if it had kept the bill. So a bank will not want to sell to the government unless it has a great need of cash.

In recent years the Bank of England has favoured buying eligible securities as a last resort facility.

18.5.3 Choice facing a bank

We have discussed the last resort facility as if it were only to be used in an emergency. In fact, banks regard the last resort facility as another way of ensuring that they can meet their cash requirements. The other two ways of doing this are to hold cash or to hold liquid assets.

Each method of meeting its cash requirement involves a cost to the bank:

(a) Cash reserves make no interest. So an increase in the cash ratio implies that the interest received by the bank is reduced.
(b) Liquid assets generally pay less interest than other loans, because borrowers are prepared to pay more interest to avoid the prospect that they may have to make a rapid repayment.
(c) Use of the last resort facility involves payment of the minimum lending rate on loans, or selling assets at a price that implies a loss.

A bank can therefore choose between opportunities that differ in uncertainty and in expected profit. If a bank has a relatively high cash ratio or high liquidity ratio, it sacrifices interest, so that its profits are lower but it is fairly certain that it will not need to use the last resort facility. If its cash ratio or liquidity ratio is lower, it sacrifices less interest but its profits may be reduced because there is a greater likelihood that it will need to use the last resort facility. So a risk-averse bank chooses a higher cash ratio than a risk-neutral or a risk-preferring bank. (Note that the risk-aversion, neutrality or preference involved is the bank's attitude to its own profit. The risk of failing to meet its cash requirement is removed for all banks that have access to the last resort facility.)

18.6 Credit creation

Banks keep only a fraction of their total assets in the form of cash and liquid assets. If a bank receives more cash, or makes more liquid loans, its liquidity ratio rises. If the bank then makes more long-term (non-liquid) loans, the liquidity ratio falls again. So a bank that acquires additional cash or liquid assets can maintain its liquidity ratio at the desired level by making more long-term, non-liquid loans. These additional long-term loans are a form of **credit creation**:

> A bank can create credit up to the limits implied by its holdings of cash and liquid assets, and its desired liquidity and/or cash ratios.

For example, suppose that a bank has total assets of £100 million, of which £25 million are cash and liquid assets. Its liquidity ratio is 25 per cent (column 1 in table 18.4). If the bank acquires an additional £5 million in cash (column 2) it can make an additional £15 million in long-term loans and retain its liquidity ratio at 25 per cent (column 3). The bank creates credit of £15 million on the basis of the expansion in its cash. It can do this because it needs to keep only a fraction of its total accounts in cash or liquid form, because its cash requirement is only a fraction of its total liabilities.

A bank receives additional cash if its account-holders deposit cash, or if its account at the central bank increases because it receives payments from other

Table 18.4 Credit creation after cash inflow

	1		2		3	
	£ million	%	£ million	%	£ million	%
Cash and liquid assets	25	25	30	28.6	30	25
Other assets (i.e. loans)	75	75	75	71.4	90	75
Total assets	100	100	105	100	120	100

banks or from the government. If bank M receives cash that was withdrawn from bank N, or if M's account at the central bank is credited with money paid to it by N, M's cash reserves increase and N's fall. The cash reserves of the whole banking system are unchanged. M can create credit by increasing its long-term loans, but N must reduce its long-term loans because its reserves have fallen. There is no increase in the total long-term loans by banks. This total can increase only if the total cash reserves of all banks increase.

The cash reserves of all banks increase if the government creates more cash. This increase occurs in two ways:

(a) Some of the newly created cash is credited to banks' accounts at the central bank as the government transfers the cash from its own account to make its expenditures.
(b) The remainder of the newly created cash is paid directly as notes and coins to households. However, much of this is eventually paid into banks: for example, a household that receives a transfer payment spends most of it at shops that pay the notes and coins into their bank accounts.

This additional cash allows for the creation of additional credit up to the limit given by the banks' desired cash and liquidity ratios.

A bank can also create credit if it acquires more liquid assets. For example, if a bank has £100 million in cash, £200 million in liquid assets and £700 million in other assets, its cash ratio is 10 per cent and its liquidity ratio (including cash) is 30 per cent. If it then acquires another £60 million in liquid assets, with no reduction in its cash, it can maintain a liquidity ratio of 30 per cent by creating credit (and so increasing its other assets) of £140 million. Table 18.5 records the change in its assets during this process. The bank's cash ratio falls to 8.33 per cent. Column 4 in the table shows the outcome if the bank wants to compensate for the lower cash ratio by increasing its liquidity ratio to 32 per cent. The bank can create credit of £65 million, and so its cash ratio becomes 8.89 per cent and its liquidity ratio is 32 per cent.

We can conclude that the total additional credit created by banks depends on their total cash reserves and their total holdings of liquid assets.

Table 18.5 Credit creation after an increase in liquid assets

	1		2		3		4	
	£ million	%	£ million	%	£ million	%	£ million	%
Cash	100	10	100	9.43	100	8.33	100	8.89
Other liquid assets	200	20	260	24.53	260	21.67	260	23.11
Total liquid assets	300	30	360	33.96	360	30	360	32
Other assets	700	70	700	66.04	840	70	765	68
Total assets	1,000	100	1,060	100	1,200	100	1,125	100

18.6.1 Credit creation and the supply of money

When a bank lends it does so by increasing the amount that the borrower can withdraw from the bank. So credit creation implies an increase in total bank accounts, and an increase in M1 and all measures that include M1. So:

The supply of money increases when banks create additional credit.

18.7 Credit creation and pure monetary policy

The government uses a pure monetary policy if it changes the method by which it finances a deficit of given size. Suppose that the government decides to reduce its cash creation and to borrow more. When we analysed a pure monetary policy without considering the banking sector, we concluded that an increase in borrowing and reduced cash creation implies an increase in interest rates and a reduction in national income, either because the increase in interest rates reduces aggregate demand (macroeconomic analysis), or because the reduced supply of money reduces national income as in the quantity theory of money (market analysis).

In an analysis that allows for the operations of the banking sector, the effects of a pure monetary policy depend on how and from whom the government borrows.

18.7.1 Borrowing from the non-banking private sector

If a household or firm (outside the banking sector) buys a bond from the government, it is likely to pay for it by cheque. So the household's bank must transfer money to the government: the bank's account at the central bank is reduced and the government's account is increased. So the bank's cash reserves fall and it must reduce its lending if it is to restore its liquidity ratio to the previous level. The bank must reduce its credit creation, and the supply of money falls. Furthermore, the additional supply of bonds reduces the prices of bonds and increases interest rates. So:

The government reduces the supply of money and increases interest rates by selling bonds to the non-banking private sector.

This method of affecting the money supply and interest rates is known as **open market operations**, because changes in the supply of money are brought about by government operations in the bond market.

18.7.2 Borrowing from the banking sector

If the government sells bonds or Treasury bills for £1,000 to a bank, the bank receives a liquid asset and pays the government from its account at the central bank. So the bank's cash reserves fall by £1,000 and its liquid assets increase by the £1,000 bill or bond. Its cash ratio falls but its liquidity ratio is unchanged. The bank may reduce its total assets a little by creating a little less credit because its cash ratio has fallen, but unless the cash ratio has fallen below the required level it is likely that this form of monetary policy leads to little change in the supply of money. The increased supply of bonds from the government leads to an increase in interest rates. So:

If the government borrows from the banking sector, interest rates increase and there is little change in the supply of money.

This conclusion is different from that obtained when the government borrows from the non-banking private sector, and differs from the conclusion that was obtained from the analysis of pure monetary policy without considering the banking sector.

18.8 Monetary and fiscal policy

If the government increases its expenditure, it may pay more cash to households (particularly if it has increased transfer payments), and it is likely to pay more cheques and bank transfers to households and firms, so that it must transfer cash to banks at the central bank to cover these payments. So increased expenditures imply that banks' cash reserves increase. Similarly, if the government reduces taxes, households and firms pay less by cheque to the government and so banks transfer less cash to the government at the central bank. So banks' cash reserves increase compared with a situation in which taxes are not reduced. Therefore any fiscal policy that increases the government's deficit increases banks' cash reserves and their ability to create credit.

Any such fiscal policy has an accompanying monetary policy that determines the way in which the additional deficit is financed. This monetary policy can involve three methods of financing:

(a) Borrowing from the non-banking private sector. The bonds sold to finance this borrowing are bought using cheques drawn on bank accounts, and so banks must transfer the money lent to the government and their cash reserves fall by the amount of the loan. If the entire additional deficit is financed in this way, the monetary policy reduces banks' cash reserves by the same amount that the fiscal policy increases them.

(b) Borrowing from the banking sector. Again, banks must transfer cash to the government, and if the entire additional deficit is financed in this way, banks' cash reserves are unchanged. However, the additional bills and bonds bought by the banking sector add to their liquid assets, and to their ability to create credit.

(c) Issuing more cash. There is no transfer from banks to the government, and if the entire additional deficit is financed in this way the amount of additional cash in the economy equals the additional deficit so that banks can create additional credit.

So:

The supply of money increases if the additional deficit is financed either by creating additional cash, or by borrowing from the banking sector.

The opposite conclusions hold if the government reduces its deficit by cutting its expenditures, or increases taxation.

18.9 Credit creation and control of the supply of money

The preceding description of the relationship between credit creation, the money supply and reserves of cash and liquid assets is somewhat mechanical. It would appear that increases in cash reserves or in banks' liquid assets automatically imply increases in credit, and that decreases in cash and liquid assets automatically imply decreases in credit. If this were so, the government could control the amount of credit and the supply of money by controlling the amounts of cash and liquid assets in the economy using its fiscal and monetary policies to control the size of the deficit and the method of financing it.

This mechanical conclusion would be true if banks kept rigidly to predetermined cash and liquidity ratios. However, the cash or liquidity ratio that is required by the government or that is necessary to meet cash requirements is a minimum figure. Banks are at liberty to hold more than the minimum amounts of cash and liquid assets. Why should a bank wish to do this, given that increased lending implies an increased interest income for the bank?

If banks keep rigidly to predetermined ratios, they increase their lending when they receive more cash or liquid assets, and decrease lending (by making fewer new loans than are needed to replace maturing loans) when they have less cash or liquid assets. However, it is not always easy to decrease lending, nor necessarily profitable to do so. A firm that has borrowed to finance an investment may rely upon renewing the loan because the investment project has not yet proved profitable. If it cannot renew the loan, because its bank is reducing lending, the firm may face a cash flow crisis. In some cases, this may imply that the firm cannot repay the principal on the loan to the bank, and so the bank loses money. To avoid this possibility, a bank is likely to leave itself a little flexibility: when its cash reserves or liquid assets increase, the bank does not increase its lending up to the limit implied by its desired (or required) cash ratio or liquidity ratio. So when cash reserves or liquid assets fall the bank is not forced to make so great a reduction in its lending. The bank prefers to sacrifice some interest by lending less than the maximum to avoid the possibility that firms are unable to repay loans.

This flexibility in the use of the cash ratio and the liquidity ratio implies that the government cannot control exactly the amount of credit creation by changing the amount of cash and liquid assets in the economy. In particular, a reduction in cash and liquid assets may not lead to a proportional reduction in credit and so, to this extent, the government cannot control the supply of money.

An even more extreme conclusion is that credit created and the supply of money may *increase* when the government *reduces* the amount of cash or liquid assets, and at the same time increases sales of bonds to the non-banking private sector or banks. The increased sales of bonds increase interest rates, so that firms must pay more interest on loans. This increases the probability that a firm will face a cash flow problem. The firm's bank may decide to lend it more to avoid bankruptcy (if the firm goes bankrupt the bank may lose the principal on previous loans), so that the amount of credit created increases despite the reduction in cash and liquid assets. This increase can occur only if the bank can reduce its cash and liquidity ratio because it has not previously lent up to the maximum possible.

The last conclusion emphasizes the difficulty that the government has in controlling the supply of money (or the extent of private sector liquidity). Money and liquidity are affected by the actions of the banking sector: the government controls the supply of cash and liquid assets, but these do not necessarily give the government complete control over the supply of money. As we shall see in the next chapter, this complicates the analysis of monetary policies designed to affect national income, inflation and employment.

18.10 Other aspects of monetary policy

The government can influence the banking sector and its creation of credit by methods other than changes in cash creation and borrowing. These methods are also a part of the government's monetary policy:

(a) If the government makes the last resort facility more expensive (by increasing the minimum lending rate or reducing the prices paid for assets) a bank is likely to reduce the probability that it will use the facility by increasing its cash ratio or its liquidity ratio. It can then lend less with given cash reserves or given liquid assets. The bank's ability to create credit is reduced, and so the supply of money is reduced.

(b) If the government requires an increase in the cash and/or liquidity ratios, credit creation and the supply of money are reduced with given cash reserves and liquid assets.

(c) The government may 'freeze' a part of a bank's account at the central bank (**special deposits**), and tell the bank that the frozen amount cannot be included in its cash reserves. The bank must reduce its total assets to preserve its cash ratio, and so the supply of money is reduced. This method has not been used in the UK since July 1980.

(d) Banks may be asked to agree to reduce their total lending, or to lend more to firms and less to households to encourage private investment. These voluntary agreements can work because banks know that other measures (such as special deposits) could be used if the central bank's request is ignored.

18.11 Summary

The banking sector complicates the operation of monetary policy compared with the situation considered in chapter 17. This complication arises because the supply of money includes items other than notes and coins – although there is no single definition of the supply of money that is generally accepted – and because banks can increase the supply of money by lending. Banks can lend a multiple of their cash reserves and liquid assets because their cash requirement is only a fraction of their total deposits. So if the government expands the supply of cash to finance its budget deficit, the supply of money, including bank accounts, increases. Banks include loans to the government among their liquid assets, and an increase in bank lending to the government increases the supply of money. Government control of the supply of money is made more difficult because banks do not want to maintain rigidly predetermined cash or liquidity ratios.

Topics and problems

(1) What would happen if the government discontinued the last resort facility?

(2) What would happen to 'broader' measures of the supply of money (such as M3 and M4) if the government were able to maintain rigid control over M0? What would happen to interest rates given the inevitable fluctuations in the government's deficit?

(3) How could additional money be supplied (to finance increased numbers of transactions) if the government maintained a balanced budget?

(4) 'Banks make large profits because they lend other people's money, so bank charges should be abolished.' Discuss.

(5) 'Competition ensures that banks all pay similar interest rates and charge similar interest rates on loans.' 'UK banks form a collusive oligopoly that ensures that no bank undercuts any others.' Which of these explanations of similarities between banks' interest rates do you favour?

(6) A bank maintains a cash ratio of 15 per cent. How much extra credit can it create if it receives an additional £3 million cash? What additional liquid assets does the bank need to preserve a 40 per cent liquidity ratio?

Chapter Nineteen

Imperfections and government policy

Competition policy — nationalization and privatization — pricing decisions of nationalized firms — profits and losses of nationalized firms — external effects — social cost–benefit analysis

---

19.1 Introduction

Governments use a wide variety of policies that affect particular firms, industries or markets. These policies may be introduced to deal with a particular problem, such as the abuse of monopoly power by a firm, or they may be introduced as part of a market approach to macroeconomic policy. In this chapter we examine the microeconomic effects of these policies, and return to their role in 'supply-side' macroeconomics in chapter 21.

As well as having specific microeconomic effects, all government policies also affect the income distribution. For example:

(a) If the government is successful in limiting the market influence of a firm, its owners' income from supernormal profit is reduced.
(b) If a firm is nationalized, the profits from operating it are received by the government and not by private shareholders.

The redistributional effects of these policies are generally less important than the redistributional effects of the taxation and social security systems that we shall examine in the next chapter.

Apart from the policies that we discuss in later parts of this chapter, the UK government uses policies to reduce or offset the influence of other imperfections. For example:

(a) It attempts to spread information on job vacancies.
(b) It attempts to reduce discrimination through legislation, including equal pay laws, which attempt to enforce the payment of similar wages to men and women who do similar jobs.

Governments act in ways that increase some imperfections. For example:

(a) The Common Agricultural Policy of the European Community keeps the prices of some goods above their equilibrium levels by ensuring that surplus goods can be sold to the EC, which stockpiles them. This policy is intended to protect the incomes of farmers and reduce dependence on food imported from outside the EC.

(b) Some activities require central or local government permission in the form of licences: for example, operating taxis in many areas. The incomes of the licence-holders are increased if the price of their good is kept above its equilibrium level by a restriction in the number of licences.

(c) Governments allow individuals and firms to hold patents on inventions and copyright on books, music and other written output. These restrictions prevent the freedom of information required for free operation of markets. They are preserved to give inventors, writers etc. incentives to continue to produce without fear that others will immediately copy their ideas.

Government activities can themselves be imperfections. In particular, the government affects labour markets and many goods markets because it finances much of its expenditure through income taxes and VAT.

19.2 Competition policy

Few industries approximate to the conditions of perfect competition, which requires that there is a large number of small firms and that there is freedom for new firms to enter the market. Few firms have the market influence of a pure monopolist, because most face some competition from the producers of substitute goods. Many markets are supplied by oligopolistic firms and, as we saw in chapter 13, these firms may compete by using price or non-price competition, or they may collude openly or covertly. Most competition policy is directed against oligopolists.

19.2.1 Competition policy in the UK

UK competition policy is operated by the **Director General of Fair Trading**, who has overall responsibility for policies designed to limit the market influence of firms and to protect consumers, and by the **Monopolies and Mergers Commission**, which investigates the effects of the market influence of firms as they exist, or as they intend to exist after two or more firms have joined together in a merger.

The Office of Fair Trading is empowered to investigate market influence and to make recommendations in cases where it feels that an imperfection is against the public interest because, for example, prices are too high or information is limited. For example, a 1982 report on opticians recommended the removal of restrictions on advertising to increase information and competition. The report concentrated on these imperfections, and was less concerned about the effects of the licensing of opticians that restricts entry to the industry, because the Office did not feel that this imperfection had significant effects contrary to the public interest.

Firms or whole industries can be referred to the Monopolies and Mergers Commission by government ministers. A firm can be referred to the Commission if it sells more than 25 per cent of the total sales in the market (reduced from 33 per cent in 1973), and a merger between two or more firms can be referred if the merging firms would supply more than 25 per cent of the total in the market. The Commission seeks evidence from interested parties (including firms in the industry and others who feel that they are affected by the potential or actual market influence), and makes recommendations to the government, which can then act as it sees fit. The Commission may recommend controls on the prices of goods sold or on the profit that the firm can achieve (as, for example, in the case of the Commission's 1982 investigation of the London Rubber Company, which sold about 90% of all contraceptive sheaths sold in the UK, and whose profits were regarded as a matter of concern by the Commission). It may also recommend the ending of restrictive practices (for example, the Commission recommended in 1982 the ending of the exclusive buying agreement that restricts franchised car dealers from buying car parts from suppliers other than the franchising supplier).

Restrictive practices are also monitored by the Restrictive Practices Court and are the subject of various European Community laws. These practices are generally illegal, although some are permitted if they can be shown to be in the public interest – that is, if their advantages outweigh their disadvantages. One restrictive practice that remains is Resale Price Maintenance on books, but the producers of most other goods are not permitted to dictate the prices at which their goods are sold by retailers, and they are not allowed to refuse to supply a retailer on the grounds that he or she sells the good at a lower price than the producer would like.

19.2.2 Control of monopoly power

The government can deal in a straightforward way with restrictive practices and other activities that it believes to be against the public interest by prohibiting them. However, some aspects of market influence must be dealt with in less direct ways:

(a) By limiting the price that a firm may charge, or the profit that a firm may make.
(b) By splitting an existing firm into parts that are required to compete with one another or, similarly, by preventing a proposed merger. Given that many references to the UK Monopolies and Mergers Commission are proposed mergers, this policy is frequently available.
(c) By obtaining a voluntary agreement from a firm to refrain from using its potential market influence, perhaps by publicizing the disapproved activities.

It is simplest to trace the potential effects of these policies by considering their effects on a monopolist. In figure 19.1(a) the profit-maximizing output is A, where marginal cost equals marginal revenue, and the firm sells at price C. The supernormal profit is area BCDE.

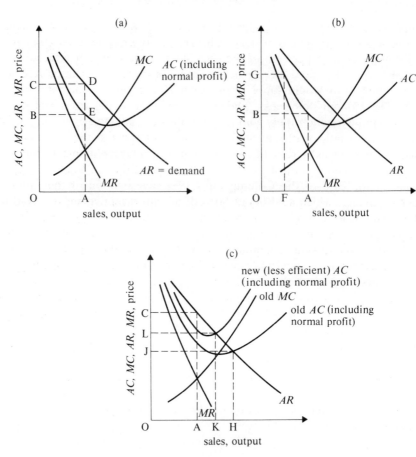

Figure 19.1 Monopoly and competition policy
(a) shows an unregulated profit-maximizing monopolist (b) shows the effect of dividing
the firm (c) shows the effect of a profit limitation.

19.2.3 Division of firms (or prohibition of mergers)

If the government orders a firm to divide into two (or more) parts, a monopoly
becomes an oligopoly. The advantage of this division is that the parts of the
firm may compete with one another, so that each has much less market
influence than a monopolist and the price charged to consumers is likely to be
lower. Of course, if the parts of the firm are able to collude, the division has
little effect on their collective market influence. The disadvantage of splitting
a firm (or of preventing a merger) arises if there are significant economies of
scale. In figure 19.1 the average cost of producing the monopolist's output A
is less than the average cost of producing any smaller output. So if, for
example, the monopoly were split into two parts, each producing at F (half of
output A as in figure 19.1(b)), the average cost of production in the industry
increases from B to G. So the two firms use more resources to produce the

output of the monopolist. Of course, if they compete the firms may each produce more than F, but average costs will increase unless (as seems unlikely) each firm produces A, thus doubling the output of the industry.

19.2.4 Profit and price restrictions

If competition policy requires a firm to reduce its profits to an agreed level, the firm may initially do this by reducing its price and selling more as the government intended. However, a firm in this position has little incentive to remain efficient or to introduce new methods of production, because it is not allowed to increase its profit by reducing its costs. The alternative, that the government should monitor the firm and allow some profit increases (those caused by reduced costs) but not others (those caused by the use of market influence), may be very costly to administer.

Suppose that the government requires that a monopolist makes no more than normal profit. In figure 19.1(c), the firm must sell H at price J so that its average revenue equals average cost (including normal profit). If the firm becomes less efficient, or gives its workers a wage increase, its average cost curve rises. The firm can maintain its profit at the normal level by reducing its output to K and increasing its price to L.

If a firm is required to reduce its price from the profit-maximizing level, it retains an incentive to reduce its average costs by improving its efficiency and introducing new methods of production. However, the government may calculate the allowed price by allowing the firm to achieve a reasonable profit and, if the firm's profits increase substantially, the government may reduce the allowed price. If the government reacts in this way, a policy that limits the firm's price is similar to one that limits its profits, and the firm's incentive to maintain or improve its efficiency is removed.

These examples show that it may be difficult to assess the effect of competition policy on the public interest because the effects of increased competition or of restrictions on market influence must be offset against potential inefficiencies and the removal of the incentive to innovate and reduce average cost.

19.3 Nationalization and privatization

In the UK, particularly in the years immediately following the Second World War, the government **nationalized** (or took a major shareholding in) a number of firms that had previously been privately owned. The government owns these firms, provides money for investment and receives their distributed profits. If a nationalized firm makes a loss, the government is responsible for its debts.

Nationalized firms generally fall into two categories:

(a) A monopoly supplier of a good that is formed when all firms in an industry are nationalized. Many of the nationalizations in the 1940s were of whole industries, including the railways, electricity production and distribution, and gas production and distribution. These nationalized firms have (or had) considerable market influence, although many face competition from firms (nationalized or privately owned) producing substitute goods. For example, nationalized railways compete with bus companies.

(b) A single nationalized firm that faces competition in an oligopolistic market from privately owned firms producing similar goods. Nationalizations involving a single firm in an industry included British Airways and BL cars (now the Rover group).

Firms in the first category are often known as **nationalized industries**, and we use this term when we distinguish the first category from the second. Note that many of the firms nationalized before 1979 have been **privatized** or **denationalized**.

19.3.1 Reasons for nationalization

Firms have been nationalized in the UK (and elsewhere) for four main reasons:

(a) To preserve them when they would otherwise have closed because of bankruptcy (for example, BL). Closure would cause a loss of jobs both in the firm itself and in its suppliers, and it might have strategic implications if the alternative suppliers of the good were firms in other countries.

(b) To provide finance for major investment programmes. This was particularly important for several major industries (including British Rail) after the Second World War, because there had been no major investment (and considerable destruction and depreciation) during the war. It was unlikely that private owners could raise the necessary finance to replace and modernize the industry's equipment. Similarly, in nationalizing BL, the government committed itself to a major investment programme to try to ensure that the firm could compete successfully.

(c) To control market influence. This was considered particularly important in industries such as gas, electricity and water supplies, where a single firm has a natural monopoly caused by economies of scale (see section 12.2).

(d) Ideology. A major part of the traditional socialist view of the best method of organizing economic activities is public ownership, particularly of larger firms. This view is based partly on the value judgement that it is wrong for people to receive incomes from the ownership of equipment, land and firms (see section 10.9.4), and partly on the view that the economic system works more efficiently if the government plans many economic activities. This planning can be carried out more easily if the government owns major firms.

19.3.2 How are firms nationalized?

In revolutionary times, factories have been seized by the state and the owners have received no compensation, but in the UK the former owners of nationalized firms have been compensated by the government for the loss of ownership and the loss of income. The nationalization of a firm or an industry usually requires an Act of Parliament that sets out the terms of compensation, and ensures that the government gains full control of the firm or industry.

In principle, the price that the government must pay to compensate the previous owners depends on the circumstances of the firm being nationalized. If a firm would otherwise be bankrupt, its shareholders might receive little or nothing after the firm's assets have been sold and its debts paid. In this case, the firm's shares would have a very low price. On the other hand, if a firm was nationalized to control its market influence, its share price would be high, reflecting the supernormal profit that the firm could achieve.

19.3.3 Privatization

In the UK since 1979, and in other countries too, the government has sold nationalized firms to private shareholders. The revenue from selling shares in nationalized industries can be used to help meet the government's budget deficit; recent figures for the UK are given in table 19.1. However, this is not the only reason put forward for privatization.

Table 19.1 UK government privatization proceeds 1986–9

Financial year	£ billion
1986–7	4.4
1987–8	5.1
1988–9	7.0

Source: *Financial Statistics*

The main additional reasons are:

(a) The market view of macroeconomics is that the economy operates best when markets are free to operate without government interference. Privatization implies that the firm's shares are traded on the stock exchange and, in theory, this implies that funds for investment are allocated to the firm only if it is profitable. Investment decisions are taken out of the government's control and are instead market related. Privatization reduces the government's ability to interfere in the profit-maximizing activities of firms, and so they become more responsive to changes in consumers' tastes.

(b) Nationalized industries operate inefficiently. This is partly because competition makes firms operate at lower average costs and in some cases at least, privatization has been accompanied by increased competition for previously nationalized monopolies. The second reason for inefficiency is that the incentive to make greater profits and to avoid losses is greater for a privately owned firm than for a nationalized firm. In particular, nationalized firms are less likely to resist demands for wage increases, since a nationalized firm can make a loss without risking going out of business.

The first of these reasons is more applicable in circumstances where privatization leads to greater competition. If the government privatizes a monopoly by selling shares in a single firm, it becomes a privately owned monopoly (British Gas was criticized for abuse of market power by the Monopolies and Mergers Commission in 1988, only two years after it was privatized). If it is split into several firms, thereby gaining some benefits from competition, the firm may lose benefits from economies of scale. In fact, the issues of increased competition and privatization need not be decided simultaneously: privately owned firms may be allowed to compete with nationalized firms that have previously had a monopoly. For example, private bus operators may be allowed to run services in competition with public sector operators; the extent of competition to the BBC in both radio and television broadcasting has increased considerably over the past 30 years.

19.3.4 Privatized share prices

The government does not know in advance the equilibrium price at which the demand for the shares in a nationalized firm will equal the number that it supplies.

If the price is set below the equilibrium level, the excess demand increases the price of the shares on the Stock Exchange, and those who have bought from the government can resell their shares at a profit. This occurred in 1984 when the UK government sold shares in British Telecom. The price was set below the equilibrium level, and the demand was four times the supply. The price increased by 85 per cent immediately trading began. In this circumstance, the government loses revenue from the sale, and is likely to face criticism for allowing speculators to profit from the fact that the price is below its equilibrium level.

If the price is set above the equilibrium level, some shares remain unsold. The government fails to denationalize the firm completely, although it may not lose revenue if the sale is underwritten by financial institutions that agree to buy unsold shares at a previously agreed price. This occurred in the UK in 1987 when the government sold shares in BP and overestimated the equilibrium price, because prices of all shares fell dramatically in October 1987 between the decision to sell and the time of the sale. Few of the shares were sold on the open market; the remainder were bought by the underwriters.

The difficulty for the government of setting the selling price may be overcome if the government offers the shares for sale by asking people (and banks, pension funds and other financial institutions) to submit bids stating the price that they would pay, and the quantity that they would buy at that price. The government sells the shares at the price for which the number of shares bid for at that price and at higher prices equals the supply. Note, however, that this process takes time (between asking for bids and allocating shares) and the buyers would take the risk that there would be a general fall in share prices during that time, such as happened in October 1987. If such a fall occurs, buyers might regret their bids.

Suppose, for example, that the government wants to sell 100 shares, and Alan bids for 80 shares at £5 each, Bill bids for 20 shares at £4 each and Charles bids for 30 shares at £3 each. The government sells 80 shares to Alan and 20 to Bill, all at £4 each, and it sells nothing to Charles. Note that all buyers pay the same price, even if they have bid more, because people would be unlikely to bid at all if they knew that they may have to buy at a price that exceeds the equilibrium level. The price at which they could resell on the Stock Exchange is likely to move rapidly to the equilibrium, and few people would take the risk of buying at a higher price.

19.4 Pricing decisions of nationalized firms

In the UK, a nationalized firm has a sponsoring ministry, which is a government department that monitors the performance of the firm, consults with it about its plans for pricing and investment, and deals with such matters as the appointment of its senior managers. Major aspects of the operation of a nationalized firm are set out in the Act of nationalization and in a series of White Papers (statements of government policy), of which the latest two were published in 1967 (Cmnd 3437) and 1978 (Cmnd 7131). These White Papers contain guidelines on the prices that nationalized firms should charge and on the criteria that they should use for evaluating investment projects.

The prices set by nationalized firms for the goods that they sell affect the economy in a variety of ways. These effects are likely to be significant, because nationalized firms sell their goods to many households and to many other firms. The major effects are on:

(a) Efficiency. The price of a good determines how much of it is bought, and so determines the amounts of resources that are used to produce it. This may affect the efficiency with which the nation's resources are used.

(b) Inflation. Nationalized firms supply goods that form a considerable part of total household expenditure, so that price increases by nationalized firms affect the rate of inflation. In the UK in 1989, 4.6 per cent of all expenditure on consumer goods was on goods produced by nationalized firms (this fraction is falling as firms are privatized; it was 11 per cent in 1983). Table 19.2 shows the changes in the prices of these goods in recent years.

(c) Income distribution. Goods such as coal and electricity form a larger part of the expenditure of poor people than of richer people. In the UK these goods account for 15 per cent of the expenditures of people who rely for their incomes mainly on the government pension, compared with 5.4 per cent of the expenditures of all households. Table 19.2 shows how the prices of these goods have increased more rapidly than the average of other retail

Table 19.2 Changes in prices of goods produced by nationalized firms (figures are index numbers, and all indices = 100 in January 1974)

Date	Average of all prices	Prices of goods sold by nationalized firms	Fuel and light
Jan. 1974	100	100	100
Jan. 1979	207.2	234.5	233.1
Jan. 1984	342.6	445.8	469.3
Jan. 1989	437.9	556.8	527.4

Source: *Department of Employment Gazette*

prices, and so the rate of inflation experienced by poor people has exceeded that experienced by richer people.

(d) Fiscal and monetary policies. The price charged by a nationalized firm affects its profit or loss. This in turn affects the revenue received by the government from a profitable firm, and affects the subsidy that the government must pay to a loss-making firm. Thus the profits and losses of nationalized firms affect the government's budget. Table 19.3 shows the

Table 19.3 Combined accounts of UK public corporations, 1985–8 (figures are in £ million)

	1985	1986	1987	1988
Operating revenue	52,952	47,474	37,753	37,468
Other income (net)	1,617	892	848	2,821
Expenditure	−47,414	−39,619	−31,483	−30,983
Balance	7,155	8,747	7,118	9,486
Subsidies	3,409	2,379	1,960	1,830
Taxes and royalties paid	−1,605	−1,824	−1,002	−1,063
Balance	8,959	9,302	8,076	8,719
Interest and dividends paid to central and local government	2,633	2,246	2,205	2,067
Other interest and dividends	1,080	1,034	903	886
Undistributed income	5,246	6,032	4,968	5,766
Privatizations during year		Br. Gas	Br. Airways, Royal Ordnance, Br. Airports	Br. Steel Various Bus Companies

Source: *UK National Accounts*

combined accounts of UK public corporations (most of which are nationalized firms).

19.4.1 Average cost pricing

Perhaps the simplest principle that a nationalized industry could follow is to set is price equal to its average cost of production (normal profit, in this case, is interest on the money lent by the government). So in figure 19.2 the firm sells output A at price B, because the average cost of producing A is B. The average cost pricing principle implies that the firm is not taking advantage of its market influence to gain supernormal profit, and there is no need for a government subsidy. The firm operates without 'exploiting its customers' (because it makes only normal profit) and without 'being a burden on other parts of the economy' (because it requires no subsidy). However, as we shall see below, average cost pricing does not necessarily lead to the efficient use of resources.

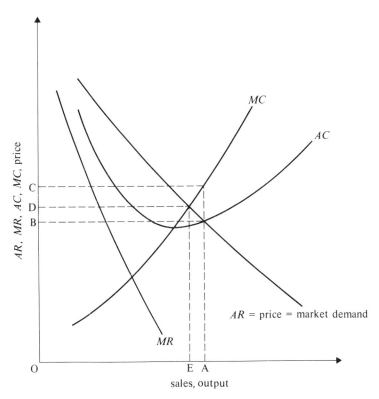

Figure 19.2 Pricing policy of a nationalized firm
Average cost pricing gives output A and price B; marginal cost pricing gives output E and price D.

19.4.2 Marginal cost pricing

If the price of a good is reduced by a small amount, more is sold and consumers obtain an additional benefit that can be measured as the price that they are willing to pay for the additional goods (see section 9.7 on consumers' surplus). If the price exceeds marginal cost, the additional benefit exceeds the cost of the resources used to produce these additional goods, and so there is a positive advantage to society from the price reduction. According to this argument, if the price exceeds D in figure 19.2, it should be reduced at least to D, where output is at E and the price equals marginal cost.

A similar argument shows that if the price is reduced below D the additional benefit is less than the additional cost. Consumers obtain an additional benefit, measured by the price that they are willing to pay for the additional goods, that is less that the cost of the resources needed to produce the additional goods. According to this argument, the price should not be below D. So:

> Maximum social advantage is obtained when the price of a good equals its marginal cost.

This **marginal cost pricing principle** is supported by the conclusion (see section 8.7) that in a perfect market system that is in long-run equilibrium the price of each good equals its marginal cost of production. Since a perfect market system in long-run equilibrium is efficient, the marginal cost pricing rule promotes the efficient allocation of resources in the economy. So, if a nationalized industry is required to behave as if it is a part of a perfect market system in an attempt to allocate resources efficiently, it should set its price equal to marginal cost.

In a perfect market system in long-run equilibrium, the prices of all goods equal both their average and marginal costs of production (see section 8.6). However, this does not provide equal support for the average cost pricing principle, because price equals average cost (but not marginal cost) in the long-run equilibrium of, for example, a monopolistically competitive industry (see section 12.6), but such an industry does not use resources efficiently.

The 1967 White Paper on Nationalized Industries placed greater emphasis on the use of marginal cost pricing than did the 1978 White Paper. The latter recognized the principle but allowed for the possibility that the price might be altered to ensure that a nationalized firm meets other targets set by the government, particularly targets for its profit or loss (see section 19.5.1). The 1978 White Paper recognized that at least some nationalized firms must take account of the prices set by their competitors. In particular this applies to firms such as BL, but it also applies to firms that have market influence but that face considerable competition from suppliers of substitute goods. For example, British Coal faces competition from oil suppliers, because customers could switch from burning coal to burning oil. So British Coal must take account of the price of oil when it sets the price of coal. British Coal also faces competition from foreign suppliers of coal, and as long as it does not have protected markets it must set its own price in line with those of its foreign competitors.

It may then be possible to adjust the output of the nationalized firm to the level where the marginal cost of production equals the externally set price, but such output changes may not be desirable in the light of other targets that the firm faces.

19.4.3 Long-run marginal cost

A perfect market system operates efficiently when it is in long-run equilibrium and prices equal long-run marginal costs. The **long-run marginal cost** of a good includes both:

(a) The additional operating cost of producing additional ouput.
(b) The additional cost of expanding the firm's equipment to supply the additional output in the least expensive possible way.

For example:

(a) The long-run marginal cost of increasing the output of electricity from 1,000 to 1,001 units is the cost of generating the additional unit, plus the difference between the cost of the equipment (power stations and transmission lines) needed to supply 1,001 units and the cost of the equipment needed to supply 1,000 units.
(b) The long-run marginal cost of carrying on additional 100 passengers per day on a railway includes the additional fuel and ticketing costs plus the additional cost to the railway of buying, say, a nine-car rather than an eight-car train.
(c) Calculations of the long-run marginal cost of coal must take into account that if additional coal is used now, less coal is available to future users. So the current long-run marginal cost of coal is the value of coal to these future users who are deprived if more coal is used now. However, more coal can be used now in the UK without affecting future consumption by depleting UK reserves of coal if more coal is imported. So it is possible to estimate the long-run marginal cost of coal as the cost of buying and delivering imported coal to customers.

19.4.4 Peak-load pricing

Despite the general principle that prices should equal long-run marginal costs, there are frequently occasions when a nationalized industry can produce much more than it can sell if it sets its price equal to long-run marginal cost. This excess capacity occurs because the industry faces a **peak load**. For example, suppliers of electricity have the capacity to meet demand on cold winter evenings, and so they have much more capacity than is needed on warm summer days.

The marginal cost pricing principle implies that different prices should be charged (if this is administratively and technically possible) at times of peak and off-peak demands: this is **peak-load pricing**. The principle ensures that a household buys a unit of a good only if it is willing to pay a price equal to the cost of the resources needed to produce an additional unit. If the supply of an additional unit requires additional equipment, then the price should equal long-run marginal cost, but if an additional unit can be supplied using existing equipment, the principle implies that the price should equal **short-run marginal cost**, which is the additional cost of producing an additional unit using the existing equipment.

For example, this principle implies that the price of a rush hour train journey should equal long-run marginal cost given that trains are fully used in the rush hour. Demand is much lower at other times, and then the price should be set at the short-run marginal cost of carrying an additional passenger on trains that are not full. The marginal cost pricing principle implies that anyone who is willing to pay the short-run marginal cost is able to travel at off-peak times.

19.5 Profits and losses of nationalized firms

If a firm sets its price equal to marginal cost it may make a profit or a loss, depending on the relation between average and marginal cost. Two possibilities are illustrated in figure 19.3:

(a) In figure 19.3(a), average cost exceeds marginal cost at output A. Total revenue (OA × OB = OBEA) is less than total cost (OCDA) so that the firm makes a loss (BCDE) when it sets its price equal to marginal cost.
(b) In figure 19.3(b), output is H if price equals marginal cost, and at that output marginal cost exceeds average cost. Therefore total revenue (OGJH) exceeds total cost (OKFH) and the firm makes a profit (KGJF).

These two cases differ, in that in figure 19.3(a) marginal cost is less than average cost, so that average cost is falling at output A, while in figure 19.3(b) average cost exceeds marginal cost, and so average cost is increasing at output H. So figure 19.3 illustrates the conclusions that:

(a) If price equals marginal cost and if average cost is decreasing at the chosen output level, the firm makes a loss.
(b) If price equals marginal cost and if average cost is increasing at the chosen output level, the firm makes a profit.

If average cost is decreasing there are economies of scale, because an increase in output would reduce average cost. So figure 19.3(a) is likely to illustrate the position of a nationalized natural monopoly.

19.5.1 Target profit or loss

Among the criteria for setting prices set out in the 1978 White Paper is that a nationalized firm must meet the target for its profit or loss. A target of no profit and no loss implies that the firm sets its price equal to average cost. Examples of a target profit and a target loss are given in table 19.4 and figure 19.4:

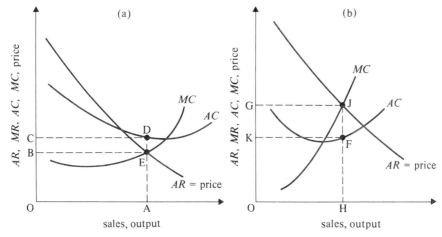

Figure 19.3 Marginal cost pricing, profit and loss
(a) shows a loss because average cost C exceeds average revenue B at the output A given by marginal cost pricing (b) shows a profit because average revenue G exceeds average cost K at output H given by marginal cost pricing.

(a) AA is the firm's average cost curve and BB represents the average cost plus average profit target (column 5) if the firm is required to make a profit of £5,600. Output must then be 1,600 so that total revenue is £80,000, total cost is £74,400 and the profit equals the target.
(b) CC represents column 7, which is average cost minus the average permitted loss if the firm is permitted to make a total loss of £1,800. Output is 1,800,

Table 19.4 Target profit and loss for a nationalized firm

1	2	3	4	5	6	7
			Target profit = £5,600		Target loss = £1,800	
Output	Average revenue = price	Average cost	Target profit ÷ output	Average cost + profit	Target loss ÷ output	Average cost − loss
1,000	65	50	5.6	55.6	1.8	48.2
1,200	60	48	4.67	52.67	1.5	46.5
1,400	55	47	4	51	1.29	45.71
1,600	50	46.5	3.5	50	1.13	45.37
1,800	45	46	3.11	49.11	1	45
2,000	40	48	2.8	50.8	0.9	47.1

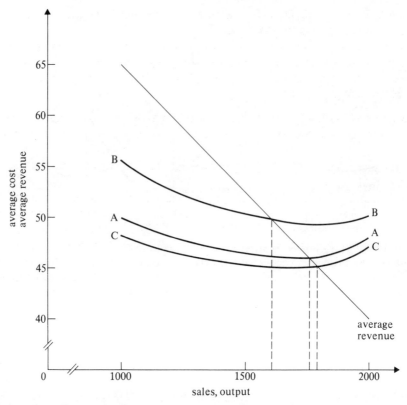

Figure 19.4   Target profit or loss for the nationalized firm of table 19.4
The average cost curve AA shifts up to BB to allow for a target profit, or down to
CC to allow for a target loss.

price is £45 and total cost is £82,800, which exceeds its total revenue of
£81,000 by the amount of the permitted loss.

A firm can use the marginal cost pricing principle and meet a target only if
the target equals the profit or the loss that it makes when price equals marginal
cost. A profit target may be made compatible with the marginal cost pricing
principle, because the government may use the principle when it sets the target.
The UK White Papers refer to marginal cost pricing, and they are used by
sponsoring ministries to provide guidelines when they are involved in setting
targets, so that in some cases the target profit or loss may be compatible with
the marginal cost pricing principle.

19.5.2 Targets and macroeconomic policy

The use of targets for the profits and losses of nationalized firms is partly,
perhaps mainly, designed to ensure that nationalized firms contribute to the
government's macroeconomic policies, particularly when, as in recent years in

the UK, the government has a target for its budget deficit as a part of its monetary policy (see section 17.4.1).

The prediction of the outcome of an increase in a firm's target profit depends on the method of analysis used. Suppose that the target profit for a nationalized firm is increased by £100 million, and it meets this target by increasing its prices:

(a) Macroeconomic analysis predicts that the increase in profit reduces national income and reduces employment through the multiplier process. The effects are similar to those of an increase in taxation (see section 17.3.2), because the price increase implies that households pay more money to the government.
(b) Market analysis predicts that the increase in price reduces output and employment in the nationalized firm, and that the increase in profit reduces government borrowing. So interest rates fall and the exchange rate depreciates. Investment by private firms and exports increase and imports decrease until the involuntary unemployment disappears. Alternatively, the reduced deficit leads to a reduction in the amount of money created and this reduces the inflation rate.

19.5.3 Wages in the public sector

Local and national government employs a large number of workers (approximately 7 million or 30 per cent of the total labour force in the UK in 1988) in nationalized firms, as civil servants, teachers, doctors and elsewhere. Wage payments form the major part of the costs of many nationalized firms, and so there is a close relation between the prices set by nationalized firms, the wages that they pay and the profits that they contribute to the government (or the subsidies that they require). Wage negotiations by workers in nationalized industries (and by other government employees, including teachers, doctors and civil servants) are concerned with the size of the target profit or the allowed subsidy, or with the amount that the government is prepared to pay to run its services (such as health and education) and government departments. So government policies on the prices, profits and losses of nationalized firms imply a policy (whether this is admitted or not) on the wages of workers in those firms.

19.6 External effects

An **external effect** (or **externality**) arises when the action of one person or firm affects other people or firms, other than through changes in supplies or demands that affect prices. Examples of external effects include:

(a) Pollution, including the discharge of waste into the atmosphere, seas, lakes and rivers.

(b) The noise of aircraft, vehicles and factories.
(c) The effects of coal and asbestos dust on workers.
(d) The visual effects of waste tips, pylons etc., and the pleasure given by the design of some buildings, or by the use made of land.
(e) Congestion caused by road users.

19.6.1 Private and social costs and benefits

In assessing the effects of external effects it is useful to distinguish:

(a) **Private costs** (or **financial costs**) and **private benefits** (or **financial benefits**), which include only the costs and benefits to the person or firm that carries out the activity. When considering the activities of a firm, private costs and benefits are generally only the monetary costs and revenues of the activities.
(b) **Social costs** and **social benefits**, which include the private costs and benefits and the costs and benefits caused by externalities.

Whenever an activity causes external effects, the social cost differs from the private cost, and/or the social benefit differs from the private benefit. For example:

(a) If a factory discharges waste into a river at no cost to itself, the discharge of waste is not included in the firm's private cost. If the pollution prevents people from fishing downstream, the social cost includes the loss of amenity to those who want to fish.
(b) The private benefit to a firm that builds a railway includes the revenue from selling tickets. The social benefit includes the time saved by road users if the railway reduces road congestion.

An activity is carried out by a person or a firm if the private benefit exceeds the private cost. However, if the social cost exceeds the social benefit the activity does not benefit society as a whole. For example, a firm may build an airport and operate it profitably (private benefit exceeds private cost) at a place where the noise affects a large number of people (so that social cost exceeds social benefit). A government may then decide to prohibit the building of the airport, or to restrict the number of flights from it.

Government policy is also needed to ensure that a project goes ahead when the social benefit exceeds the social cost, but no privately owned firm will invest in the project because the private cost exceeds the private benefit. For example, a privately owned firm would not build a railway that could not be operated profitably, but the railway might be socially desirable if it saves travellers' time by reducing road congestion.

19.6.2 Policy options

The most straightforward policies open to a government are banning undesirable activities and requiring nationalized firms to carry out projects in which privately owned firms would not invest, but for which the social benefit exceeds the social cost. For example, the UK government has paid a subsidy to British Rail to keep open some rural railway lines that would close if the decision were made entirely on the basis of the private cost and private benefit.

Some undesirable activities are not prohibited, but are penalized by higher charges, by taxes or by requiring compensation for those affected. For example, the British Airports Authority charges airlines more to land a noisy aircraft than to land a quieter aircraft. The airlines are made aware of the social cost of noisy planes because their private costs are reduced if they use quieter planes. The additional charge brings the private cost closer to the social cost, and so brings private decisions more closely into line with socially desirable decisions. Some of the revenue from the higher charges is used to compensate people who live nearby by, for example, providing double-glazed windows.

It may be impossible to ban activities that pollute because the activities are felt to be very desirable in other ways. An alternative, market-related, method of regulating pollution and other undesirable activities is to sell licences permitting a limited amount of pollution. The government decides that it will allow, say, 100 units of pollution to be released into a river, and sells a licence to release the pollutant to the highest bidder. No other firm can then release the pollutant, and the firm that buys the licence is forced to take account of the social cost of the pollution through the higher private cost.

19.7 Social cost–benefit analysis

How does the government decide whether to prohibit, restrict or encourage an activity, or whether to require a nationalized firm to invest in a project when the private cost and/or private benefit differ from the social cost and/or social benefit? In practice the answer may be entirely political, because it is based on the interests of pressure groups or the needs of political parties. However, **social cost–benefit analysis** has been developed to try to give an answer that is based, at least in part, on economic criteria:

> Social cost–benefit analysis attempts to evaluate social costs and benefits in terms of money, so that the advantages and disadvantages of external effects can be balanced against the private cost and private benefit.

Social cost–benefit analysis raises a variety of questions, including:

(a) How can monetary values be placed on external effects such as noise, pollution and road congestion?
(b) What **discount rate** should be used to take account of the fact that costs and benefits occur at different times? The method of discounting used in social cost–benefit analysis is the same as that used by privately owned firms to evaluate investment projects (see section 8.8). However, privately owned firms discount only the private costs and private benefits of an investment project, whereas in social cost–benefit analysis the figures to

be discounted from the future to the present include the values placed on external effects.

19.7.1 The valuation problem

Some external effects can be valued in a relatively straightforward way. For example, if a new railway line reduces the travelling time of 5,000 people by half an hour each week, and the average way is £4 per hour, the time saved has a value of 5,000 × 1/2 × £4 = £10,000 per week. This external effect is added to the private benefit (the revenue from ticket sales) in a social cost–benefit analysis of the project.

It is less easy to place monetary values on some other external effects. Suppose, for example, that we want to place a value on the noise suffered by people who live near the site of a proposed road. There are two approaches that we could use:

(a) We could observe the amount that people have spent on noise insulation in similar circumstances, and how much they have lost because of the reduction in the prices of their properties, and conclude that these amounts measure the monetary cost associated with the noise. However, this conclusion is of limited relevance because it depends on the extent to which people can afford to buy insulation and on the extent to which they prefer to buy other goods and suffer the noise.
(b) We could ask people how much money they need to compensate them for the increased noise, and assume that the total amount represents the monetary cost of the noise. However, people who are asked questions of this kind have two incentives to overstate the compensation required. First, overstatement is advantageous if they are actually paid the compensation for which they ask. Second, even if the compensation is not paid (or is paid at a lower level), overstatement increases the calculated social cost of the project and reduces the chance that the social benefit exceeds the social cost. So, by overstating, those who are adversely affected can reduce the likelihood that the project is carried out.

The difficulties of valuing external effects imply that we cannot be confident that the figures used in a social cost–benefit analysis are absolutely correct. However, it is possible to perform a **sensitivity analysis** of the project by varying some of the figures used. For example, suppose that the social benefit of an airport exceeds the social cost if the effects of noise are valued at £1 million. If the social benefit outweighs the cost even if the value of the effects of the noise is increased to £2 million, then the valuation of the external effect is not critical to the recommendation of the social cost–benefit analysis. Alternatively, it may be that the social cost exceeds the social benefit if the value of the effects of the noise is increased to £1,050,000. In this case the valuation of the external effect is critical to the decision. If the valuation of some external effect is critical in this way, the social cost–benefit analysis does not give a clear signal to the government on whether the project should go ahead. The social cost and social benefit are finely balanced, and so a decision to go ahead with the project is likely to be based on other grounds than the social cost–benefit analysis.

19.7.2 Choice of discount rate

A firm making a decision on an investment project is likely to base its choice of discount rate on the interest rate that it pays to borrow (see section 8.8). A government could use the interest rate on, say, long-term government bonds as the discount rate for assessing projects in social cost–benefit analysis. However, this interest rate is affected by a change in the supply of savings or in private investment, or by the government's monetary policy. In practice, the government is likely to assess a project using several discount rates to find whether the outcome is particularly affected by the choice of discount rate. If the discounted sum of social benefits exceeds the discounted sum of social costs using a wide range of discount rates, then the decision on the project is not sensitive to the choice of the discount rate and the social cost–benefit analysis gives a clear indication of the social desirability of the project.

The sorts of sensitivity analysis that a government may use are illustrated for the Channel Tunnel project in table 19.5. These estimates were made before the present project started. The growth referred to is the growth rate of national income (low growth is an average of approximately 1.5 per cent per year from 1981 to 2000; high growth is an annual average of approximately 2.5 per cent), which affects the demand for Channel crossings. The discounted social benefits of both projects listed in the table exceed their discounted social costs in all cases, except for the bridge when the growth rate is low and the discount rate is at the highest level used. This reflects the fact that a bridge would be more expensive to build than a tunnel, and so it would not be judged desirable if Channel crossings are expected to increase only slowly (low growth),

Table 19.5 Sensitivity analysis of alternative Channel links (figures are net present value (see section 8.8) over 50 years, quoted in £ million)

Growth	Discount rate (%)	Bridge	Tunnel
Low	3	2,642	5,898
	5	759	3,084
	10	−573	643
High	3	6,977	8,948
	5	3,183	4,770
	10	135	1,172

Source: *Report of the Transport Committee of the House of Commons* 1980–1 (HCP 155)

and if future benefits are given a low weight compared to current costs (high discount rate).

19.7.3 Social cost–benefit analysis and income distribution

Social cost–benefit analysis evaluates projects in monetary terms. Private costs and private benefits are valued using the market prices of goods and of factors of production, and as we have seen, social costs and social benefits are frequently valued either according to the prices that people are observed to pay or according to the prices of goods that they would buy with their compensation. All the costs and benefits therefore depend on the prices of goods and factors, and so they are all based on the current income distribution (see section 10.8), which influences supplies, demands and prices. So the recommendation from a social cost–benefit analysis depends on the existing income distribution. The recommendation might be different if the distribution was different, because the prices of goods and factors change when the income distribution changes.

Social cost–benefit analysis cannot be used to evaluate policies that are designed to redistribute income. Consider a very simple example: an income tax takes £1 million from the richest 10 per cent of the population, and this money, minus £10,000 in administrative costs, is given to the poorest 10 per cent of the population through the social security system. The cost to the rich is £1,000,000, and the benefit to the poor is £990,000. If the cost and benefit of the policy are expressed in monetary terms, the social cost exceeds the social benefit. The same conclusion would be true for any redistributional policy, and so social cost–benefit analysis automatically recommends against all redistributional policies. In section 22.2.2 we shall discuss a possible modification of social cost–benefit analysis that might be used to evaluate redistributional policies.

19.7.4 Social cost–benefit analysis and unemployment

One of the social benefits of an investment project may be the employment of the workers involved in carrying it out, and it may be desirable to include this benefit in a social cost–benefit analysis. Indeed, macroeconomic analysis predicts that a major investment project (such as building a cross-Channel link or a third London airport) would have an expansionary multiplier effect (see section 17.3) that would increase employment further. However, market analysis predicts that the increase in employment on the proposed project is offset by employment crowded out elsewhere (see section 17.6.2), so that there is no change in total employment. Therefore the decision on whether to include increased employment as a social benefit of a project depends on the method used to analyse macroeconomic aspects of economic systems.

19.8 Summary

The government can use a variety of policies to limit the effects of imperfections, but all government policies cause some interference in the operation of markets because taxes must be raised or borrowing increased to finance the policies.

Firms are nationalized so that the government can control important parts of the economy and limit the power of natural monopolies, and so that bankrupt firms do not close. The 1980s policies of privatization can be traced to the market approach to macroeconomics, to the view that nationalized firms are less efficient than privately owned firms, and also to the government's desire to raise money to help meet its deficit. The pricing decisions of nationalized firms affect the efficiency of the allocation of resources: a policy of marginal cost pricing makes nationalized firms appear to behave as if they were competitive. However, marginal cost pricing implies that a firm makes a loss if marginal cost is less than average cost, so that it must receive a subsidy. The profits and losses of nationalized firms affect the size of the government's deficit, and have macroeconomic implications.

Privatization is carried out for reasons opposite to those for nationalization, and in particular because nationalized industries are considered to be inefficient. Privatization of natural monopolies leads to the possibility of private monopoly power. A major problem for the government is setting the price of the shares of newly privatized firms to ensure that the shares are sold without sacrificing revenue. The revenue from privatization can be used to help meet the government's budget deficit.

The government can regulate external effects if it can change private costs and benefits to match social costs and benefits more closely. The desirability of projects that involve significant external effects can be assessed using social cost–benefit analysis. However, the outcome from such an analysis may not be clear cut if some external effect is difficult to value, because the valuation may be critical to the decision. Similarly, the discount rate may also be critical to the decision.

Topics and problems

(1) Should monopolies be regulated on either distributional or efficiency grounds?

(2) 'Many industries were nationalized to limit the market influence of natural monopolies.' 'Nationalized industry prices have risen faster than most others over the past 25 years.' Has nationalization therefore failed?

(3) Should the government nationalize failing firms and privatize profitable firms?

(4) 'Everyone owns a nationalized industry so everyone benefits from its success.' 'Shareholders in a privatized firms gain profits from the sales of goods that people want to buy.' Are these statements compatible?

(5) Should the government subsidize the prices charged by nationalized firms supplying energy and transport to help the poor?

(6) 'The peak-load pricing of energy is unfair because it increases prices when energy is needed most.' Do you agree? How else might a nationalized energy firm meets its peak demands on very cold days?

(7) Is it right to suppose that the inflation rate can be reduced by increasing nationalized firms' selling prices?

(8) Is the most desirable level of pollution zero?

(9) Many projects (such as investment in medical equipment and in motorway crash barriers) are principally designed to save lives. Not all such projects can be carried out because resources are scarce. Is it desirable (or ethical) to attach a money value to lives that are saved in order to carry out a social cost–benefit analysis to see whether a life-saving project is worthwhile? If this is to be done, what method should be used?

(10) A bridge is proposed that would have a current cost of £750,000. It is expected to last for 20 years, with an annual maintenance cost of £5,000. The social benefit to each person using the bridge is £10. Is the project socially desirable if the discount rate is 10 per cent, and if (a) 5,500 people use the bridge each year (b) 8,500 people use it each year (c) 10,500 people use it each year? How do your answers change if the discount rate is reduced to (i) 8 per cent   (ii) 5 per cent   (iii) zero?

Chapter Twenty

Incentives and redistribution: taxes and benefits

Redistribution of income — incentives — indirect taxes and subsidies — cash benefit or subsidized goods?

20.1 Introduction

In section 17.3 we considered the multiplier effects of taxes and government expenditure, and their relations to fiscal and monetary policy. Taxes and benefits also affect the income distribution (and are often introduced precisely for that reason) and incentives to work. The effects of taxes and benefits on incentives are a major part of supply-side economic policies that are intended to have a macroeconomic impact on employment and growth. In this chapter we look at these other aspects of government activities.

Total taxes are mostly made up of:

(a) **Direct taxes**, which are mainly income tax and national insurance contributions.
(b) **Indirect taxes**, which are mainly Value Added Tax (VAT) and excise duties on alcohol, tobacco and petrol.
(c) **Capital taxes** on gifts and inheritance.
(d) Taxes collected by local government. At the time of writing the UK government is implementing a major change from the use of **rates** (taxes on the value of property) to a **community charge** (commonly known as a poll tax) supplemented by rates on commercial and industrial property.

Government expenditures include:

(a) Payments for **consumer goods** (current goods and services) and **investment goods** (capital formation).
(b) **Transfer payments** paid to pensioners, the unemployed, people who are sick or disabled.
(c) **Interest** payments on previously issued government bonds.

Table 20.1 lists the major sources of tax revenue and expenditures that make up the UK government's budget.

Table 20.1 Major government revenues and expenditures (£ billion)

	1985	% of GDP	1986	% of GDP	1987	% of GDP	1988	% of GDP
GDP (at market prices)	354		379		414		464	
Revenues								
Taxes on income	52	14.6	52	13.8	55	13.4	61	13.1
Social security contributions	24	6.8	26	6.9	28	6.9	31	6.7
Indirect taxes	57	16.0	63	16.6	68	16.4	75	16.2
Other	14	4.1	13	3.3	14	3.1	19	4.1
Total	147	41.5	154	40.6	165	39.8	186	40.1
Expenditure								
Consumer goods	74	20.9	80	21.1	86	20.8	92	19.8
Investment goods	7	2.0	7	1.9	6	1.5	5	1.1
Transfer payments	50	14.1	53	14.0	56	13.5	57	12.3
Interest	17	4.8	17	4.5	18	4.3	18	3.9
Other	8	2.3	6	1.5	5	1.2	10	2.1
Total	156	44.1	163	43.0	171	41.3	182	39.2

Source: *UK National Accounts*

20.1.1 Average and marginal tax and benefit rates

In section 17.2, we defined the average and marginal tax rates for the society as a whole. It is convenient to extend these definitions to individuals and to make similar definitions for benefits:

(a) The **average tax rate** for an individual is his or her total tax payment divided by his or her income before the tax is paid.
(b) The **marginal tax rate** for an individual is the additional tax that he or she pays when his or her income increases by one unit (£1).
(c) The **average benefit rate** for an individual is his or her total income from transfer payments divided by his or her income before the payments are received.
(d) The **marginal benefit rate** for an individual is the additional benefit that he or she receives when his or her income increases by one unit.

The marginal benefit rate is, in most cases, zero or negative: people receive smaller transfer payments when their other incomes increase.

20.2 The redistribution of income

The effects of a tax system or a benefit system on the income distribution are often summarized as being **progressive, neutral** or **regressive**. We use these words only to describe, and our use of them implies no approval or disapproval.

A tax system is:

(a) **Progressive** if the average tax rate increases as people become richer because the marginal tax rate exceeds the average tax rate.
(b) **Neutral** if the average tax rate is the same at all levels of income because the average tax rate equals the marginal tax rate.
(c) **Regressive** if the average tax rate falls as people become richer because the average tax rate exceeds the marginal tax rate.

Similarly, a benefit system is:

(a) Progressive if the average benefit rate falls as people become richer.
(b) Neutral if the average benefit rate is the same at all levels of income.
(c) Regressive if the average benefit rate increases as people become richer.

A progressive tax or benefit system reduces the inequality of the income distribution; one sign of this is that the Gini coefficient (see section 6.3.2) is lower after tax has been paid than it was before. So by this criterion a progressive tax system (or a progressive benefit system) tends to equalize the income distribution.

Table 20.2 shows the effects on the income distribution of benefits and taxes in the UK. Some transfer payments (such as child benefit in the UK) are **universal benefits** that are paid to everyone in a particular category, regardless of income. These benefits form a larger proportional addition to poor people's incomes than to richer people's incomes, and so they are progressive, but they are not as progressive as **means-tested benefits** that are paid only to people whose other income is below a specified level. Table 20.2 shows the redistributive effects of transfer payments in the UK: they form almost all of the gross income of the poorest group, and are highly progressive.

The UK income tax rate structure is progressive: table 20.2 shows that the average tax rate increases from almost zero to 22 per cent for the five groups considered (and is higher for people with incomes well above £25,470, which is the average income of the richest 20 per cent of the sample of households). However, most countries' direct tax systems (including that of the UK) have become very complicated because they grant total or partial exemptions from tax for some categories of incomes (for example, in the UK income from National Savings Certificates does not have to be declared for income taxation, so that they are a very attractive form of saving for rich people) and they make allowances for certain expenditures (for example, in the UK some of the interest paid on mortgages can be deducted from income before tax is calculated; in Canada, people who move home when they change their jobs deduct moving expenses from their incomes before tax is calculated). The

Table 20.2   Redistributive effects of taxes and benefits in the UK

	Lowest 20%	Next 20%	Next 20%	Next 20%	Next 20%	Gini coefficient
1 Original income (£) plus	130	2,800	8,030	13,180	24,790	0.48
2 Transfer payments (£) equals	3,370	2,270	1,250	870	680	
3 Gross income (£)	3,500	5,070	9,280	14,050	25,470	0.36
(2 as % of 1) minus	2,592	81	16	7	3	
4 Direct tax (£) equals	10	330	1,490	2,880	5,650	
5 Disposable income (£)	3,490	4,740	7,790	11,170	19,820	0.33
(4 as % of 3) minus	0.3	6.5	16	20	22	
6 Indirect tax (£)	880	1,540	2,280	2,900	4,250	
(6 as % of 5) plus	25	32	29	26	21	
7 Benefits in kind (£) equals	1,520	1,950	1,510	1,670	1,690	
8 Final income (£)	4,130	5,150	7,020	9,940	17,260	0.29
(8 as % of 5)	118	109	90	89	87	
(8 as % of 1)	3,177	184	87	75	70	

Source: *Social Trends*

complications imply that no existing system ensures that, without exception, a richer person pays a larger proportion of his or her income in tax than does a poorer person.

20.2.1 Redistributive effects of indirect taxes

Of total tax revenue in the UK, 43 per cent is raised from VAT and other indirect taxes, and these taxes can be regressive in that poor people may pay a higher proportion of their incomes in indirect taxes than do richer people. This conclusion would certainly be true if:

(a) All goods were subject to an indirect tax at a standard rate.
(b) Richer people save a larger fraction of their incomes than poorer people.

For example, suppose that 15 per cent of the price of every good is paid in indirect tax. If Alan has an income of £5,000 and saves 10 per cent of his income, and if Bill has an income of £15,000 and saves 20 per cent of his income, then Alan spends £4,500, of which 15 per cent (= £675) is indirect tax, and Bill spends £12,000, of which £1,800 is indirect tax. So Alan pays 13.5 per cent of his income in indirect tax, and Bill pays 12 per cent. In practice (see table 20.2, in which the average tax rate is lower for the poorest group than for the next poorest, but declines for richer groups), this conclusion is modified by the facts that:

(a) Not all goods are subject to indirect tax. For example, food, electricity, gas and coal are all exempt from VAT in the UK. Most of the goods on which no indirect tax is charged are necessities on which poorer people spend a larger fraction of their incomes than richer people. So these exemptions from indirect taxes have a progressive effect.

(b Some goods are subject to indirect taxes at a higher rate than others. For example, alcohol, tobacco and petrol are all subject to excise duties that increase the indirect tax rate on these goods above the general rate of VAT. The system of Purchase Tax, which was replaced by VAT in the UK in 1973, levied taxes on different goods at different rates, in an attempt to tax luxuries at a greater rate than necessities. A similar policy was used when VAT was introduced in the UK and is used in other European Community countries, but since 1979 the rate of VAT in the UK has been uniform for all goods on which the tax is paid. If the government charges a higher rate of tax on luxuries than on necessities, richer people, who buy a greater proportion of luxuries, pay a higher average tax rate than poorer people. Excise duties on alcohol and tobacco are likely to be less progressive; for example, in the UK tobacco accounts for 3.3 per cent of the expenditure of the poorest group in society and only 2.6 per cent of the average person's expenditure. So the poorer people pay a higher than average fraction of their incomes through the tax on tobacco.

Despite these modifications indirect taxes are regressive and, as table 20.2 shows, this offsets a considerable part of the progressive nature of direct taxes in the UK.

20.2.2 Freely provided goods and the income distribution

In principle a **freely provided good** (or **benefit in kind**), such as state-provided health care and education in the UK, which is supplied to everyone on the same basis, has a similar effect on the income distribution to a transfer payment that is paid to everyone. Each person receives a service that is worth the same amount of money, and this represents a larger proportional increase in income for a poor person than for a richer person. In practice, the distributional effects depend on whether the same amount is actually provided to each person, whatever his or her income (or, in the case of health services, whether each person has similar access to the service if it is needed). Some studies (see for example that of J. Le Grand, *The Strategy of Equality*, listed in the bibliography) indicate that the supply of freely provided goods is greater (per head) in areas

Table 20.3 Income–leisure combinations for figure 20.1

Leisure time (hours)	Situation 1 (lower tax rates)			Situation 2 (higher tax rates)			Compensated situation (higher tax rates and additional hours)		
	Income before tax (£)	Tax rate (£)	Income after tax (£)	Income before tax (£)	Tax rate (%)	Income after tax (£)	Income before tax (£)	Tax rate (%)	Income after tax (£)
0	80	25	60	80	43	45.6	90	48	46.8
2	70	20	56	70	38	43.4	80	43	45.6
4	60	16	50.4	60	32	40.8	70	38	43.4
6	50	12	44	50	28	36	60	32	40.8
8	40	10	36	40	24	30.4	50	28	36
10	30	6	28.2	30	20	24	40	24	30.4
12	20	2	19.6	20	15	17	30	20	24
14	10	0	10	10	10	9	20	15	17
16	0	—	0	0	—	0	10	10	9
18	—	—	—	—	—	—	0	—	0

with a higher average household income, so that the redistributive effects are not as great as if there were equal provision.

Table 20.2 shows that the amount of benefits in kind received by richer people are greater than those of poorer people (although the average benefit rate falls, so that the benefits are progressive). This may be because areas with higher average incomes have a larger supply of these services, but it may also be because of other factors, such as the possiblity that the richer group have, on average, more children in education. We cannot identify the cause of the increase in benefits in kind for richer people without further information.

20.3 Incentives

A government that wants to make a considerable redistribution of income could introduce a very progressive tax system. However, it is often argued that high rax rates reduce people's incentives to work. If this is so, a very progressive tax system reduces national income, which may imply that everyone, including the poor, is worse off than if the tax system were less progressive, because the lower national income implies that there is less tax revenue available to finance benefits.

We can discuss whether an increase in tax rates reduces the number of hours that people are willing to work by using the techniques developed in section 10.3. Table 20.3 and figure 20.1 show the effects of two alternative tax systems on a person who receives a wage before tax of £5 per hour. The lines GH and GJ represent the combinations of income and leisure that are available in the two situations. These lines are curved because the tax system is progressive: the household's after-tax income rises at a decreasing rate as it works more hours because the average tax rate increases. Suppose that in situation 1 he chooses to work for 8 hours per day, taking 8 hours leisure (and 8 hours sleep), so that his post-tax income is £36. He is at point A in figure 20.1. He works fewer hours in situation 2 than in situation 1 if he chooses a point on GJ that is to the right of B.

To use the income and substitution effects of sections 9.4 and 10.3, we introduce the compensated situation represented by curve DC. In this situation, total working and leisure time is 18 hours, the tax rates are those of tax system 2, and he can have the combination of post-tax income and leisure that he chooses in situation 1 (curve DC passes through A). Then:

(a) The **substitution effect** is the movement from A to the point chosen in the compensated situation.
(b) The **income effect** is movement from the point chosen in the compensated situation to that chosen in situation 2.

The axiom of revealed preference (see section 9.4.3) implies that he does not choose a combination on AC in the compensated situation. A combination such as E (4 hours leisure, £43.4 income after tax) is inferior to F (4 hours, £50.4), and he has revealed by his choice of A in situation 1 that he prefers

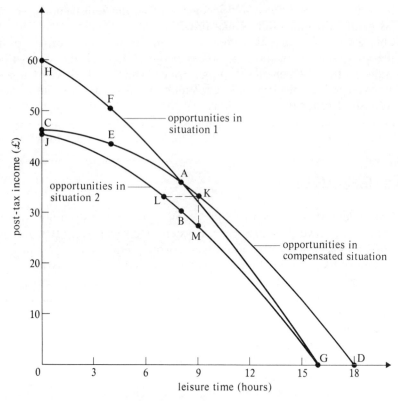

Figure 20.1   Income tax and incentives from table 20.3
Situation 1 involves lower taxes than situation 2. Both situations allow 16 hours for work and leisure. The compensated situation involves the tax rates of situation 2, with an additional 2 hours of working plus leisure time.

A to F, because he chooses A when F is available. He prefers A to E, and does not choose E when A is available. So, in the compensated situation, he chooses a point on AD, showing that:

> The substitution effect of an increase in tax rates increases leisure time and reduces post-tax income.

Situation 2 has the same tax rates as the compensated situation, and he has fewer hours available in total. So he is likely to reduce both working and leisure time:

> The income effect of an increase in tax rates is likely to reduce both leisure time and post-tax income.

Hence if he chooses point K in the compensated situation, he chooses a point between L and M in situation 2.

The total effect on his leisure time and working time depends on the relative sizes of the two effects:

(a) If he chooses a point to the right of B in situation 2, the substitution effect exceeds the income effect, and the increase in tax rates increases his leisure and reduces his working time.

(b) If he chooses a point to the left of B in situation 2, the income effect exceeds the substitution effect and the increase in tax rates reduces his leisure and increases his working time.

If we accept the argument that the supply curve of labour is backward-bending (see section 10.3.3), the substitution effect exceeds the income effect for richer people, and so the incentive to work less when tax rates increase is more likely to apply to people with high incomes than to people with lower incomes. Richer people may be prepared to sacrifice some post-tax income when tax rates increase, and to take more leisure, because the reward for working an additional hour is reduced by higher taxes. Poorer people may work more hours to maintain their post-tax incomes when tax rates increase.

The disincentive effects of tax increases are usually discussed in terms of direct tax systems. However, if people make decisions on the hours that they work on the basis of their real incomes, the effects of increases in indirect taxes can be analysed in a similar way. An increase in the average price level that is caused by increases in indirect taxes reduces real incomes as does an increase in direct taxes.

20.3.1 Benefits and the natural rate of unemployment

An obvious disincentive to work occurs if social security benefits available to unemployed people increase relative to the wages that they could earn in employment. This will be an individual calculation, both because different individuals have different earning potential and because many social security benefits depend on family size and other sources of income (such as spouse's earnings). The size of benefits in relation to earnings is one of the imperfections that may prevent full employment in modified market analysis, and so the natural rate of unemployment can be reduced by making benefit payments less generous relative to average earnings.

It is possible to make a more sophisticated argument on the effects of unemployment benefits when there are successful trades unions who increase their members' wages above the market equilibrium. This implies that fewer people are employed at these higher wages, and so the supply of workers for other, non-unionized jobs increases. This depresses wages for non-unionized jobs so that more people have an incentive to remain unemployed. The relevance of this argument depends on the growth of union power as well as the level of benefits relative to wages.

20.3.2 Poverty trap

Means-tested benefits can give rise to a very large negative marginal benefit rate at certain levels of income. If a particular benefit is paid only when a household's other income is below some threshold level, the benefit is completely lost when other income rises above the threshold. The household's income including benefits may even fall if it works more hours so that its income excluding benefits increases. If a person's income including benefits falls, or rises only a little when he works more, plainly he has a strong disincentive to work more hours. So means-tested benefits can cause a **poverty trap** that reduces or removes the incentive to earn more.

For example, if a person receives a transfer payment of £5 only if her other income is not more than £50, her income including benefits is £55 if her income excluding benefits is £50, but if she works harder and increases her income excluding benefit to £51, her income including benefits falls to £51. Her marginal benefit rate is minus 400 per cent.

The disincentive effect can be reduced if the amount of the means-tested benefit is reduced gradually as other income increases. However, even a gradual reduction can decrease the reward for working harder. For example, suppose that the benefit is £5 for incomes up to £50, and is reduced by £0.50 for every additional £1 of other income. Income after benefits therefore increases by £0.50 when the person earns an additional £1 at each income level between £50 and £59. The marginal benefit rate is minus 50 per cent.

In practice the marginal benefit rate for some individuals remains very large (and negative) because, as a person's income increases, he or she loses part or all of several benefits (the income at which this happens varies from one individual or family to another since benefit payments may vary with the size of the family and other factors). In addition, in the UK the income tax system adds to the poverty trap, because people begin to pay income tax at much the same level as they begin to lose means-tested benefits.

20.3.3 Negative income tax

The effects of the poverty trap could be reduced significantly if the income tax and transfer payment systems were amalgamated into a **negative income tax system**. Table 20.4 gives an example of such a system, and its effects are illustrated in figure 20.2. People who have incomes below £40 per week receive a payment from the government; people with incomes above £40 per week pay tax to the government. As pre-tax income increases, the average benefit rate falls, and then the average tax rate increases. So the system is progressive. Furthermore, each successive increase of £10 in income before tax and benefit yields at least an additional £6 in income after tax and benefit. There is no poverty trap, in the sense that there is no income level where benefits are reduced or taxes increased so rapidly that all, or even more than all, of a £10 increase in income is lost. In fact, the marginal tax rate in the example given increases from 20 per cent to 40 per cent as incomes increase, so that the average benefit rate falls more rapidly and the average tax rate increases more rapidly than they would if the marginal rate were constant. The system is progressive.

A negative income tax system could take account of different personal circumstances, just as the current income tax system and system of transfer

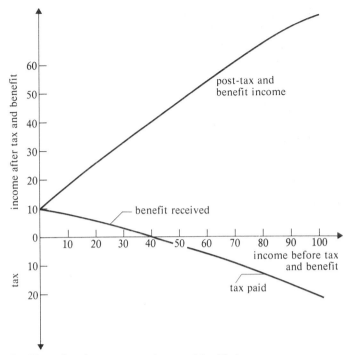

Figure 20.2 Negative income tax from table 20.4
Benefit is received up to income of £40; thereafter, tax is paid at an increasing average rate.

Table 20.4 Example of a negative income tax system

Income before tax and benefit (£ weekly)	Tax paid (−) or benefit received (+) (£ weekly)	Income after tax and benefit (£ weekly)	Average tax (−) or benefit (+) rate (%)	Marginal tax rate (%)
0	+10	10	infinite	—
10	+8	18	+80	20
20	+6	26	+30	20
30	+3	33	+10	30
40	0	40	0	30
50	−3	47	−6	30
60	−6	54	−10	30
70	−9	61	−12.9	30
80	−13	67	−16.3	40
90	−17	73	−18.9	40
100	−21	77	−21	40

The marginal tax rate is calculated for a £10 increase in income before tax and benefit. For incomes below £40, the marginal tax rate is the negative of the marginal benefit rate: it reflects the reduction in benefit. For incomes above £40, the marginal tax rate reflects the additional tax paid.

payments do. If the government decides that a person with children should receive more benefit and/or pay less tax than someone with no children, a person with children can be given an allowance that reduces his or her taxable income. Then, his or her tax or benefit is calculated on the basis of his or her taxable income, so that, in the example, if taxable income is less than £40, he or she receives money from the government, even if actual income exceeds £40. Similar allowances could be given for any other purpose, including mortgage interest, dependent relatives, pension contributions, relieving handicaps and so on, so that the system can allow for special needs.

20.3.4 Incentives and macroeconomics

The possible incentive effects of tax cuts have been incorporated into the **supply-side** theory of macroeconomic policy. This theory assumes that:

(a) If income tax rates are reduced, people work much harder, so that there is a substantial increase in outputs. This requires that the substitution effect of a tax change exceeds the income effect for the great majority of people.
(b) If taxes on profits are reduced, privately owned firms invest more.

There are other aspects of supply-side theories – all of which are related to the view that the economy operates best if markets are competitive and free from government interference. We discuss these in chapter 21.

These two incentive effects cause an increase in national income and in employment as people want to work more and firms create more jobs through their increased investment, and so saving increases. This reduces interest rates, which provides an additional stimulus to investment.

Multiplier analysis agrees to some extent with the macroeconomic effects of tax reductions predicted by the supply-side theory, because tax reductions cause an expansionary multiplier effect (see section 17.3.2). However, macroeconomic analysis implies that the increases in national income and in employment are mainly the result of increases in demands for goods caused by increased disposable incomes, and are the result of the incentive effects of lower taxes only in so far as firms increase their investment expenditure because they become more optimistic as national income increases.

Supply-side theories assume that the economy works more efficiently if there are fewer imperfections. All taxes are imperfections, so that lower taxes improve the efficiency of the economy, increase employment and increase outputs. However, tax reductions that are not accompanied by reductions in government expenditure imply an increase in the government's budget deficit or a reduction in its surplus. If this is financed by an increase in borrowing, interest rates rise and offset some of the effects predicted by supply-side analysis.

An extreme supply-side response to this problem is that the increase in national income induced by the reduction of taxes and removal of other imperfections is large enough for total tax payments to increase, even though the tax rates fall. For example, if the government reduces the average tax rate for society from 25 per cent to 20 per cent, and if national income is initially £100 million, so that total tax payments are £25 million, the extreme supply-side argument predicts that the tax reduction increases national income to at least £125 million, so that total tax revenue would not fall below £25 million. In practice, the deficit would fall even if the effect on tax revenues were not quite as large as this example implies, because any increase in employment reduces government expenditure on transfer payments.

The supply-side theory has been used to support the tax-cutting policies of the US government since 1980 (personal income tax rates, for example, have been reduced by approximately 25 per cent since 1980, and many other tax rates have also been reduced). Since 1982 there has been an increase in real national income, and for some of the period the unemployment rate has fallen. However, the government budget deficit increased very rapidly from 1980 to 1985, and there is little evidence to suggest that tax reductions can lead to a large enough increase in national income to reduce the government's deficit, and so reduce borrowing. Less extreme supply-side theories argue that investment increases if interest rates fall, and this can occur only if the government cuts its expenditure as well as tax rates to reduce its borrowing.

20.4 Indirect taxes and subsidies

We have seen that indirect taxes in the UK are regressive. There are three other aspects of these taxes that we can consider using partial equilibrium analysis, which assumes that the price moves rapidly to its equilibrium level when the tax is imposed:

(a) How much revenue does the government raise from an indirect tax?
(b) How much does the price paid by buyers increase when an indirect tax is imposed on a good (or an existing tax is increased)?
(c) How much does the price received by sellers fall when an indirect tax is imposed or increased?

The second and third questions together involve the **burden** (or **incidence**) of an indirect tax:

> The burden of an indirect tax falls on the buyers in so far as the price that they pay increases, and on the sellers in so far as the price that they receive falls.

Table 20.5 and figure 20.3 show the effect on the supply curve for a good of the imposition of an indirect tax of 25 per cent. The imposition of the indirect tax shifts the supply curve to the left (from SS to TT). This shift occurs because, given the price paid by buyers, sellers receive less when there is an indirect tax then when there is not. So, for example, the supply is 7 units when the buyers pay £12 and there is no tax, and the supply is also 7 units when the buyers pay £16, of which £4 is tax, so that the sellers receive £12.

We can answer our three questions using figure 20.3:

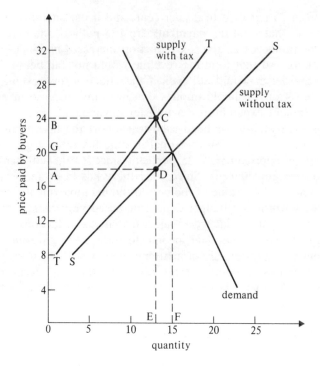

Figure 20.3   Effect of an indirect tax for example of table 20.5
Supply and demand are related to the price paid by buyers, so that supply falls when a tax is imposed. The effect on the suppliers is the reduction GA in the price received; the effect on the demanders is the increase GB in the price paid. Tax revenue is ABCD.

Table 20.5   Effect of an indirect tax on supply

| Price paid by demanders | No tax | | Tax = 25% of price paid | | |
	Demand	Supply	Tax	Price received by suppliers	Supply
4	23	0	1	3	0
8	21	3	2	6	1
12	19	7	3	9	4
16	17	11	4	12	7
20	15	15	5	15	10
24	13	19	6	18	13
28	11	23	´7	21	16
32	9	27	8	24	19

(a) The quantity sold after the tax is imposed is E, and the price paid by buyers is B. So total expenditure on the good is OBCE. The suppliers receive price A (curve SS shows that they supply E when they receive A, and after the tax is imposed they receive A when the buyers pay B) and so their total revenue is OADE. The government receives tax revenue of OBCE − OADE = ABCD.

(b) The price paid by buyers increases from G to B. Note that this is not the full amount of the tax (in the numerical example, B is £24, G is £20 and the tax is £6).

(c) The price received by the sellers falls from G to A.

20.4.1 Indirect tax and price-elasticity of demand

Figure 20.4 shows two alternative demand curves for a good.

(a) In figure 20.4(a), the price-elasticity of demand for the good is low, so that the demand curve is nearly vertical. The government receives a revenue ACGF; the price paid by buyers rises from B to C, and the price received by the sellers falls from B to A.

(b) In figure 20.4(b), the price-elasticity of demand is high, so that the demand curve is nearly horizontal. The government receives a revenue XZTU; the price paid by buyers rises from Y to Z, and the price received by sellers falls from Y to X.

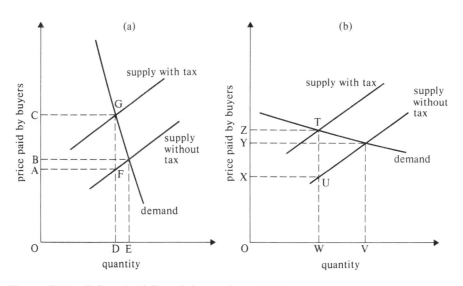

Figure 20.4 Price-elasticity of demand and indirect tax
(a) shows an inelastic demand curve, for which the majority of the burden is on the buyers (b) shows an elastic demand curve, for which the majority of the burden is on the sellers.

So:

(a) The tax revenue is higher in the low price-elasticity of demand case.
(b) The rise in the price paid by buyers is larger and the fall in the price received by sellers is smaller in the low price-elasticity of demand case.
(c) The burden of the indirect tax falls more on the buyers and less on the sellers in the low price-elasticity of demand case.

If the government's principal reason for levying indirect taxes is to raise revenue, it imposes taxes on goods for which the price-elasticity of demand is low. This is one reason for the high excise duties on alcohol, tobacco and petrol (although high taxes on the first two might also be justified on health grounds, and high taxes on petrol might be justified on the grounds that it is necessary to reduce the use of petrol in order to conserve oil for the future or to limit pollution). The conclusion that little revenue is raised from goods that have a high price-eleasticity of demand may explain why the government abandoned the policy of taxing luxuries at a higher rate of VAT. A luxury is a good with a high income-elasticity of demand, and goods with high income-elasticities of demand are likely to have high price-elasticities of demand, because of the income effect of the price change (see section 9.4.6).

20.4.2 Subsidized goods

Governments subsidize purchases of some goods to reduce the prices paid by the buyers, so that more people can afford to buy them. If the goods are supplied by privately owned firms, the subsidy is paid to the firms for each unit sold. In the case of goods supplied by nationalized firms, the size of a subsidy is ambiguous unless we are prepared to say what the correct unsubsidized price is. For example, if we were to say that the correct price, based on efficiency criteria, for a good is its marginal cost (see section 19.4.2), any decision to set the price below marginal cost implies that the government is subsidizing the good for some other reason, such as the desire to change the income distribution. However, this may not imply that the government pays money to the industry, because it is quite possible for an industry to price below marginal cost and make a financial profit. So when we discuss the effects of subsidies on purchases of these goods we need to decide on the correct, unsubsidized price before we can state the size of the subsidy.

If the government subsidizes purchases of a good, it reduces the price paid by the buyers from B to A in figure 20.5. The price received by the sellers increases from B to E, and so the subsidy per unit sold is AE. The total subsidy paid is AE × OD = AEFG.

20.4.3 Goods supplied without charge

Some goods, notably health care and education in the UK, are provided 'free' in the sense that there is no charge at the time of use of the service. Of course, these goods require resources to produce them, and they are by no means free

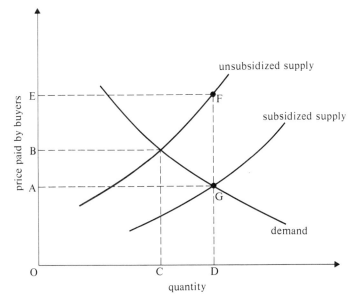

Figure 20.5   Effect of a subsidy
The subsidy shifts the supply curve to the right, so that the equilibrium quantity increases from C to D and the equilibrium price paid by the buyers falls from B to A. The cost of the subsidy is AEFG.

to society as a whole, because they involve an opportunity cost of other goods that could have been produced instead. However, the separation of the act of using the goods from the act of paying for the costs of production affects the economic principles that apply to them.

The macroeconomic effects of expenditure to produce goods that are supplied free of charge to the user are similar to the macroeconomic effects of other forms of government expenditure. The main problem arises because the demand for a good that is provided without charge is likely to exceed the supply that the government is willing to provide, given the nation's resources. How is demand to be rationed to equal the available supply, given that the good is provided free?

The demand for a good that is supplied without charge can be rationed to equal the supply in two ways:

(a) By **limiting quality**. For example, in education the quality of provision is affected by the number of students per teacher, by the equipment and books available, and so on. Given that the service is provided without charge, demanders would like to have small classes and large amounts of equipment. The government limits its expenditure on education by limiting the quality of the service.

(b) By **queueing** or **delaying**. For example, in the health service there are waiting lists for many services. The time spent queueing acts as a price, because people must sacrifice time that they could have spent on some other activity in order to wait in line – just as the payment of a money price involves a sacrifice of some other good that people could have bought instead. People pay for private health care partly to avoid the costs of delay.

Neither method of rationing indicates the quantity of the good that the government should supply. This decision requires that the government makes a value judgement on the extent to which the resources of the economy should be devoted to the provision of goods without charge, rather than to the production of other goods.

20.5 Cash benefit or subsidized goods?

Is it possible to say which method of providing social benefits is preferable? The word 'preferable' involves a value judgement, and so we cannot answer the question without stating the value judgement on which the answer is based.
  Consider two policies:

(a) The government makes a transfer payment of £100 to a household.
(b) The government pays the first £100 of the household's electricity bill.

From the household's point of view the cash benefit can never be worse than the subsidy because it can, if it wants to, use the cash to pay for £100 of electricity, which would leave the household in the same position as the subsidy (effectively with £100 of free electricity). However, if it prefers, the household could spend some or all of its £100 on goods other than electricity. So the household may be better off with the transfer payment than with the subsidy, because it prefers to spend less than £100 on electricity and to use the remainder of the cash to buy other goods.
  The government makes the cash payment if it makes the value judgement that it is better for people to choose what to buy, rather than to be forced to receive benefit only if they consume particular goods. A government might not make this value judgement, because it believes that people might spend cash benefits on undesirable goods. For example, the government might judge that it is better to give people free food, rather than an equivalent sum of money that they might spend on tobacco and alcohol. This alternative value judgement is **paternalistic**, because it implies that the government is a better judge of what is good for people than the people are themselves.

20.6 Summary

Direct and indirect taxes, cash transfer payments, subsidized goods and goods supplied without charge all cause changes in the income distribution. In the main, the UK income tax system and the provision of benefits are progressive, and the indirect tax system is regressive.

A reduction in income taxes increases the incentive to work as long as the substitution effect outweighs the income effect. Benefits, and particularly means-tested benefits, can give a disincentive to work because the reward for working more is low when benefits are reduced or withdrawn. Supply-side theories predict that a general reduction in taxation leads to an increase in national income because people work harder and firms are encouraged to invest. The revenue from and distribution of the burden of an indirect tax depend on the price-elasticity of demand.

Goods that are supplied without charge must be rationed in some way, either by limiting quality or by queueing. In general a person is better off if he or she receives a cash payment rather than an equal-sized subsidy on a good that he or she may, or may not, want to buy.

Topics and problems

(1) Should the government redistribute income?

(2) 'Income tax is a tax on what people put into the economy in the form of work, indirect taxes are a tax on what people take out from the economy in the form of consumer goods, so direct taxes are less desirable than indirect taxes.' Discuss.

(3) Income taxes and indirect taxes affect people's decisions on labour supply and demand for goods and so they affect the allocation of resources. Are there any possible taxes that do not affect people's economic decisions? (Consider, for example, a tax on economic rent; see section 10.6.2.)

(4) Is the government's desire for revenue from the tax on tobacco products consistent with its anti-smoking campaign?

(5) How would you explain the finding that people in richer areas receive more goods supplied without charge than people in poorer areas?

(6) Would it be desirable to abolish all subsidies to individuals and replace them with either a means-tested cash benefit or a universal cash benefit?

(7) One of the objectives of the single European market is the reduction in differences between countries' rates of VAT. What happens if the VAT rate of a good is 15 per cent in one town and zero in another town 10 miles away (across an unrestricted frontier)? Does your answer depend on the market structure for the goods or the quality of the roads between the towns?

(8) 'The imposition of VAT on children's clothes and food would be unfair and inefficient.' Do you agree?

Chapter Twenty-one

Major themes in government policy

Objectives of government policy — free market strategy — interventionist strategy — exchange of views — ISLM analysis

---

21.1 Introduction

In previous chapters we have discussed a range of government policies and two main alternative analyses of the operation of the economy. In this chapter we bring these together to give an overview of different policy strategies and alternative views of their outcomes. We consider two alternative general strategies:

(a) **Free market strategy**, which is based on the view that the economy works best if competitive markets are left free to operate without intervention. Thus the government's main policies involve reductions in the extent of its intervention in the economy, although competition policies and powers to reduce the monopoly influences of trades unions are more positive policy implications of this strategy.

(b) **Interventionist strategy**, which is based on the view that it is possible for the government to intervene successfully to shift the outcome of the economy towards the government's desired goals. Typically this involves fiscal, monetary and other policies that lead to changes in national income and employment.

The two strategies obviously parallel the two main methods of analysis: the free market strategy can be associated with market analysis; the interventionist strategy can be associated with macroeconomic analysis. In practice, no government has a completely single-minded view of policies to pursue, and elements of both strategies appear in policy statements. However, the division into two main strategies helps to highlight many of the areas of economic (and hence political) debate.

21.2 Objectives of government policy

The two strategies aim to fulfil the objectives of the government. We could make general statements that the government wants 'to promote the general welfare of the people' – which is, presumably, true, but is vague enough to be open to a variety of interpretations. In the economic context, general welfare is likely to involve:

(a) **Employment and unemployment**: a general desire to reduce unemployment and to match demands and supplies in various labour markets.
(b) **Income distribution**: implying at least a desire to provide support for individuals who are unable to earn a sufficient income for basic necessities, and quite possibly a much more radical view of income and wealth redistribution. A policy on redistribution implies decisions on tax and benefit systems and on freely provided goods, such as health and education services.
(c) **Economic growth**: partly to ensure that national income increases at least as fast as the population, and partly to enable an increase in average living standards. This increase may allow redistribution in relative terms towards one group without needing to reduce others' living standards. The promotion of economic growth requires policies to increase productivity, including investment in new machinery and in human capital.
(d) **Inflation**: the possible disadvantages of inflation (see section 6.5) include the uncertainty that it can cause, which might reduce investment and hence economic growth. Inflation may also have redistributive effects that offset other redistributive policies.
(e) **Exchange rates**: although not necessarily directly affecting welfare, rapid changes in exchange rates can lead to uncertainties for exporters, and lead to lower investment and lower economic growth. At some times (such as the period from 1945 to 1971) governments try to have a **fixed exchange rate policy**, which avoids all but minor changes in exchange rates; at other times, they allow changes, but not necessarily the fluctuations that could arise from a **freely floating exchange rate policy**, in which there is no government intervention in foreign exchange markets.

No set of policies can simultaneously achieve full employment, rapid growth, zero inflation, a constant exchange rate and some desired income distribution. So a government must set priorities and decide the extent to which it wants to meet one objective rather than another. In the next chapter we shall discuss **public choice**, which shows some of the difficulties involved in reaching agreement on the mix of objectives. In this chapter we discuss the two strategies in relation to these five aims.

The five objectives listed above are themselves **instruments** for improving the welfare of the population. Governments often phrase their policy objectives in terms of other targets that are instruments used to try to achieve one or more of the objectives listed. These include, in particular, targets for the rate of increase in the supply of money (related closely to the inflation rate in the monetarist view; see section 11.5) and targets for the exchange rate (which affects import prices and hence inflation and the level of exports, and hence employment).

21.3 Free market strategy

The free market strategy argues that the government should intervene as little as possible in the economy and, where it does so, its role should be to reduce imperfections in the economy. Much of the strategy involves supply-side policies, such as reductions in tax rates and measures to increase competition and to privatize nationalized industries and public services such as health and education.

21.3.1 Employment policy in a free market strategy

In market analysis involuntary unemployment disappears because labour markets reach equilibrium quickly. Taking such a view implies that the government can do nothing to affect the level of unemployment, except perhaps to help increase the speed of information flows in the economy through a network of efficient (but perhaps privately owned) employment agencies. Then those who are temporarily unemployed and those entering the labour market from school or college are aware of vacancies and so frictional unemployment is short-lived.

The modified market view is that markets move as near to equilibrium as imperfections allow, and unemployment reaches its natural rate quickly (see section 16.5.1). Policies to increase employment are designed to try to reduce the natural rate, and include:

(a) Strategies for training and retraining to bring demands and supplies in different labour markets into balance. These can include both the provision of training courses and support for students on them. The free market strategy is likely to support private training initiatives, including industrial funding of schools and colleges.
(b) Limitations on union power to ensure that wages are not kept above their equilibrium level. If wages are above equilibrium, some people who want a job cannot get one. Various limitations are possible, including restrictions on secondary picketing (picketing suppliers or customers of the firm in dispute, for example), restrictions on single union agreements and closed shops, legal liability on unions for the losses caused by strikes, secret ballots before strikes and so on. Many such limitations have been introduced or reinforced in the UK during the 1980s.
(c) Reductions in social security benefits for the unemployed to increase their incentive to work.
(d) Changes in housing legislation to enable people to move easily from one area to another in search of work. These changes may affect private and

publicly owned rented housing and also the cost and process of buying and selling houses.

21.3.2 Inflation policy in a free market strategy

The simplest inflation policy most closely associated with the free market strategy is monetarist. The government controls the supply of money, and this enables the government to control the inflation rate in the way indicated by the quantity theory of money.

Since our initial discussion of the quantity equation $MV = PT$ in section 11.5.4, we have developed a much more complicated analysis of the economy. In particular, we have seen that the 'supply of money' is not easily defined. The ambiguities in the definition of the supply of money and the difficulties of controlling any chosen measure lead to several policy strategies for the government if it is trying to reduce the inflation rate. The government can use one or more measures of the supply of money as **targets**, by setting a range for the target annual increase in that measure. If the actual outcome appears to be outside the target range, then the government takes steps to meet the target.

Attempts to control any measure of the supply of money imply equivalent attempts to control the demand for money because demand and supply must be equal. In section 14.7.3 we saw that the demand for money falls if the interest rate increases, and any form of monetary control by the government implies changes in the interest rate, which may have effects on private investment, consumption and saving.

Policy options for the control of the supply of money include the following, of which the government may choose several since they are not mutually exclusive:

(a) **Control using the cash ratio**. To some extent this might be done by direct control over the production of notes and coins, and so the government would try to reduce the inflation rate by reducing the production of money and insisting on a particular cash ratio. Indeed, the government could legislate an increase in the cash ratio. Then if there is no increase in cash, banks must reduce their lending to comply and so broader measures of the supply of money (which reflect more closely the funds available for spending) are also reduced. We saw in section 18.9 that banks need not respond as the government would like if their actual cash ratios are not kept at a minimum legal or desirable level.

(b) **Control using the liquidity ratio**. The government controls not only the cash in circulation, but also the volume of many of the assets that banks regard as liquid (see section 18.5.1). Many of the eligible liquid assets are supplied by the government, including bonds and Treasury bills, and so this strategy requires that the government reduces its borrowing from the banking sector specifically to reduce the volume of eligible liquid assets.

If the government does this, banks have fewer eligible securities, and they reduce their lending to maintain their liquidity ratios.

(c) **Control through the last resort facility**. Banks that are faced with a potential cash or liquidity shortage may decide to risk more frequent use of the last resort facility. The government cannot refuse to fulfil its obligations to be a provider of last resort funding because a refusal would reduce public confidence in banks. So it must dissuade banks from wanting to use the facility by increasing minimum lending rate and reducing the prices at which it will buy eligible securities from banks that need cash. Again banks reduce their lending and the interest rate increases.

(d) **Controlling the budget deficit**. This is an extension of policy (b) that recognizes that the government is likely to create more money and borrow more from banks if it has a large deficit to finance. So, apart from free market views that the role of government should be reduced (and so government expenditure and taxation should be reduced), the desire to control the supply of money may also point towards a small or zero deficit, or even to a budget surplus (which would permit a repayment of previous loans). Note that free market strategy and small budget deficits do not always coexist – in the 1980s, the USA has had a very large deficit with a free market strategy.

(e) **Interest rate policy**. Since the interest rate must increase if the government wants to reduce the supply of money (see section 17.5), it might choose simply to increase the interest rate when inflation is higher than desired without responding to any particular measure of the supply of money. An increase in the interest rate reduces the demand for money – and this allows a reduction in the supply, however it might be measured. The government can do this because it controls some interest rates (such as those on National Savings and minimum lending rate) directly, and can affect the interest rate on bonds through its own sales and purchases in the bond market. An increase in the interest rate reduces aggregate domestic demand because consumption and investment are reduced by the increased cost of borrowing, and then it is arguable whether the counter-inflationary effects of an increase in the interest rate arise through the reduction in the supply of money and the monetarist mechanism, or whether the reduction in aggregate domestic demand causes a reduction in prices in the way that macroeconomic analysis predicts. It may not matter much which analysis is the true description, in that both indicate a reduction in inflation, except that if the reduction in aggregate demand is the prime cause, then it may be argued that tax increases or reductions in government expenditure would also be effective (and perhaps more desirable for distributional reasons).

Control of the supply of money and an increase in the interest rate reduce inflation only if forces tending to cause an inflationary spiral are not strong. Free market strategy is based on the assumption that markets move rapidly as near to equilibrium as possible, so that prices rather than outputs fall to make the demand for money equal to a reduced supply. If the forces leading to an inflationary spiral are strong, then reductions in consumption and investment demand are likely to lead to reductions in outputs rather than in prices. In addition, if an increase in the interest rate leads to an appreciation in the exchange rate, then exports fall (as they become less competitive on world markets) and this further reduces demands for domestically produced goods.

Note finally that, in the UK, an increase in the interest rate leads to an increase in the Retail Prices Index because payments of interest on mortgage loans are included in the items that affect the cost of living. So the published inflation rate *increases* when the interest rate increases. Free market strategy relies on the assumption that the eventual decrease in the inflation rate caused by a reduction in the increase in the supply of money is permanent and more than offsets the increase caused by higher mortgage interest payments.

21.3.3 Exchange rates in a free market strategy

If monetary policy leads to changes in the interest rate, exchange rates will change too. The exchange rate between the pound and another country's currency appreciates if the UK interest rate increases relative to the interest rate on equivalent loans in the other country because foreigners demand pounds to lend to the UK government. So any attempt to reduce the inflation rate by reducing the supply of money causes the exchange rate to appreciate. Imports become cheaper (which helps to reduce the inflation rate as imported goods and materials are less expensive) and exports become more expensive for foreigners to buy, so that aggregate domestic demand falls. Reduced demand for exports and increased competition from imports is likely to reduce outputs and employment. However, the free market view implies that this reduction is only temporary, and that the temporary reduction in employment reduces real wages, which helps to restore the competitiveness of domestic goods against their foreign competitors. Employment increases again as demand for domestic goods increases, although the restoration of full employment may require that resources transfer from one sector to another. The free market view implies that this happens rapidly so that there is no long lasting unemployment.

Note that if the government changes the interest rate frequently to try to maintain some measure of the supply of money within a target range, exchange rates are likely to change frequently too. This might reduce foreign trade because people are less willing to buy goods from abroad if the exchange rate on the day of purchase is uncertain. To some extent this uncertainty can be offset by suitable purchases in forward exchange markets (see section 14.6.2), but frequent changes in the interest rate and in exchange rates do cause uncertainty for those making decisions on outputs and investment.

The desire to ensure stability in foreign exchange markets can lead directly to a policy of trying to maintain an exchange rate (say between the pound and the US dollar) at or near a predetermined level. Then changes in the interest rate are made to try to offset other changes in the exchange rate and not directly to control the supply of money or inflation. The various measures of the supply of money then respond to changes in the interest rate and, according to monetarist theory, the inflation rate changes as the supply of money changes. However, the stability of the prices of imports caused by the unchanging exchange rate will help to reduce cost-push inflationary pressures.

21.3.4 Growth policy in a free market strategy

In a market economy the rate of economic growth is determined by the level of investment, which is, in turn, determined by the interest rate on borrowed funds and, where there is uncertainty, by the optimism or pessimism of firms.

In a mixed economy the government may influence the interest rate by its monetary policy. *Ceteris paribus* an increase in the interest rate reduces investment and reduces the growth rate of national income. So monetary policies to reduce inflation may lead to a reduction in investment as the interest rate increases. However, market analysis argues that uncertainty and pessimism reduce inflation, and that these result from inflation. So firms become more confident in the future because inflation is reduced, and therefore invest more.

The government can also influence investment through its taxation policies. The profitability of an investment to an entrepreneur is affected by the level of taxes on profits, the extent to which expenditure on investment goods can be offset against tax liability, and the extent to which firms are encouraged to keep undistributed profits because they are taxed less than distributed profits. The types of investment that occur are also affected by the tax system: if tax relief is given for some kinds of investment (on housing for example) but not on others (such as support for students) then the tax system affects the pattern of investment. Finally, of course, the levels of direct and indirect taxes faced by consumers influence their demands for goods, and so affect the sales of firms and the potential profitability of investments. The free market strategy calls for the lowest possible tax rates and generally for few tax reliefs for special purposes, and argues that the supply-side effects of lower taxes lead to higher private investment.

21.3.5 Redistribution in a free market strategy

A full scale free market strategy does not involve policies that are deliberately designed to influence the income distribution. However, the choice of tax rates and the need to help groups with low incomes, such as the sick and the old, still leave some scope for the government to exercise discretion on the income distribution.

Policies that reduce rates of income tax are likely to reduce its redistributive effect, particularly if the maximum marginal rate is reduced towards the average rate paid by most people, as has happened in the 1980s in the UK and the USA. Obviously, policies that reduce social security benefits that are paid to unemployed people to try to persuade them to take employment have two redistributive effects:

(a) Those who do not find a job are made worse off by the cut in benefits.

(b) The lowest level of wages that employers need to pay is reduced.

The free market strategy also involves the privatization of nationalized industries and services that were previously supplied by the public sector. If health care or education services are privatized, and are available only to those who can afford to pay for them, then poorer people lose and richer people gain compared with a situation where these services are supplied to everyone by the state.

Supporters of the free market strategy claim that the incentive effects on employment and on growth of lower taxes will, at least in the long run, increase national income more than would otherwise occur. This additional national income is then available to increase the incomes of everyone, and so ultimately everyone, including poor people, is better off. Likewise, vigorous attempts to reduce inflation help to reduce unemployment and increase investment, so that national output increases. Again, the long-run increase in outputs could benefit everyone.

Despite these possible benefits from the supply-side policies of a free market strategy, there is no mechanism that guarantees that an increase in national income will benefit everyone. This can only occur if the government introduces policies that, for example, increase the real value of pensions and expenditure on health services for the poor as national income increases.

21.4 Interventionist strategy

The free market strategy argues that the government should reduce its role in the economy as far as possible, by cutting taxes, privatizing industries and so on, and that the government can reduce the inflation rate using monetary policy. The interventionist strategy, on the other hand, argues that the government may need to increase its expenditure and/or tax rates as a part of its policies on employment, inflation and growth. Supporters of the strategy are also likely to argue that some investments can best be made by the public sector, and that the government can have a positive policy on the redistribution of income.

21.4.1 Employment policy in an interventionist strategy

Macroeconomic analysis assumes that macroeconomic equilibrium national income can occur at less than the full employment level and that the government can use fiscal policy to increase employment by increasing its expenditure and/or reducing taxes to stimulate a multiplier process. The interventionist strategy argues that the government can use fiscal policy in a systematic and reasonably flexible way to increase employment when otherwise there would be considerable unemployment.

Interventionist governments have used fiscal policy to stimulate employment at least since the great depression in the USA (Keynes' *General Theory of*

Employment, Interest and Money provided some of the theoretical justification for this strategy). The objective is to attempt to keep the level of aggregate domestic demand, and hence national income, close to the full employment level. Government expenditure and taxation must be adjusted to try to offset changes in private investment and exports and, if necessary, in the propensities to save and to import. The use of this policy implies that national income responds quickly to changes in fiscal policy. If there are long time lags, the policy may turn out to be **destabilizing**: for example, a reduction in taxes designed to offset a fall in private investment may not affect national income until private investment has risen again.

Changes in fiscal policy require changes in monetary policy (see section 17.6), and this is likely to affect the interest rate. However, macroeconomic analysis argues that investment (and hence employment through the multiplier) is not greatly affected by changes in the interest rate and so fiscal policy is the most powerful policy available to the government.

21.4.2 Inflation policy in an interventionist strategy

An increase in government expenditure or a tax reduction increases the government's deficit. This causes an increase in borrowing by the government as its deficit rises, and hence to the possibility that the supply of money (M0 if the government creates more cash; M3 if the government borrows more from banks) increases. However, macroeconomic analysis rejects the use of the quantity equation, and uses the Phillips curve analysis to argue that inflation does not increase if aggregate domestic demand increases as long as the economy is not close to full employment. The increase in the supply of money is offset by a reduction in the velocity of circulation as people and firms hold more money.

In reality, outputs may not increase rapidly following an expansionist fiscal policy, so that there may be at least a temporary increase in inflation if the government attempts to expand employment too quickly. This increase in inflation may be offset in the longer term when firms can increase their outputs but, on the other hand, the initial inflation may remain in an inflationary spiral. In these circumstances, attempts to expand employment more quickly than firms can increase their outputs can lead to long-lasting inflationary pressures.

The interventionist strategy argues that the government can also use fiscal policy to reduce inflation by cutting aggregate domestic demand. An increase in taxation or a reduction in government expenditure reduces national income and hence reduces the inflationary gap. The Phillips curve shows that this is likely to reduce inflation as long as unemployment is low. However, it may be difficult to overcome the forces that give rise to an inflationary spiral, and a reduction in government expenditure or tax increase may reduce employment rather than inflation. Some interventionists argue that the inflation rate can be reduced only by a prices and incomes policy which places legal restraints on increases in wages and prices. Such a policy directly affects the forces that maintain the inflationary spiral in the economy, but can be successful only if the government can maintain it in the face of both market forces (which may imply changes in prices and wages because of changes in demands and supplies) and pressure from trades unions that reject restraints on their members' incomes.

21.4.3 Growth policy in an interventionist strategy

To some extent investment and hence growth are stimulated by fiscal policy that maintains full employment (as long as this does not greatly increase the interest rate and so make firms more uncertain and less optimistic). In addition, the government may adapt its fiscal policy to give firms incentives to invest by, for example, allowing tax reductions when a firm uses profits to finance investment rather than distributing them.

Many supporters of the interventionist strategy would argue that the government should itself invest to increase the growth rate. The private sector does not, it is argued, invest as much as is socially desirable, and so the government must invest too. If there is unemployment the government can increase both employment and the growth rate by increasing its own expenditure on investment goods. As we have discussed above, the borrowing implied by this policy may increase the interest rate, but this does not reduce private investment significantly. Macroeconomic analysis rejects the idea of crowding out when there is unemployment.

Macroeconomic analysis argues that firms' expectations rather than the interest rate are the major determinants of investment, and so private investment is likely to increase when firms expect that the government will use its fiscal policy to expand employment. So if the government wants to reduce unemployment, it may be able to give a small stimulus through its fiscal policy, and allow this to cause an increase in private investment that further expands national income and employment.

21.4.4 Exchange rates and foreign trade in an interventionist strategy

Fiscal policy that expands employment by increasing aggregate demand is also likely to lead to an increase in imports. This is particularly likely if aggregate demand expands more rapidly than firms can expand domestic outputs, so that some of the excess demand is met by imports. The balance of trade deteriorates and the exchange rate depreciates. On the other hand, if government borrowing increases because it has a larger deficit, the increase in the interest rate leads to an inflow of foreign currency from foreign lenders so that the exchange rate appreciates. The government can use monetary policy to change the interest rate to maintain a target exchange rate, particularly if it believes that changes in the interest rate have very little effect on investment and national income. Thus the government has two policies (fiscal and monetary) that it can use to try to meet two objectives (full employment and a stable exchange rate). It can set its expenditure and taxes to try to reach full employment, and set the interest rate to ensure that borrowing from abroad is sufficient to meet the resulting trade deficit at the target exchange rate. The government can use this dual policy as long as foreign lenders are willing to continue to lend despite the ongoing trade deficit; if they lose confidence, the government needs to cut expenditure or increase taxes to reduce the demand for imports.

The problem of ensuring full employment without a balance of trade deficit would be solved if the country could establish **export-led growth**. If exports increase because productivity has increased, the quality of goods has increased or the exchange rate has depreciated, then the export multiplier increases national income and employment, and the balance of trade also improves. Export-led growth has obvious advantages, although it may be difficult to achieve in practice, and other countries may also try to benefit from it, leading to successive depreciations as each country tries to make its exports more competitive.

21.4.5 Redistribution in an interventionist strategy

An interventionist government has much more scope for redistribution of national income than a government committed to a free market strategy. The government is not committed to lower government expenditure as a matter of strategy, and so it has considerable scope for increasing social security payments and spending on health and education services. This expenditure on its social policies also increases employment through the multiplier process. Indeed any redistribution from rich to poor is likely to increase the average propensity to consume as poor people save a smaller fraction of their incomes than rich people.

21.5 Exchange of views

These two strategies are very different, and each is the subject of considerable criticism by the others. Some of these disagreements are based on differences in opinion on the result of policy changes (for example, will an expansion in M3 lead to inflation or to a reduction in the velocity of circulation of money?). Other disagreements are based on different analyses of why things happen (for example, national income rises if taxes are cut; is this a supply-side outcome from greater incentives, or a demand-side multiplier effect?). Both of these sources of disagreement can be traced to differing views on the role of markets and prices: the free market strategy is based on the view that markets can (and should) operate efficiently; the interventionist strategy is based on the view that prices are slow to change and, particularly, that real wages do not fall quickly when there is unemployment.

21.5.1 Free market view of interventionist strategy

The interventionist strategy argues for active use of fiscal policy to affect employment and inflation. The free market view is that this can have, at best, a short-term effect, and that increases in one component of aggregate demand are soon crowded out by reductions in some other component. If the government increases its expenditures, demands for goods increase. Then, according to the free market view:

(a) The interest rate increases, private investment and consumption fall.
(b) The exchange rate appreciates because the interest rate rises, and so exports are reduced and imports increase.
(c) In so far as the extra government expenditure is financed by printing extra money or borrowing from banks, the supply of money increases and so prices rise.

The first two of these effects are crowding out (see section 17.6): they reduce other components of aggregate domestic demand, and so total outputs, and hence employment, do not increase. The third effect is likely to lead to continued inflation, which can only be offset by deflationary monetary policy.

21.5.2 Employment increases and accelerating inflation

The interventionist strategy argues for the use of fiscal policy, accompanied if necessary by increases in the supply of money, to increase employment. A tax reduction, for example, increases average real incomes, and so demands increase. The free market strategy argues that the increased demands lead, in the short term, to higher outputs as well as higher prices. In the longer term, households and firms become accustomed to the higher rate of inflation and make their decisions on the assumption that the new higher rate of inflation will continue; prices increase both as a result of the extra demands and because firms face higher wages, and real incomes return to their original level, with a higher inflation rate.

The short-term gains in employment are lost as the economy returns to equilibrium at the natural rate of unemployment. Unless it can use supply-side policies to increase incentives to work and remove imperfections that cause unemployment, the government can maintain the higher level of employment only by a further stimulus to demand that will maintain the higher outputs and increase the inflation rate further. Free market strategists argue that the Phillips curve relation (which implies that, if unemployment is lower, inflation is at a higher constant rate) is not valid. Instead, unemployment can remain below the natural rate only if the government is willing to cause accelerating inflation. Conversely, the government can reduce the inflation rate by contracting its deficit and the supply of money. In the short term outputs and employment are likely to fall, but unemployment returns to the natural rate as firms and households build the new inflation rate into their expectations.

This debate highlights the differing underlying assumptions: the free market criticism is valid if there is little scope for reducing involuntary unemployment, either because there is none (labour markets are in equilibrium) or because the economy is operating at the natural rate of unemployment, which might be reduced by supply-side policies but not by fiscal policy except in the short term.

The interventionist strategy on inflation is criticized by free market strategists because it does not give sufficient emphasis to the supply of money. Tax increases or reductions in government expenditure can reduce inflation only if the resulting smaller government deficit (or increased surplus) implies that there is less money in circulation because the government creates less cash or borrows less from banks (see section 18.8). The reduced deficit does not have multiplier effects because other expenditure is 'crowded in' (the opposite of crowding out) when government expenditure is reduced or taxes are increased.

21.5.3 Interventionist view of free market strategy

A free market strategy that cuts taxes to give greater incentives will, according to interventionists, increase national income through the multiplier. In this case, the direction of the predicted effect is the same, but the reason for the increase in employment is different.

The free market view argues that the incentive effect remains even if the government reduces its expenditure to the same extent that tax revenues fall. Indeed, free market strategies might well argue that the supply-side effects on national output are increased if the government reduces its expenditure. For example, reduced social security benefits increase incentives to work. Macroeconomic analysis, however, predicts that reductions in government expenditure cause reductions in employment – and that equal reductions in taxation and expenditure lead to a fall in national income (see section 17.3). So if the free market strategy succeeds in reducing government intervention in the economy, interventionists argue that national income and employment fall.

The use of monetary policy to reduce inflation is also criticized by interventionists because the velocity of circulation is not predictable. If the government attempts to reduce the supply of money (or its rate of increase) by reducing its deficit, then the multiplier leads to less employment; if the interest rate increases, the exchange rate appreciates and exports fall, again reducing outputs and employment through the multiplier. Thus monetary policy leads to a reduction in employment as well as to a reduction in the inflation rate. Indeeed, if the forces maintaining the inflationary spiral are strong, the main consequence of the restrictive monetary policy is a reduction in employment. Inflation will begin to fall only when there is sufficient unemployment for workers and their unions to be prepared to accept a cut in real wages (and hence break the inflationary spiral) rather than further job losses.

UK experience in the early 1980s suggests that a very considerable increase in unemployment is likely to occur as a result of contractionary monetary policy. Between June 1978 and June 1980, the interest rate on UK Treasury bills rose from 9.1 per cent to 15.8 per cent and the exchange rate (annual average) between the pound and the US dollar appreciated from £1 = $1.91

to £1 = \$2.33. These changes occurred because the government was attempting to reduce the rate of increase in the supply of money. Unemployment in 1978 was (as officially measured), 5 per cent of the labour force. By 1981, allowing the policy time to be effective, unemployment had risen to 9 per cent (an additional one million unemployed people).

Supporters of the free market strategy argue that the experience of the early 1980s does not illustrate the potential effectiveness of their favoured strategy in reducing inflation without a major increase in unemployment. The economy was not operating as a market economy can (and in their view should). There were many imperfections in markets, including union activity that prevented rapid adjustments in real wages and social security benefits and a tax system that reduced incentives to work and to invest. The supply-side policies of reducing union influence, privatization and direct tax reductions have, it is argued, increased the effectiveness of market forces later in the 1980s. Having reduced these imperfections and reduced the inflation rate, free market strategists argue that the economy can benefit from supply-side policies with reduced unemployment and low inflation.

21.6 ISLM analysis

Some aspects of the debate between the two strategies can be summed up using an ISLM analysis. This analysis is illustrated in a diagram based on two curves:

(a) The IS curve shows the combinations of interest rates and national income that give macroeconomic equilibrium. If the interest rate rises, saving increases, investment falls and government expenditure may increase as more interest must be paid on Treasury bills and other government debt. Tax revenues may change (savers have higher incomes, but borrowers are likely to have lower incomes), imports may rise and exports may fall if the exchange rate appreciates. Aggregate domestic demand therefore falls, and national income must fall to restore macroeconomic equilibrium.
(b) The LM curve shows the combinations of interest rates and national income that ensure that the demand for money equals the supply. If the interest rate increases, the demand for money falls, and so national income must increase to increase transactions demand and so increase demand to equal supply.

These two curves (IS_1 and LM_1) are shown in figure 21.1. These curves intersect at C, where national income is A and the interest rate is B.

21.6.1 Fiscal and monetary policies

A pure monetary policy involves no change in the position of the IS curve, because there is no change in government expenditure or in tax rates. If the government increases the supply of money, the LM curve shifts outwards from LM_1 to LM_2 in figure 21.1, because either national income must increase for

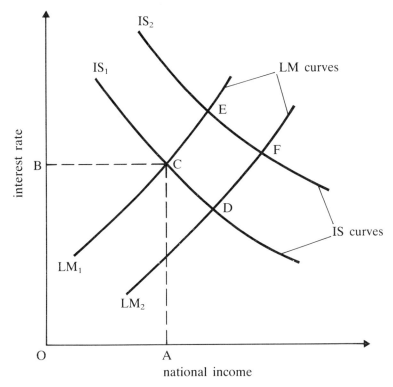

Figure 21.1 ISLM analysis
A change in fiscal policy shifts the IS curve; a change in monetary policy shifts the LM curve.

a given interest rate, or the interest rate must fall at a given national income, to ensure that the demand for money increases to equal the increased supply. So, as we should expect, an expansion of the supply of money increases national income and reduces the interest rate (point D).

A change in fiscal policy affects the IS curve. If the government increases its expenditure, or reduces tax rates, desired injections increase at each interest rate, and so national income increases. So the IS curve shifts from IS$_1$ to IS$_2$. If the additional deficit is financed entirely by additional borrowing, the LM curve is unchanged (LM$_1$) and the intersection is at E. If some or all of the additional deficit is financed by the creation of additional money, the LM curve also shifts, from LM$_1$ to LM$_2$. The creation of additional money causes a greater increase in national income and a smaller increase in the interest rate than a policy of financing the additional deficit entirely by borrowing (intersection at F).

21.6.2 Free market strategy

The free market view is that fiscal policy is relatively ineffective unless there is an accompanying monetary policy. In figure 21.2, the LM curves are vertical,

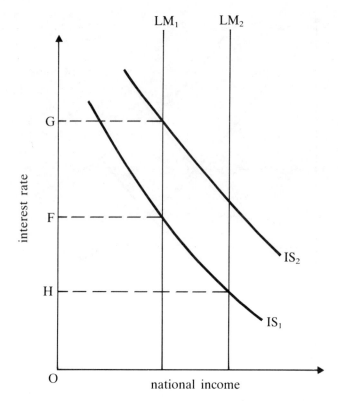

Figure 21.2 ISLM analysis in free market strategy
The LM curves are vertical as in figure 14.3.

implying that national income is unchanging given an unchanging supply of money. If there is an expansionary fiscal policy, the IS curve shifts from IS_1 to IS_2. If there is no change in the supply of money, the interest rate increases from F to G, and there is no change in national income. This reflects crowding out: the expansion in government expenditure generates an equal and opposite contraction in private investment so that aggregate demand is unchanged.

If there is an increase in the supply of money the LM curve shifts to LM_2. The downward slope of the IS curve implies that the interest rate falls from F to H, so that private investment increases. The increase in private investment increases national income to the extent implied by the increase in the supply of money. The free market view is that this increase in national income arises through price rises as there is no scope for an increase in employment, but this distinction between output and price increases is not captured by the ISLM diagram.

21.6.3 Interventionist strategy

The Keynesian interventionist view is based on the assumption that private investment and national income do not change much when the interest rate changes, so that the IS curve is nearly vertical as in figure 21.3. An expansionary fiscal policy shifts the IS curve from IS$_1$ to IS$_2$ and changes national income from Q to R if there is no change in the supply of money. If the government increases the money supply, but there is no change in fiscal policy, the LM curve shifts from LM$_1$ to LM$_2$ (with the IS curve remaining at IS$_1$) and there is a change in national income to S. The nearly vertical IS curve reflects the Keynesian view that fiscal policy is much more effective in changing national income (and hence employment) than monetary policy.

The conclusions from the two methods of analysis and their associated policy strategies are reflected in the different slopes of the curves. To some extent, therefore, it is legitimate to say that the debate between the strategies is a debate about the slopes of the curves. However, the different conclusions on the possibilities for increasing employment rather than inflation are lost in the ISLM diagram.

Box 11 shows the mathematical background for deriving the slopes of the IS and LM curves.

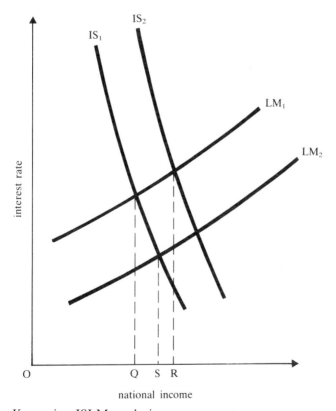

Figure 21.3 Keynesian ISLM analysis
The IS curves are nearly vertical, illustrating the small influence of the interest rate on investment.

Box 11   ISLM analysis in equation form

The IS curve is based on the national income equation

$$I + G + X = S + T + M \tag{21.1}$$

and on the relationships between these variables, national income and the interest rate.

(a) $I = I(r)$, with $\delta I/\delta r < 0$
(b) $S = S(Y,r)$, with $\delta S/\delta Y > 0$ and $\delta S/\delta r > 0$
(c) $T = T(Y)$, with $\delta T/\delta Y > 0$
(d) $X = X(r)$ (exports depend on the exchange rate, which in turn depends on the interest rate), with $\delta X/\delta r < 0$ (interest rate rises, exchange rate appreciates, exports become more expensive abroad)
(e) $M = M(Y,r)$ (imports increase if national income increases, and imports also depend on the exchange rate), with $\delta M/\delta Y > 0$ and $\delta M/\delta r > 0$.

Now $I + G + X = J$ (injections) and $S + T + M = W$ (withdrawals) and (a) to (e) above imply $\delta J/\delta Y = 0$, $\delta J/\delta r < 0$, $\delta W/\delta Y > 0$ and $\delta W/\delta r > 0$. So, if initially $J = W$ and then r rises, $W - J$ becomes positive. Equality between W and J can be restored only by a reduction in Y. So if r rises Y must fall to maintain macroeconomic equilibrium, and so the IS curve slopes down. The slope of the IS curve depends on the sizes of the various derivatives involved.

The LM curve is based on the demand for money or liquidity preference function $L = L(Y,r)$, with $\delta L/\delta Y > 0$ (transactions demand increases as Y increases) and $\delta L/\delta r < 0$. If the money supply is fixed, and r increases, L falls and Y must increase to restore equality in the money market. So the LM curve slopes upwards. The extreme monetarist argument is that $\delta L/\delta r = 0$, so that an increase in r has no effect on L, and the LM curve is vertical.

21.7 Summary

The free market strategy is based on market analysis and concludes that supply-side measures are most effective at reducing unemployment and increasing the growth rate. The government's monetary policy determines the inflation rate, and fiscal policy is largely ineffective because of crowding out. Redistributive policies introduce more government intervention and so make the economy operate less efficiently.

The interventionist strategy is based on macroeconomic analysis and concludes that fiscal policy can be effective in reducing unemployment, and that monetary policy is much less effective than fiscal policy. The government can stimulate growth through its own investment, and redistribution from rich to poor is likely to increase spending and so can also help to stimulate employment.

Topics and problems

(1) 'It is absurd to stick rigidly to one policy strategy; a mixed analysis must be better.' 'The government should stick rigidly to a single set of policies so

that fear of policy changes does not increase uncertainty and so reduce investment.' Comment.

(2) Trace the effects of an increase in unemployment benefits using each method of analysis.

(3) Examine the case for and against the means testing of state benefits.

(4) Should we welcome the single European market as a move towards free trade, or reject it as a threat to British jobs?

(5) 'State provision makes sure that everyone gets the health care and education that they need.' 'Private provision introduces competition so that people get what they want at the lowest price.' Discuss.

(6) Do figures for the UK economy on inflation and unemployment bear out the view that inflation accelerates when the government tries to maintain unemployment at too low a level?

(7) What do the two methods of analysis say about the consequences of reducing the extent of tax relief on housing mortgages?

(8) Use the two methods of analysis to trace the effects of an increase in the price of oil on the UK economy (the UK is a net exporter of oil).

(9) Use the two methods of analysis to trace the effects of an increase in the price of oil on the French economy (France is not an oil producer).

Chapter Twenty-two

Public choice

Utilitarianism — democratic methods of making public choices — liberalism — libertarianism — socialism in a mixed economy

---

22.1 Introduction

Most of this part has been devoted to a discussion of policies that governments use, or might use, to affect various aspects of the economy. We have concentrated on positive economics (what happens if...?) and prescriptive economics (how can the government...?). In this chapter we examine more closely the basis of some of the value judgements that underlie normative economics (the government should...). We examine how the government's choice of policies might reflect at least some of the views of its citizens.

The value judgements that we examine fall into two broad categories:

(a) Those that attempt to make public choices between policies on the basis of individuals' views of the outcomes of the available policies. These include **utilitarianism**, and choices based on methods of **voting**. Thus, when there is a vote between candidates (or, as in the USA for example, between proposals for alternative tax policies), individuals vote according to which of the outcomes they most prefer.

(b) Those that attempt to make a public choice on the basis of a principle that may or may not be reflected in individual views. These include **liberalism**, **libertarianism** and **socialism**, which are all political systems that approve of some policies or activities and disapprove of others. Socialists, for example, are likely to approve of taxes on profits and disapprove of privatization as issues of principle.

We use terms such as 'liberal' and 'socialist' with no intention of making a direct identification of these terms with the policies of similarly named political parties in the UK and elsewhere. In our discussion, the terms are used to describe particular sets of value judgements.

The two types of public choice mechanism are not directly identifiable with the two main policy strategies examined in the previous chapter. The interventionist strategy might result from a socialist viewpoint or from the outcome of some voting mechanism that reflects the views of interventionist citizens. Similarly, the free market strategy can be (and frequently is) the result of liberal or even libertarian convictions, but might also result from voting.

22.2 Utilitarianism

Utilitarianism is a method for making public choices that was developed in the nineteenth century by Jeremy Bentham (see section 9.6), James Mill (born in Forfar, Scotland, in 1773, died in 1836; employee of the East India Company 1819–36) and his son John Stuart Mill (born in London 1806, died in 1873; employee of the East India Company 1823–58), who is also associated with the development of liberalism (see section 22.4).

The utilitarian value judgement approves of the use of the policy that gives the greatest total of utility.

The value judgement requires that:

(a) Every person can express his or her preference for policies in the form of cardinal utility (see section 9.6.2). Each person must assign a number to each policy that reflects both the order of preferences (higher number is more preferred), and the intensity of preferences (a larger difference in utility between two policies implies a more intense preference).
(b) The cardinal utilities of different people can be added. This implies that one unit of utility has the same social value for each person.

Cardinal utility gives no more information that ordinal utility when we are concerned with individual choices between combinations of goods (see section 9.6). However, the additional information conveyed by cardinal utilities is crucial for the utilitarian value judgement. Table 22.1 compares the utilitarian choice for two lists of utilities. Columns 1 and 4 contain identical information on the order of Alan's preferences, and columns 2 and 5 contain identical information on the order of Bill's preferences, but the addition of the utilities of columns 1 and 2 implies that policy Y gives the greatest total utility, and

Table 22.1 Alternative utilitarian calculations

			Utilities			
Policy	1 Alan	2 Bill	3 Sum	4 Alan	5 Bill	6 Sum
X	6	1	7	10	2	12
Y	5	8	13	3	3	6
Z	1	9	10	2	16	18

so Y is the utilitarian public choice. The addition of the utilities of columns 4 and 5 shows that Z is the utilitarian public choice in these circumstances. The public choice of policy changes, although the order of the individuals' preferences has not changed.

22.2.1 Utilitarianism and income distribution

The utilitarian value judgement approves of a policy of taxation and transfer payments if the utility gained by those who receive the transfer payment exceeds the utility lost by those who pay taxes. This statement appears to require that we measure the size of the change in each person's utility. This may be judged to be impractical, either because we make the judgement that it is impossible to measure utility in any satisfactory way, or because it is very difficult to obtain information on the utilities of a large number of people. However, even if we cannot obtain information on the change in each person's utility, some redistributional policies are approved by the utilitarian value judgement if we make the following assumptions:

(a) Each person gains the same utility from each income level. This assumption does not imply that each person would buy the same goods if all incomes were the same. People's preferences can show diversity in determining the collections of goods that they buy from a given income, but not in the amount of utility gained from the income.
(b) The marginal utility from an additional unit of income decreases as the level of incomes increases (this is the assumption of the **diminishing marginal utility of income**). This assumption implies that £1 gained or lost by a richer person has less influence on the public choice than £1 gained or lost by a poorer person.

Table 22.2 shows an example in which these two assumptions hold. If Alan has an income of £7 and Bill has an income of £11, total utility is 40 + 100

Table 22.2 Utility scale with diminishing marginal utility of income

Income	Utility (common scale)
6	20
7	40
8	58
9	74
10	88
11	100
12	110

= 140. If a policy takes £2 in tax from Bill and gives it as a transfer payment to Alan, total utility increases to 148, and so the utilitarian value judgement approves the policy.

These assumptions do not approve all policies that make the income distribution more equal, because taxes levied to redistribute incomes may reduce incentives (as the free market strategy suggests; see section 21.3), and therefore reduce the total income that is available for distribution. If, in our example, a policy of equalizing incomes reduces total income to £16, so that each has £8, total utility is 116, which is less than total utility when Alan has an income of £7 and Bill has an income of £11.

The utilitarian value judgement is likely to approve of redistributive policies as long as the disincentive effect is not large, and as long as we accept the assumptions that each person obtains the same utility from each income level and that the marginal utility of income is diminishing. This inexact statement may be the strongest conclusion that we can reach on utilitarian principles because of the difficulties involved in measuring everyone's utilities in sufficient detail to use the utilitarian value judgement in a more exact way.

22.2.2 Utilitarianism and social cost–benefit analysis

If it is possible to use the utilitarian method, it can replace the social cost–benefit analysis in the assessment of projects hat have significant external effects. The project is accepted if the total utility gained over the life-time of the project exceeds the total utility lost. However, the utilitarian value judgement does not automatically reject policies that transfer income from one person to another (as social cost–benefit analysis does; see section 19.7), because the utilitarian value judgement assesses the effects of a policy in terms of utility, and not in terms of money. Even if utilities cannot be measured in the detail required, the assumption of the diminishing marginal utility of income can be incorporated into social cost–benefit analysis by giving greater weight to the monetary values of the gains or losses of poorer people than to those of richer people.

22.2.3 Utilitarianism and other policies

There is no clear-cut answer to the question of whether the utilitarian value judgement always approves or always disapproves of policies designed to increase employment or to control monopoly power, or of a particular way of running nationalized firms (such as the use of marginal cost pricing). In each case, the use of the value judgement requires that we assess the balance between the utility gained and the utility lost, and so no conclusion is possible in the absence of specific information on people's utilities.

22.3 Democratic methods of making public choices

The example of table 22.1 shows that we cannot make public choices in a consistent way by adding together numbers that represent ordinal utilities, because the same preferences give different public choices if they are represented by different numbers. However, adding utilities is not the only way of combining individual preferences. All political voting systems, for example, attempt to combine individual preferences between candidates to determine who wins the election. Is it possible to use a similar method to make a public choice between economic policies on the basis of a referendum, in which people are given a list of possible economic policies, and asked to state their preference between them in an ordinal way? We refer to these methods as **democratic** – not with any intention of implying that other methods are necessarily undemocratic, but to reflect the similarity of these methods to the methods of elections in democratic states and of resolving differences of opinion in other democratically organized groups.

In order to use any democratic method of making public choices, it is necessary that each person can state a preference between any two policies A and B (one of which may simply involve no change in the current policy – the *status quo*): he or she prefers A to B, he or she prefers B to A, or he or she is indifferent between A and B (see section 9.5).

22.3.1 Unanimous choices

A public choice between A and B can be made easily if all people state the they prefer A to B, and we make the value judgement that the public choice should agree with any unanimously expressed opinion of this kind. We could extend the idea of unanimity a little to include the possibility that some people prefer A to B and the remainder of the population is indifferent between A and B. No one expresses a preference for B over A and so, if the public choice is A in these circumstances, those who prefer A to B are satisfied, and those who are indifferent do not mind which of the two is the public choice.

Unaminous judgements can be made only after each person has taken account of all aspects of a policy. This implies that policy A is not necessarily chosen on the basis of unanimity simple because everyone has more goods if A is chosen than if B is chosen. Some people may prefer B to A even in these circumstances because of the effects of the two policies on the income distribution. For example, suppose that a policy involves reducing taxes paid by the rich and reducing transfer payments to the poor, and that this policy has the supply-side effect of increasing national income and employment so that everyone has more goods. The rich gain very much more than the poor from the policy. Some may disapprove of this policy because it makes the income distribution less equal. This implies that there need not be unanimous approval even of a policy that improves the efficiency of the operation of the economic system, because some people may disapprove of its effect on the income distribution.

22.3.2 Conflicts of opinion

In a society consisting of a large number of people it is unlikely that many, if any, policies would be unaminously approved. There is likely to be conflict of opinion on most, if not all, policy proposals. How can a democratic public choice be made in these circumstances?

   In political and committee decision-making, conflicts are often resolved by agreeing that the view of the majority prevails over the view of the minority. It is possible to use majority voting to make a public choice of an economic policy, but there are at least two possible objections to this use of majority voting:

(a) It ignores the strength of people's feelings. The minority may be passionately opposed to a policy, whereas the majority favours it, but no member of the majority has particularly strong views.
(b) It may be inconsistent if there are several possible policies, and if people have widely differing views. For example, the government puts forward three possible sites, X, Y and Z, for an airport and the judgement is to be made by 20 people (it could, of course, be 20 million), whose preferences are given in table 22.3.
   Then if a series of votes is taken, we find that:

   (i)   12 people prefer X to Y, and 8 prefer Y to X. So a majority prefers X to Y.
   (ii)   13 people prefer Z to X, and 7 prefer X to Z. So a majority prefers Z to X.
   (iii) 15 people prefer Y to Z, and 5 prefer Z to Y. So a majority prefers Y to Z.

The government faces a problem: whichever site it chooses, there is always some other site that is preferred by a majority.

Table 22.3 Preferences giving inconsistent majority decision

Number of people	Most preferred policy	Middle policy	Least preferred policy
8	Y	Z	X
7	X	Y	Z
5	Z	X	Y

22.3.3 Tactical voting behaviour

Majority voting is not the only democratic method of making public choices when people have conflicting views. For example, each person could be given one vote that he or she can allocate to a policy that he or she likes best, and the public choice is the policy that receives the most votes (this is the method of voting in most UK political elections). In the example of table 22.3, 7 people would give their single vote to X, 8 to Y and 5 to Z. Site Y is the public choice.

A major difficulty with this method of making the public choice is that the five people who give their votes to Z may realize that Z will not be the public choice. If these 5 people give their votes to site X, then X has 12 votes and Y has 8 votes, so that X is the public choice. By giving their votes to X rather than to Z, these 5 people can ensure that X is the public choice, instead of Y. Since these five people prefer X to Y, they have an incentive to vote for X (so that X is the public choice), rather than for Z (in which Y is the public choice). These 5 people can influence the outcome of the procedure for selecting the public choice by **tactical voting**, rather than by revealing their true preferences.

The possibility of tactical misrepresentation of preferences arises in other methods of making public choices, including some, such as social cost–benefit analysis, that are not democratic methods in the sense that we have used the term. If a person is aksed how much money he requires to compensate him for some harmful external effect, he has an incentive to overstate the amount to influence the outcome in his favour (see section 19.7.1). Wherever it arises, the incentive to state untrue preferences has serious implications for public choice, because a policy appears to be the best for society as a whole although it is not truly the best. If society decides to use a particular method (such as voting or social cost–benefit analysis) to evaluate policies, it is undesirable that the outcome is in fact the result of untruthful statements of preferences.

22.3.4 'Impossibility problem'

We have seen that a variety of methods of making public choices can run into difficulties: majority voting may not give a clear public choice (as in table 22.3); the allocation of a single vote and the use of social cost–benefit analysis may be open to the tactical misrepresentation of preferences. Is there any way of making public choices that avoids both these difficulties, and yet reconciles conflicting views in an acceptable way?

The answer to this question is no, there is no way of making a public choice that satisfies the following four conditions:

(a) The method ensures the public choice agrees with unanimously stated preferences.
(b) At least some conflicting views are reconciled, in the sense that more than one person's preferences affect the public choice. That is, the method

ensures that there is no individual who can always dictate the public choice between policies.

(c) The public choice is clearly made: the method ensures that, whatever preferences people express, there in one policy that is the clear public choice. The method must rule out the difficulty raised by the preferences of table 22.3 for the method of majority voting.

(d) The method excludes the possibility that any person, or group of people, can affect the outcome by a tactical statement of untrue preferences.

This result stems from the work of Kenneth Arrow (born 1921; professor of economics, Harvard and Stanford Universities; Nobel prizewinner in economics 1972), who demonstrated a related conclusion to the one stated here in *Social Choice and Individual Values* (1951; listed in the bibliography). The examples that we have given do not constitute a proof of the conclusion (proofs of results of this kind are fairly complex mathematically), but they demonstrate the difficulties that can arise if we attempt to base the public choice of economic policies on people's stated preferences. The attempt to avoid the difficulty of measuring and comparing cardinal utilities raised by the utilitarian method of making public choices has led to other difficulties.

22.3.5 Democratic methods and the choice of policies

If we are prepared to use a democratic method, even though it may give no clear public choice, or it may be open to tactical statements of untrue preferences, the choice of policies depends on individual preferences. It is impossible to say, in advance of detailed knowledge of preferences, what sorts of policies are likely to be approved. The use of the method reflects the difficulty of making judgements of policies from which some people gain and others lose. However, the use of democratic method of making public choices implies that the government is prepared to accept the use of policies that have harmful effects on some people: the democratic method allows the possibility that people 'suffer for the social good'. We shall see in section 22.5 that this possibility is not approved by all value judgements that might be used to make public choices.

22.4 Liberalism

An alternative approach to that of the previous two sections involves making public choices according to a principle that may or may not give public choices that reflect the preferences of people in society. The first of these that we consider is liberalism (see the note on terms at the end of section 22.1).

The liberal value judgement of the nineteenth century supported the free market views of Adam Smith and his followers. The essential point of the liberal value judgement is that each person should be free to make the best of his or her own resources. A person's opportunities should be restricted only to the extent necessary to ensure that everyone else is also free to make the best use of his or her own resources. There is a close relation between this value judgement and support for the free market strategy, which aims at the removal or limitation of imperfections, the limitation of market influence, the control of external effects and the reduction of government intervention beyond that needed to remove or limit imperfections.

22.4.1 Liberalism and income distribution

As we have seen in discussing the free market strategy, the value judgement that each person should be free to make the best use of his or her own resources is opposed to many policies that redistribute incomes. Government intervention should be kept to a minimum, and so policies that redistribute can be justified by the liberal value judgement only on some restricted grounds:

(a) Policies that redistribute income by reducing monopoly profits and other incomes derived from imperfections are approved by the liberal value judgement, because the redistribution is the result of making the system more nearly perfect.
(b) Policies that give incomes to the very poor may be approved by the liberal value judgement if it is argued that a person who is starving, or close to starving, is not free to make the best use of his or her own resources. So to give some freedom of choice to everyone, some people may need transfer payments, and some taxes may be needed to finance these.

In so far as redistribution to reduce poverty is justified by the liberal value judgement, the redistribution should be made through cash payments. The purpose of the redistribution is to promote freedom for people to make the best use of the resources that they have, and this freedom is enhanced if they are given money that they can spend how they like, rather than if they are given goods at subsidized prices (see section 20.5).

The liberal approval of cash payments rather than subsidies extends to goods that are provided without charge by the state. If a redistributive policy is needed to ensure that everyone receives some eduction, the liberal value judgement approves a policy of giving people money that they can spend on education supplied by privately owned firms (at the school of their choice) rather than providing schooling without charge. Similarly, if a redistributive measure is needed to ensure that everyone has the opportunity for adequate health care, the liberal value judgement approves cash payments that enable everyone to buy private health insurance, for use in privately owned hospitals, rather than the supply of a state health service.

A difficulty with the liberal view of redistribution is that taxpayers may be unwilling to approve cash payments rather than subsidies on goods. The liberal value judgement states that no one has the right to say how another person should spend his or her money, but it is probable that many people take a paternalistic view of redistributive policies because they are unwilling to pay taxes to finance transfer payments to people who then spend the money received on goods that the taxpayers believe to be undesirable. This paternalistic feeling is likely to cause difficulties for a political party in a democratic state that proposes to substitute cash payments for state-supplied or state-subsidized goods.

An intermediate solution that compromises on this difficulty is the provision of **vouchers**: people receive vouchers that they must spend on, say, education but they retain the freedom to buy education from whatever school they choose. The liberal value judgement approves the freedom of choice involved in this policy, and it also approves the likelihood that there would be a number of firms supplying schooling in an area, so that no school has significant market influence and society benefits from competition between them. These schemes are, however, largely untried in practice, perhaps because of the administrative complications of setting them up and the vested interests of the present suppliers of eduction and other goods that are subsidized or supplied without charge by the government.

22.5 Libertarianism

The liberal value judgement is based on the view that each person should be free to choose how to use the income that he can make by using his own resources. The only restrictions on what an individual may do come from the necessity to ensure that others are also free and, in the liberal view, this implies the removal of imperfections and the redistribution of income to remove at least the most extreme poverty. The libertarian value judgement goes further: it states that all forms of government intervention are wrong, because they force people to act in ways that they would not otherwise act. For example, people do not pay taxes voluntarily. They are **coerced** into doing so by the power of the state.

Government actions are imposed on some people, except in the rare circumstances that a government action is unanimously agreed to be desirable. According to the libertarian value judgement, all coercive acts are undesirable, so that the only role for government is as a co-ordinator of voluntary actions. For example, a group of people may be prepared to pay a fraction of the cost of installing and operating street lights, and be willing to delegate the administrative aspects to an elected town council. According to the libertarian value judgement, those who want street-lighting cannot force others to pay a part of the cost of providing it, and the only legitimate function of the town council is co-ordination.

22.5.1 Libertarianism and property protection

In its most extreme form, the libertarian value judgement excludes even the limited government intervention allowed in our discussion of market economies in parts II and III: the provision of property protection and the enforcement of contracts. Of course, it is likely that most people want these services, and if everyone is willing to pay an equal share of the costs of providing them, the state can act in a co-ordinating role without coercion. The extreme libertarian value judgement does not approve of a policy that provides these services to anyone who is unable, or unwilling, to pay his or her share of the cost. To provide services to those who cannot afford them requires that others pay more than they would wish to do, and so they are coerced. According to the libertarian value judgement, people are free to pay a protection agency that helps to protect their property and enforce their contracts by taking retribution against thieves and contract breakers. Those who cannot pay, or do not want to pay, must protect their property or enforce their contracts through their own efforts.

Some people, including Robert Nozick in *Anarchy, State and Utopia* (see the bibliography), who otherwise support the libertarian value judgement, make an exception of these basic legal services. They justify this exception on the grounds that people whose property is not protected, and who cannot seek legal help to enforce contracts, can be coerced by those who do have these protections. If Alan's property is not protected and Bill's property is protected, then Alan is coerced by Bill if Bill takes goods that Alan has made, because Bill can obtain legal protection if Alan tries to seize them back. So some libertarians regard state intervention as necessary to avoid this sort of coercion.

22.5.2 Libertarianism and poverty

The UK system of redistributive taxation and transfer payments would undoubtedly not be approved by the libertarian value judgement. However, it is likely that most people, perhaps everyone, would agree to participate in an insurance scheme that, for example, gives an income to anyone who becomes too ill to work, and the libertarian value judgement approves of state coordination of this voluntary insurance. In addition, the libertarian value judgement approves of voluntary payments to help the poor, and so a version of the libertarian view lies behind the idea that people and families should 'help themselves' rather than relying on transfer payments from the state.

The libertarian value judgement presents a challenge even to those who do not agree with it, because it raises the fundamental question of the right of the state to intervene. No other value judgement that we discuss does this: the utilitarian value judgement, the value judgement that lies behind democratic methods of public choice, the liberal value judgement and the socialist value judgement discussed in the next section all assume that the state has the right to intervene in certain circumstances. The libertarian value judgement rejects this assumption, and those who do not agree with it must justify the right of the state to intervene in a coercive way that prevents people from acting as they would like to do.

22.6 Socialism in a mixed economy

The socialist value judgement of the public choice of economic policies is based mainly on two statements:

(a) Workers in privately owned firms are exploited because some income is paid to the suppliers of factors other than labour (see section 10.9.4). This exploitation contributes to an unjust income distribution.
(b) Market economic systems are far from perfect, and so they are likely to be inefficient (because, for example, persistent unemployment occurs).

On the basis of these statements, the socialist value judgement approves of:

(a) The nationalization of firms and of the land. This contributes to the reduction of exploitation, because the profits of nationalized firms are not paid to capitalists but can be used to pay for social benefits. The government can direct nationalized firms to invest in projects as a way of increasing employment.
(b) Macreconomic policies that are designed to increase employment. Those who make the socialist value judgement are likely to use macroeconomic analysis rather than market analysis because of the belief that market systems are far from perfect, and so they believe that macroeconomic policies, particularly fiscal policies, can be effective in increasing employment.
(c) Policies that redistribute national income through taxes and social benefits. Increases in social benefits imply increases in government expenditure, and this contributes to the increase in employment.
(d) Government planning of at least the most important economic activities to improve the efficiency of the economic system.

In chapter 24 we shall examine the economic systems in which the socialist value judgement causes all major activities to be centrally planned.

22.7 Summary

Governments have a range of alternative policies available, and the analysis of public choice is concerned with the way in which the government chooses between these policies. This choice involves a value judgement, which may be that public choices should be based on individual preferences, or on some principle that may or may not be supported by a large number of people.

All the value judgements considered, except the libertarian, approve of some government intervention in the economic system. The liberal value judgement generally approves of policies designed to improve the efficiency of the process of allocating resources, and may approve some policies that redistribute incomes. The utilitarian and democratic methods and the socialist value judgement may approve of a much broader range of redistributive policies.

The utilitarian method is difficult to use in most circumstances because it is very difficult, if not impossible, to measure utilitiies. Democratic methods do not require the measurement of cardinal utilities, but some people can influence the outcome in their own favour by stating untrue preferences. Alternatively, some democratic methods (including the use of majority decisions) do not provide consistent public choices in all circumstances.

Topics and problems

(1) 'Everyone wants the economic system to allocate resources efficiently, but people disagree strongly about the desirable income distribution. So governments should concentrate on policies to increase efficiency, and ignore policies that can change the distribution.' Discuss.

(2) Are government actions coercive? If so, is this coercion undesirable?

(3) Many states have (nominally or actually) an established or dominant religion. Can, and should, these countries base their public choices on that religion? If so, what might be the outcome?

(4) A market system operates efficiently only if the owners of all scarce resources receive an income. Does this imply that the socialist view that workers are exploited is unfounded?

(5) 'Market economies may be inefficient and unjust, but planned societies are worse.' Discuss.

(6) How might a system of vouchers for higher and further education in the UK be operated? Would such a system be desirable?

(7) Individuals have the preferences listed in table 22.4.

Table 22.4 Preferences for use in problem 7

Individual	Most preferred	Next	Next	Least preferred
Alan	w	x	y	z
Bill	x	z	y	w
Colin	y	z	w	x

What, if any, is the public choice given by the method of majority voting?

What, if any, is the public choice if each person has one vote that he can give to one alternative? The votes are then added and the public choice is the policy that gets the most votes. Ties are resolved by giving Bill an additional, casting vote.

Does any person have an incentive to give his vote to other than his most preferred policy in the second of the methods of public choice above?

Part V

Development and planning

We discussed the principles that lie behind the international division of labour in chapter 2, and in various subsequent chapters we have analysed international economic transactions. International specialization and transactions affect the distribution of income between countries, and the most striking aspect of that distribution is the contrast between the incomes of developed and underdeveloped countries. We examine some of the problems of these countries in chapter 23, including the effects of trade between rich and poor countries, aid from richer to poorer, the advantages and disadvantages of investment by multinational firms in less developed countries, and international indebtedness.

Finally, in chapter 24, we examine planned economies, both to examine the ways in which they operate and to compare them with the market and mixed economies that have been the subject of the remainder of the book.

Chapter Twenty-three

Economic development

Major aspects of development — investment by multinational firms — international trade and development — international debts and development

23.1 Introduction

We have discussed market and mixed economies mainly in the context of richer countries, using UK examples. However, many countries are not in the fortunate position of the UK because their national incomes (per head of population) are smaller and in some cases national income is rising less quickly than the population. In many less developed countries the majority of the population works on the land, and so we can ask a fundamental question:

> How can a country move from the situation of many less developed countries, in which most of the population produce agricultural goods using methods that are very inefficient in comparison with those used in richer countries, to a situation in which it has gained at least some of the benefits of specialization and exchange?

There are approximately 50 countries (including the most populated, China and India), whose reported national income per head was less than US $500 in 1984. In comparison, the US national income per head was $15,500 in that year, and that of the UK was $8,500. These figures reveal the gap between the developed and the less developed countries of the world. However, figures of national income per head do not give an exact reflection of the size of the gap (although it is not clear whether the gap is overstated or understated by national income per head). There are several problems involved in comparing national income statistics:

(a) The figures quoted are all converted into US dollars, but exchange rates do not reflect the relative purchasing powers of currencies. The quantities of goods that can be bought with a dollar in the USA may be very different from the quantities of goods that can be bought in India with the rupees that can be bought for a dollar.

(b) If the conversion to US dollars is done at the market exchange rates (or at official exchange rates where markets do not operate) the figures for national income per head change when exchange rates change. For example, if the rupee depreciates by 10 per cent against the dollar, the reported Indian national income falls by 10 per cent when measured in dollars, even though there is no change in Indian national income measured in rupees.

(c) Many countries' national income figures are either estimated on the basis of very incomplete information or exclude some goods. For example, it is extremely difficult to record the production of goods by farmers when they consume many of the goods themselves. There is no market transaction to record and little possibility of obtaining the information accurately. This problem also arises in richer countries, but on a much smaller scale, because a much smaller fraction of the total output of the economy is used by the producer.

In addition, national income figures do not describe all aspects of the outcome of a country's economic system (see section 6.7), and so they do not reveal all aspects of the difference between developed and less developed countries. There are many non-economic aspects of development that are beyond the scope of this book, but that may affect the extent to which people are prepared to adapt their traditional economic system and adopt new methods of production.

23.2 Major aspects of development

The development of the economy of a less developed country has at least three aspects.

(a) The **agricultural sector** must provide more food using fewer resources, so that people working on the land can do other jobs needed for development. In principle this may not be difficult, because there is **disguised unemployment** in the agricultural sectors of many less developed countries. The marginal product of labour in agriculture is low (possibly zero), so that the removal of some people from the land would not reduce total agricultural output significantly. A family farm may provide jobs for all the family but could be run with a smaller workforce. The practical problems of reducing the agricultural workforce and of increasing the efficiency of those who remain are considerable, particularly because people are unlikely to be willing to move from the land if they are unsure how they will then obtain food, and they are unlikely to be willing to specialize in growing one crop if they fear a harvest failure.

(b) The country must build up its **infrastructure**, including transport links, water supply and drainage, electricity supply, medical provision and eductional facilities to improve the skills of the workforce. The improvement of transport and communications is vital to development because more goods must be traded if people specialize, and they are unlikely to be willing to specialize if they are unsure whether they will be able to obtain the other goods that they need.

(c) The country must build up some industries other than its agricultural sector. If a country can develop a very efficient agricultural sector, and export enough food so that it receives sufficient foreign currency to buy all the imports that it needs, the country may not need to **industrialize** to develop. However, the prices of agricultural goods fluctuate, and a poor harvest may reduce the country's export earnings very considerably. A similar problem is faced by countries that rely heavily on exports of one basic material. For example, over 90 per cent of Zambia's exports are of copper, the price of which fell by more than 50 per cent relative to prices of other goods (that Zambia would like to import) between 1973 and 1982. So most countries want, if possible, to diversify by building up other industries.

The main constraint on development is likely to be a lack of equipment, skills, energy and materials, which are available abroad but which the country cannot buy because it has little foreign currency and little prospect of selling goods abroad to obtain foreign currency.

Improvements in the efficiency of the agricultural sector, and the development of industries other than agriculture, might be left to privately owned firms, particularly those based in other countries that have the necessary equipment, skills and foreign currencies to invest in major projects. However, infrastructure projects are less likely to be undertaken by privately owned firms because the private cost exceeds the private benefit (because the beneficiaries can afford to pay very little for using roads or water pipes), even though the social benefit exceeds the social cost. The International Development Agency, and other organizations that provide official and private aid, finance projects without expecting a commercial return.

23.3 Investment by multinational firms

A privately owned firm may look beyond its own country when it is considering investment projects. A firm that operates in more than one country is a **multinational firm**, and most large firms are multinationals. An important criterion for a multinational firm that is deciding on the location of an investment project is the cost and availability of the necessary inputs, including materials, labour and land. A less developed country may have abundant unskilled labour, available at wages far below those in richer countries (particularly if the poorer country has restrictions on the activities of trades unions) and this makes investment in less developed countries attractive to multinational firms. In addition, the less developed country may supply some of the materials needed. However, a firm must weigh these potential advantages against the costs involved in:

(a) Bringing in or training workers with the skills needed to build the factory and to operate the necessary equipment.

(b) Importing equipment that is unavailable in the less developed country.
(c) Transporting the goods produced to the firm's main markets, which are likely to be in richer countries.

The benefits to a country of private investment by firms based abroad are mainly the effects of increased employment. Macroeconomic analysis predicts that the increase in employment has a multiplier effect on national income, so that the outputs of and employment in domestically based industries are increased by the foreign investment. Firms based in the less developed country or its government may not be able to increase investment and employment, because investment requires the use of skilled labour and equipment that a multinational firm can obtain easily, but that may not be available to domestic firms or the government because the country has no foreign currency with which to pay for the imports.

23.3.1 Transfer pricing, profits and taxation

The multiplier effects of foreign investment are reduced to the extent that some of the incomes generated in the less developed country by the multinational firm are paid to shareholders abroad and to skilled workers who send wages back to their own country. A less developed country may try to reduce the outflow of profits by taxing the profits of multinationals, so that more of the benefits of its operations remain within the country. However, the extent of a multinational firm's profits in any single country is ambiguous, and the firm can use that ambiguity to reduce its tax bill and to repatriate profits to the country where the multinational firm is based, as the following example shows.

Suppose that a multinational firm produces its product in two stages. Stage 1 (processing materials into partly finished goods) takes place in less developed country Alpha. Stage 2 (processing the partly finished goods into finished goods) takes place in richer country Beta, where all the goods are sold. The firm's average cost of production in Alpha is 200 units of Alpha currency (written as $A200), and its average cost of production in Beta is 100 units of Beta currency ($B100). These costs include all payments for labour, land, materials and equipment, but do not include normal profit. The exchange rate is $A2=$B1. The firm's average revenue (selling price) in Beta is $B300.

The firm's average cost, measured in Beta-currency, is $B200 ($A200 × 1/2 + $B100) and its profit per unit of output is $B100. Simple arithmetic suggests that half of this profit is made in each country, so that firm's accounts would show that its factory in Alpha made a profit per unit of $A100 ($B50) as in the first column of table 23.1. The factory in Alpha is credited with the **transfer price** of the partly finished good, which is $B150 = $A300. This transfer price is then a part of the costs of the factory in Beta.

However, suppose that the government of Alpha taxes firms' profits at a higher rate (50 per cent) than the government of Beta (25 per cent). If the firm credits each factory with an equal profit, using a transfer price of $A300 ($B150), the firm pays a total of $A50 + $B12.5 (=$B37.5) in tax. If the firm

Table 23.1 Effects of transfer pricing on firm's accounts in Alpha and Beta, and on tax payments

	$A	$B	$A	$B
Transfer price	300	=150	220	=110
In Alpha				
Average revenue				
(= transfer price)	300	(=150)	220	(=110)
Average production cost	200	(=100)	200	(=100)
Profit per unit	100	(=50)	20	(=10)
Tax paid per unit (rate 50%)	50	(=25)	10	(=5)
In Beta				
Average revenue				
(= selling price)		300		300
Average cost				
(= average production cost				
+ transfer price)		250		210
Profit per unit		50		90
Tax paid (rate 25%)		12.5		22.5
In Alpha and Beta (converted to $B)				
Average revenue				
(= selling price)		300		300
Average production cost		200		200
Profit per unit		100		100
Tax paid per unit		37.5		27.5

sets a lower transfer price ($220, as in columns 3 and 4 of table 23.1), it increases the apparent profit in Beta and reduces it in Alpha, thus reducing its total tax bill. In the absence of regulation of the firm's transfer price, it avoids tax altogether in Alpha by setting its transfer price at $A200.

A multinational firm might extend this principle by using a **tax haven**. In our example, the firm established a subsidiary in Gamma, where it has an office but does not perform any part of the production process of the good. One unit of Gamma currency ($G) exchanges for $A10 or $B5. The firm can then transfer the partly finished goods from Alpha to Gamma at transfer price of $A200 ($G20), and then transfer them again for $G40 ($B200) as in table 23.2. The firm appears to make no profit in Alpha or Beta. All of its profit appears to accrue to its subsidiary in Gamma, where its profit per unit is $G20 ($B100). If Gamma charges no tax on this profit, the firm escapes paying tax.

Most countries have legislation that is designed to try to prevent firms from using transfer pricing and tax havens to avoid taxes, but it is not easy for any country (particularly a less developed country) to investigate a multinational firm to see whether it is using a fair transfer price. The major problem is that the partly finished goods are not sold on a market from one factory to another

Table 23.2   Effects of using tax haven

	$A	$G	$B
In Alpha			
Average revenue (= transfer price to Gamma)	200		(= 100)
Average production cost	200		(= 100)
Profit per unit	0		
In Gamma			
Average revenue (= transfer price to Beta)		40	(= 20)
Average cost (= transfer price from Alpha)		20	(= 100)
Profit per unit		20	(= 100)
Tax paid		0	
In Beta			
Average revenue (= selling price)		300	
Average cost (= average production cost + transfer price)		300	
Profit per unit		0	
In all countries (converted to $B)			
Average revenue (= selling price)		300	
Average production cost		200	
Profit per unit		100	
Tax paid per unit		0	

(as they would be if the factories in the two countries were owned by different firms), and so there is no market price that can be used to establish a transfer price to value goods that a multinational firm produces in one country and transfers to another.

23.3.2 Multinational firms and exchange rates

The activities of multinational firms can have significant effects on exchange rates. In the short term, multinationals can transfer large amounts of liquid funds (hot money) from one currency to another. These funds move according to the firms' expectations of changes in exchange rates (see section 14.6). For example, the increase in liquid funds held by oil-producing firms (and by oil-exporting countries) after the oil price increases of 1973–4 and 1979 had significant effects on changes in exchange rates.

In the longer term, investment, production and sales in a country affect foreign exchange markets in several ways:

(a) The firm demands the country's currency to pay the costs of establishing a factory.
(b) When a firm produces and sells in a country its revenue in the country may exceed its cost there, so that it has a surplus that it may want to transfer out of the country to pay as dividends to shareholders or to use for investment in other countries. The firm supplies the country's currency.
(c) If the firm's revenue in a country is less than its costs in that country, it must transfer money into the country to continue production there. So the firm demands the country's currency.

A multinational firm's investment plans in a country depend both on its expectation of future costs and revenues in the country and on its expectations of changes in exchange rates. A depreciation reduces the cost of buying the currency to establish a factory and to pay any excess of costs over revenues in the country; a depreciation also reduces the value of money repatriated from the country.

23.3.3 Regulating multinational firms

A government is likely to want to regulate the activities of multinational firms to attempt to reduce the outflow of profits, both to increase the size of the multiplier effect of their investment and to prevent a depreciation of the currency. However, a multinational firm is in a strong position to negotiate favourable terms with a government, because it can threaten to withdraw from the country and close its factories there. This may have serious effects on employment in the country, and a government may be unwilling to face the possibility that the firm will withdraw. This problem is not faced only by less developed countries: multinational firms have obtained aid from governments of industrialized countries on threat of withdrawal (for example, Chrysler obtained £162 million from the UK government in 1976 as a part of an agreement to continue to produce in the UK).

Some governments threaten to nationalize the assets of multinational firms (perhaps without compensation), and to some extent this provides the country with a counter-threat to a multinational firm's threat to withdraw. However, many factories operated by multinational firms rely on the firm's own skilled labour, which is not readily available elsewhere, on the firm's factories elsewhere for materials, and on the firm's established sales network to sell the goods produced. A nationalized firm may have none of these advantages, and so nationalization is not always a viable counter-threat for a less developed country.

23.4 International trade and development

A country that is attempting to build up an industrial sector needs to be able to sell the goods produced. To some extent firms can sell within the country, but the principle of comparative advantage (see section 23.2) and the benefits of the division of labour imply that a country should not attempt to build up a large number of different industries. Instead, it should concentrate on some to gain the advantages of specialization, and export some of the goods produced to obtain foreign currencies to pay for imports of other goods. However, this is not necessarily easy for two reasons:

(a) Firms need time to grow to an efficient size.
(b) Foreign firms may attempt to exclude the new firms from their markets.

23.4.1 Infant industry tariffs

While a firm is growing to its most efficient size its average production costs are higher than they eventually will be, and the firm is not competitive with established firms in other countries. The **infant industry** argument for tariffs is often applied here: the firm in the less developed country should be protected from international competition, at least in its own domestic market, while it grows. However, a firm that has protection when it is an infant industry may never become efficient enough to compete with firms in other countries, because it does not reduce costs below the protected level. For example, if a tariff of 50 per cent is placed on a good that foreign producers supply for £10, the domestic firm can sell profitably in the domestic market as long as its average cost is less than £15. If the firm finds it very difficult to reduce its average cost to £10, it may decide to continue to produce only for the protected domestic market, so that it does not export at all. If the government threatens to remove the tariff, the firm can argue that it would close down, thus increasing unemployment, and increasing imports as foreign firms supply the market, so that the currency depreciates. So infant industry tariffs may never be removed, and the firm may never be able to sell exports in competition with firms from other countries.

23.4.2 Foreign competition

The tactics that foreign firms can use to prevent the entry of firms from less developed countries to their markets are similar to those discussed in the context of oligopoly in section 13.3:

(a) The existing firms can cut their prices, or threaten to cut their prices, to reduce the new entrant's revenue.
(b) The existing firms can advertise, and use other forms of non-price competition, to increase the new entrant's costs.

A government may support these moves to prevent firms from other countries from entering a market in order to protect its existing firms, particularly if a firm in a less developed country can benefit from lower labour costs, and so sell at a lower price than existing firms. Some protection of this kind is the subject of international agreements that may place quotas on imports from less developed countries, or that provide equal access: the less developed country imports goods from the richer country in exchange for free access for its goods to the richer country's market.

23.4.3 Dumping

Governments often accuse other countries of subsidizing exports so that they can export goods at prices that are below average cost. This practice is known as **dumping**, and is plainly an attractive policy for a government that wants to increase export revenues, or for a government that has other policies that give rise to surpluses of goods (such as the EC Common Agricultural Policy and the US agricultural policy, both of which give rise to surpluses of agricultural goods).

The advantage of receiving dumped goods is that the importing country buys goods very cheaply: its terms of trade improve so that it receives more imports for each good that it exports. However, countries do not always welcome dumped goods (and international agreements attempt to restrict dumping in some circumstances), because the cheap imports compete with domestically produced goods and may cause unemployment as households buy cheaper imports.

Dumping can be a particular problem for less developed countries. At first glance, it might seem to be desirable for the EC or the USA to sell their excess food cheaply to less developed countries, particularly if a country suffers a harvest failure or other disaster that reduces the availability of domestically produced food. However, if excess food is sold very cheaply to a less developed country over a long period, the supply of food in the less developed country increases and the price of food falls. This is beneficial to those who buy the food, but may prove to be a disaster for farmers in the less developed country who can no longer sell food at a profit. In the long run, farmers leave the land and domestic food production falls, so that the country has to continue to rely on imports of food. Without the cheap imports, the price of food might have been high enough to give farmers a sufficient incentive to improve domestic agriculture and to reduce the long-term need to import food, so that the country could spend its foreign currencies on other goods.

Subsidized sales of food also affect countries that produce food for their own use and export any surplus. The increased supply of food at very low prices reduces the world price of food, and this reduces the export earnings of countries that sell food abroad. So less developed countries that are attempting to develop by selling agricultural goods are less able to do so when richer countries sell their surplus food cheaply.

This problem would not arise if rich countries dumped goods that less developed countries do not produce, including the investment goods that less developed countries need to build up an industrialized sector. However, industrialized countries have no incentive to subsidize sales of these goods, because cheap imports of investment goods to less developed countries enable them to develop industries that would then compete with established firms in richer countries. The dumping of food is in the interest of the dumpers, because they obtain at least some revenue from the surplus produced by their agricultural policies. The dumping of other goods is not in their interest, and so subsidized sales of equipment occur only in the context of foreign aid.

23.4.4 Trade or aid?

Poor countries need to trade to benefit from specialization, and the benefits to them are increased if rich countries are prepared to:

(a) Allow firms based in less developed countries to sell goods in the richer countries without import restrictions and without facing competition from firms based in richer countries that receive government subsidies.
(b) Tolerate the use of tariffs by less developed countries to protect infant industries.
(c) Avoid depressing the prices of goods (particularly agricultural products) by dumping surpluses.

All these policies require that rich countries refrain from using government policies to change the international income distribution in their own favour.

The effect of this restraint by governments in richer countries is, in some ways, analogous to the effect of government policies to reduce firms' market influence on the income distribution within a country. However, anti-monopoly policy can be carried out by a government that represents the interests of households and others who are affected by the market influence. There is no international organization that can act on behalf of poorer countries and ensure that richer countries do not use their influence.

An alternative (or a supplement) to voluntary agreements on international trade is **aid** given by rich countries to less developed countries. This aid may be in the form of gifts of money, loans at low interest rates, particularly to finance infrastructure projects, subsidies for students from less developed countries who want to study in richer countries and support for skilled workers who work in less developed countries. Some aid is directed to international aid organizations such as the International Development Agency. In 1985, UK aid amounted to approximately 0.35 per cent of national income; some developed countries (such as Holland and Norway) give approximately 1 per cent of their national incomes as aid.

Aid may benefit the donor country as well as the recipient countries. Some aid is **tied** to purchases of goods from the donor country, and may help to increase employment and national income there. A less developed country might prefer **untied** aid, because it can use it to buy goods from the cheapest source, but it is unrealistic to suppose that donor countries would be as willing to give untied aid as they are to give tied aid.

23.5 International debts and development

A less developed country wants to increase its national income, and macroeconomic analysis predicts that it can do this by increasing government expenditure or by using policies that encourage private investment. However, the additional government deficit or private investment requires financing.

Some of this finance can come from the increase in saving caused by the increase in national income, although the marginal propensity to save is likely to be low because many people are very poor. The remainder must be financed either by an increase in cash creation or by borrowing from abroad.

23.5.1 Cash creation

An increase in the amount of cash in use causes an increase in the supply of money, some of which may be held in households' portfolios of savings, but people with low incomes save little, so that much of the increased supply of money is used to finance transactions. So either the velocity of circulation of money is reduced or national income rises. If national income rises faster than the country can produce additional goods (because the investment projects that are financed using the additional money have yet to produce goods), then the increase in the supply of money causes inflation.

23.5.2 International debts

In recent years, attention has been focused on the accumulated foreign debts of some countries. At the end of 1987, Brazil and Mexico both had foreign debts in excess of US $100 billion (compared to GNPs of $314 billion and $140 billion respectively), and several other countries had difficulties making interest payments and principal repayments. The debt service ratio of a country is the ratio of payments of interest and repayments of principal on foreign debt to the country's export receipts. The average debt service ratio of 17 highly indebted countries was approximately 25 per cent. On average, these countries needed to pay 25 per cent of total export receipts to meet interest and capital repayments on their foreign debts – leaving very little foreign currency for the imports needed to continue their development programmes.

These debts are the result of borrowing by governments and by privately owned firms, and one reason why such large debts have accumulated is that, until recently, there was little co-ordination of lenders or borrowers. The lenders (mainly banks in richer countries) did not know how much other banks were lending, and the government of the borrowing country did not know the extent of its own borrowing and that of privately owned firms.

The debt service ratios of poor countries also increase as interest rates rise. The monetary policies of many countries have led to higher interest rates in the 1980s than in previous decades. If there is fear that a country may be unable to meet its debt repayments, it can borrow (if at all) only at interest rates above the level paid by other countries.

23.5.3 Default

A country could refuse to pay interest or to repay loans by defaulting on its liabilities. This would immediately resolve the country's difficulties of finding the necessary foreign currencies and would, of course, imply that the country would be unlikely to be able to borrow so easily in the future.

The most important consequences of default are on the banks that have loans that are not repaid. If a bank has lent a large amount to a country that defaults, it may go bankrupt because it is not receiving expected interest and loan repayments. If a few banks go bankrupt for this reason, and people lose faith in banks, they demand to withdraw from their accounts in cash, so that all banks face a very large cash requirement. Some bankers, economists and politicians have argued that a default by one of the major debtor countries could cause a major upheaval in the banking systems of many Western countries. So far no default has occurred, probably because this fear prevents creditors from declaring debtor countries bankrupt.

In the face of a major default, banks in developed countries may be forced to make extensive use of the last resort facility, and so governments must create additional cash to lend to banks or to buy liquid assets from them (see section 18.5.2). The supply of money would rise in many countries, and market analysis predicts that this would lead to inflation. Even economists who use macroeconomic analysis would probably not disagree about the inflationary effects of a sudden, major increase in the supply of money.

A default changes the international income distribution in favour of the defaulting country, because it has obtained goods on credit and given nothing in return. The amount of the default is, in a sense, enforced aid from the countries whose banks have lent the money.

23.5.4 Rescheduling

The possible consequences of default are so unpleasant for the lending countries (up until the time of writing) default has been avoided by **rescheduling** the debts. This generally involves the postponement of the maturity date of bonds, or agreed delays in interest payment. In some cases (such as that of Brazil in 1983), the agreement involves further loans to the country both from lending banks and from the **International Monetary Fund (IMF)**. These loans are made to enable the country to pay interest and principal on previous loans, and may also be designed to help the country to continue its development programme so that it is better able to earn foreign currencies by exporting goods in the future. The country's long-term need is to reduce imports and increase exports so that it has a surplus of foreign currencies that it can use to pay interest and repay principal on its debts. Loans from the IMF are generally given only on the condition that the borrowing country uses fiscal and monetary policies to reduce national income (and increase unemployment) to reduce imports, and to reduce the inflation rate so that its exports become less expensive. The country may also be required to devalue its currency by having lower target exchange rates, which should increase exports and reduce imports.

Lending banks favour rescheduling because they do not then have worthless assets. The rescheduling forces them to continue to lend to the debtor country, when they might prefer to lend elsewhere, but they prefer rescheduling to default. A country with a very large debt is therefore in a very strong position to negotiate terms for rescheduling, because it can negotiate better terms by threatening to default if its wishes are not met. This reverses the usual power relationship between a debtor and a lender, essentially because the international legal system has little or no effect on a defaulting country in the way that a national legal system can impose sanctions on a firm or household that defaults on loans.

23.6 Summary

In may less developed countries the majority of the workforce is employed on the land, and agricultural productivity is low. The country generally needs to improve agricultural productivity to develop infrastructure and an industrial sector. One way of increasing the pace of industrialization is to allow foreign-owned multinational firms to build factories to take advantage of low labour costs in less developed countries. However, the country may find it difficult to regulate the activities of these firms and, in particular, to obtain a share of the profits through taxation because of the problem of transfer pricing. In addition, a multinational firm may affect exchange rates by moving large sums of hot money. Richer countries may help poorer countries by giving preferential trading agreements, but they may also cause considerable problems for farmers in poorer countries by dumping cheap food from their agricultural surpluses.

In recent years some developing countries have accumulated large inter-national debts, and have had difficulty repaying these and paying interest on them, particularly because the world recession has cut their export earnings and because interest rates have increased. Some of these debts have been rescheduled, but the threat of default remains, which may have very serious consequences for banking systems in richer countries.

Topics and problems

(1) How much of its national income should a rich country give in aid to poorer countries?

(2) EC farmers gain at the expense of consumers and at the expense of farmers

in other, much poorer, countries. Should the EC agricultural policy therefore be abolished?

(3) Should students from poorer countries receive subsidized education in richer countries?

(4) The effectiveness of marcroeconomic policies in developed countries depends on the speed with which firms change their prices and outputs. How effective are these policies likely to be in less developed countries?

(5) Do the effects of investment by multinational firms in poorer countries differ from the effects of the political imperialism of earlier times?

(6) Why are population growth rates higher in poor than in rich countries?

(7) Economic development destroys the culture and social structure of less developed countries. Should rich countries therefore not help to develop poorer countries?

(8) Does the economic development of poor countries imply that people in richer countries must reduce their standards of living?

Chapter Twenty-four

Planned economies

Major aspects of planned economies — perfect planned economy — information and implementation — other aspects of central planning — decentralized planning

---

24.1 Introduction

The outcome of a mixed economy is determined by individual decisions that interact in markets, and by government influence on these decisions. However, in a mixed economy, the government does not attempt to replace many markets by a system in which people are told what to do. In a planned economy, government intervention does replace most markets, and important aspects of the economy are the result of people's reactions to a central plan.

Major parts of the economies of socialist countries are centrally planned, and this planning is based on value judgements similar to those that support the use of socialist policies (such as nationalization; see section 19.3.1) in mixed economies. These judgements are:

(a) Incomes from sources other than labour are unjustified, and are the result of the appropriation of goods and land and the exploitation of workers (see section 10.9.4).
(b) A capitalist economy, even with considerable government intervention, is inefficient because of imperfections.

Many of the topics discussed earlier in this book are relevant to an analysis of planned economies, because all economic systems face the fundamental problems of allocating resources and distributing incomes. However, many of our conclusions must be reinterpreted in the institutional conditions of a planned economy.

Although planned economies are associated with Marxist political views, Marx himself wrote little on the subject of the operation of a planned economy. His writing was much more concerned with the deficiencies of a capitalist economy that would, in his view, lead to the (probably violent) overthrow of the capitalist system and the introduction of a system in which workers control production and distribution. These deficiences concerned both the injustice of exploitation and the likelihood of cycles in which periods of high employment alternate with periods of considerable unemployment. Marx argued that the unemployment rate would increase in successive cycles, until the workers' situation had become so intolerable that their only possible action was violent revolution, such as those that have subsequently occurred in the USSR and China.

24.2 Major aspects of planned economies

A planned economy contains three important groups:

(a) The **planners**, who establish the plan (under instructions from politicians).
(b) The **factory managers**, who organize factories on the basis of their instructions from the planners. Unlike shareholders (and many managers) in a capitalist economy, these managers do not own the factories or the land or equipment used in them.
(c) The **workers**, who are instructed by factory managers.

This economic hierarchy is, in practice, only a part of the structure of a socialist society. The Communist Party in the USSR and elsewhere has a national, regional and local organization that is also concerned with production and other economic decisions. However, the economic analysis of a planned economy is most simply carried out by examining the actions of, and the interrelations between, planners, managers and workers.

A plan for the use of a country's resources has four main features:

(a) An **objective**, which states what the plan is intended to achieve.
(b) **Information flows**, which provide the planners with information on available resources, and on the technology available that determines the inputs of materials and factors needed in production.
(c) A **method of formulation**, which involves calculating the amounts of goods that must be produced. The formulation must take account of the materials produced in one factory that are used in other factories (for example, coal is used in the production of steel, electricity is used in the production of most goods). The planned outputs of goods must be consistent so that the achievement of one target is not thwarted by failure to supply the necessary inputs.
(d) A **method of implementation** that attempts to ensure that factory managers and workers carry out the requirements of the plan.

24.3 Perfect planned economy

We began our examination of market economies in part II by looking at perfect market economies that involve a number of simplifying assumptions. In a perfect market economy, no one has market influence and all necessary information is available.

We can define a perfect planned economy as one in which:

(a) All necessary information is available.
(b) No factory manager or worker uses influence to alter the outcome of the economy in his or her own favour. Factory managers and workers provide information truthfully, and implement the plan as the planners want.

A perfectly planned system is a simplification of real world planned economies, in the same sense that a perfect market economy is a simplification of real world market economies. The simplification enables us to examine the objective and the formulation of the plan, without concern for the difficulties of obtaining the necessary information and implementing the plan. As we shall see in section 24.4, there are similarities between imperfections in a market economy and imperfections that prevent planners from achieving the aims of the plan.

24.3.1 Objective of the plan

In a perfect market economy, the market supply of each good depends on the profitabiltity of producing it, which depends on market demands. In a planned economy, planners must decide (or be told by their political superiors) how much of each good is to be produced.

A fundamental part of the objective of a plan is the division of national output between consumer goods and investment goods. In practice, countries that have planned economic systems have given priority to the production of investment goods over the production of many consumer goods, because a major objective has been to increase the rate of economic growth. So the objective has consisted of target outputs for basic investment goods such as steel, coal and transport, and for some basic consumer goods such as food and housing. Any resources that remain after these high-priority targets have been met are used to produce other consumer goods.

The objective of a plan could, in principle, be designed to take account of the preferences of people in the country, both in the decision on the resources to be devoted to investment and in the decisions on the outputs of various consumer goods. To incorporate individuals' preferences into a plan, however, the planners face some of the problems outlined in our discussion of democratic (or utilitarian) methods of making public choices in a mixed economy. For example, they may use a method (such as majority voting) that gives an inconsistent conclusion in some circumstances, or they may use a method that could allow some people to influence the outcome in their own favour by stating untrue preferences. In any case, the major basis of existing planned economies is the socialist value judgement, which may be supported by a large number of people, but which does not necessarily base public choices on individual preferences.

24.3.2 Formulating a plan: input–output analysis

To formulate a plan the central planners must know what can be produced in each factory with specified inputs of materials and factors of production, and the resources of land, equipment, materials and labour of various kinds that are available.

We considered a 'plan' for the two person case of Alan and Bill in chapter 2, where it is easy to establish their comparative advantages and the desirable pattern of specialization, given the goods that are wanted. Central planners want to do this for an economy of many more people, in which there are other inputs (materials and factors) to be allocated between competing uses. In principle, they need to know the outcome of all possible patterns of specialization and to choose that which best meets the objective of the plan.

A major problem faced by planners is the avoidance of **bottlenecks**. A bottleneck arises when one target cannot be met because there is a shortage of some necessary input. For example, a target for the output of steel implies a requirement of coal and other materials, and a bottleneck arises if there is insufficient coal available for use in the steel industry. The planners must make sure that the necessary quantities of these inputs are available in the right places at the right times.

The technique of **input–output analysis** has been developed to represent the requirements of one industry for the goods produced in another. Input-output analysis was developed by Wassily Leontief (born in 1906 in St Petersburg, Russia; a professor of economics at New York University; Nobel prizewinner in economics in 1973), and its principal tool is an **input–output table**, which records the amounts of goods needed as inputs by each industry.

For example, suppose that an economy contains four industries: agriculture, coal mining, steel making and machine production. Table 24.1 is its input–output table, which shows that:

(a) The agriculture industry requires inputs of agricultural goods (as seed), and of machines (tractors).
(b) The coal mining industry requires machines and steel (for example, for pit-props).
(c) The steel making industry requires machines and coal.
(d) The production of machines requires machines, coal and steel.
(e) The goods available for final use include agricultural goods and coal for consumption, and steel and new machines for use as investment goods.

In a more realistic example (using a larger table), we could record other inputs needed in each industry, and divide the industries into parts to allow for differences between the inputs needed to produce each kind of food or machine. However, the essential feature of an input–output table is that it records each good both as an output and as an input to the production of other goods. Some goods may not be used as inputs in some industries; for example, in table 24.1, agricultural goods are not an input in the coal industry.

Table 24.1 Input–output table

	Food	Coal	Steel	Machines	Final use	Total output
		Sector production				
Food	100	0	0	0	400	500
Coal	0	0	300	200	500	1,000
Steel	0	700	0	400	400	1,500
Machines	100	300	600	400	600	2,000

The rows of the table show the uses made of the total output of each good.

The table can be used to trace the effects of changes in target outputs. If the target for the production of agricultural goods is increased by 50 per cent, then:

(a) More agricultural goods are needed as inputs to the agricultural sector. So if the target for agricultural output in 1991 is increased, people can consume less food in 1990, because more seed must be saved for the next year.
(b) More tractors are needed, and these can be produced only if more machines, steel and coal are available, and so on.

Notice that there can be feedbacks from a sector to itself. If the target output of steel is increased, more coal is needed, and this additional coal requires more steel for use in the mines. So the output of steel must increase by more than the increase in the target to ensure that there is sufficient additional steel for use in mining the additional coal.

To calculate the sizes of the increases in the outputs of each industry following an increase in the target output of one industry requires information on the technology of each industry. The simplest case to consider is that in which the inputs to an industry increase in proportion to the output from it (there are **constant returns to scale**): if output increases by 1 per cent, then the inputs required also increase by 1 per cent. In this case, there are:

(a) No economies of scale that would permit an increase of more than 1 per cent in the output of an industry if its inputs increase by 1 per cent.
(b) No diseconomies of scale that require an increase of more than 1 per cent in inputs to achieve a 1 per cent increase in outputs.

Table 24.2 uses the assumption of constant returns to scale, and shows the effects of an increase of 50 per cent in the target output of food compared to the situation of table 24.1. The table shows the effect on all industries, given the inputs needed by each industry. So the total output of steel must increase by 25 units to ensure that there is sufficient steel to meet the increased needs of other industries. In table 24.2:

(a) The ratio of each input to the output in each industry is the same as it is in table 24.1.

Table 24.2   Input–output table: final use of food increased

| | Sector producing | | | | | Total output |
	Food	Coal	Steel	Machines	Final use	
Food	150	0	0	0	600	750
Coal	0	0	305	208	500	1,013
Steel	0	709	0	416	400	1,525
Machines	150	304	610	416	600	2,080

The rows of the table show the uses made of the total output of each good.

(b) The amount of agricultural goods available for final use is 50 per cent greater than in table 24.1.
(c) The amounts of coal, steel and machinery available for final use are the same as in table 24.1.

24.3.3 Outcome of a perfect planned economy

If the planners can formulate a plan that makes the best use of the nation's resources given the objective of the plan, **a perfect planned economy is efficient**. In addition, the objective can, in principle, give rise to any income distribution that the government wants, so that the potential criticism of a perfect market economy (that it may include widespread poverty), cannot be levelled at a perfect planned economy. In a market economy, the distribution depends on people's endowments of labour and other factors of production that they can sell or hire out to obtain an income. In a perfect planned economy, the income distribution is whatever the government wants it to be (although this may not coincide with what many people want).

Both a perfect planned economy and a perfect market economy are efficient in their use of resources in that it is not possible to produce more of one good without producing less of another or using more resources. However, in a perfect market economy, few resources are needed to organize the economic system, because the outcome is determined by unco-ordinated individual decisions. Some communication is required to establish markets, but is is likely that a planned economy uses far more resources (of labour, computers and communications equipment in particular) to formulate and implement the plan. So a planned economy requires resources that cannot be used to produce investment or consumer goods.

24.4 Information and implementation

Once the planners have decided on the goods that are to be produced, including those produced by one industry for use in another, they must tell the factory managers what to produce and allocate inputs to them. In a perfect planned economy the planners are certain that the managers will implement the plan as the planners want. In reality, a major imperfection of planned economies is that managers are likely to attempt to influence the outcome of the plan for their own benefit.

In keeping with the basic method of this book (see section 1.6.3), we assume that factory managers make decisions based on their preferences and the opportunities open to them. The planners in a large economy are unlikely to be able to limit managers' opportunities far enough for them to have no scope to depart from the plan, and so the planners must try to ensure that managers are motivated to make the decision that the planners want. The planners must devise a system of **incentives** to implement the plan.

Incentive schemes are likely to involve rewards to factory managers who fulfil their target outputs and sanctions on those who do not. However, the target must be carefully specified, and must include aspects of both the quality and the quantity of goods produced, or the managers have no incentive to improve the reliability of the goods produced. The target must be specified in considerable detail; for example, if the target output of nails from a factory is specified in millions, the factory is likely to produce only small nails because these are easier to produce given the inputs allocated to the factory. If the target is specified in tonnes of nails, the factory is likely to produce only large nails because these are easier to produce.

24.4.1 Information

The preceding problem requires that instructions to managers are detailed, and leave them few opportunities to deviate from the plan. However, a much more serious problem arises because the factory managers are able to influence the formulation of the plan. The central planners require information on the amounts of inputs that a factory needs to achieve a target output so that the plan avoids bottlenecks. In many cases, the only source of this information is the managers of factories, and so the planners can find out information relevant to their control of the managers only by asking the managers themselves.

If a manager has an incentive to ensure that the factory produces its target using the inputs allocated (and if he faces sanctions if the factory does not produce its target), he has an incentive to overstate the amounts of inputs that the factory needs to produce a target output. If the planners have no way of checking the accuracy of the manager's replies, the factory is likely to receive more inputs than it needs to achieve its target. So one or more of the following happens:

(a) The factory uses the additional inputs in a way that is technologically inefficient.

(b) The additional inputs are used to produce additional outputs. This is likely only if managers and workers are given incentives (in the form of bonuses) to exceed the target. However, increased production reveals that the manager overstated the amounts of inputs needed to produce the target, and this may lead to reductions in inputs in the future as the planners learn that the manager has previously overstated his needs. So the incentive to produce more than the target now must be offset against the possible reduction in the future allocation of inputs.

(c) The excess inputs are sold illegally (on a black market) for the manager's personal gain.

If a factory manager overstates the amount of inputs that he needs in order to achieve the target more easily or to gain personally by selling the excess inputs, he uses his power to influence the outcome of the planning process. This power arises because he is the source of the information on which the plan is based.

Individuals have the power to influence the outcome of market and mixed economies as well:

(a) In a market economy, the owners of any firm or the members of any trade union that has market influence can influence the outcome of the economy in their own favour (see chapter 12).

(b) In a mixed economy, methods of making public choices (including social cost–benefit analysis and democratic methods) can give some people an incentive to provide untrue information about their preferences, in order to influence the outcome of the decision-making processs in their favour (see sections 19.7.1 and 22.3.3).

Each of these possibilities (including the possible incentive to factory managers in a planned economy) involves the power to influence the outcome of the economy. People may feel constrained not to use such power by their own moral views, but economists must recognize the incentive that materially motivated people have to use such power to their own advantage.

24.4.2 Small-scale production

The ability of factory managers to influence the outcome of the economy depends on the planners' alternative sources of information. In an industry where one or a few large plants produce a good, the factory managers may be able to use considerable influence. In industries (such as agriculture) where goods are produced in small-scale units, the planners have a large amount of information from a number of different producers. So it is likely that no single producer can make great gains from overstating its input requirements, because the planners can check its needs against those of other factory managers producing similar goods.

This does not imply that it it easier for the central planners to control the outputs of goods produced in many small factories than those produced in a few large factories. In such an industry, the planners must provide a very large amount of information, or else they must use the price system to try to obtain the desired outputs. If the price is set too low, the producers have an incentive to produce little beyond their own needs; if the price is too high, the producers make a large profit, which is contrary to the socialist value judgement that profit is an unjustified source of income. The producers may not employ and exploit workers (because they run very small farms or factories), but they are able to buy the goods produced by other workers and obtain the benefits of exploiting these other workers.

24.4.3 Consumption and wages

If the planners made a detailed enough plan, they could issue instructions to each individual concerning the job that he or she is to do. In addition, the planners could allocate a ration of each consumer good to each person. In practice, workers in all Eastern Europe planned economies are paid wages, and buy many consumer goods in markets so that the planners do not need to allocate rations of all goods.

The problem of incentives and information also arises here. The planners must ensure that the wages paid do not destroy the incentive to do, or to train for, difficult or unpleasant jobs. If someone has a comparative advantage in doing a difficult or unpleasant job, and she knows that her wage is the same whatever job she does, she may deny that she has the skill needed to do the job. So the wage paid to those who do more difficult or unpleasant jobs must be sufficiently greater than the wage paid for other jobs for people to have an incentive to supply the necessary skills. The income distribution may in fact be determined by the need to ensure that various skills of labour are available, rather than by the objective of the plan. The outcome of a planned economy is then similar to that of a market economy in which wages change to reflect shortages of various skills. However, in a socialist planned economy, no one receives an income (legally) from any source other than wages.

24.5 Other aspects of central planning

In practice, workers receive wages in the form of money and buy consumer goods with that money. This saves the need for an extremely complex system of rationing. However, the planners set wages and prices, and unless they choose to set prices at their equilibrium levels (and are successful in calculating the equilibrium prices), some goods will be in shortage, and so other methods of allocating goods are likely to be important:

(a) People queue to try to obtain goods that are in excess demand. In extreme cases (as appears to have happened in the early 1980s in Poland) people spend so long queueing for scarce goods that less labour is supplied, and so total outputs fall, which adds to the shortages.
(b) Some goods are allocated only to those in certain occupations. In practice, factory managers and those high in the political hierarchy are better able to obtain scarce goods that other people.
(c) Some goods are sold on black markets. People who obtain scarce goods at the official price (or illegally) resell them at a higher price, or barter them for other scarce goods.

24.5.1 Inflation

In principle, a planned economy can be entirely free from inflation, but in practice there are at least two reasons why price rises may occur:

(a) Some goods are imported, and so the country is not immune to inflation imported from other countries.
(b) Average wages tend to increase, because there is resistance to wage reductions and the higher wages that arise from promotions and bonuses are unlikely to be offset by lower wages arising from demotions and penalties for failures. So money incomes rise and, if prices are held constant, there are ever-increasing shortages of consumer goods. The government may not be prepared to tolerate the alternative methods of allocation listed above, and so it increases prices.

24.5.2 Unemployment

A perfect planned economy has no unemployment (neither does a perfect market economy) because the planners are able to find a job for everyone according to his or her comparative advantages. If the planned economy has imperfections, people may work where their marginal product is very low, and so there is considerable hidden or disguised unemployment. This is another result of the incentive that factory managers may have to give false information on their needs for inputs, including labour.

24.6 Decentralized planning

Our discussion of planned economies has been based on the assumption that, as far as possible, the planners reject the use of prices and the profit motive as a way of organizing economic activities. However, it is possible to conceive of an economy that is planned but that uses prices to implement the plan.

The operation of **decentralized** planning is based on three conclusions from the analysis of perfect market economies:

(a) A perfect market economy in long-run equilibrium uses resources efficiently (see sections 7.5 and 8.7).
(b) Material motivation (profit maximization) leads producers to supply more of those goods for which demand has increased and less of those goods for which demand has fallen (consumers' sovereignty, see section 9.8).
(c) The demands for consumer goods depend on incomes, which are determined in factor markets.

In a system of decentralized planning the planners determine the equilibrium prices that would arise in a perfect market economy, given the demands for goods determined by the objective. The planners then announce these prices, and tell factory managers to maximize the profits made in their factories, given the prices of the goods that they produce and the prices (wages and rents) that they must pay for their inputs. As in a perfect market economy each factory makes normal profit, but none of this is paid to the factory managers (who receive a wage), because they own none of the inputs used in the factory. All of the profit (and rent on land) is paid to the government.

If more of a good is wanted, or a good becomes scarce because of a harvest failure, or if the price of an imported good or material increases, the planners increase the announced price of it. Some factory managers switch to producing it so that the supply increases, exactly as profit-maximizing perfect competitors react to price changes in a perfect market economy.

The government announces the wages of different skills of labour that are needed to ensure that sufficient of each skill is available. The government uses its revenue from rent and normal profit to buy investment goods, and perhaps to alter the distribution of incomes that arises from the announced wages of labour. It sets the prices of consumer goods to attempt to ensure that the supplies determined by producers equal the demands of wage-earners. The government can determine the supplies of consumer goods but must then set their prices to ensure that demands equal these supplies.

Decentralized planning has the advantage that the planners do not need to send detailed instructions to each factory telling it what to produce and allocating inputs to it. The planners have to determine the relevant prices and wages, but then factory managers are told to respond to those prices, and workers respond to the incentives provided by the announced wages.

To operate a system of this kind, the planners must establish the market prices and wages. They may be able to do this by trial and error: they calculate the equilibrium prices as closely as they can with the information available to them, and then ask factory managers to state their demands for inputs and supplies of outputs at those prices. If the supply of a good exceeds the demand, the planners reduce its price to encourage its use and to discourage its production; if the demand for a good exceeds the supply, the planners increase the price to discourage its use and encourage its production. These price changes continue until the prices have reached the equilibrium level. So the planners attempt to imitate the way in which perfect markets would operate.

A problem remains. Factory managers may maximize profits simply because they are told too, but the incentives of a market economy are missing: the factory managers do not themselves gain from the profitability of their factories. In practice, it is likely that they must be given incentives to act as the planners want, so that the factory managers receive incomes related to the profit of their factory. So the managers become similar to capitalists in a market economy, and this outcome may be unpalatable to those who support the use of planning on the basis of the socialist value judgement.

24.7 Summary

Planners require an objective, and need information on the productive potential of the economy. When they have these they can formulate a plan, attempting to avoid bottlenecks. Then they must devise a method of implementing the plan by giving instructions to factory managers and to workers. A major problem arises because the formulation and implementation of the plan depend on the information given to the planners, and the suppliers of information may be able to alter the plan in their own favour by giving false information, particularly by overstating their needs for materials and factors of production.

To some extent these problems can be avoided in a system of decentralized planning, which attempts to imitate the operation of a perfect market economy, but which prevents individuals from receiving incomes other than from wages.

In principle a planned economic system can operate efficiently, and the objective can include a socially desirable income distribution and a socially desirable level of investment. This conclusions can be contrasted with the outcome of a market economy that may be efficient (if it is close to perfection) but in which the income distribution and the level of investment are the outcome of market forces. In practice, planned systems use many resources simply to formulate and implement the plan, and the problems of obtaining accurate information are large. The income distribution may be considerably affected by the need to give people incentives to do certain jobs, so that the socially desired income distribution may not be achieved.

Topics and problems

(1) Capitalist economies give economic power to the managers and owners of large firms. A planned system gives political power to the senior planners. Does this mean that both systems inevitably lead to social inequalities?

(2) 'Political freedoms must be curtailed to prevent people from voicing objections to the socially desirable plan.' Is this a valid comment on all planned economic systems?

(3) Is it possible to run a planned economy with a significant number of privately owned firms? Is it desirable to do so?

(4) 'A planned economic system refuses to use prices and the profit motive explicitly, but must eventually do so implicitly.' Comment.

(5) Should a developing country attempt to use a central plan? What particular advantages and disadvantages (compared to the use of planning in richer countries) might be faced?

(6) An economy produces coal and steel. To produce a tonne of coal requires 1/4 tonne of coal and 1/2 tonne of steel. To produce a tonne of steel requires 1/3 tonne of coal and 1/3 tonne of steel.

(a) What is the input–output table for the economy if 300 tonnes of coal and 160 tonnes of steel are required for final use?

(b) How does the input-output table change if the requirement of steel for final use is doubled?

(7) What is the answer to problem 6 if instead 2/3 tonne of coal and 2/3 tonne of steel are required to produce a tonne of steel (the coal industry is as in problem 6)?

Glossary

absolute advantage a person's (or country's) ability to produce more of a good (or more of all goods, depending on the context) than another person (or country)

aggregate demand the sum of desired consumption expenditure and investment expenditure in a market economy; includes government expenditure in a mixed economy and exports in an open economy

aggregate domestic demand aggregate demand minus demand for imported goods

aggregate supply the total of goods available to meet aggregate demand

allocation the process of determining the use of resources in the economy

appreciation of a currency occurs if the exchange rate of the currency with other currencies rises so that one unit of the currency buys more units of other currencies

average cost pricing the principle that the price charged by a nationalized firm equals its average cost of production so that it makes no profit and no loss

balance of payments a record of the flows of money into and out of a country, the extent of official financing and transfers into and out of its reserves of gold, foreign currencies and Special Drawing Rights

balance of trade value of exports minus value of imports; there is a surplus on the balance of trade if the value of exports exceeds the value of imports; there is a deficit on the balance of trade if the value of imports exceeds the value of exports

balanced budget arises when government revenues equal its expenditures

bill a security representing a loan to a firm or the government, usually of shorter duration than a bond. Interest on bills is often paid by repaying the face value of the bill to the lender, who has lent less than the face value

bond a security representing a loan to a firm or the government on which interest is paid at a rate that is fixed when the bond is first sold by the borrowing firm or government

boom a period of rapid economic growth and, usually, lower than average unemployment

budget the record of government expenditure and tax revenues; if tax revenues exceed expenditure there is a budget surplus; if tax revenues are less than expenditure there is a budget deficit; if the two are equal, there is a balanced budget

building society   a non-profit-making financial institution in the UK. Its main functions are to borrow from households and to lend money for house purchase

business cycle   alternating periods of higher and lower rates of economic growth

capitalism   a market economic system in which all factors of production and all firms are privately owned

cash   notes and coins, and money that can be withdrawn immediately from a bank's account at the Central Bank

cash ratio   the ratio of cash to a bank's total assets. The ratio may be fixed by the government

central bank   a financial institution that acts as a link between the government and banks, and that carries out monetary policy. The UK central bank is the Bank of England

certainty equivalent   an individual is indifferent between an uncertain prospect and its certainty equivalent, which is usually expressed as a sum of money that is certain to be received

ceteris paribus   an assumption that all things other than those under consideration in a model are unchanged

circular flow of national income   recognition of the fact that much of national income circulates from firms to households (when firms pay wages and other incomes) and thence back to firms (as households buy goods)

collusion   agreement between two or more firms to combine their market influence

community charge or **poll tax**   tax paid at the same rate by all individuals in an area

comparative advantage   a person's (or country's) ability to produce a good at a lower opportunity cost than some other person (or country)

competition   situation in a market where there are several suppliers, each of whom offsets much of the potential market influence of the other suppliers

complement   if the price of a good falls the demand for a complement to it increases

concentration ratio   a measure of the extent of the market influence of major firms in an industry, given by the percentage of total sales made by the largest three, five or 10 firms

constant prices   term used when national income (or gross national product) is calculated for several years using prices from only one of the years. This allows comparisons of real outputs, and (approximately) cancels out the effects of inflation

constant returns to scale   a situation in which the output of a firm or an industry can be increased (by say 10 per cent) if there is an equal proportional increase (10 per cent) in the quantities of all inputs (factors and materials) used

consumers' sovereignty   a situation in which a change in the pattern of demands is followed by a similar change in the pattern of supplies and, in the long run, no increase in firms' profits

consumer's surplus   a measure of the benefit to a consumer that is received from a good in excess of the amount paid for it

consumption expenditure   the part of national income spent on consumer goods

consumption function   the relation between desired consumption expenditure and national income

cost-push inflation   inflation caused by increases in firms' payments for factors and materials that are then passed on to customers through price increases

credit control   the part of monetary policy that attempts to control the amount of lending by banks and other financial institutions

credit creation   a mechanism whereby a bank can increase lending if it receives more cash or liquid assets because its cash and liquidity ratios are less than one

cross price-elasticity of demand   percentage change in demand for one good caused by a 1 per cent increase in the price of another good. Positive for substitutes, negative for complementary goods

crowding out   a conclusion of market analysis that an increase in one component of aggregate demand must be offset by an equal decrease in some other component (if the decrease if less than the increase, there is partial crowding out)

customs union   an agreement between countries to allow free trade between them and to place a common tariff on goods imported from outside the customs union

debt crisis   the problems that arise, or may arise, because some poor countries have large international debts in relation to their national products

debt service ratio   the ratio of a country's annual repayments of and interest on loans from abroad to the country's export revenues

decentralized economy   an economic system in which production and consumption decisions are not made by central planners

decentralized planning   a system in which central planners set prices and wages, and individual consumers, workers and factory managers make decisions on consumption and production on the basis of the announced prices and wages

deflation   a situation in which national output begins to grow more slowly, or even to decline, often as a result of deflationary government policies

deflationary gap   macroeconomic equilibrium national income minus full employment national income at existing prices and money wages (when this difference is negative)

demand   the quantity (of a good, asset, factor of production) that a person or firm wants to buy at a particular price. A demand schedule and a demand curve represent demand at each price

demand-deficient unemployment   unemployment caused by a simultaneous reduction in the demands for many goods

demand-pull inflation   inflation caused by an inflationary gap in which aggregate demand exceeds the ability of the economy to supply goods

depreciation   of a currency occurs if the exchange rate of the currency with other currencies falls so that one unit of the currency buys fewer units of other currencies

depression   a period of low national income and high unemployment, particularly one that continues for a number of years

devaluation   a deliberate depreciation by a government of an exchange rate below its previous fixed or target level

direct tax   a tax on incomes, such as income tax, capital gains tax and national insurance contributions in the UK

discount rate   the annual rate (often based on an annual interest rate) used to reduce future costs and benefits to a present value when discounting

discounting   a technique for assessing projects that give rise to costs and benefit in a number of years. The technique implies a greater value of present costs and benefits compared to future costs and benefits

disguised unemployment   a situation in which people are employed even though their marginal product is very low, so that little output would be lost if they were not employed

disposable income   a household's income after taxes have been paid; also used for the total of such incomes in the economy

distribution   process of determining the share of national income received by each person

division of labour   the pattern of specialization within and between industries

domestic product   the total value of all goods produced in an economy in a given period (equals the total of the quantity of each good produced multiplied by its price)

dumping   selling goods abroad at a price that is below the cost of producing the goods

economic growth   the increase in national income caused by increases in the outputs of goods (and not by price increases)

economic principles   general statements about behaviour and its outcomes that apply in a variety of circumstances

economic rent   income received in excess of transfer earnings

economies of scale   reductions in the average cost of production that make large factories more efficient than small factories

economy or economic systems   the way in which a society organizes its economic activities

effective demand   a demand whose presence is signalled to firms in a market economy by changes in prices. If the effective demand for a good increases, the price of the good rises

efficient output level   a situation from which it is impossible to increase the output of one good without either reducing the output of another good or using more resources

elasticity   the percentage change in one magnitude that is caused by a 1 per cent change in some other magnitude

equilibrium   a situation in which there is no incentive for anyone to change the way in which he or she behaves in order to benefit from a possible change in the situation

European Community (EC)   consists of Belgium, Denmark, Federal Republic of Germany, France, Greece, Ireland, Italy, Luxembourg, Netherlands, Portugal, Spain, UK. The EC aims to establish a single market in which there are no barriers to the free trade of goods and factors of production. The EC has a Common Agricultural Policy and other social and regional policies designed to promote economic activity

European Monetary System (EMS)   an agreement between members of the EC on monetary co-ordination. Most member countries (not, at the time of writing, the UK) are members of the exchange rate mechanism of the EMS, which allows only very small variations in exchange rates between members' currencies

exchange   the process through which a person (or country) who has one good obtains other goods from other people (or countries)

exchange controls   laws that prevent or restrict the purchase of foreign currencies for specified purposes

exchange rate   the amount of one country's currency that can be obtained for one unit of another country's currency

expectation   an opinion about possible future events

expected value   the sum of each expected outcome of an uncertain event multiplied by the probability that that outcome will occur

expenditure method   a method of calculating national income that involves adding together amounts spent by households, firms and the government

exploitation   taking advantage of other people's labour, by using market influence as an individual or, in Marxist analysis, by capitalists as a class

exports   goods sold to households, firms and governments in other countries

externality or external effect   any way in which the action of one individual or firm affects the opportunities or preferences of another individual or firm, other than through changes in prices in markets

factor cost   the use of prices that exclude the effects of indirect taxes and subsidies on goods to calculate national income

factors of production   land, labour and equipment used to produce goods. Enterprise (the initiative taken to set up and run a productive activity) is sometimes included

financial assets   bonds, shares, money and other non-material items held as forms of saving

fiscal drag   a situation in which aggregate demand rises more slowly than national income because tax rates increase as people's incomes increase

fiscal policy   government policy that determines the levels of its expenditures and tax rates

fixed exchange rate system   an agreement between countries to allow no change, or only very small changes, in the exchange rates between their currencies

forward or futures contract   an agreement made now to buy or sell a good, a financial asset or a currency at a specified future date and at a specified price

free market economy   an economic system in which markets are competitive and there is little government intervention

free trade   a system in which countries do not restrict or tax imports or subsidize exports

freely floating exchange rates   a system in which governments do not intervene to change the demands and supplies of currencies in foreign exchange markets so that there is no official financing

frictional unemployment   unemployment that arises as people enter the labour market and change from one job to another, assuming that they are unemployed only for a short period

full employment   a situation in which all people work for the number of hours they would choose to work given the real wage offered to them. More colloquially, a situation in which everyone who wants a job at the current real wage level has one

full employment national income   the level of national income at which there is full employment, given unchanged prices and money wages

game theory   a method for analysing oligopoly and other situations of conflict that emphasizes the outcomes of the strategies that a firm can use, given the possible strategies of other firms

gearing ratio   the ratio of a firm's interest-paying debt (bonds and bills) to the total of its debt plus shares issued

general equilibrium   simultaneous equality of supply and demand in all markets

Giffen good   a good for which demand increases as the price increases

gold standard   an international agreement (that existed before the First World War and for a limited period after) in which each country maintained a fixed price of gold in its own currency and a fixed relationship between its supply of money and its reserves of gold

goods   things that are produced, and that households or firms want for consumption or investment. In this book goods include services

gross   (used to describe investment and national product) including investment goods bought to replace those that have worn out

hot money   liquid funds that can be transferred rapidly from one currency to another, according to changes and expectations of changes in exchange rates

imperfections   aspects of an economic system that cause it to differ from a perfect market system. Imperfections include lack of information, restrictions on opportunities (other than those cause by market prices and wages), market influence, government intervention and limitations on the speed of price changes that prevent rapid market clearing

import function   the relationship between total imports and national income

imports   goods bought from households, firms and governments in other countries

income effect   the effect of a change in a price or a wage that arises because the household becomes better or worse off as a result of the price or wage change

income-elasticity of demand   percentage change in demand caused by a 1 per cent increase in income

income method   a method of calculating domestic product and national income by adding together incomes paid by firms to households

index-linking   a system in which money wages, transfer payments or the values of and interest on bonds are increased in line with the inflation rate, so that their real value is maintained

index number   a way of expressing changes in a magnitude (such as the price level) by setting the index of the magnitude equal to 100 on some base date, and scaling the magnitude at other times correspondingly

indifference   a statement by an individual that he or she does not have a preference for one alternative (policy or collection of goods) over another; he or she is equally satisfied with either alternative

indirect tax   a tax levied when a good is purchased, such as Value Added Tax, excise duties on alcohol, tobacco and petrol and car tax

ineffective demand   demand for goods that would occur if households' incomes were higher. In a market economy there is no signal to firms (through market prices) to inform them about ineffective demands

infant industry   an industry that is smaller than (and it is hoped is growing towards) its most efficient size. The protection of infant industries is one reason put forward for import restrictions on competing goods

inferior good   a good for which demand falls as income increases

inflation   an increase in the average level of prices (and/or money wages)

inflationary gap   macroeconomic equilibrium national income minus full employment national income at existing prices and money wages (when this difference is positive)

inflationary spiral   a situation in which inflation is perpetuated because firms are able to increase prices in line with increases in their costs, and workers and trade unions are able to increase money wages in line with increases in prices

injections to the circular flow of national income   private investment, government expenditure and exports

input–output table   a table that records the production of goods in an economy and the uses of goods produced in one industry as inputs in other industries

interest   income received by lending money; the cost involved in borrowing money

interest-elasticity of demand for money   percentage reduction in the amount of money demanded when there is a 1 per cent increase in interest rates

internal rate of return   the discount rate for which a project has a net present value of zero

investment   expenditure by firms and the government on new or replacement equipment

Keynesian theory   based on macroeconomic analysis, rejecting the quantity theory of money and emphasizing the effectiveness of fiscal rather than monetary policy to change national income, employment and the inflation rate

liquidity   the speed with which the value of asset can be realized to buy other goods or other assets. Notes and coins are the most liquid assets since they can be used immediately to buy goods

liquidity preference   the relationship between the demand for money and the interest rate at a given level of national income

liquidity ratio   the ratio of liquid assets (including cash, some bills and government bonds) to a bank's total assets. The ratio may be fixed by the government

luxury   a good for which the income-elasticity of demand exceeds one

M1   a measure of the supply of money that includes notes and coins and bank accounts from which money can be withdrawn without notice

M2   M1 plus building society and National Savings accounts from which money can be withdrawn without notice

M3   M1 plus bank accounts for which the holder must give notice of withdrawal

M4   M3 plus building society accounts for which the holder must give notice of withdrawal

M5   M4 plus private sector bills

macroeconomic analysis   a method of analysing macroeconomic aspects of market and mixed economies that assumes that firms change their outputs and employment levels, rather than their prices, when there is a change in demands

macroeconomic equilibrium   a situation in which desired injections to the circular flow of national income equal desired withdrawals from it

macroeconomics   the study of the economy as a whole

marginal   concerned with the effects of a small change

marginal cost   increase in a firm's total costs caused by a small increase in output

marginal cost pricing   principle that the price of a good sold by a nationalized firm should equal its marginal cost of production

marginal product of labour   change in a firm's output caused by a small increase in the firm's employment of labour

marginal revenue   increase in a firm's total revenue caused by a small increase in sales

marginal revenue product of labour   change in a firm's total revenue caused by a small increase in the firm's employment of labour

market   the totality of all attempts to buy and sell a good, asset, currency or factor of production

market analysis   a method of analysing macroeconomic aspects of market and mixed economies that assumes that firms change prices when demand changes in such a way that all markets clear rapidly

market clearing   the movement of a market or markets to equilibrium in which total demand equals total supply

market demand   total of the demands for a good by firms and individuals

market economy   an economy in which the outcome is the result of individual decisions co-ordinated in markets and in which there is little government intervention

market equilibrium   a situation in which demand equals supply

market structure   a description of the interrelation between demanders and suppliers, the extent of influence in the market and the ease with which new suppliers can enter the market. Examples of market structures are monopoly, monopolistic competition, monopsony, oligopoly and perfect competition

market supply   total of the supplies of a good by firms and individuals

microeconomics   the study of decisions of individuals and firms, and the interactions of those decisions

mixed economy   economy in which the outcome is the result of individual decisions that are affected by significant government intervention, but in which there is no central plan

model   a system of logical relationships, based on assumptions, that is designed to simplify a situation to expose its main features

modified market analysis   method of analysing macroeconomic aspects of market and mixed economies that assumes that firms change prices when demands change, and the markets move as near to equilibrium as imperfections permit. In particular, the level of unemployment returns to the natural rate

monetarist theory   generally based on market analysis, using the quantity theory of money and emphasizing the effectiveness of monetary rather than fiscal policy to change national income and the inflation rate, and the ineffectiveness of monetary and fiscal policies designed to change the level of employment

monetary policy   government policy that determines the way in which a government finances its budget deficit (or uses a budget surplus), and that regulates the activities of banks and other financial institutions

money   anything that is widely accepted as a means of making transactions

money illusion   belief by a household that it is better off because its income measured in money has risen, even though the prices of goods that it buys may also have risen

money wage   amount of money paid for an hour's labour

monopolistic competition   market structure in which each firm has some market influence (because each sells a slightly different good), and in which new firms can enter freely

monopoly   market structure in which there is a single seller, and into which no new seller can enter

monopsony   market structure in which there is a single buyer

moral hazard   difficulty that the existence of insurance makes it more likely that the event covered by insurance will occur

multinational firm   firm that operates in more than one country

multiplier   ratio of the increase in macroeconomic equilibrium national income to an increase in desired injections to the circular flow of national income (or a reduction in desired withdrawals from the circular flow)

multiplier process   the sequence of events (predicted by macroeconomic analysis) that follows an increase in desired injections to the circular flow of national income or a reduction in desired withdrawals from the circular flow

national debt   total outstanding borrowing of the government

national income   net national product at factor cost

national product   domestic product plus net property income from abroad

nationalized firm   a firm whose shares are held by the government

nationalized industry   an industry in which all (or almost all) firms have been nationalized

natural monopoly   a situation in which one firm can produce the total output of an industry at a lower average cost than any greater number of firms

natural rate of unemployment   the level of unemployment that results (according to modified market analysis) when markets have moved as near to equilibrium as imperfections permit

necessity   a good with an income-elasticity of demand between zero and one

net   (used to describe investment and national product) excluding investment goods bought to replace those that have worn out

net present value   difference between the total discounted revenues or benefits of a project and its total discounted costs

net property income from abroad   payments of dividends and interest from abroad to domestic residents minus payments of dividends and interest by domestic firms to foreign residents

non-bank private sector   households and privately owned firms that are not involved in banking

non-price competition   advertising and other ways in which firms compete other than through price reductions

normal good   good for which demand increases when income increases

normal profit   the income received by a firm's owners because they use some of their own factors of production in the firm

normative statements   statements of what should be done

official financing   money borrowed by the government, or transferred from reserves, to offset a deficit on the balance of payments; money lent, or transferred to reserves, to offset a surplus on the balance of payments

oligopoly   market structure in which a few (more than one) firms supply the good, and in which each takes account of the effects of its rivals' actions. The entry of new firms may be restricted by the actions of firms already supplying the market

open market operations   government purchases and sales of its bonds in transactions with the non-bank private sector. This is part of monetary policy

opportunity cost   the quantity or value of goods or income that must be given up to buy, to produce or to continue to possess an item

paradox of thrift or **paradox of saving**   the conclusion of macroeconomic analysis that an increase in the desire to save causes no increase in total saving because national income falls

partial equilibrium   equilibrium in a single market, assuming that prices in all other markets are unchanging

peak-load pricing   situation in which a firm charges a higher price at a time when demand for its product is high than it charges when demand is low

perfect competition   a market structure in which no firm has market influence, and in which there is freedom of entry to the market

Phillips curve   relation between the level of unemployment and the inflation rate that was originally observed for the UK for the period 1861 to 1957.

According to this curve, unemployment increases when the inflation rate falls, and vice versa

planned economy   an economy in which the government attempts to determine the outcome by formulating and implementing a central plan

positive statements   are based on logical deductions from the assumptions of a model

poverty trap   a situation in which a household loses a number of means-tested benefits and begins to pay income taxes as its income from employment increases through a critical range. In extreme cases, a household's total income may fall because the loss of benefits and increased tax payments exceed the additonal income from employment

prescriptive statements   say what can be done (given a particular model) given particular value judgements

present value   the value of a future sum of money discounted to the present

price   the amount of money exchanged for a good

price discrimination   a situation in which the supplier of a good sells at different prices to different customers

price-elasticity of demand   percentage fall in demand caused by a 1 per cent increase in price

price-elasticity of supply   percentage increase in supply caused by a 1 per cent increase in price

prices and incomes policy   a government policy that attempts to reduce the inflation rate by limiting increases in prices and money wages

principle of voluntary exchange   the principle that a person agrees to exchange only if he or she is made better off by doing so

private sector balance   the difference between households' total savings and total investment by privately owned firms

profit   income received from owning equipment (capital goods) and firms (and shares in firms). In this book profit includes dividends

progressive tax   a tax which implies that people with higher incomes pay a larger fraction of their incomes in tax than people with lower incomes; a benefit structure is progressive if people with lower incomes receive benefits that form a larger fraction of their incomes than do rich people

public choice   a decision that one policy is socially more desirable than another, based on specified value judgements that determine what is socially desirable

public sector   central government, local government, nationalized firms and other organizations that are not privately owned

Public Sector Borrowing Requirement (PSBR)   the extent of public sector borrowing and money creation

quantity equation ($MV = PT$)   statement that the value of transactions in an economy in a period equals the amount of money in use multiplied by the velocity of circulation

quantity theory of money   a theory (based on market analysis) that the velocity of circulation is constant so that the inflation rate equals the rate of increase of the supply of money minus the rate of economic growth

quota   a restriction on the quantity of a good that may be imported

rates   property taxes in the UK, paid by firms and (until introduction of the community charge) households to local government authorities

rational expectations   expectations and predictions of future events that have no systematic bias, so that magnitudes are not consistently overpredicted or consistently underpredicted

rationing   a system of allocation that is planned by the government

real wage   amount of goods that can be bought with the money wage

recession   period of lower than average national income and higher than average unemployment, the 'low point' of a trade or business cycle

regressive tax   a tax which implies that people with higher incomes pay a smaller fraction of their incomes in tax than people with lower incomes; a benefit structure is regressive if people with lower incomes receive benefits that form a smaller fraction of their incomes than do rich people

rent   income from owning, and letting others use, land and buildings; also used to describe the income from hiring out equipment

reserve currency   a currency widely held in many countries' reserves of foreign currencies

Retail Prices Index (RPI)   the average increase in the prices of consumer goods in the UK. It is the usually quoted measure of the inflation rate

revaluation   a deliberate appreciation by a government of an exchange rate above its previous fixed or target level

revealed preference   a theory based on the assumption or axiom that people's choices are consistent. The axiom of revealed preference states that a person who has chosen opportunity A when both A and B are available will not choose B in any situation in which A is also available

risk-aversion   a preference for the certain prospect of the expected value of an uncertain prospect rather than for the uncertain prospect

risk-neutrality   indifference between the certain prospect of the expected value of an uncertain prospect and the uncertain prospect

risk-preference   preference for an uncertain prospect rather than for the certain prospect of the expected value of the uncertain prospect

risk premium   difference between the expected value of an uncertain prospect and its certainty equivalent

saving   the part of a household's income (and of national income) not spent on consumer goods or paid in taxes

saving function   the relation between total desired saving and national income

services   intangible goods

share   financial asset that represents the ownership of a fractional part of a firm. Shareholders receive profits or dividends; preference shareholders receive payment before ordinary shareholders, and the latter can usually vote at general meetings of the firm

single European market   proposal to abolish all frontier controls on movement of goods and labour within the EC. Proposed to be established by 1992

slump   a period of lower than average national income and higher than average unemployment, particularly one that has continued, or is expected to continue, for a number of years

social cost–benefit analysis   a method of assessing the social desirability of projects that takes account of social costs and benefits (mainly due to external effects), and not just of private (financial) costs and benefits

Special Drawing Rights   a form of international currency, issued by the International Monetary Fund, that governments agree to accept in payment of international debts

specialization   the process of allocating workers between occupations

stagflation   a situation of low economic growth and high inflation relative to recent periods

structural unemployment   long lasting unemployment that arises from a change in the pattern of demand for goods, and from an increase in the demand for imported goods and a reduction in the demand for domestically produced goods

substitute   if the price of a good rises the demand for a substitute for it increases

substitution effect   the effect of a change in a price or a wage that is caused by the change in relative prices or wages, when the household is compensated for the change in income that gives rise to the income effect

supernormal profit   profit received in excess of normal profit; profit attributable to ownership of the firm rather than of any assets used in it

supply   the quantity that a person or firm wants to sell at a particular price. A supply schedule and a supply curve represent supply at each price

supply and demand analysis   the examination of the interaction of decisions to buy and sell in markets

supply-side theory   a theory that the most effective method of increasing national income and employment is to reduce taxes and imperfections so that people have a greater incentive to work, and firms have a greater incentive to invest

tariff   a tax or levy that increases the price of an imported good

tax function   the relationship between total tax payments and national income

terms of trade   the ratio of the average price of goods exported from a country to the average price of goods imported in to the country

trade cycle   alternating periods of higher and lower rates of economic growth

trade union   an organization of workers that negotiates wages and working conditions collectively

trade-weighted index   an average from a number of exchange rates between the one country's currency and other currencies. Each currency is weighted according to the size of its total trade (imports and exports) with the country

transfer earnings   the wage that a worker would receive in the next best paid job that he or she is able to do

transfer price   price used in the accounts of a multinational firm to show the revenue of its subsidiary in one country and the costs to its subsidiary in another country when it transfers goods from one country to the other. The transfer price determines the firm's profitability in the two countries

Treasury bill   a bill (usually for three months) sold by the government and mainly bought by banks and other financial institutions

utilitarianism   a proposal to make public choices by adding the utility gained by each individual from each of the possible outcomes

utility   a numerical representation of preferences between goods or satisfaction received from goods

Value Added Tax (VAT)   an indirect tax used in the UK and other countries of the EC. The tax is levied on sales of many goods. If a good is produced in several stages by several firms, each firm pays a fraction of the tax, related to its contribution to the final price of the good

value judgement   a statement of opinion

velocity of circulation   the average number of times that a unit of money is used in a period

wage   income received from employment. In this book, includes salaries

withdrawals from the circular flow of national income   saving, tax payments and imports

Bibliography

1 Introductory books

There are many introductory books on economics, most of them textbooks. Those with little background knowledge of the ways that economists approach problems are recommended to:

D. Whynes, *Invitation to Economics* (Oxford: Martin Robertson, 1983)
P. Donaldson, *A Question of Economics* (Harmondsworth: Penguin, 1985)

The first successful modern style textbook is Paul Samuelson's *Economics*. The latest edition is:

P.A. Samuelson and W.D. Nordhaus, *Economics* (New York: McGraw-Hill, 13th edition 1989)

Those who have a suitable background in mathematics can learn some parts of basic economics very efficiently using:

A. Smith, *A Mathematical Introduction to Economics* (Oxford: Basil Blackwell, 1982)

A useful reference for terminology is:

G. Bannock, R.E. Baxter and R. Rees, *The Penguin Dictionary of Economics* (Harmondsworth: Penguin, 3rd edition 1984)

2 The UK economy

The study of economics is made much more interesting and relevant if you regularly read about current economic and political events. Quality newspapers or the weekly journal, *The Economist*, are essential supplements to any textbook.

There are several books devoted to the current state of the UK economy (although none can be as up-to-date as current journalism), including:

M.J. Artis (ed.), *The UK Economy: Prest and Coppock's The UK Economy* (London: Wiedenfeld and Nicolson, frequently revised, 12th edition 1989)
C. Harbury and R.G. Lipsey, *An Introduction to the UK Economy* (London: Pitman, 1983)
M.H. Peston, *The British Economy* (Oxford: Philip Allan, 2nd edition 1984)
J. Black, *The Economics of Modern Britain* (Oxford: Martin Robertson, 3rd edition 1982)
K. Smith, *The British Economic Crisis* (Harmondsworth: Penguin, revised edition 1989)
N. Gardner, *Decade of Discontent: the Changing British Economy since 1973* (Oxford: Blackwell, 1987)

3 Intermediate texts

Those who continue to study economics beyond the introductory level are likely to take intermediate courses. There are many textbooks for such courses, divided between those covering microeconomic subjects, such as:

D. Laidler, *Introduction to Microeconomics* (Oxford: Philip Allan, 2nd edition 1981)

and those covering macroeconomic topics such as:

R. Dornbusch and S. Fischer, *Macroeconomics* (New York: McGraw-Hill, 4th edition 1987)

The study of some parts of intermediate and advanced economics is easier for those with some mathematical knowledge. There are many texts that introduce mathematical techniques used by economists, including:

M. Casson, *Introduction to Mathematical Economics* (London: Nelson 1973)
A.C. Chiang, *Fundamental Methods of Mathematical Economics* (Auckland: McGraw-Hill International, 3rd edition 1984)

4 General references

The free market viewpoint is argued strongly in:

M. Friedman and R. Friedman, *Free to Choose* (Harmondsworth: Penguin, 1980)

A less enthusiastic view of the operation of markets is taken in:

J.K. Galbraith, *The Affluent Society* (Harmondsworth: Penguin, 4th edition 1987)

J.K. Galbraith, *The New Industrial State* (Harmondsworth: Penguin, 2nd edition 1974)

A Marxist view of the operation of capitalist economies can be found in:

P. Baran, *The Political Economy of Growth* (New York: Mazani and Munsell, 1962; Harmondsworth: Penguin, 1973)

For a critique of the tendency towards large-scale production see:

E.F. Schumacher, *Small is Beautiful* (London: Blond and Briggs, 1973; London: Abacus, 1974)

The relation between the UK and EC is discussed in:

D. Swann, *The Economics of the Common Market* (Harmondsworth: Penguin, 6th edition 1988)

A.M. El Agraa, *The Economics of the European Community* (Oxford: Philip Allan, 2nd edition 1985)

Issues concerning less developed economies are examined in:

M.P. Todaro, *Economic Development in the Third World* (New York: Longman, 4th edition 1989)

A.P. Thirlwall, *Growth and Development* (London: Macmillan, 4th edition 1988)

H. Singer and J. Ansari, *Rich and Poor Countries* (London: Allen and Unwin, 3rd edition 1982)

Brandt Commission, *A Programme for Survival* (London: Pan, 1983)

J.K. Galbraith, *The Nature of Mass Poverty* (Cambridge, MA: Havard University Press, 1979; Harmondsworth: Penguin, 1979)

P. Donaldson, *Worlds Apart: the Economic Gulf between Nations* (Harmondsworth: Penguin, 2nd edition 1986)

5 Works by major economists

The following books by major figures mentioned in the text are among the most important in the development of the subject. At one time, students used Marshall's *Principles* as a major text. Those who study macroeconomics beyond an introductory level are likely to read parts or all of Keynes' *General Theory*:

A. Smith, *An Enquiry into the Nature and Causes of the Wealth of Nations* (first published 1776; Harmondsworth: Penguin, 1970)

D. Ricardo, *On the Principles of Political Economy and Taxation* (first published

1817; Harmondsworth: Penguin, 1971)

K. Marx, *Capital*, 3 volumes (published in German in 1867, 1885 and 1894; many English translations available)

L. Walras, *Elements of Pure Economics* (published in French in 1874; English translation, London: Allen and Unwin, 1954)

A. Marshall, *Principles of Economics* (London: Macmillan, 1st edition 1890, 8th edition 1920)

J.M. Keynes, *The General Theory of Employment, Interest and Money* (London: Macmillan, 1936)

6 Other references in the text

The following authors and publications are mentioned in the text. Galbraith's *The Great Crash* is suitable reading on an introductory level, particularly for students interested in the operation of financial markets and the history of the 1920s and 1930s. There are some parallels with the stock market crash of October 1987. The book by Arrow and, even more, that by von Neumann and Morgenstern are mathematically difficult.

K.J. Arrow, *Social Choice and Individual Values*, Cowles Foundation Monograph 12 (New York: Wiley, first edition 1951, second edition 1963)

M. Friedman, 'The role of monetary policy'. *American Economic Review* **58** (1968), pp. 1–17

J.K. Galbraith, *The Great Crash, 1929* (London: Hamish Hamilton, 1955; Harmondsworth: Penguin, 1961)

J. Le Grand, *The Strategy of Equality: Redistribution and the Social Services* (London: Allen and Unwin, 1982)

R. Nozick, *Anarchy, State and Utopia* (New York: Basic Books, 1974)

A.W.H. Phillips, 'The relationship between unemployment and the rate of change of money wage rates in the United Kingdom 1861–1957'. *Economica* **25** (1958), pp. 283–99

J. von Neumann and O. Morgenstern, *Theory of Games and Economic Behaviour* (Princeton: Princeton University Press, 1944)

7 Sources of Information on the UK economy

The Central Statistical Office of the UK government produces a number of regular publications, including:
Annual Abstract of Statistics
Economic Trends (monthly)
Financial Statistics (monthly)
Monthly Digest of Statistics
National Accounts (annual)
Social Trends (annual)

United Kingdom Balance of Payments (annual)

The *Business Monitor* series produced by the Department of Trade and Industry includes the annual Census of Production. The *Department of Employment Gazette* contains the monthly Retail Prices Index. The *Household Expenditure Survey* produced by the Department of Employment contains details of the pattern of consumers' expenditure.

Detailed information on UK imports and exports is published monthly by the Department of Trade and Industry in *Overseas Trade Statistics of the United Kingdom*.

Financial information is presented in the *Bank of England Quarterly Bulletin*, which also contains articles on changes in monetary policy and related matters.

Government documents, such as White Papers, reports of Nationalized Industries, reports of the Monopolies and Mergers Commission and reports of the Director-General of Fair Trading, are listed annually in *Government Publications*, published by Her Majesty's Stationery Office.

Answers to selected problems

Chapter 2

(12) Case 1: 210, 36   case 2: 39, 10   case 3: 60, 16   case 4: 90, 24   case 5: 360, 44

(15) 2 (Bill)   4 (Alan)   7 (Alan)

(16) Case 1: 275   case 2: 0   case 3: 37.5   case 4: 87.5   case 5: 525

(17) Case 6: 68.75   case 8: 106

Chapter 3

(9) Bill gives cloth for food, Colin gives food for cloth, Alan gains nothing from trade

(10) 6 cloth = 5 chairs

Chapter 4

(11) 5

(12) (a) 0.375, 0.3   (b) 0.5, 0.625

(13) 7

(15) 2, 3

(16) 0.3, 0.4

(17) 1, 4

Chapter 6

(5) £2,000 (33.9%)

(6) Using 1988 prices: growth rate 4.2%, inflation rate 28.5%   using 1989 prices: growth rate 1.3%, inflation rate 32.2%

(7) (a) 31.0% (b) 23.8%

(8) Household 2 (inflation rate 55.5%)

Chapter 7

(5) (a) Case 1: 42, 0   case 2: 24, 0, 30   case 3: 24, 44   case 4: 24, 68, 0
     (b) no change   (c) case 1: 18, 16   case 2: 0, 16, 30   case 3: 0, 60   case
     4: 0, 84, 0

Chapter 8

(6) (a) zero (b) 3 (c) 7
(7) Profit-maximizing outputs: top row: 4,3,2   bottom row: 5,4,3   supply:
     top row: 3,200, 3,000, 2,500   bottom row: 4000, 4000, 3750 supernormal
     profit: top row: 0, -100, -200 bottom row: 125, 0, -125 long-run
     equilibrium: price $= 125$, $n = 1000$
(8) (a) Yes (b) yes (c) yes (d) no   internal rate of return $= 10.65\%$

Chapter 9

(7) 230 apples, 128 bananas   0.67   above 2.5
(8) £15 $-$£8
(9) 4   4 apples, 6 bananas
(10) £16   £30

Chapter 10

(7) (a) 5 man-hours (b) 3 man-hours
(9) (a) £2,000 (b) zero

Chapter 12

(6) (a) 10 units (b) 11 units (c) £10, £12
(7) Equilibrium wage in market 2 declines by £2

Chapter 13

(5) Not collude: both advertise   collude: neither advertise   £300 per cam-
     paign

Chapter 14

(6) (a) £250.2 (b) £207.1 (c) £110.0 (d) $-$£112.3

Chapter 15

(4) (a) £112.5 billion (b) £113.1 billion (c) £37.5 billion (d) £0.4 billion
(5) £3,571.4
(6) Increase of £1,500

Chapter 17

(7) £15,384.6, surplus is £1,846.2
(8) Macroeconomic equilibrium national income rises by £615.4, surplus is £1,800; macroeconomic equilibrium national income rises by £923.1, surplus is £2,077; macroeconomic equilibrium national income is £17,857.1, surplus is £11,571.4
(9) (a) £14,268 (b) £9,615.4 (c) £13,513.4 (d) £13,513.4

Chapter 18

(6) £20 million £5 million

Chapter 19

(10) 10%: no, no, yes 8%: no, yes, yes 5%: no, yes, yes zero: yes, yes, yes

Chapter 22

(7) No public choice with majority voting; x; Colin prefers w to x and has incentive to put w first so that w, not x, is the public choice

Chapter 24

(6) See table A1

Table A1 Input–output tables in answer to problem 6

		Sector producing			
		Coal	Steel	Final use	Total output
(a)	Coal	190	270	300	760
	Steel	380	270	160	810
(b)	Coal	230	390	300	920
	Steel	460	390	320	1,170

(7) The economy cannot produce the required outputs for final use because its industries require more inputs than they can produce.

Index